"Work harder" is what I keep telling myself...

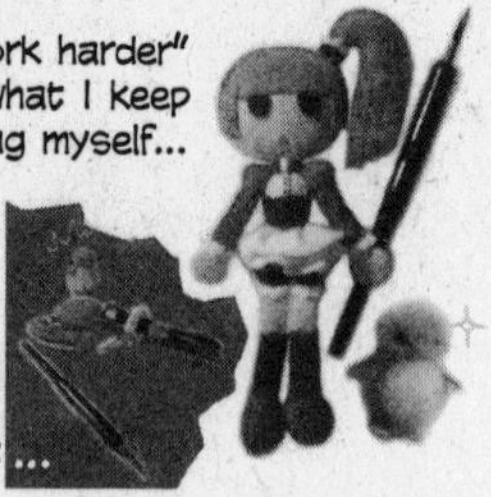

...but...

春野まこと

Makoto Haruno

Hello. ♬ I'm so happy to be able to greet you like this again in Volume 3! With lots of support and help from many people, I have been able to experience the one year anniversary of this series. Thank you very much! Whoaaa. But it's so hard to write in this high humidity and heat. Uh, but when it's cold my hands get numb. Then there's too much pollen in the air during spring. And in the fall I can't resist the temptation to overeat. You know, maybe Makoto Haruno is better suited for making stuffed animals than comics!!

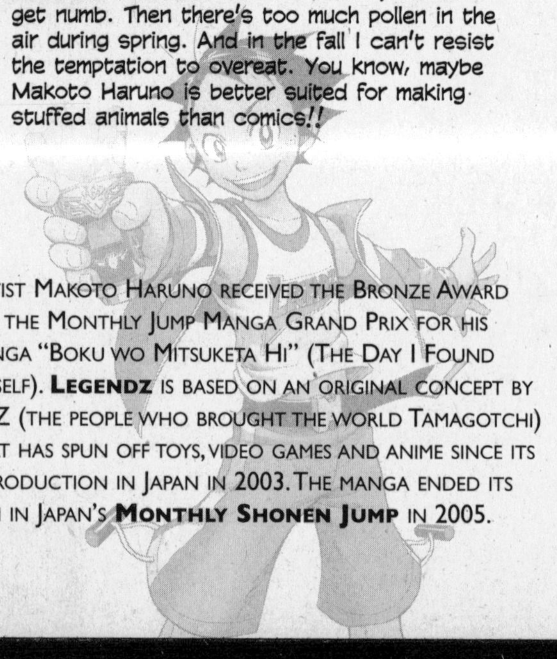

ARTIST MAKOTO HARUNO RECEIVED THE BRONZE AWARD FOR THE MONTHLY JUMP MANGA GRAND PRIX FOR HIS MANGA "BOKU WO MITSUKETA HI" (THE DAY I FOUND MYSELF). **LEGENDZ** IS BASED ON AN ORIGINAL CONCEPT BY WIZ (THE PEOPLE WHO BROUGHT THE WORLD TAMAGOTCHI) THAT HAS SPUN OFF TOYS, VIDEO GAMES AND ANIME SINCE ITS INTRODUCTION IN JAPAN IN 2003. THE MANGA ENDED ITS RUN IN JAPAN'S **MONTHLY SHONEN JUMP** IN 2005.

LEGENDZ VOL. 3
The SHONEN JUMP Graphic Novel Edition

ART BY MAKOTO HARUNO
STORY BY RIN HIRAI

English Adaptation/Shaenon K. Garrity
Translation/Akira Watanabe
Touch-up Art & Lettering/Susan Daigle-Leach
Cover Design/Sean Lee
Interior Design/Janet Piercy
Editor/Yuki Takagaki

Managing Editor/Elizabeth Kawasaki
Director of Production/Noboru Watanabe
Vice President of Publishing/Alvin Lu
Vice President & Editor in Chief/ Yumi Hoashi
Sr. Director of Acquisitions/Rika Inouye
Vice President of Sales & Marketing/Liza Coppola
Publisher/Hyoe Narita

Published by VIZ Media, LLC
P.O. Box 77010
San Francisco, CA 94107

SHONEN JUMP Graphic Novel Edition
10 9 8 7 6 5 4 3 2 1
First printing, October 2005

THE WORLD'S
MOST POPULAR MANGA

GRAPHIC NOVEL
www.shonenjump.com

www.viz.com

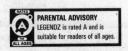

PARENTAL ADVISORY
LEGENDZ is rated A and is
suitable for readers of all ages.

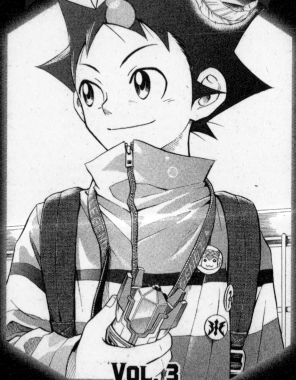

LEGENDZ

™

VOL. 3
NECROM MENACE

Art by **Makoto Haruno**
Story by **Rin Hirai**

Original Concept © WiZ 2003

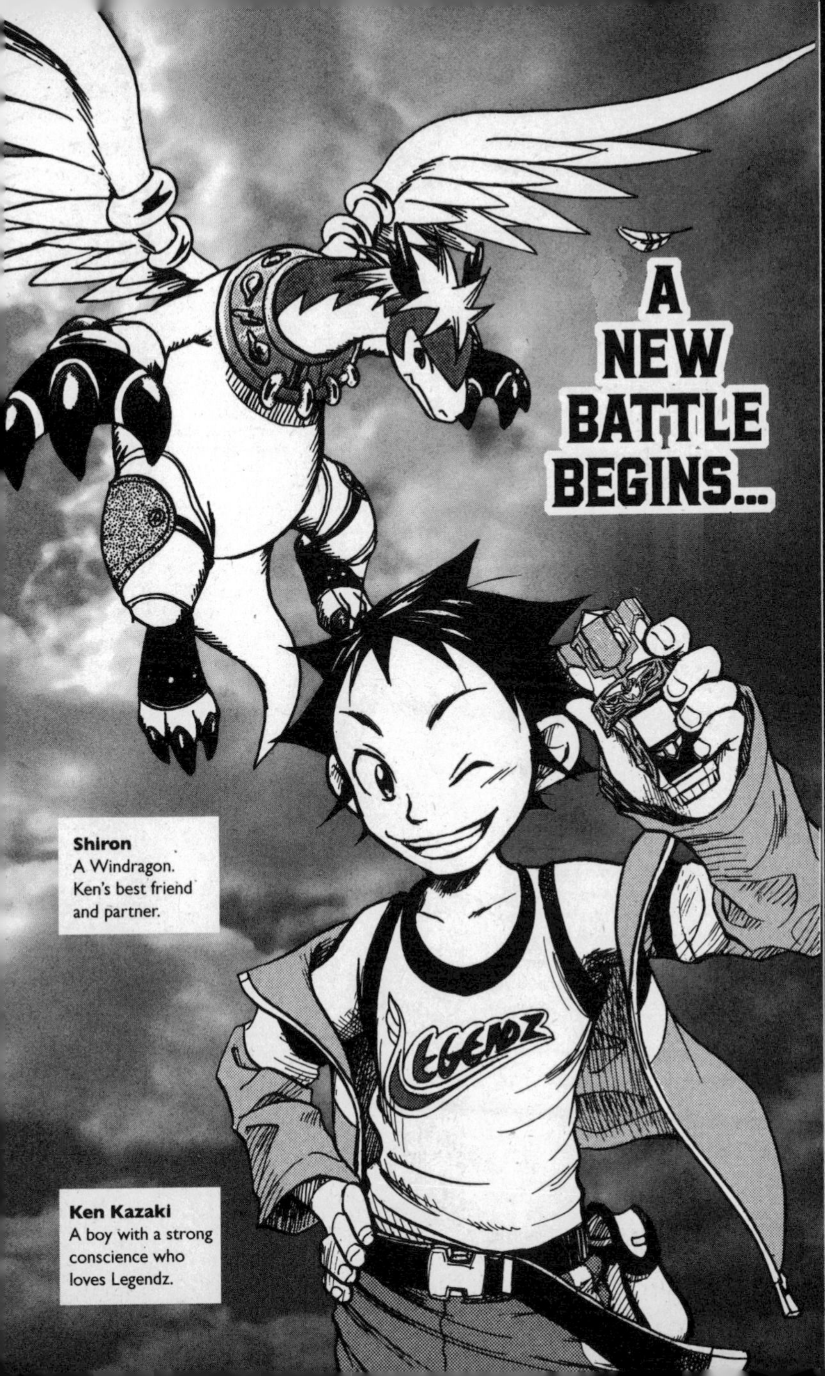
A NEW BATTLE BEGINS...
Shiron
A Windragon. Ken's best friend and partner.
Ken Kazaki
A boy with a strong conscience who loves Legendz.
LEGENDZ

LEGENDZ 3

The Story Thus Far

"Legendz" is a computerized game in which legendary monsters are reborn and raised for battle. Ken Kazaki, whose best friend is his Legendz, a Windragon named Shiron, loves the game. On his first day at Ryudo Elementary, Ken is forced to prove his abilities. His friend Ririko is kidnapped by students at Kokuryu Elementary who are after the Golden Soul Figure, which is being kept by Ryudo's top Legendz player. At Kokuryu, Ken is ambushed and fights lots of tough battles. With Shiron's help, he rescues Ririko. Ryudo's top Legendz player, Yuki, gives Ken the Golden Soul Figure, but Ken refuses to use it, saying that he wants to fight only with Shiron.

As the rescue mission ends, a helicopter appears and invites Ken to the Legendz Carnival, a huge annual Legendz tournament. Ken enters the tournament not knowing that losing means having one's Soul Figure—and the Legendz inside it—destroyed. In the first round, Ken witnesses this harsh rule being enforced as the Soul Figures of dozens of other players break. Ken makes it to the second round, in which the goal is simply to survive for three days. During this round, Ken meets Kaoruko Goshika, an injured player. Together, Ken and Kaoruko acquire a mysterious crystal…

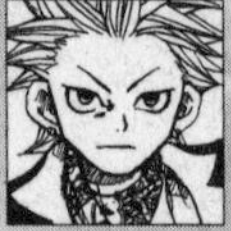

Leo Engokuin
Heir to the DWC and sponsor of the Legendz Carnival.

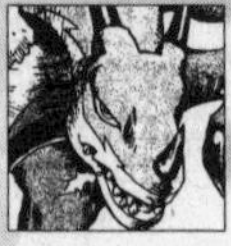

Greedo
Leo's Legendz—a Blazedragon that possesses tremendous destructive power.

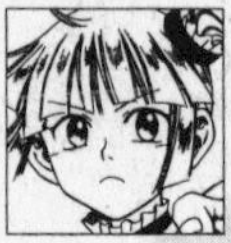

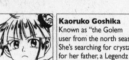

Kaoruko Goshika
Known as "the Golem user from the north seas." She's searching for crystals for her father, a Legendz researcher.

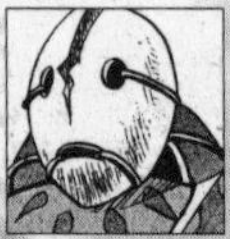

Bjork
A Golem. It can control plant life. Kaoruko's partner and Legendz.

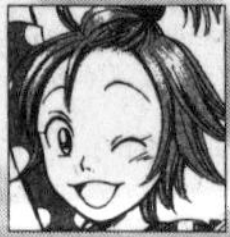

Ririko Yasuhara
A top-notch Legendz wielder at her school.

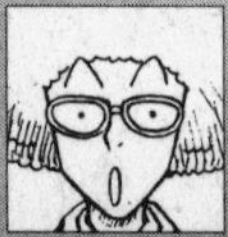

Namio Curly
Leo's assistant and the Legendz Carnival convention officer.

LEGENDZ™

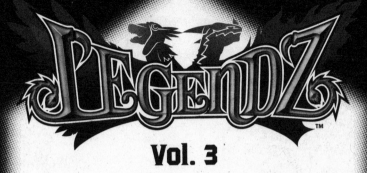

Vol. 3

CONTENTS

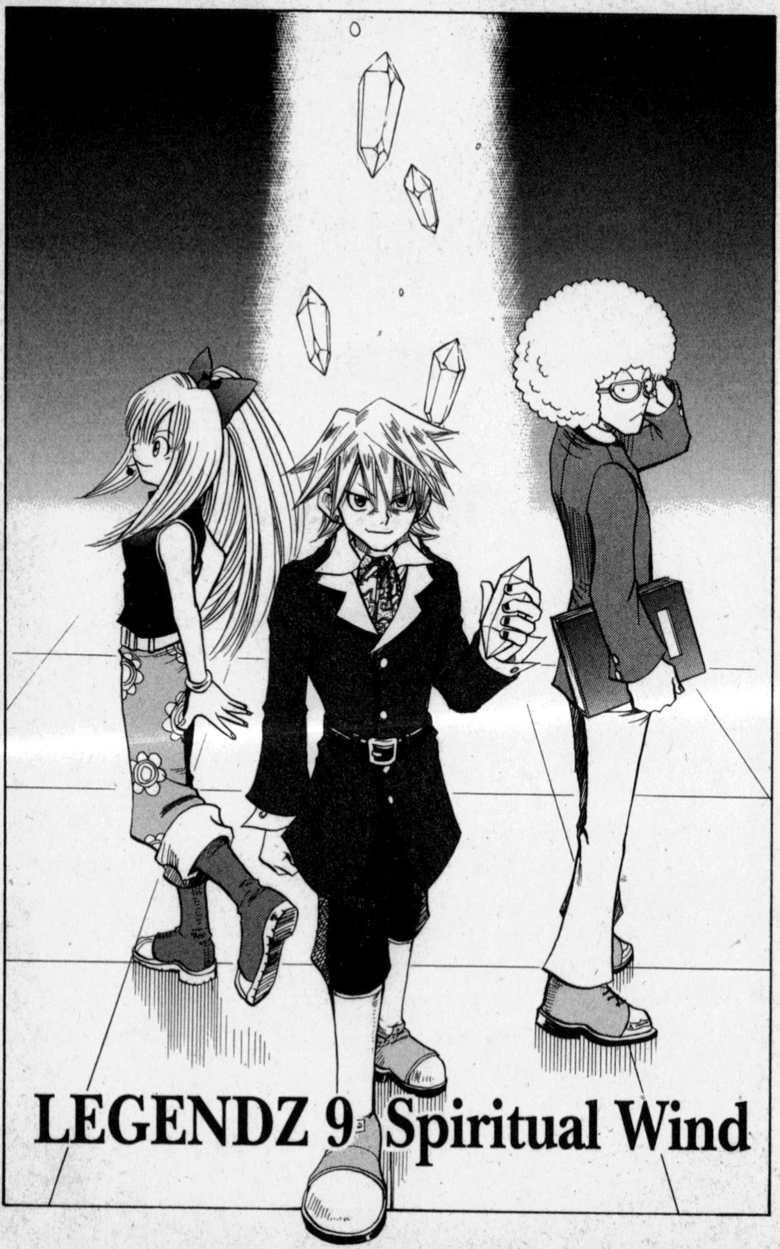

LEGENDZ 9 Spiritual Wind

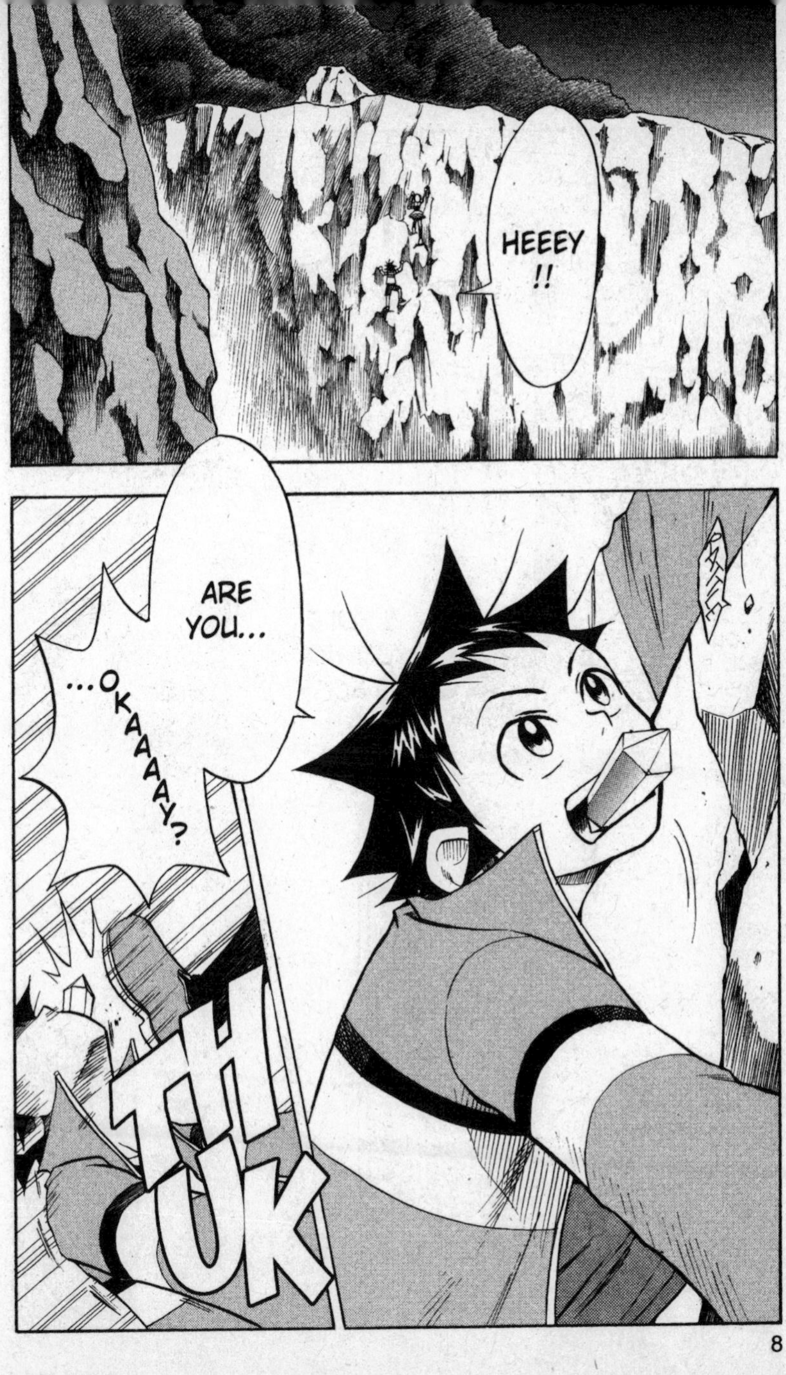
HEEEY !!
RATTLE
ARE YOU...
...OKAAAAAY?
THUK

READ THIS WAY

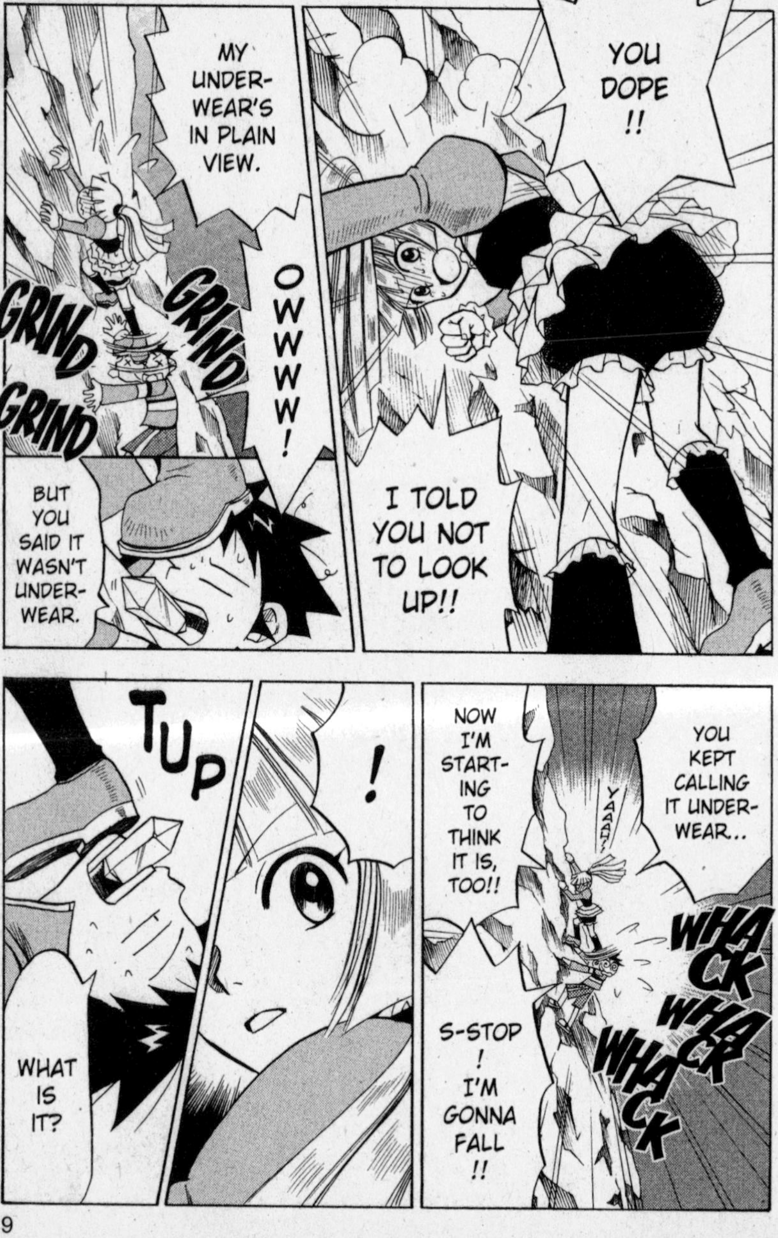
YOU DOPE!!
I TOLD YOU NOT TO LOOK UP!!
MY UNDER-WEAR'S IN PLAIN VIEW.
OWWWWW!
GRIND
GRIND
GRIND
BUT YOU SAID IT WASN'T UNDER-WEAR.
YOU KEPT CALLING IT UNDER-WEAR...
NOW I'M START-ING TO THINK IT IS, TOO!!
YAAAH!?
WHACK WHACK WHACK
S-STOP! I'M GONNA FALL!!
!
TUP
WHAT IS IT?

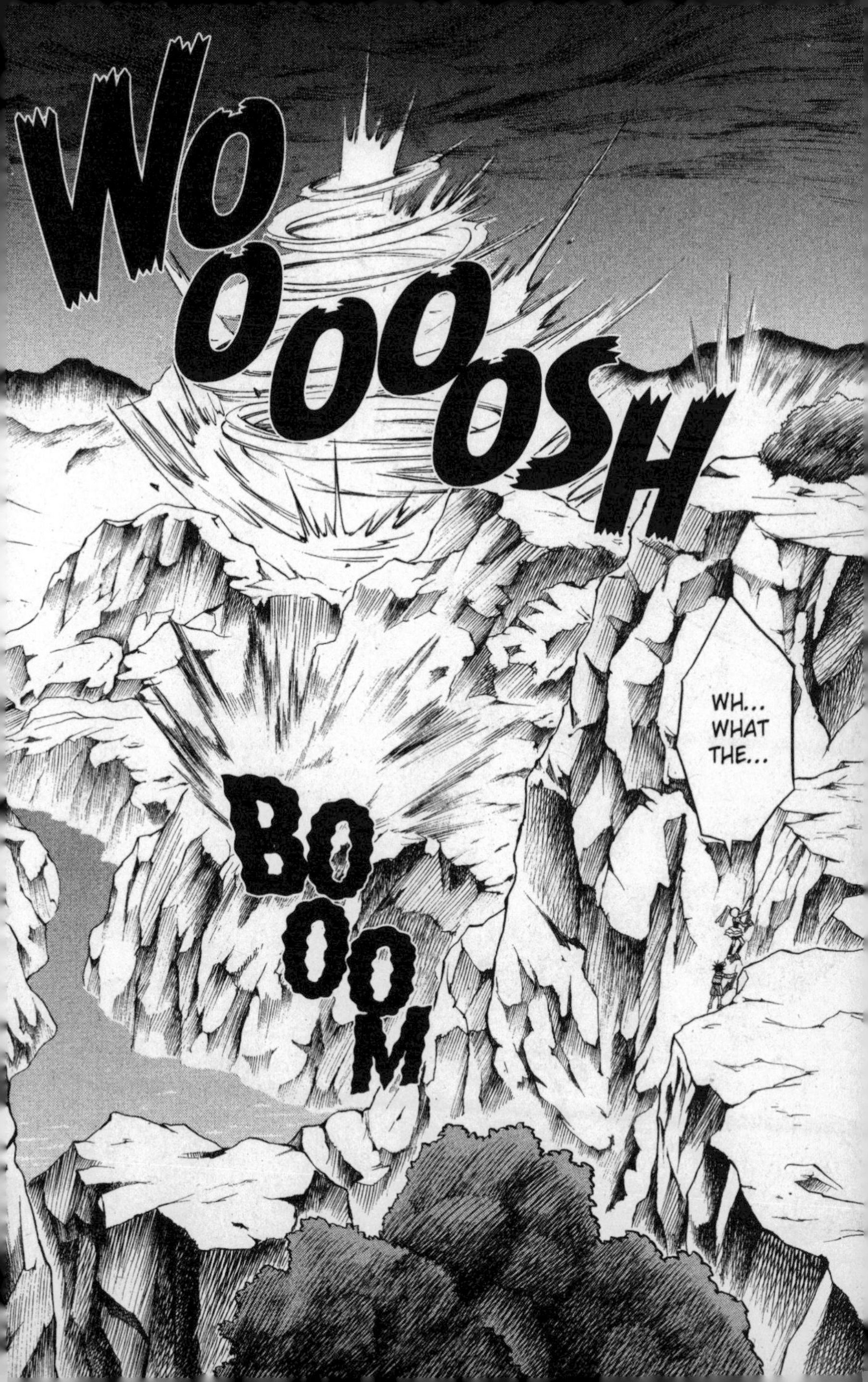
WOOOOOSH
BOOOOM
WH... WHAT THE...

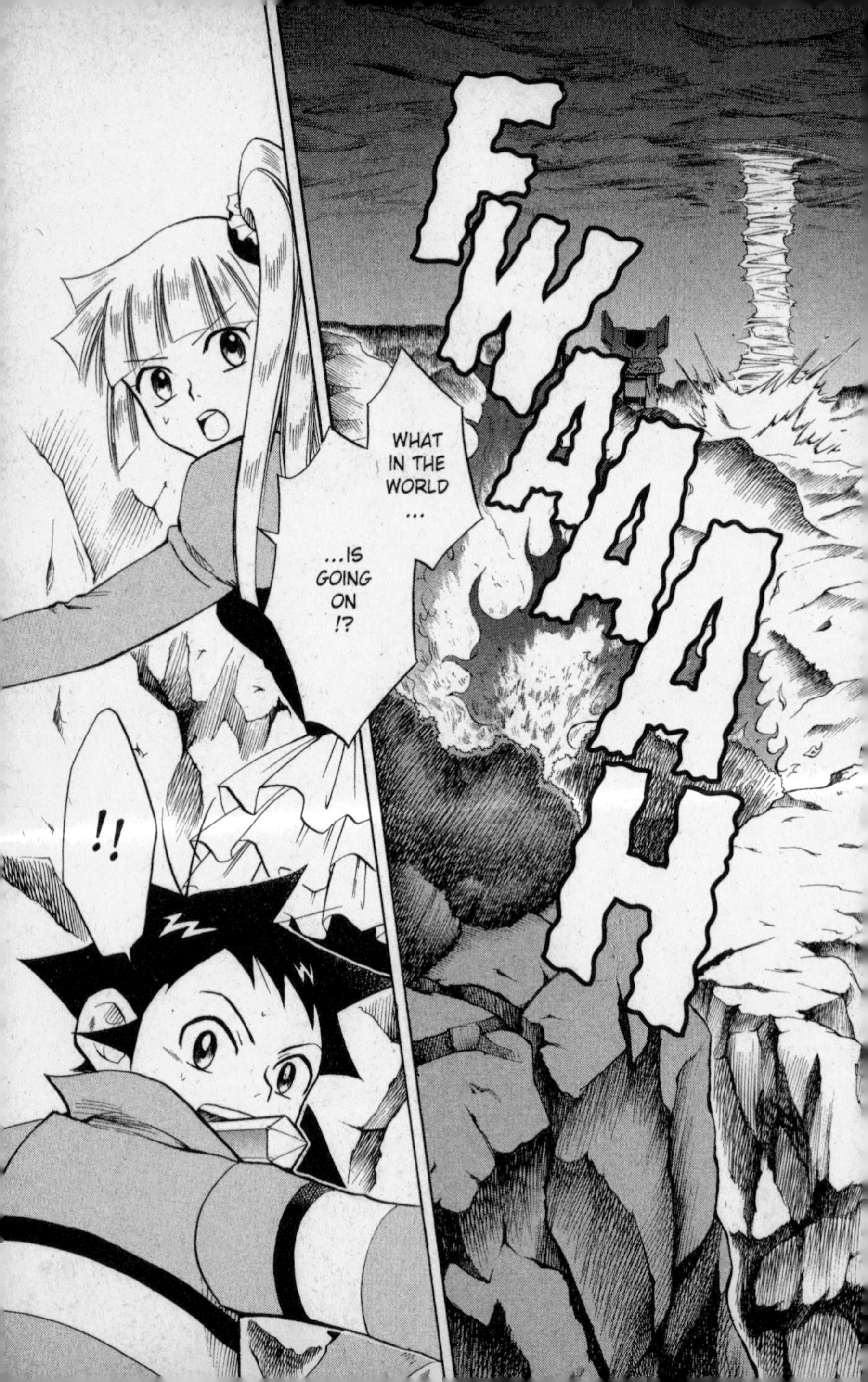
FWAAAH
WHAT IN THE WORLD ...
...IS GOING ON !?
!!

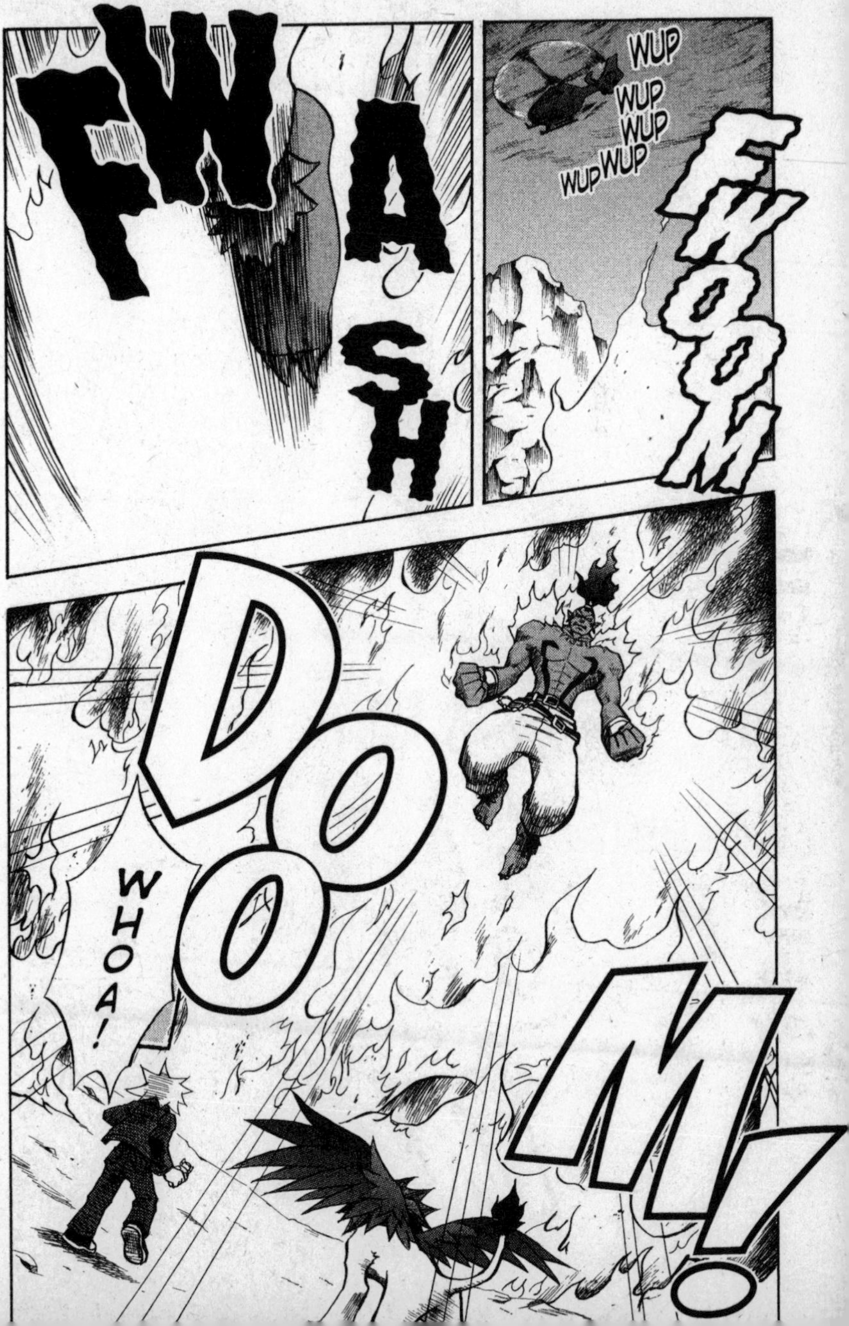
WUP
WUP
WUP
WUPWUP
FWOOM
FWASH
DOOM!
WHOA!

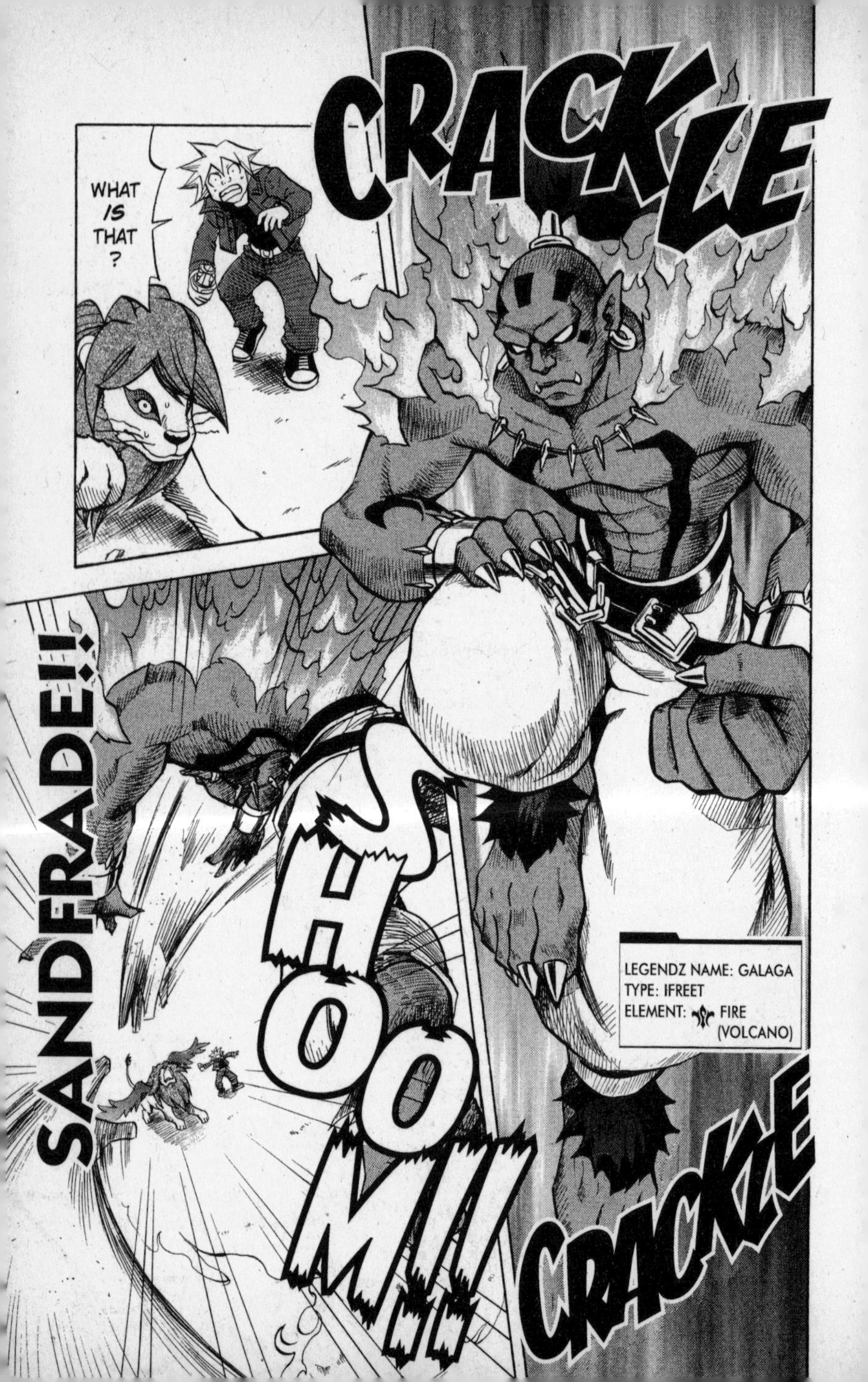
CRACKLE
WHAT IS THAT?
LEGENDZ NAME: GALAGA
TYPE: IFREET
ELEMENT: FIRE (VOLCANO)
CRACKLE
SHOOM!!
SANDFRADE!!

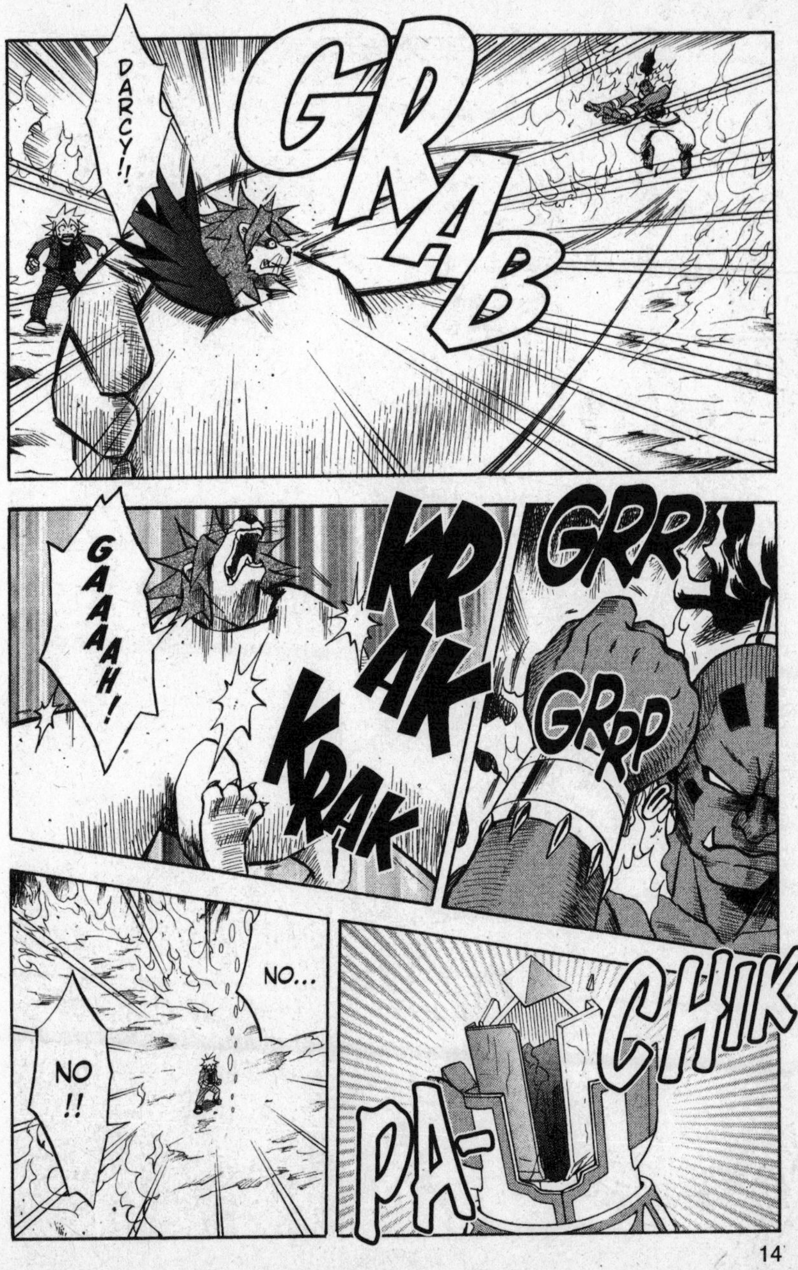
GRAB
DARCY!!
GRRR
GRRP
KRAK KRAK
GAAAAAH!
CHIK
PA-
NO...
NO!!

READ THIS WAY

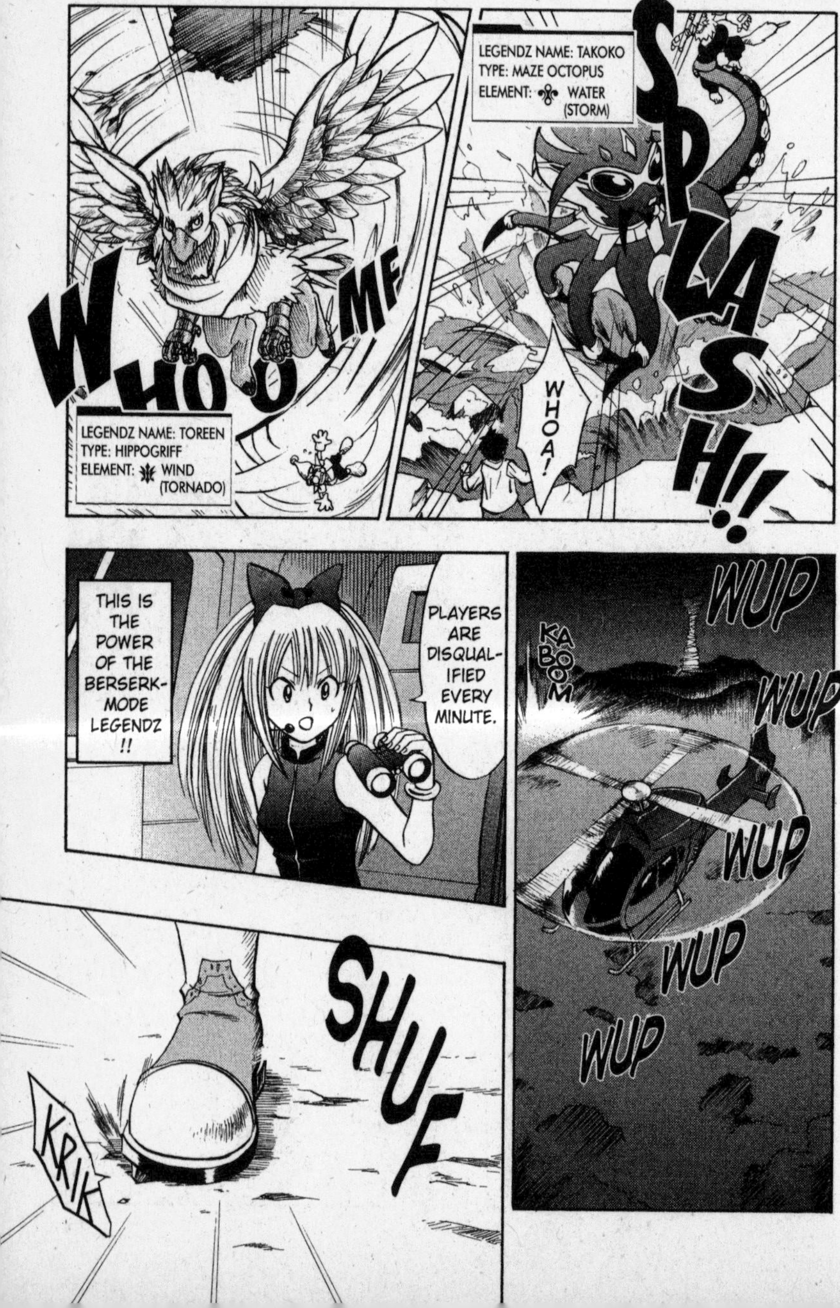
LEGENDZ NAME: TAKOKO
TYPE: MAZE OCTOPUS
ELEMENT: WATER (STORM)
SPLASH!!
WHOA!
WHOOMF
LEGENDZ NAME: TOREEN
TYPE: HIPPOGRIFF
ELEMENT: WIND (TORNADO)
KABOOM
WUP
WUP
WUP
WUP
WUP
PLAYERS ARE DISQUAL-IFIED EVERY MINUTE.
THIS IS THE POWER OF THE BERSERK-MODE LEGENDZ!!
SHUF
KRIK

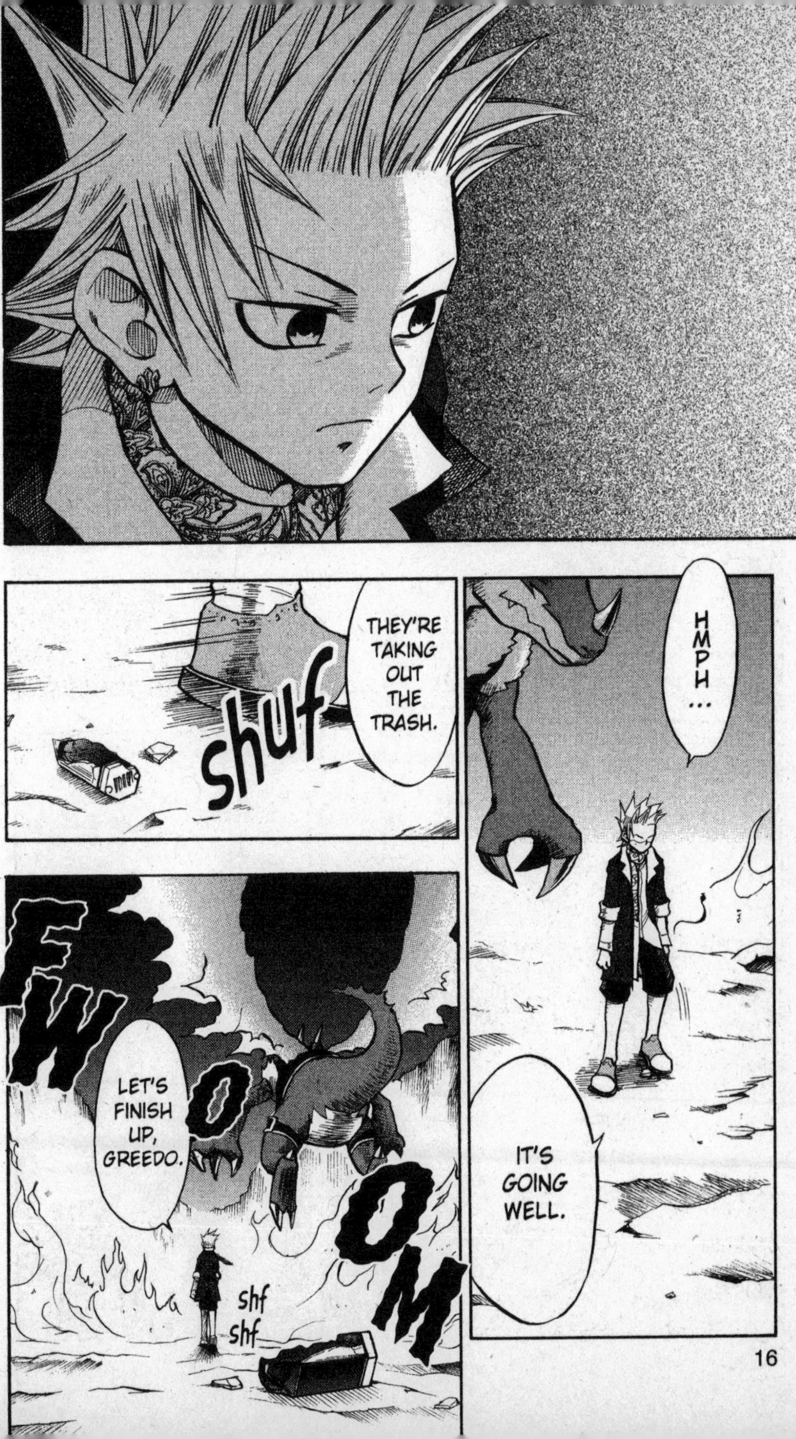
HMPH...
IT'S GOING WELL.
THEY'RE TAKING OUT THE TRASH.
shuf
FWOOOM
LET'S FINISH UP, GREEDO.
shf shf

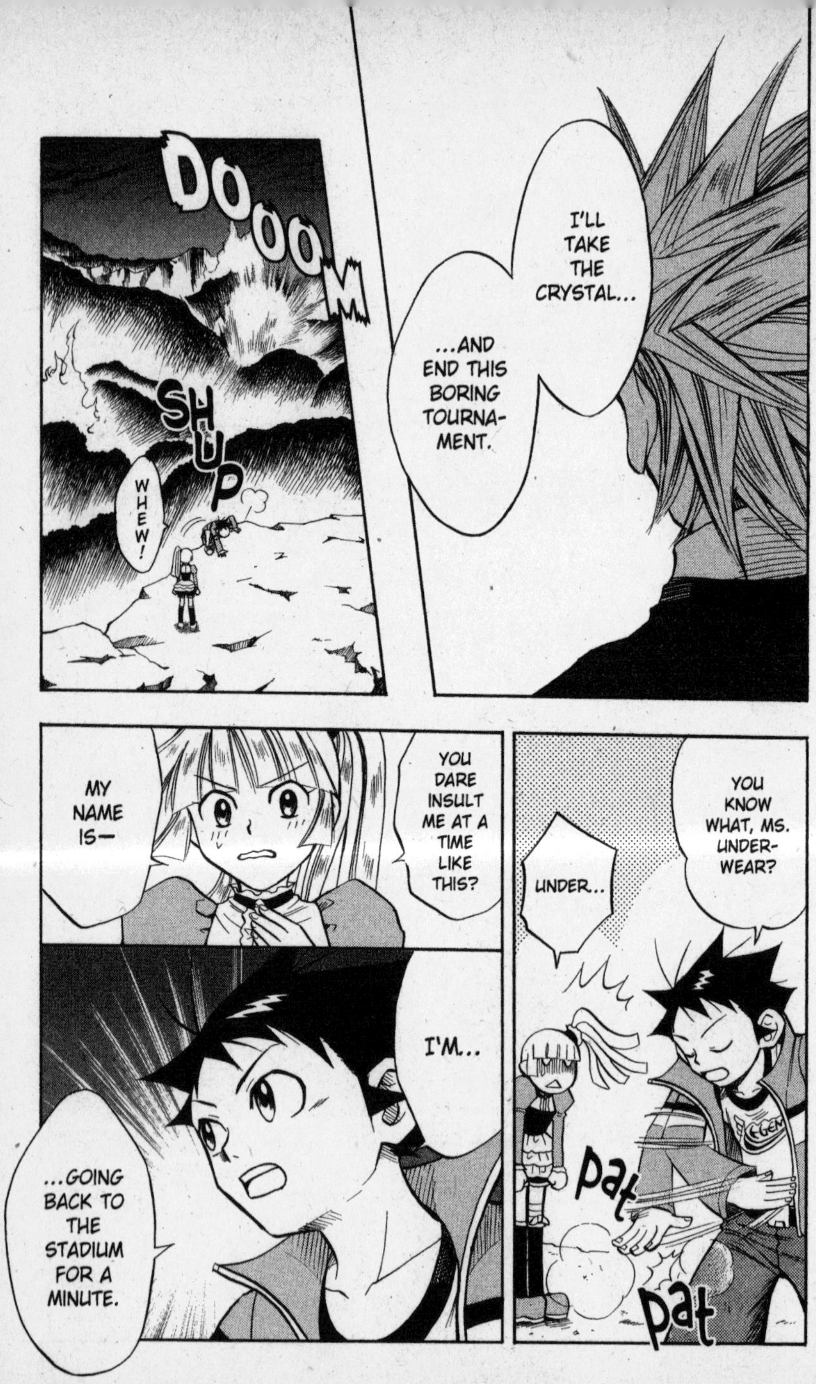
I'LL TAKE THE CRYSTAL...
...AND END THIS BORING TOURNAMENT.
DOOOOM
SHUP
WHEW!
YOU KNOW WHAT, MS. UNDERWEAR?
UNDER..
YOU DARE INSULT ME AT A TIME LIKE THIS?
MY NAME IS—
pat
pat
I'M...
...GOING BACK TO THE STADIUM FOR A MINUTE.

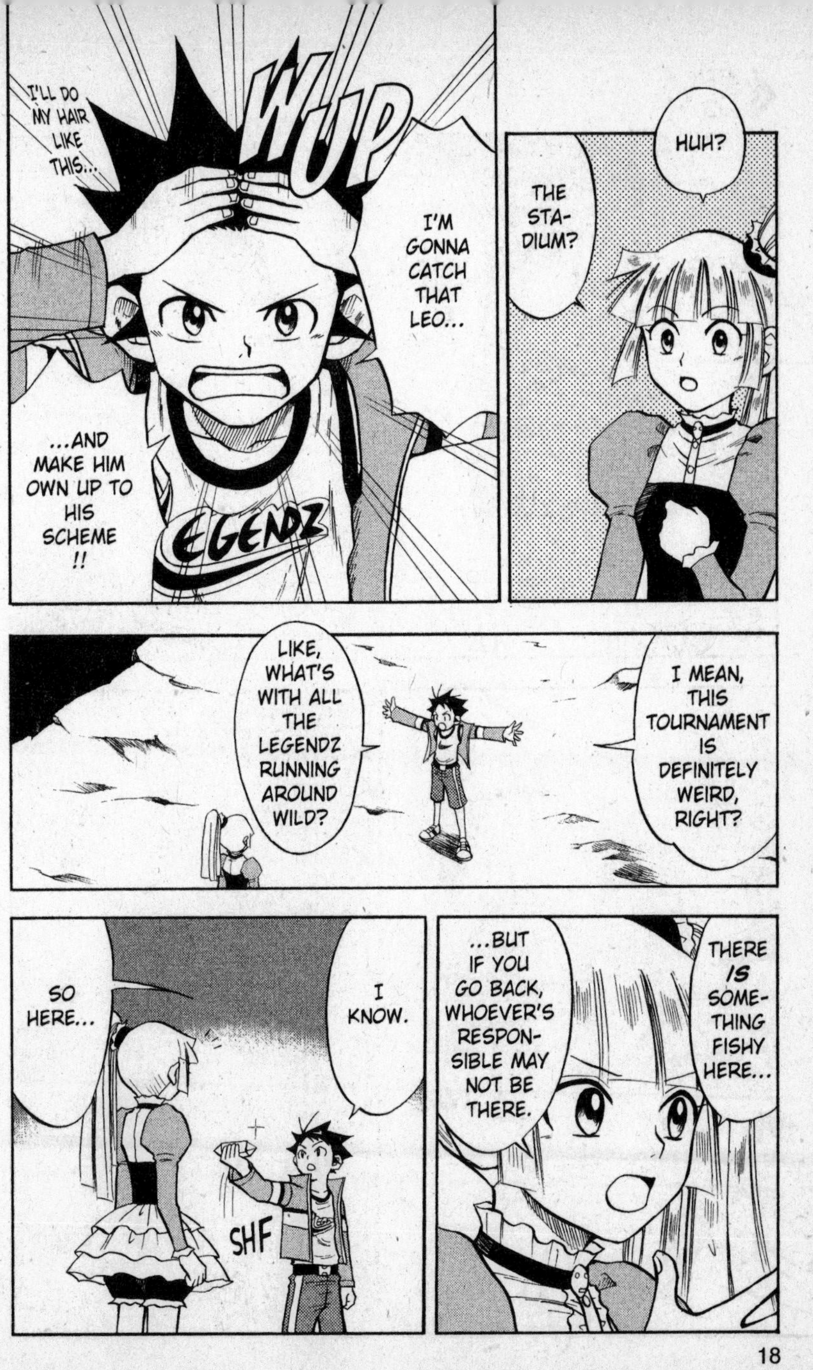
HUH?
THE STADIUM?
I'LL DO MY HAIR LIKE THIS...
WUP
I'M GONNA CATCH THAT LEO...
...AND MAKE HIM OWN UP TO HIS SCHEME!!
EGENDZ
I MEAN, THIS TOURNAMENT IS DEFINITELY WEIRD, RIGHT?
LIKE, WHAT'S WITH ALL THE LEGENDZ RUNNING AROUND WILD?
THERE *IS* SOMETHING FISHY HERE...
...BUT IF YOU GO BACK, WHOEVER'S RESPONSIBLE MAY NOT BE THERE.
I KNOW.
SO HERE...
SHF

READ THIS WAY

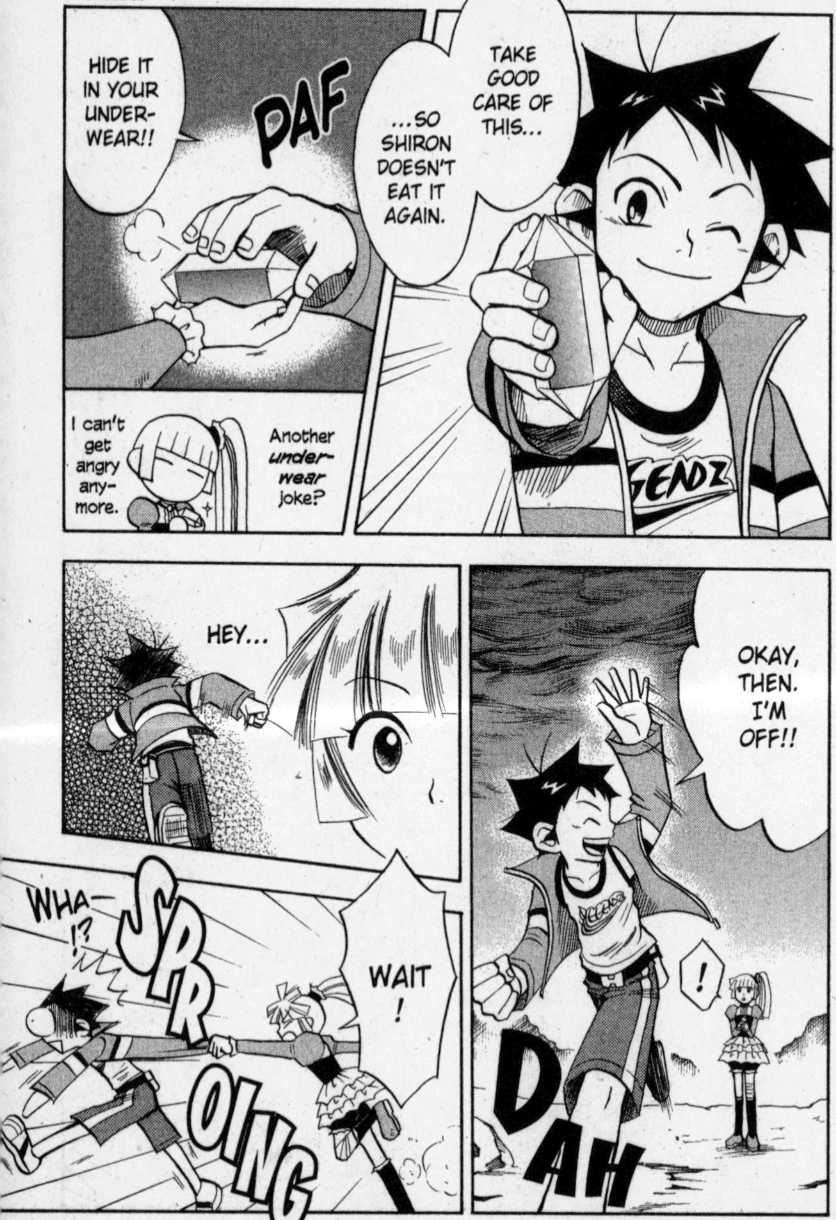
TAKE GOOD CARE OF THIS...
...SO SHIRON DOESN'T EAT IT AGAIN.
PAF
HIDE IT IN YOUR UNDER-WEAR!!
Another underwear joke?
I can't get angry anymore.
OKAY, THEN. I'M OFF!!
!
DAH
HEY...
WAIT!
SPROING
WHA-!?

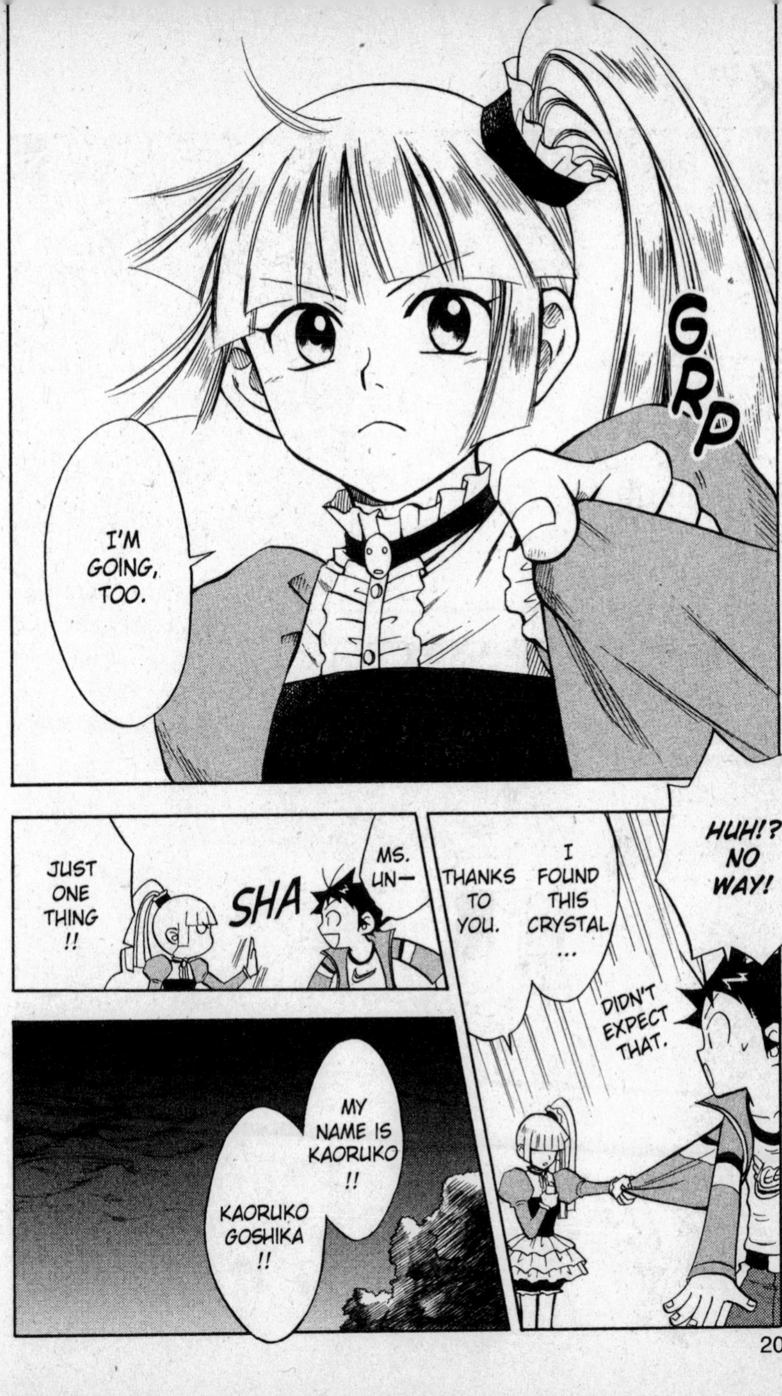
GRP
I'M GOING, TOO.
HUH!? NO WAY!
I FOUND THIS CRYSTAL...
THANKS TO YOU.
DIDN'T EXPECT THAT.
MS. UN—
SHA
JUST ONE THING!!
MY NAME IS KAORUKO!!
KAORUKO GOSHIKA!!

READ THIS WAY

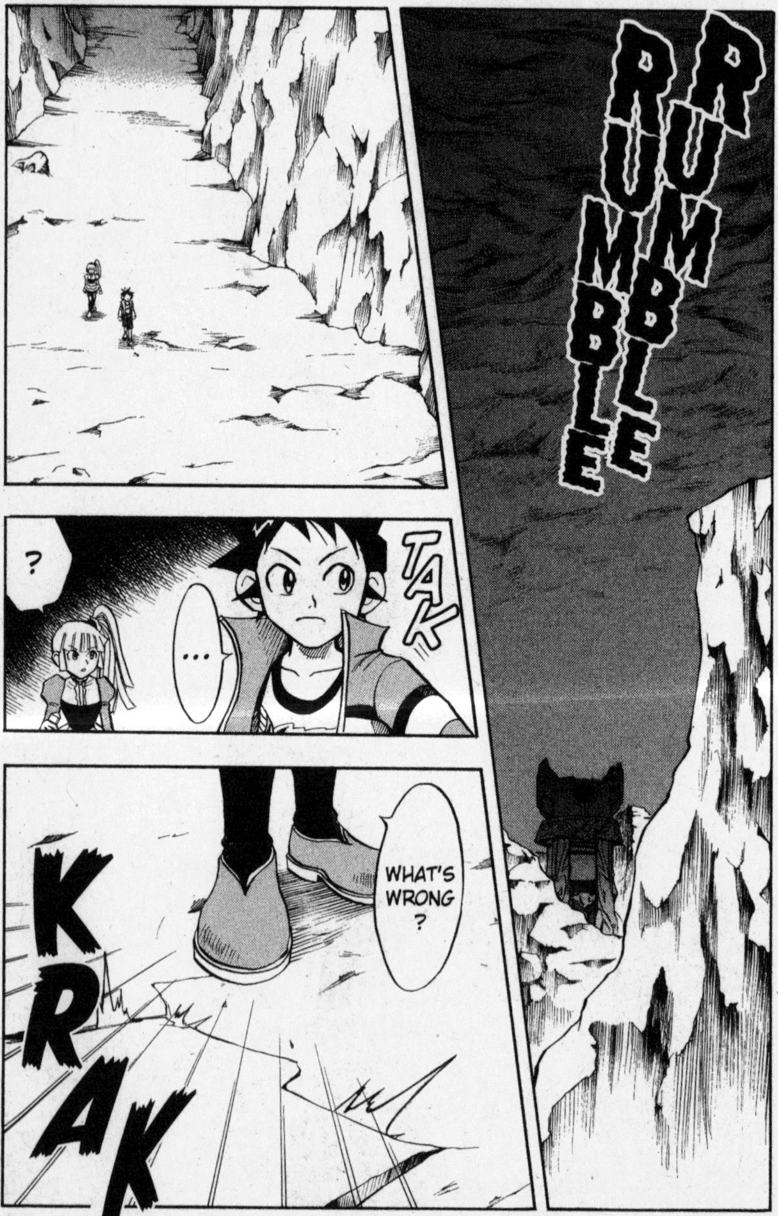
RUMBLE
RUMBLE
TAK
...
?
WHAT'S WRONG?
KRAK

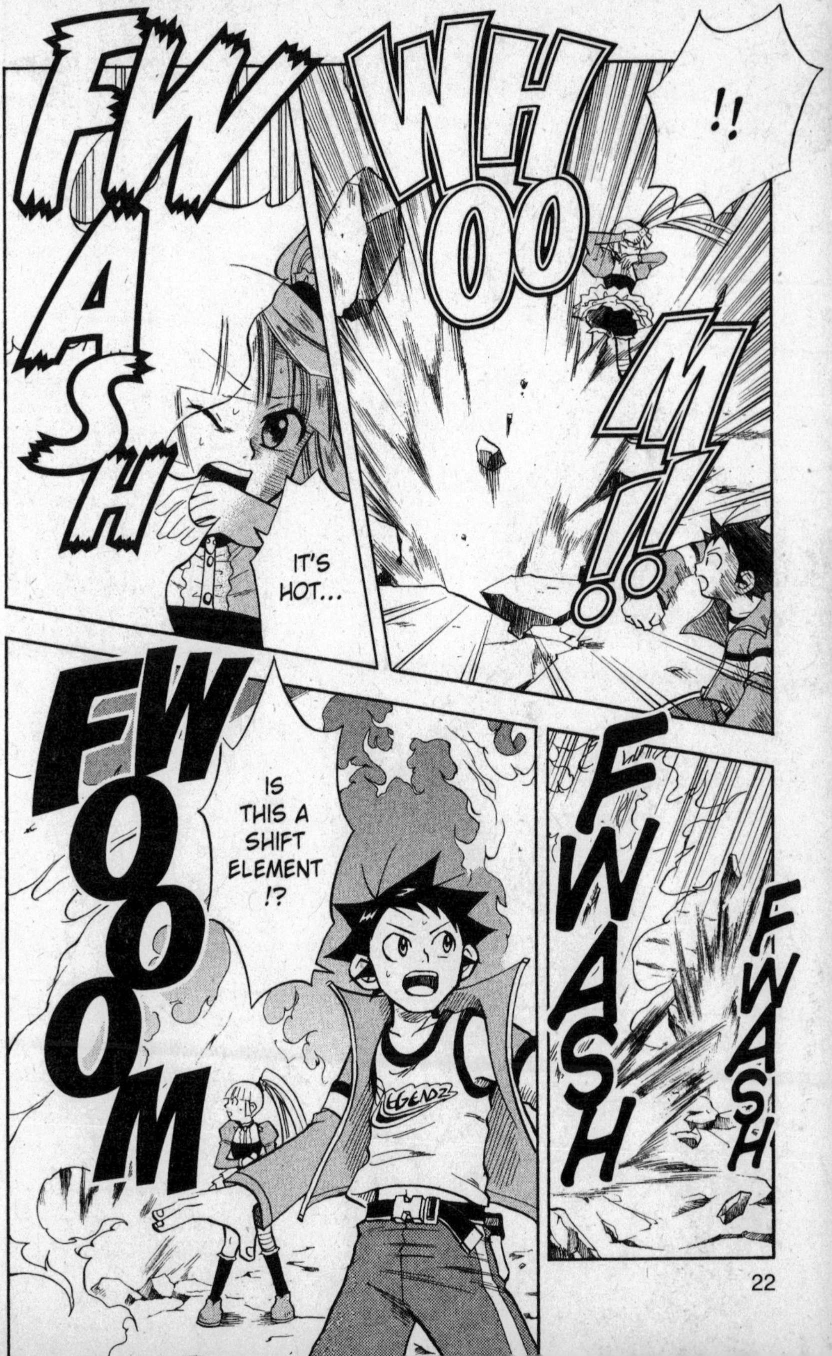
!!
WHOOM!!
FWASH
IT'S HOT...
FWASH
FWASH
FWOOOM
IS THIS A SHIFT ELEMENT !?

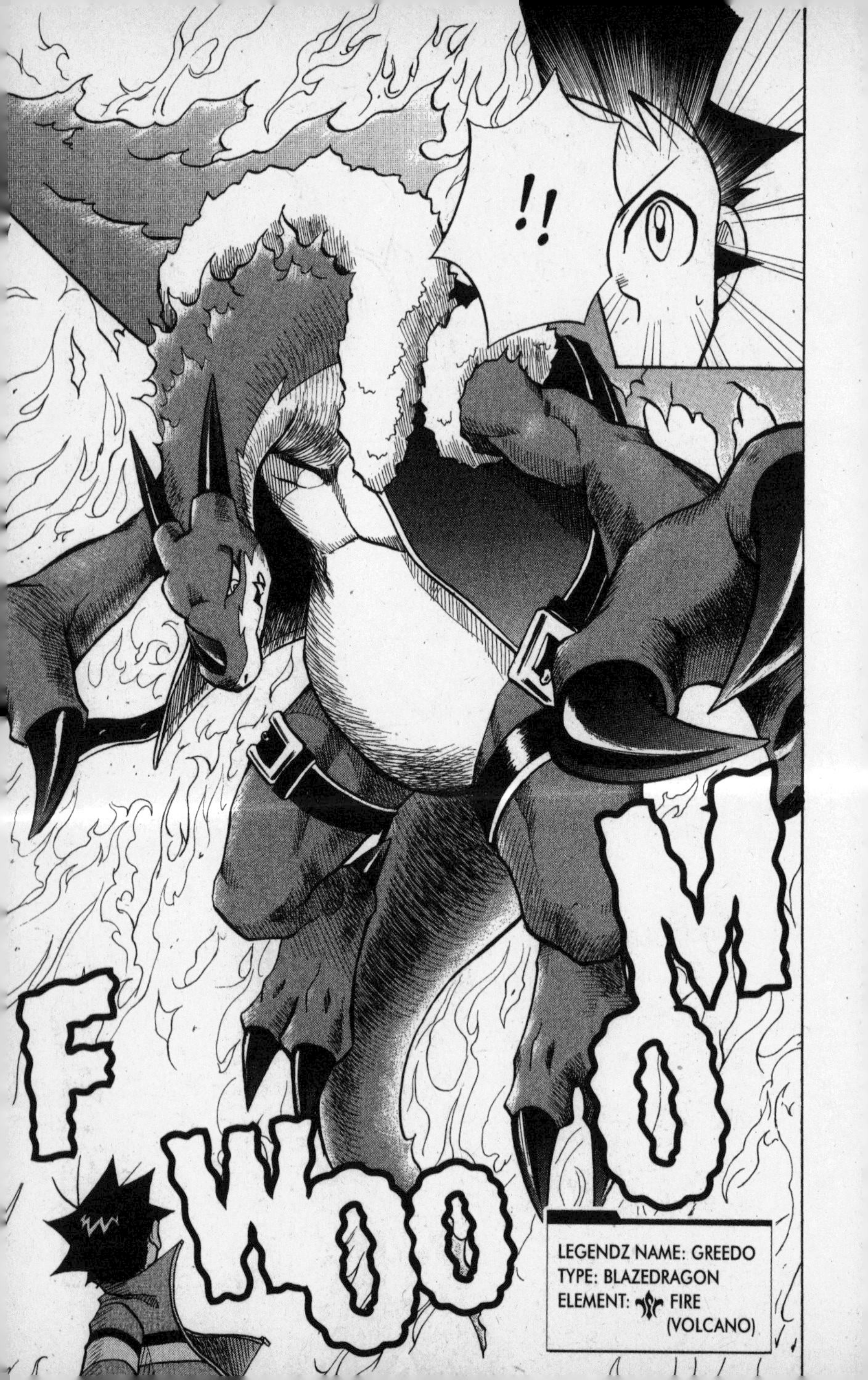
!!
FWOOM
LEGENDZ NAME: GREEDO
TYPE: BLAZEDRAGON
ELEMENT: FIRE (VOLCANO)

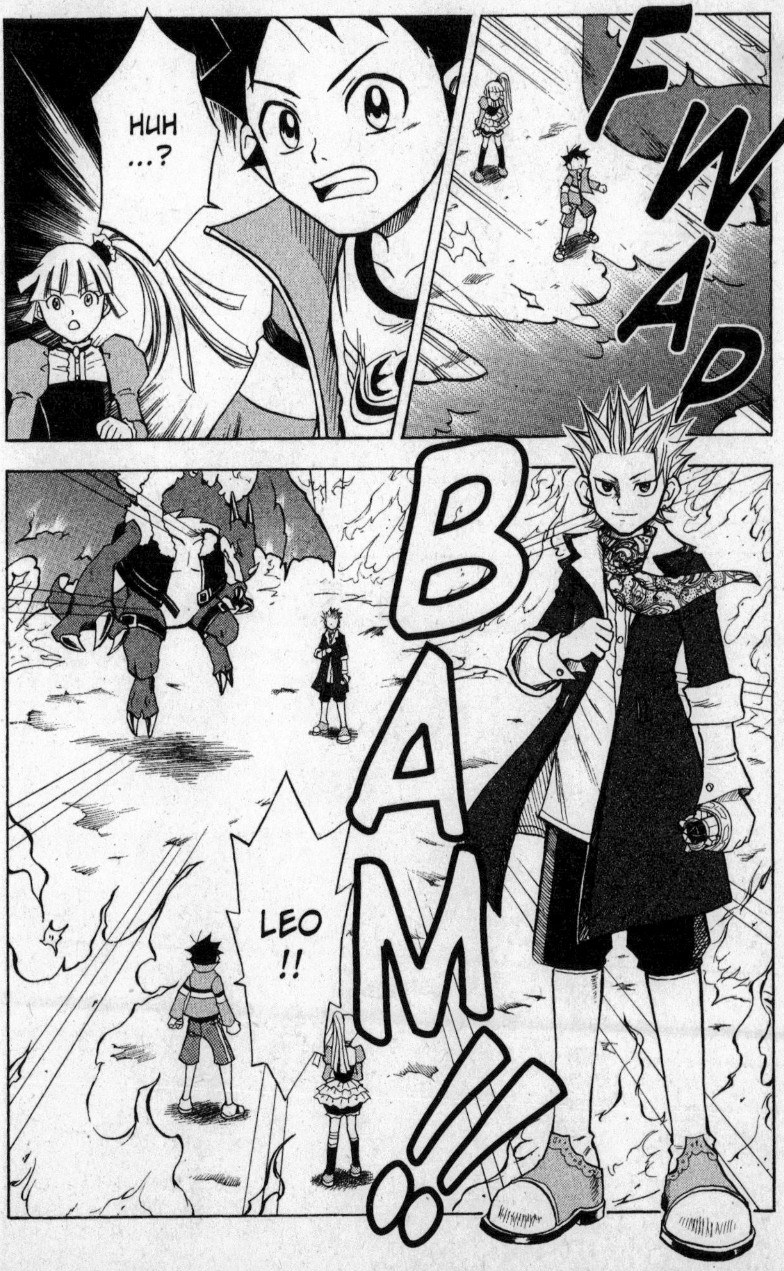
FWAP
HUH ...?
BAM!!
LEO !!

READ THIS WAY

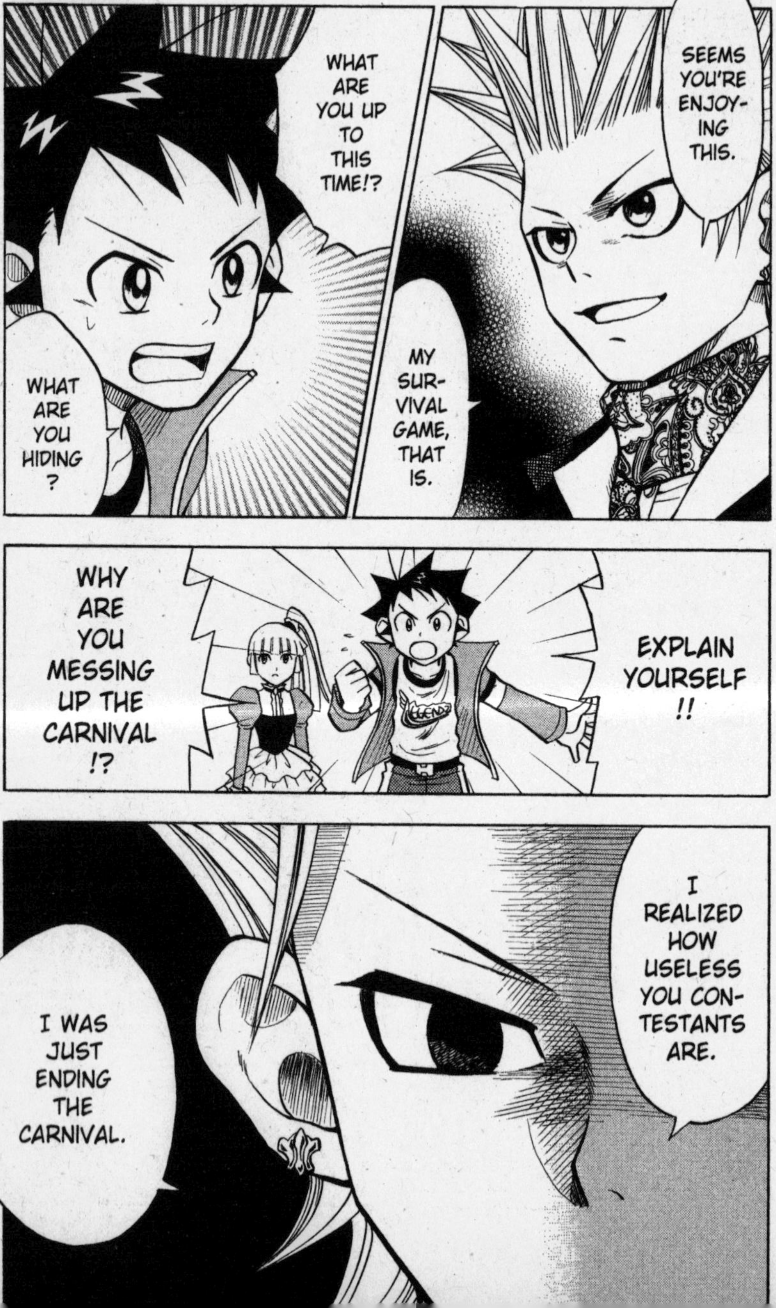
SEEMS YOU'RE ENJOYING THIS.
MY SURVIVAL GAME, THAT IS.
WHAT ARE YOU UP TO THIS TIME!?
WHAT ARE YOU HIDING?
EXPLAIN YOURSELF!!
WHY ARE YOU MESSING UP THE CARNIVAL!?
I REALIZED HOW USELESS YOU CONTESTANTS ARE.
I WAS JUST ENDING THE CARNIVAL.

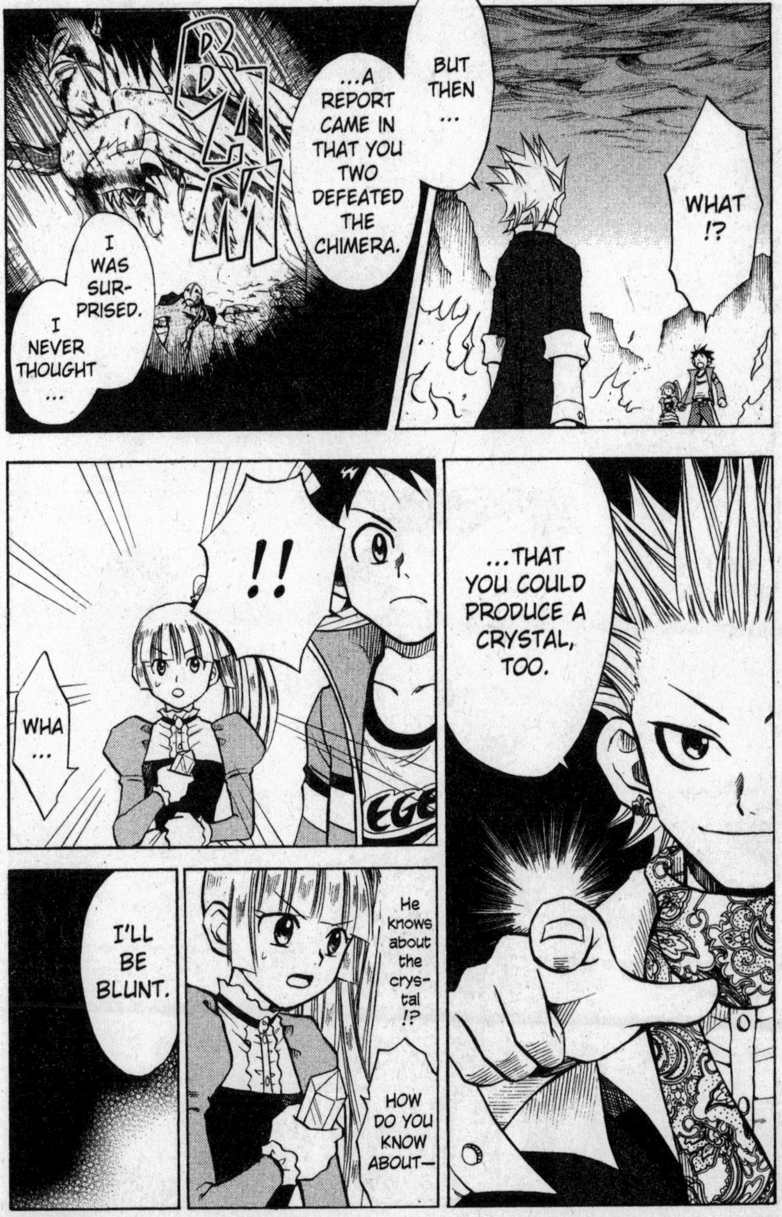
WHAT!?
BUT THEN...
...A REPORT CAME IN THAT YOU TWO DEFEATED THE CHIMERA.
BAM
I WAS SURPRISED.
I NEVER THOUGHT...
...THAT YOU COULD PRODUCE A CRYSTAL, TOO.
!!
WHA...
He knows about the crystal!?
HOW DO YOU KNOW ABOUT—
I'LL BE BLUNT.

READ THIS WAY

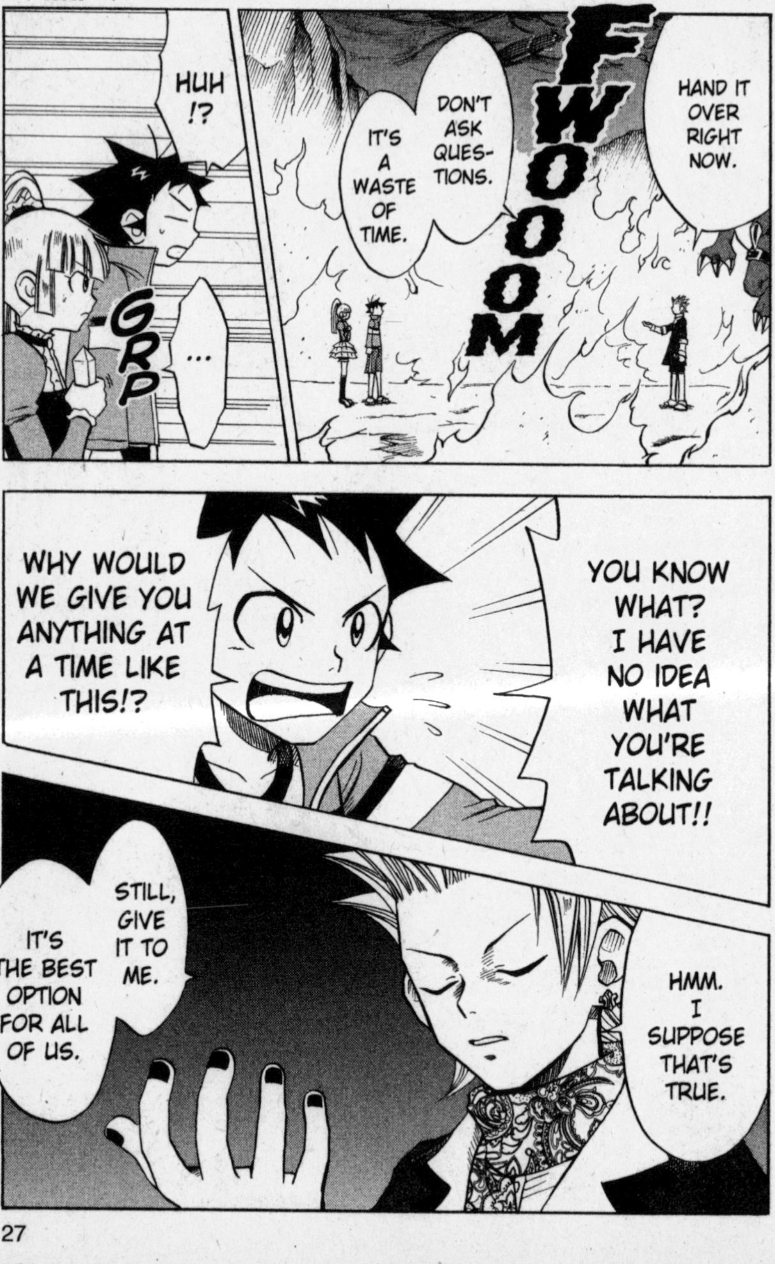
HAND IT OVER RIGHT NOW.
FWOOOOM
DON'T ASK QUES-TIONS.
IT'S A WASTE OF TIME.
HUH !?
...
GRP
YOU KNOW WHAT? I HAVE NO IDEA WHAT YOU'RE TALKING ABOUT!!
WHY WOULD WE GIVE YOU ANYTHING AT A TIME LIKE THIS!?
HMM. I SUPPOSE THAT'S TRUE.
STILL, GIVE IT TO ME.
IT'S THE BEST OPTION FOR ALL OF US.

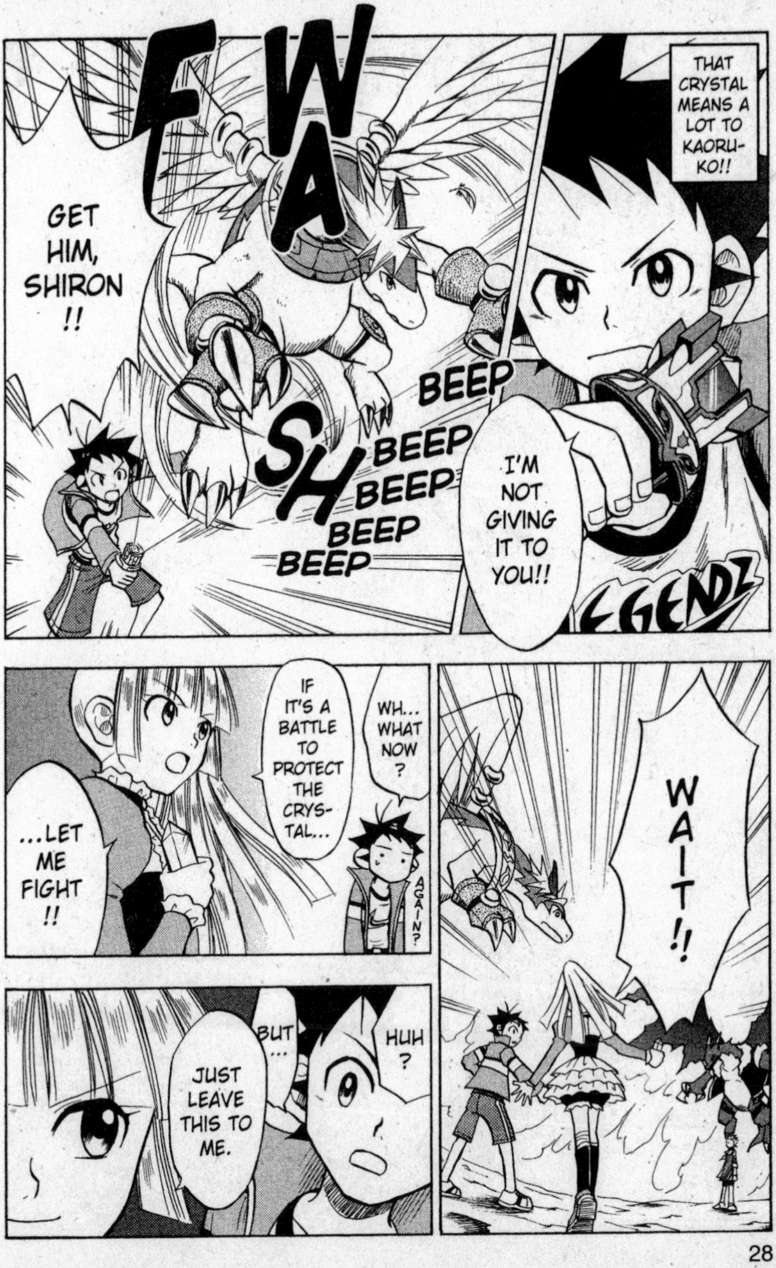
THAT CRYSTAL MEANS A LOT TO KAORU-KO!!
I'M NOT GIVING IT TO YOU!!
FWA
GET HIM, SHIRON!!
BEEP
SH
BEEP
BEEP
BEEP
BEEP
WAIT!!
WH... WHAT NOW?
IF IT'S A BATTLE TO PROTECT THE CRYS-TAL...
AGAIN?
...LET ME FIGHT!!
HUH?
BUT...
JUST LEAVE THIS TO ME.

READ THIS WAY

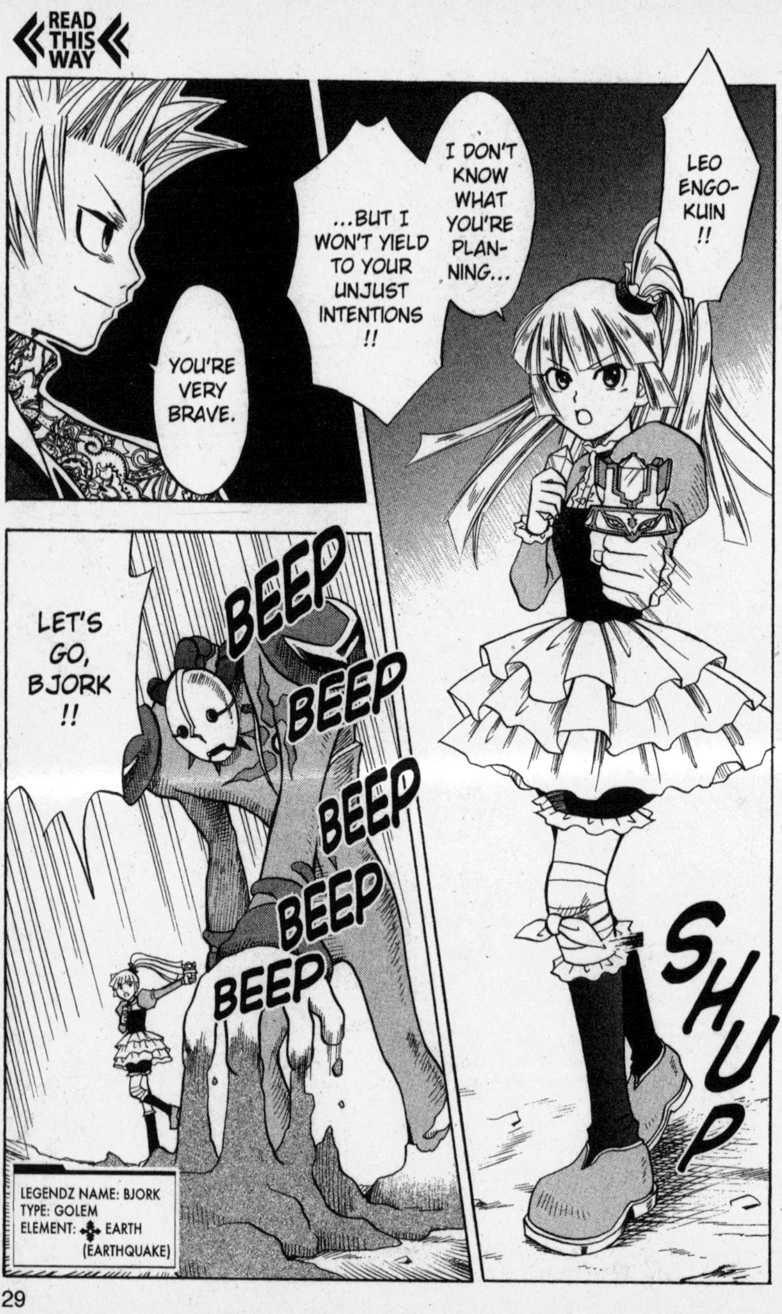
LEO ENGO-KUIN !!
I DON'T KNOW WHAT YOU'RE PLAN-NING...
...BUT I WON'T YIELD TO YOUR UNJUST INTENTIONS !!
SHUP
YOU'RE VERY BRAVE.
LET'S GO, BJORK !!
BEEP
BEEP
BEEP
BEEP
BEEP
LEGENDZ NAME: BJORK
TYPE: GOLEM
ELEMENT: EARTH
(EARTHQUAKE)

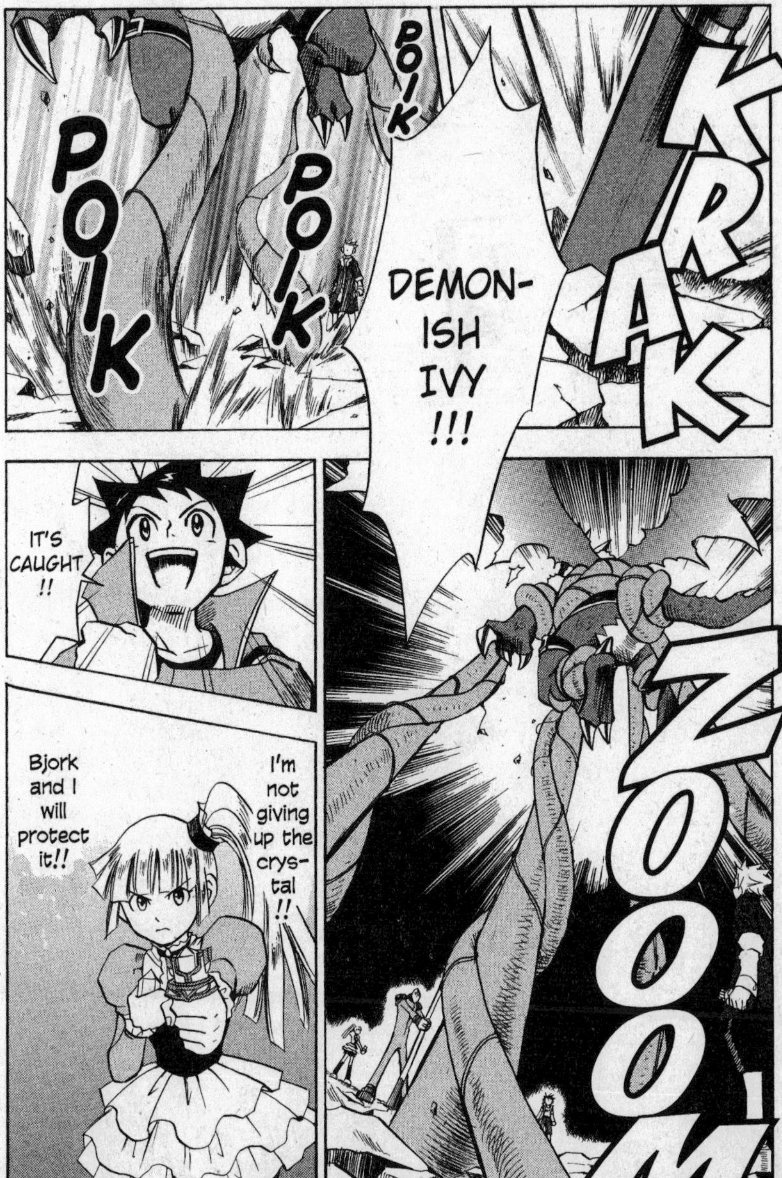
KRAK
POIK
DEMON-ISH IVY!!!
POIK
POIK
ZOOM
IT'S CAUGHT!!
I'm not giving up the crys-tal!!
Bjork and I will protect it!!

READ THIS WAY

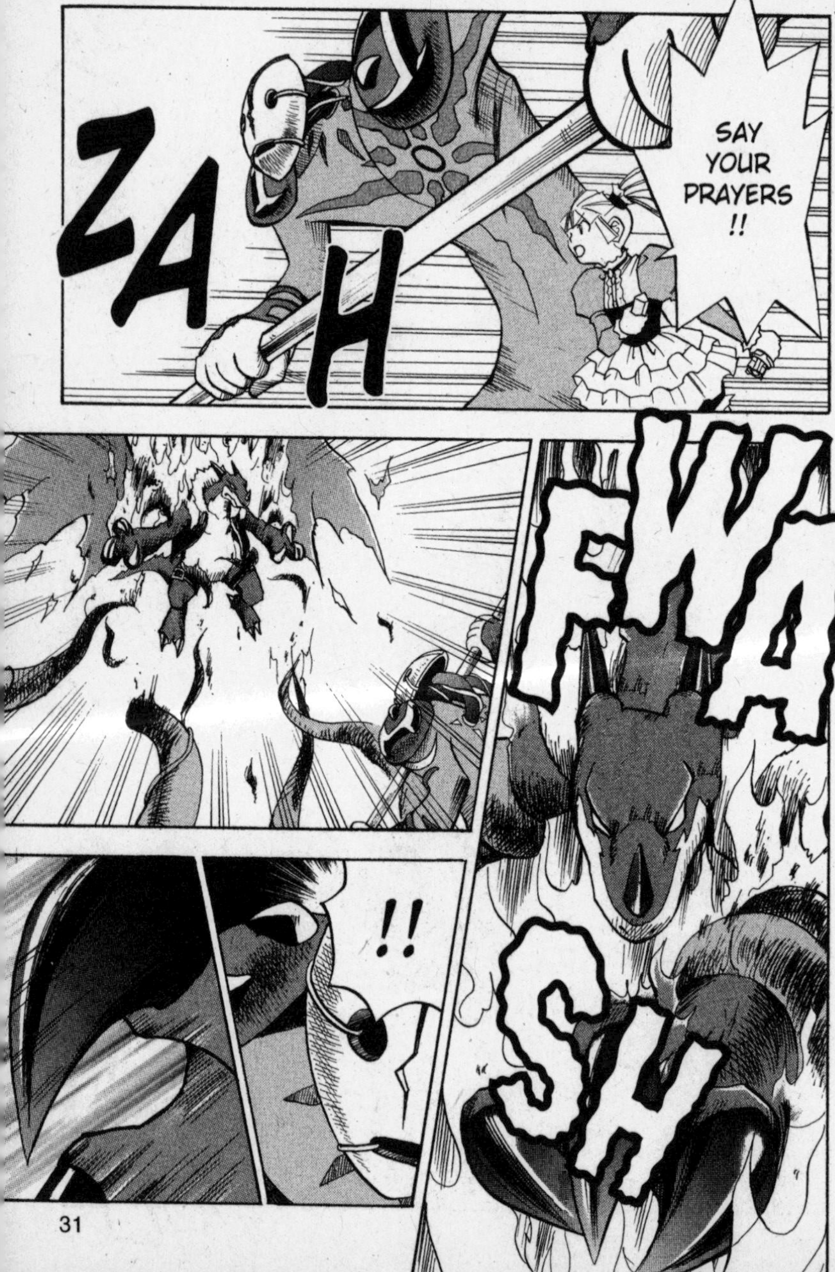
SAY YOUR PRAYERS !!
ZAH
FWASH
!!

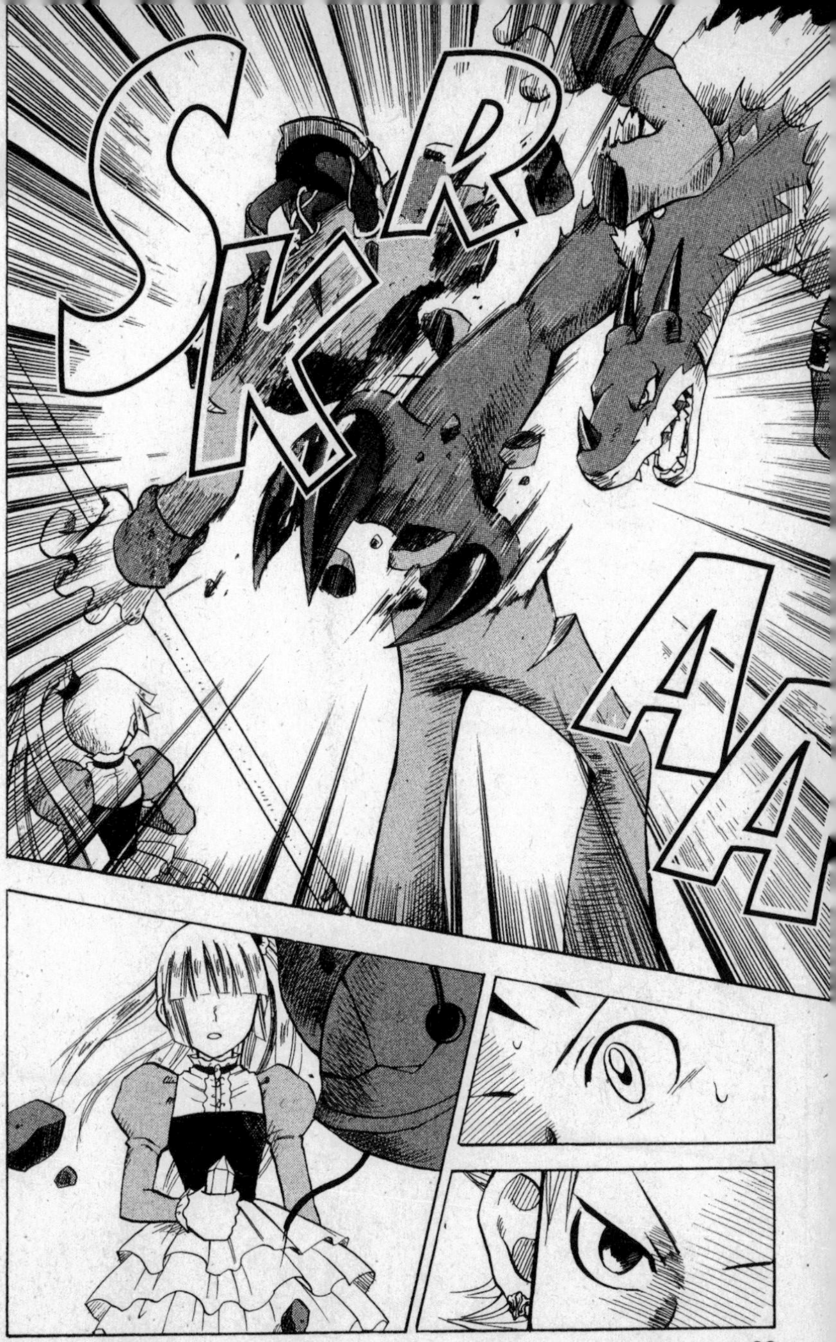
SKRK
AA

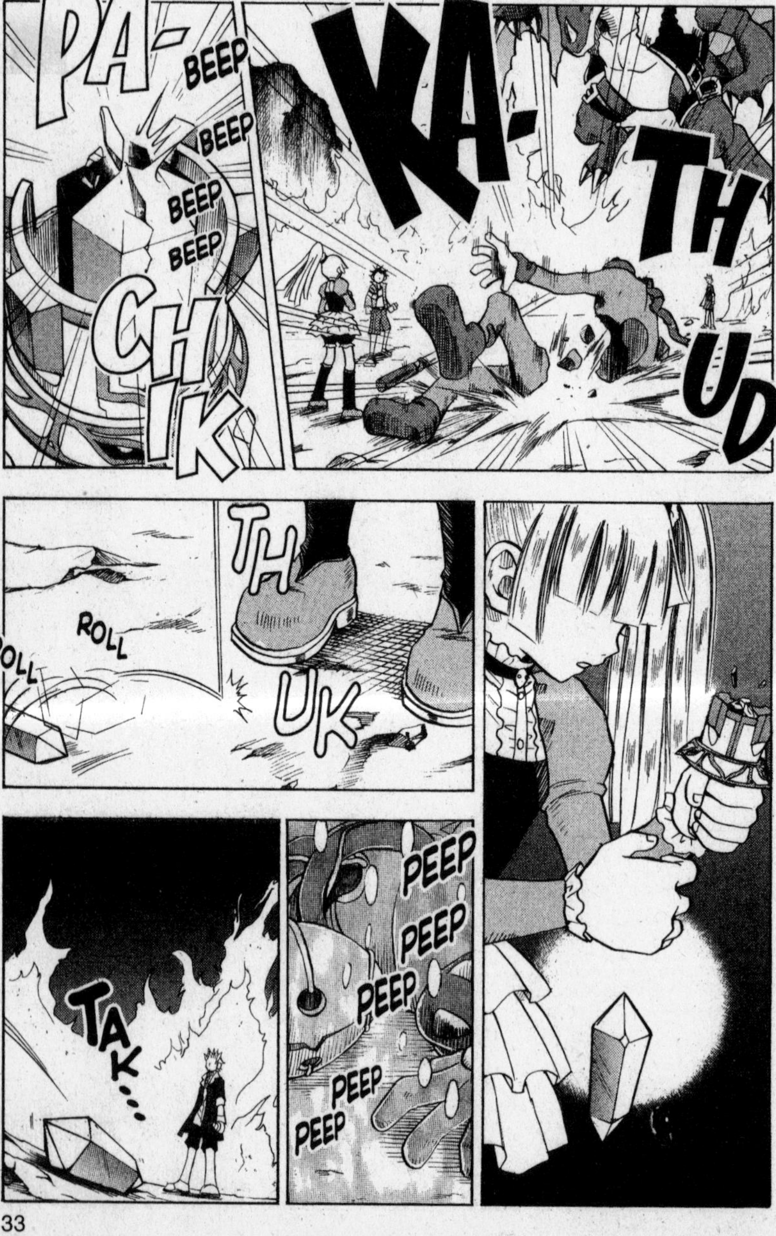
KA-
THUD
PA-
BEEP
BEEP
BEEP
BEEP
CHIK
THUK
ROLL
ROLL
PEEP
PEEP
PEEP
PEEP
PEEP
TAK...

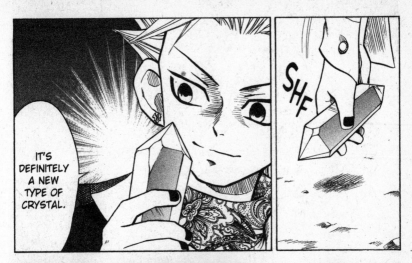

IT'S DEFINITELY A NEW TYPE OF CRYSTAL.

SHF

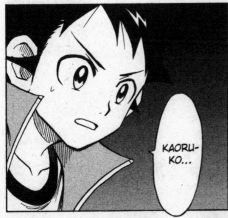

KAORU-KO...

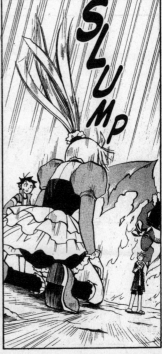

SLUMP

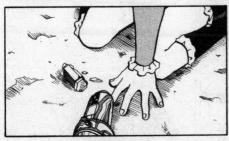

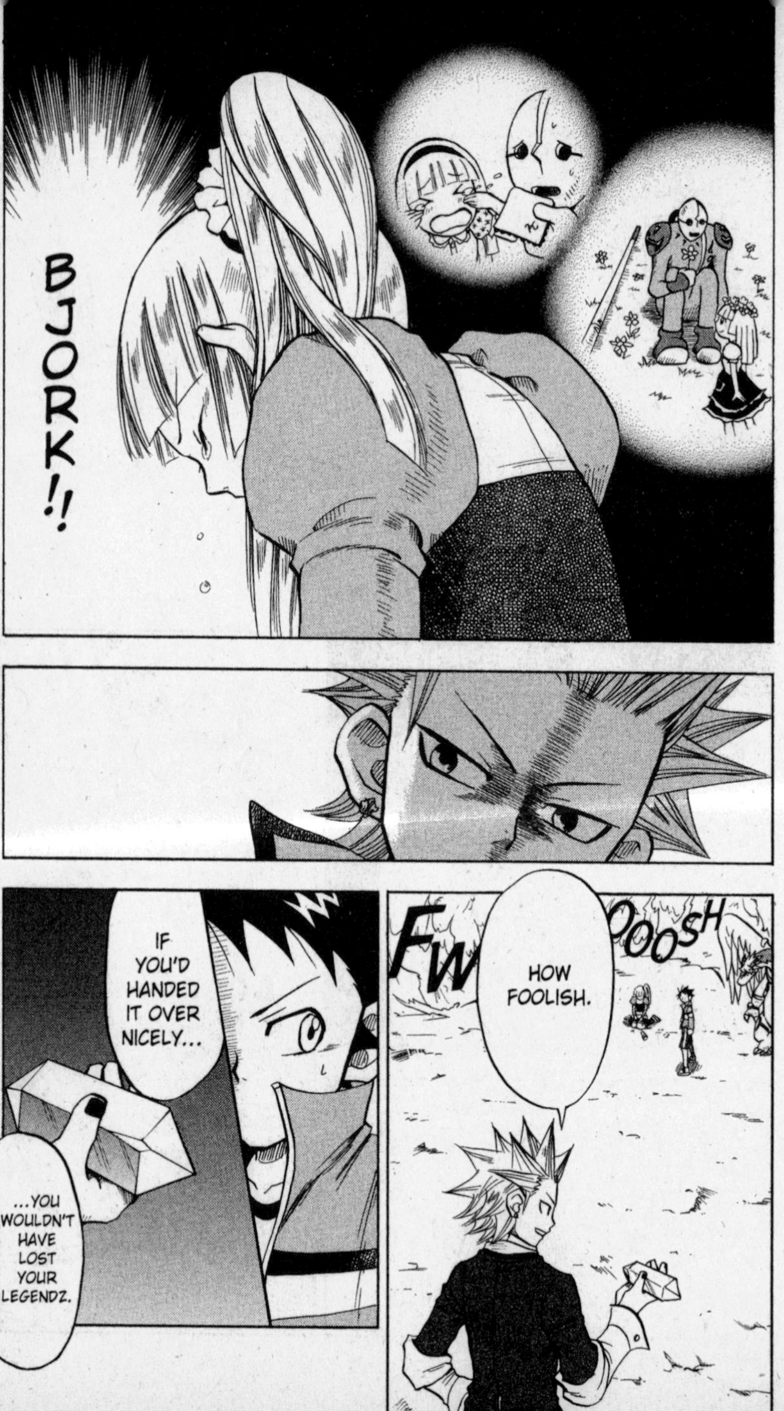
BJORK!!
FWOOOOSH
HOW FOOLISH.
IF YOU'D HANDED IT OVER NICELY...
...YOU WOULDN'T HAVE LOST YOUR LEGENDZ.

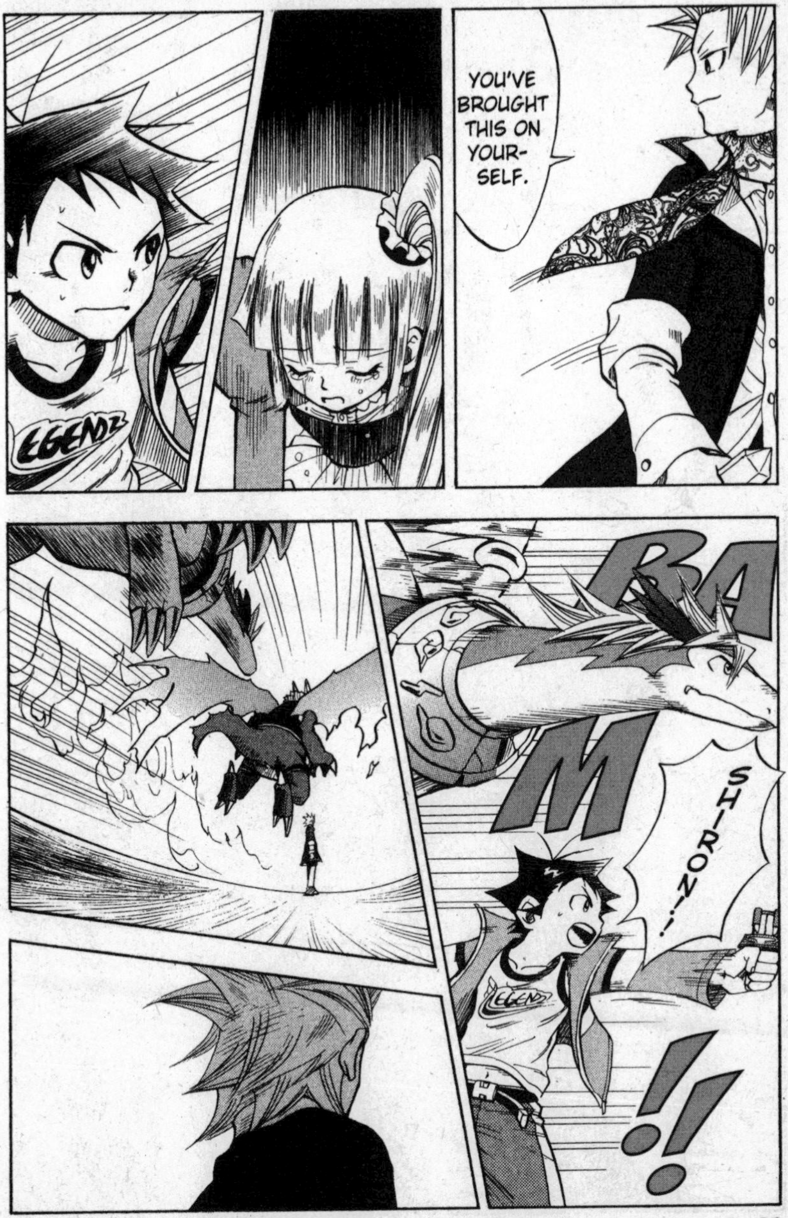
YOU'VE BROUGHT THIS ON YOUR-SELF.
BAM
SHIRON!!
!!

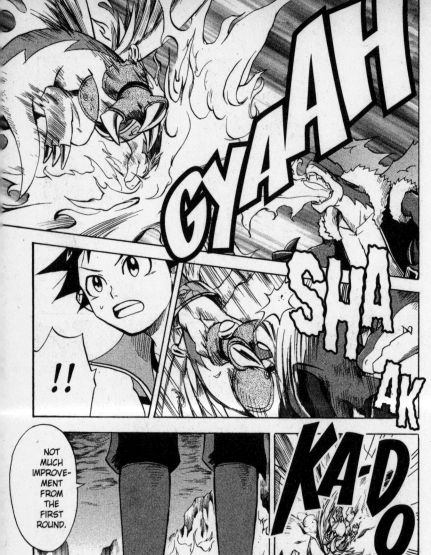

GYAAH!

SHAAK

!!

NOT MUCH IMPROVEMENT FROM THE FIRST ROUND.

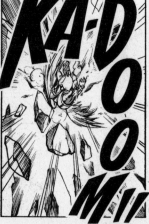

KA-DOOM!!

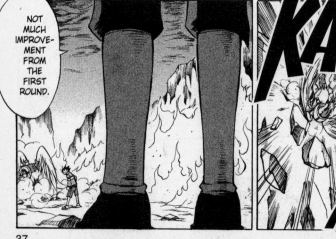

IS THAT IT?
RR RR ...
HE... HE'S TOUGH!!
AT THIS RATE...
...HE'LL TAKE KAORUKO'S CRYSTAL!
!
THUD
SHIRON!?

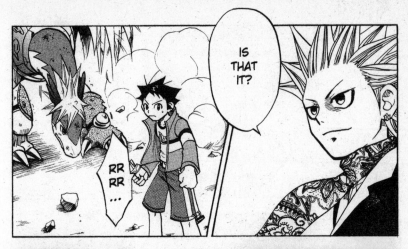

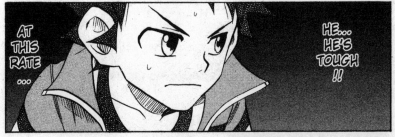

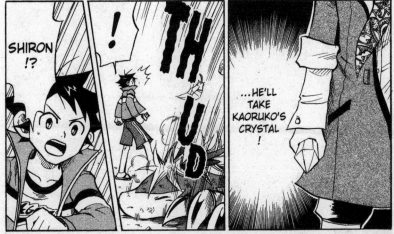

READ THIS WAY

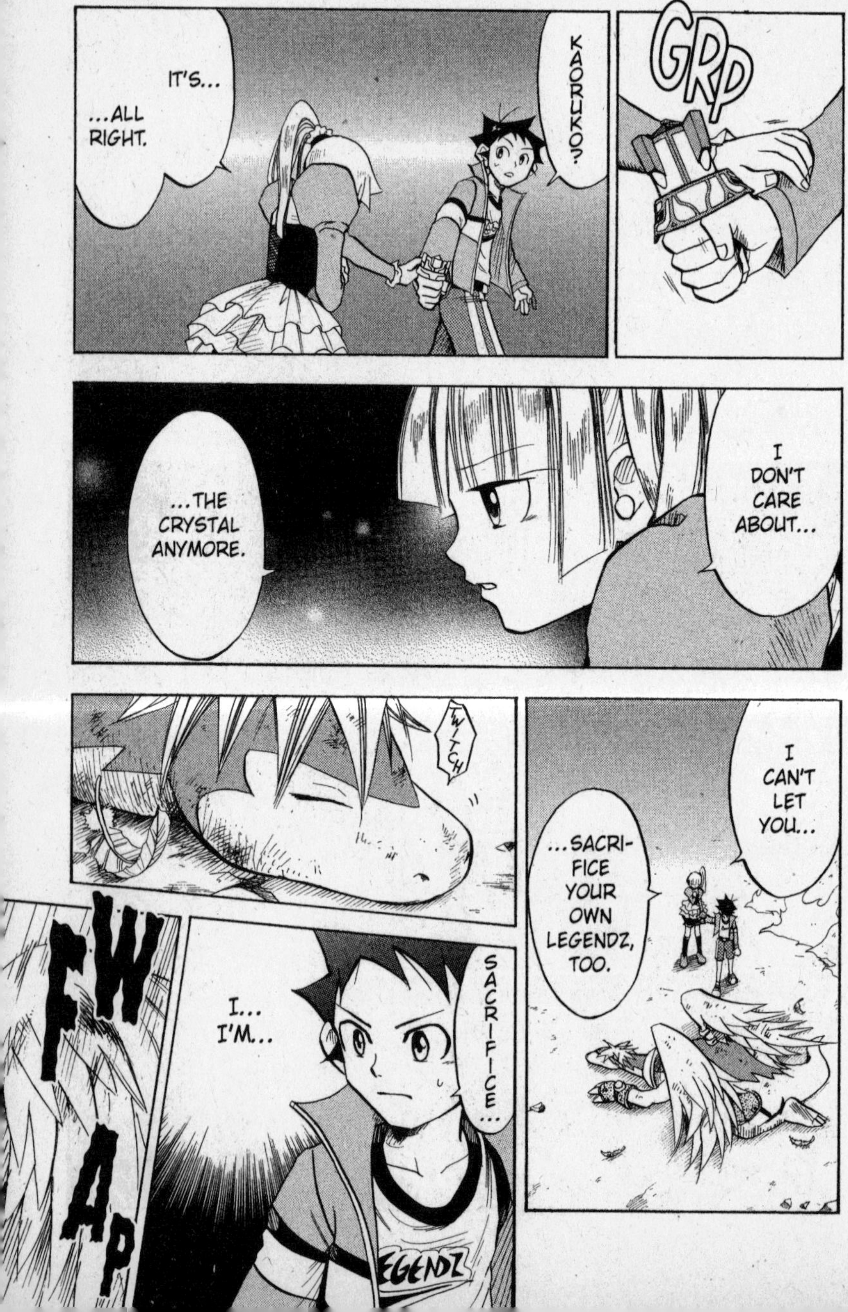
GRP
KAORUKO?
IT'S...
...ALL RIGHT.
I DON'T CARE ABOUT...
...THE CRYSTAL ANYMORE.
I CAN'T LET YOU...
...SACRIFICE YOUR OWN LEGENDZ, TOO.
TWITCH
SACRIFICE...
I... I'M...
FWAP

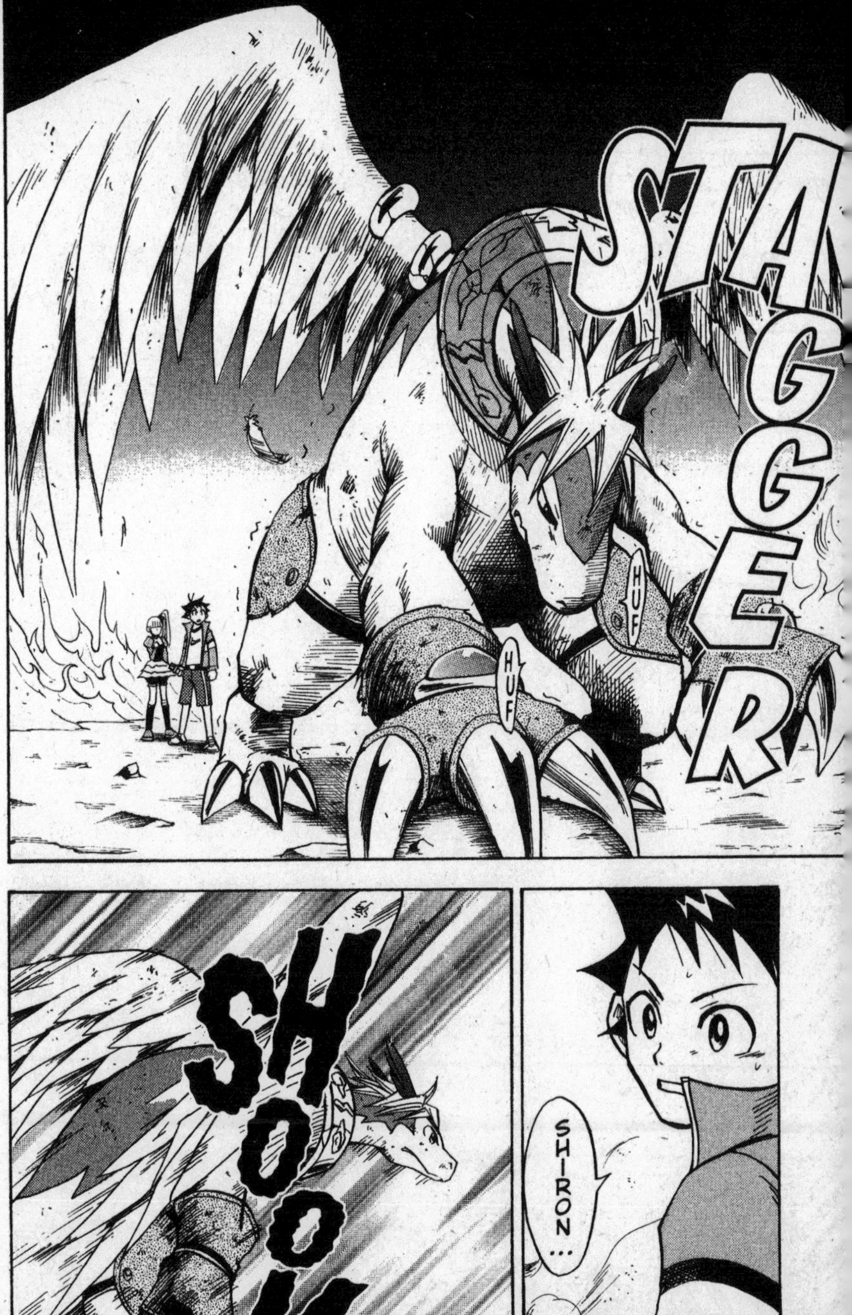
STAGGER
HUF
HUF
SHIRON...
SHOOOM

READ THIS WAY

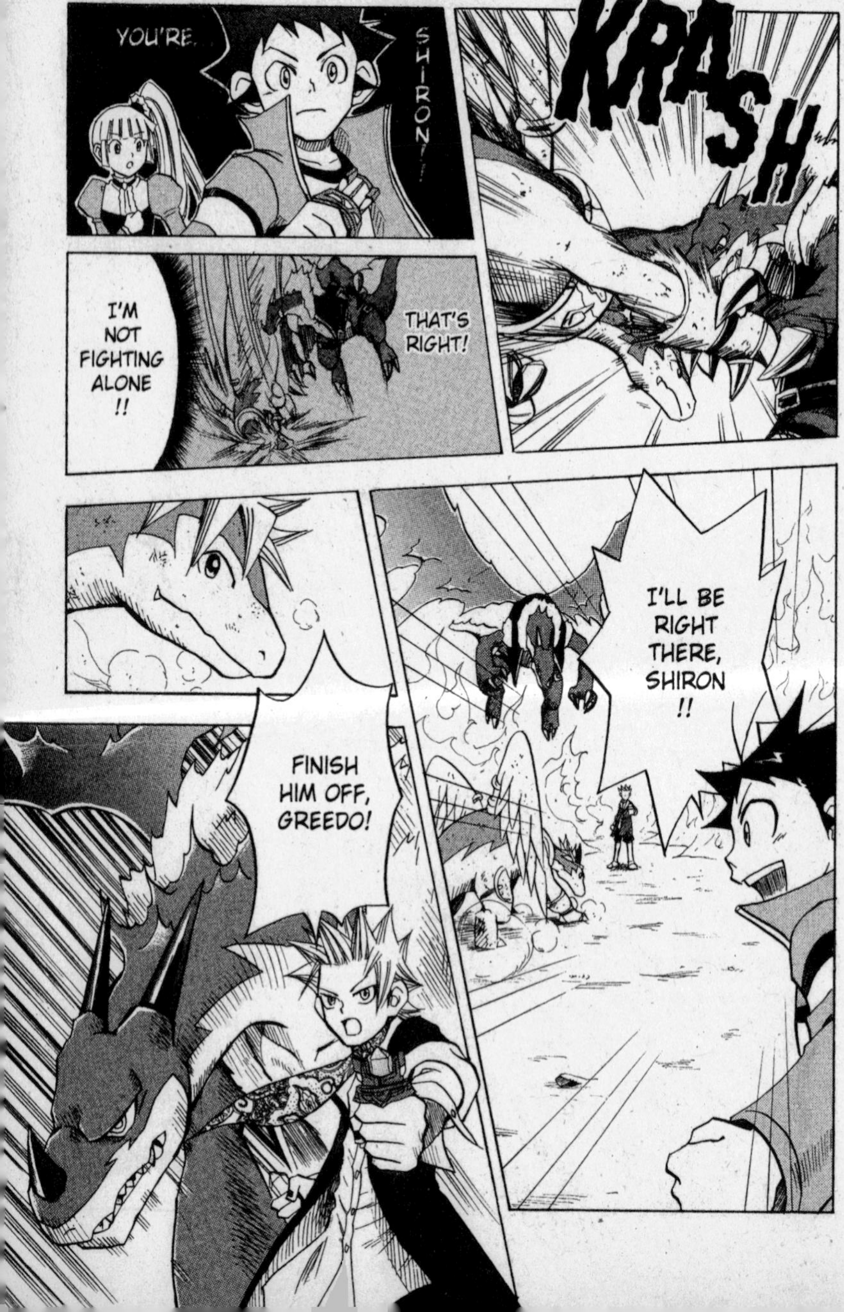
KRASH
SHIRON!!
YOU'RE...
THAT'S RIGHT!
I'M NOT FIGHTING ALONE !!
I'LL BE RIGHT THERE, SHIRON !!
FINISH HIM OFF, GREEDO!

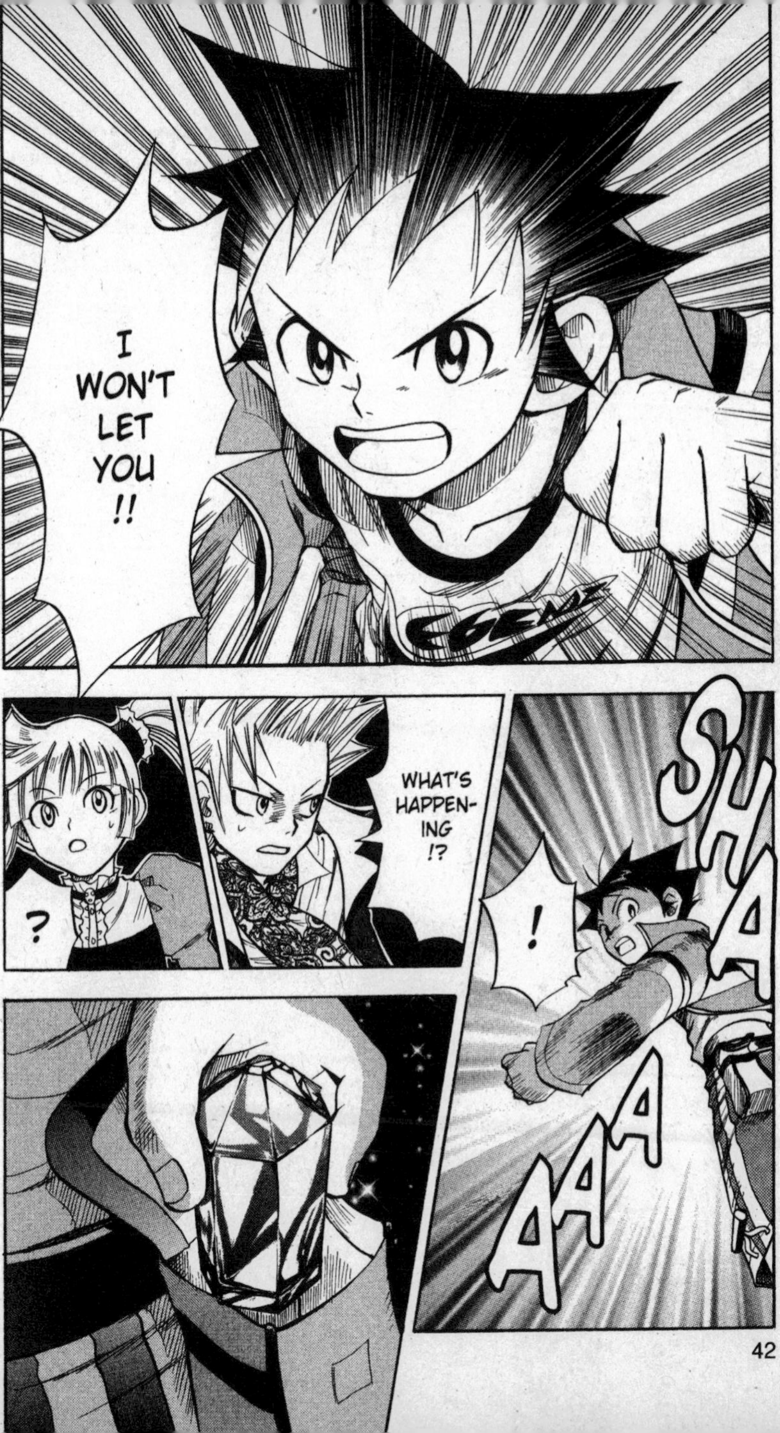
I WON'T LET YOU !!
SHAAAAA
!
WHAT'S HAPPEN-ING !?
?

READ THIS WAY

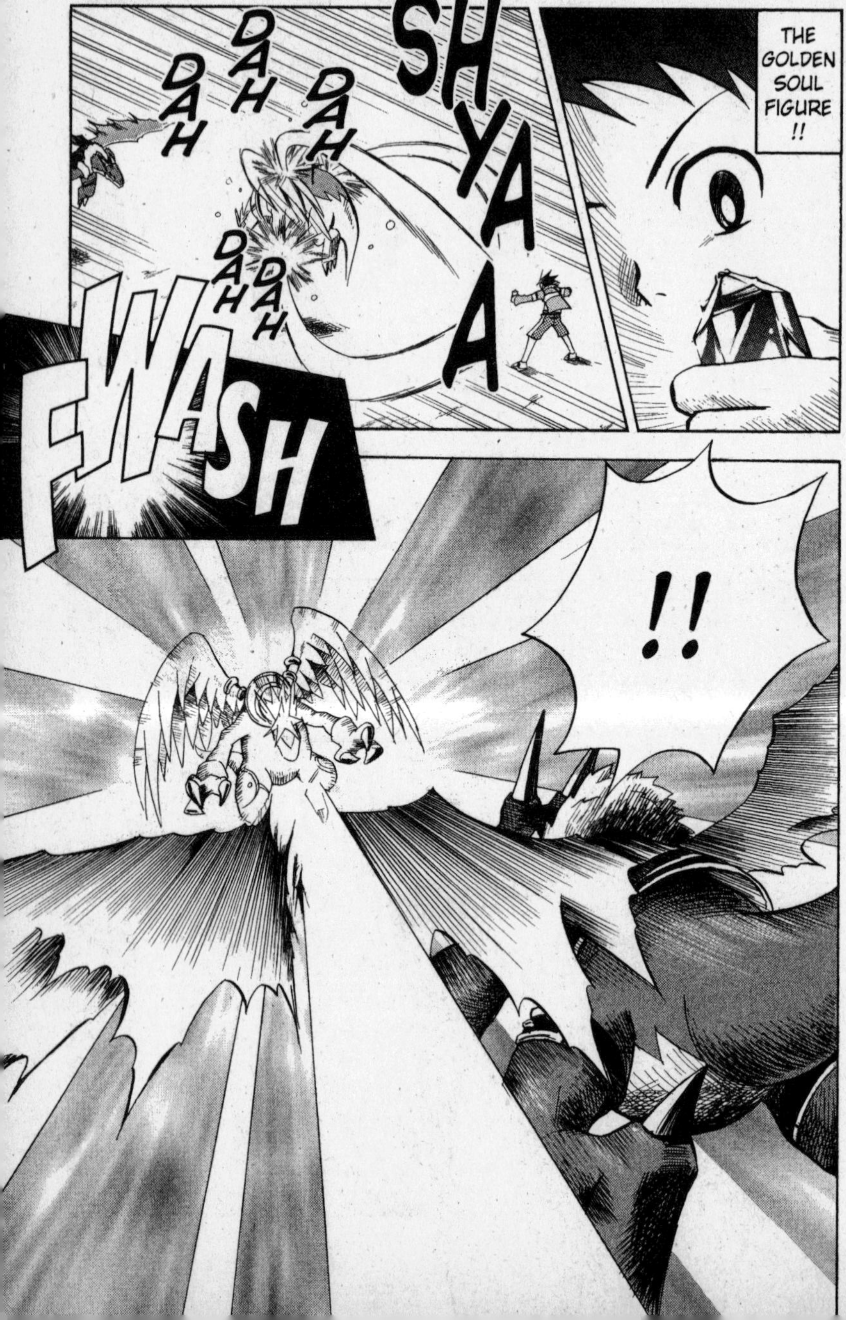
THE GOLDEN SOUL FIGURE !!
SHYAA
DAH
DAH
DAH
DAH
DAH
FWASH
!!

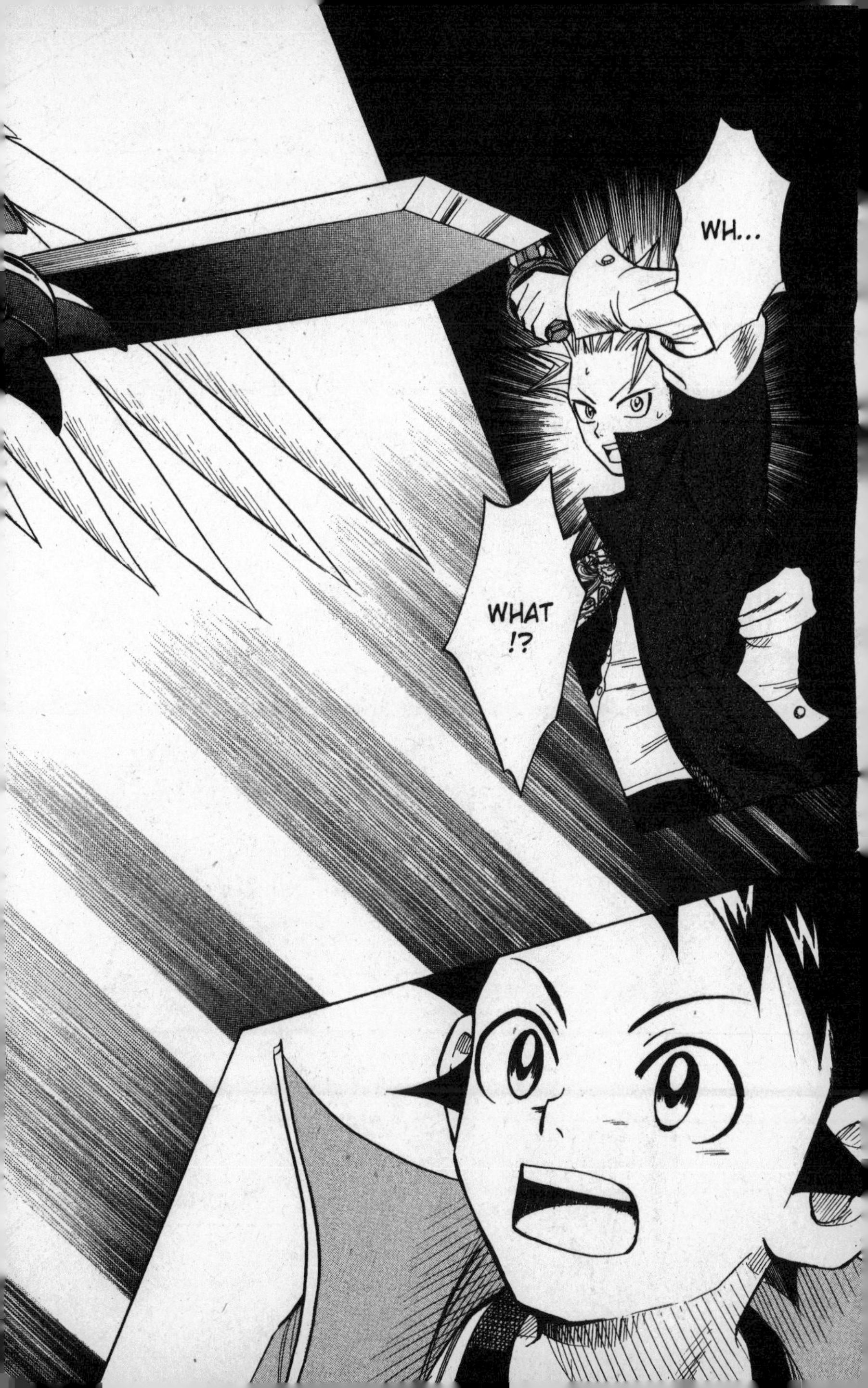
WH...
WHAT !?

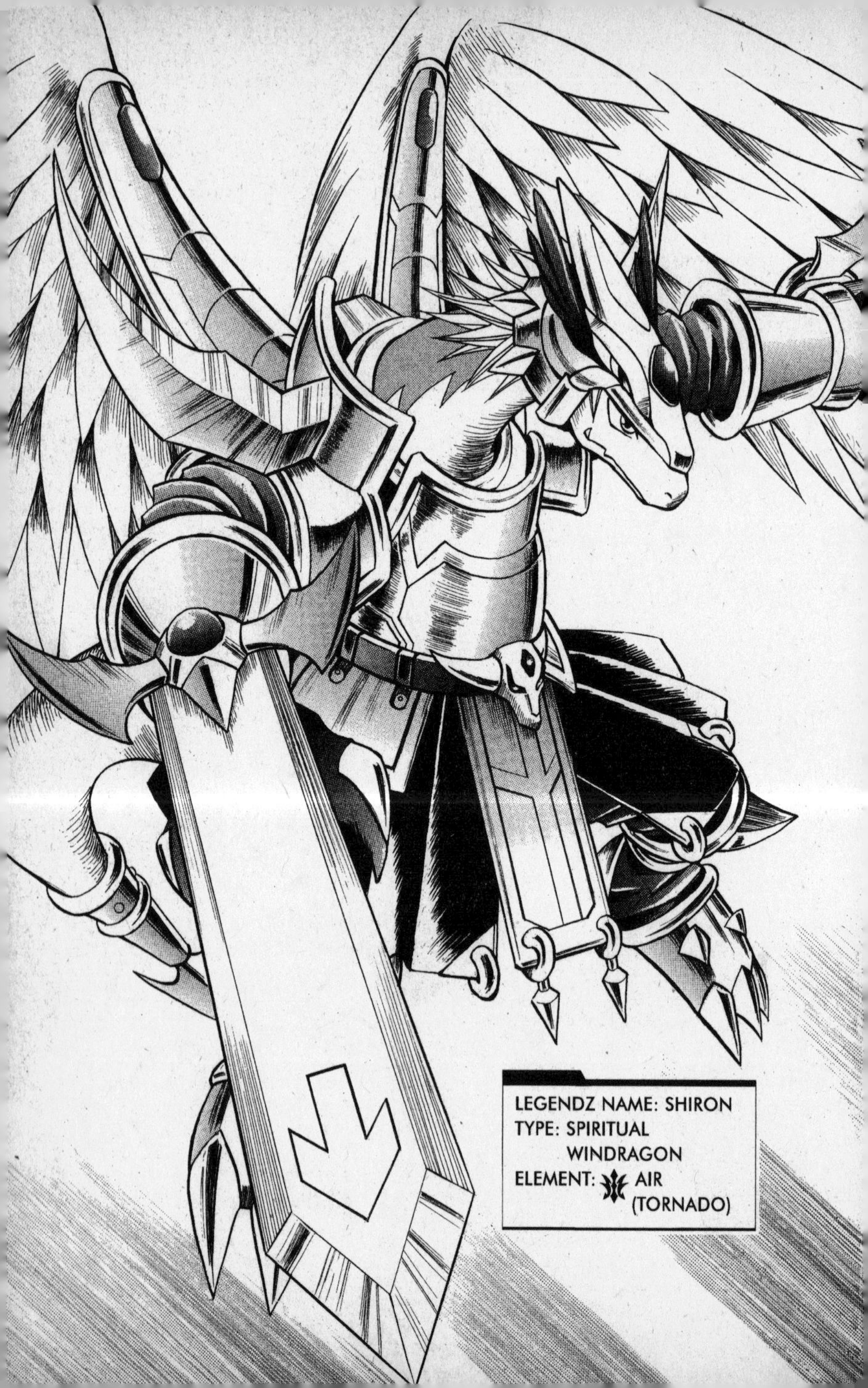
LEGENDZ NAME: SHIRON
TYPE: SPIRITUAL WINDRAGON
ELEMENT: AIR (TORNADO)

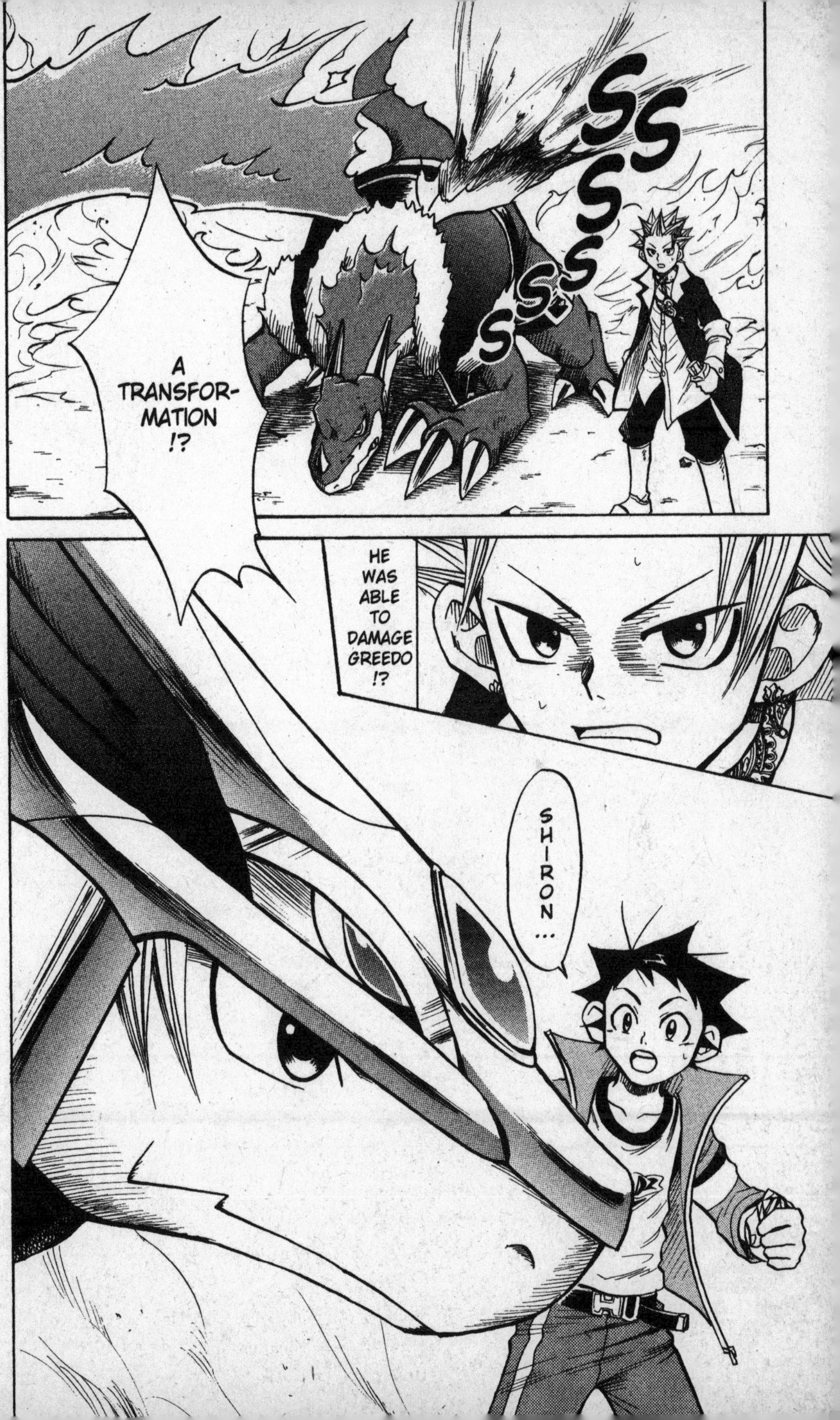
SSSSSSS
A TRANSFORMATION!?
HE WAS ABLE TO DAMAGE GREEDO!?
SHIRON...

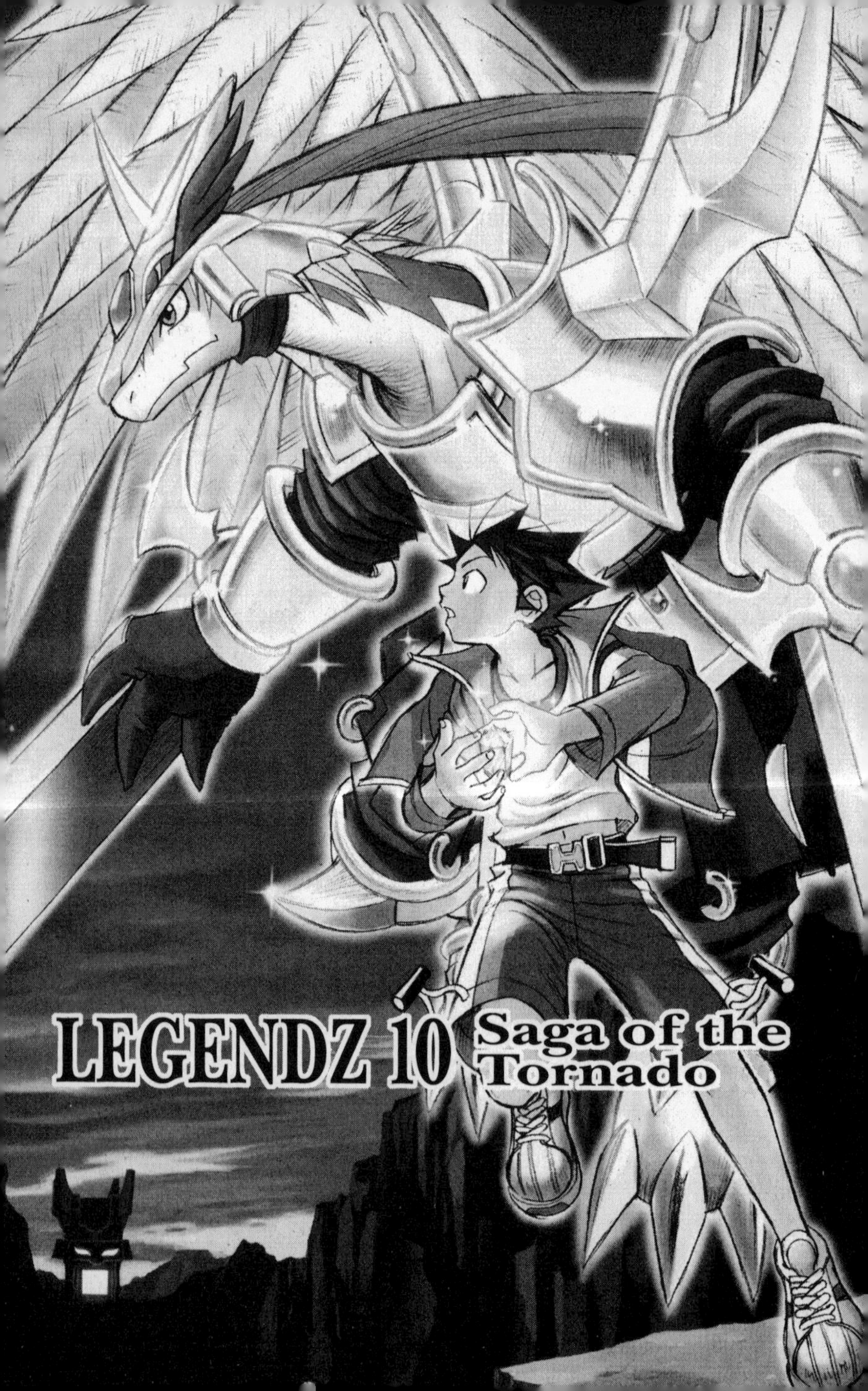
LEGENDZ 10
Saga of the Tornado

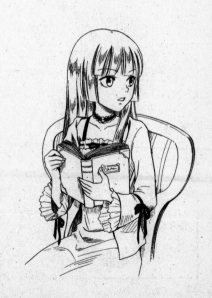

READ THIS WAY

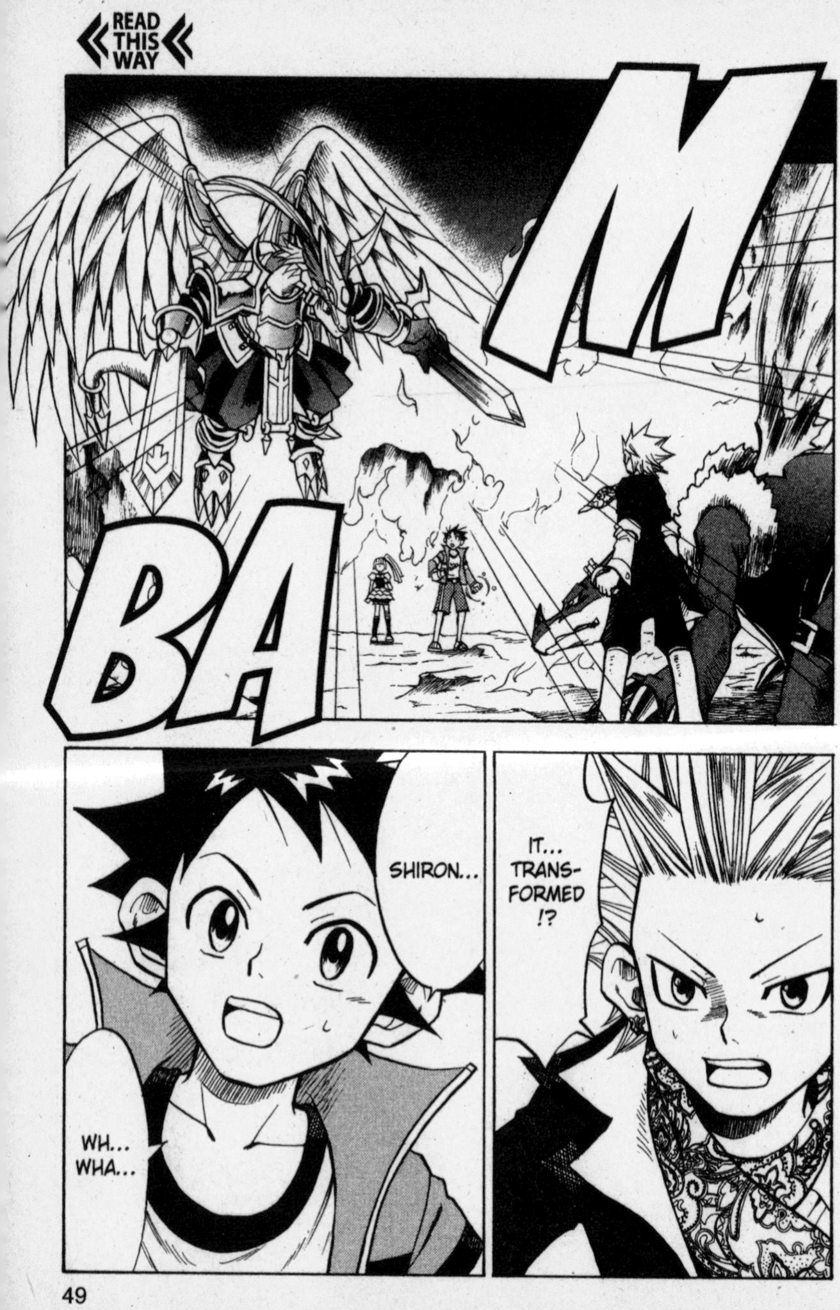
BAM
IT... TRANS-FORMED!?
SHIRON...
WH... WHA...

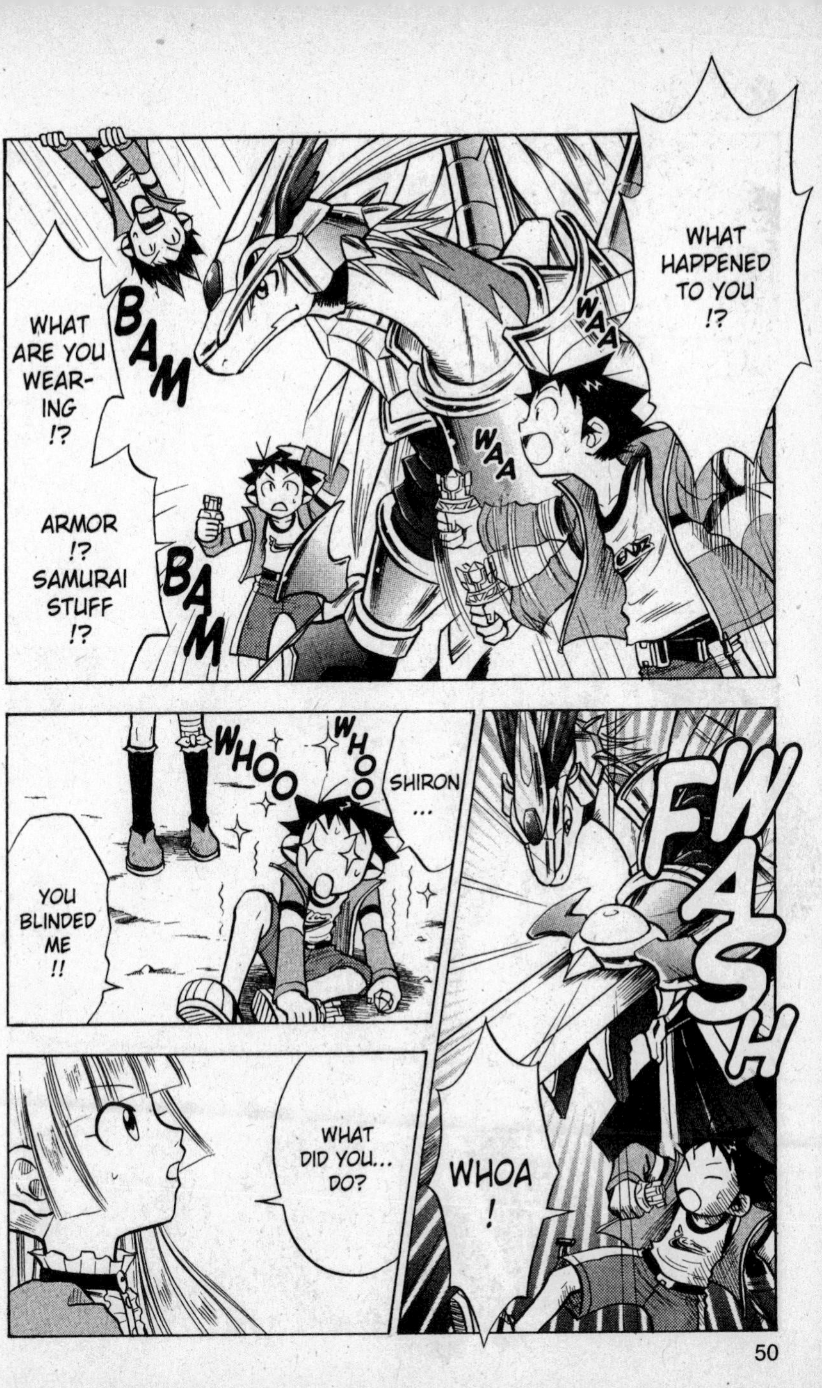
WHAT HAPPENED TO YOU !?
WAA
WAA
WHAT ARE YOU WEAR-ING !?
BAM
ARMOR !? SAMURAI STUFF !?
BAM
FWASH
WHOA !
SHIRON ...
WHOO
WHOO
YOU BLINDED ME !!
WHAT DID YOU... DO?

READ THIS WAY

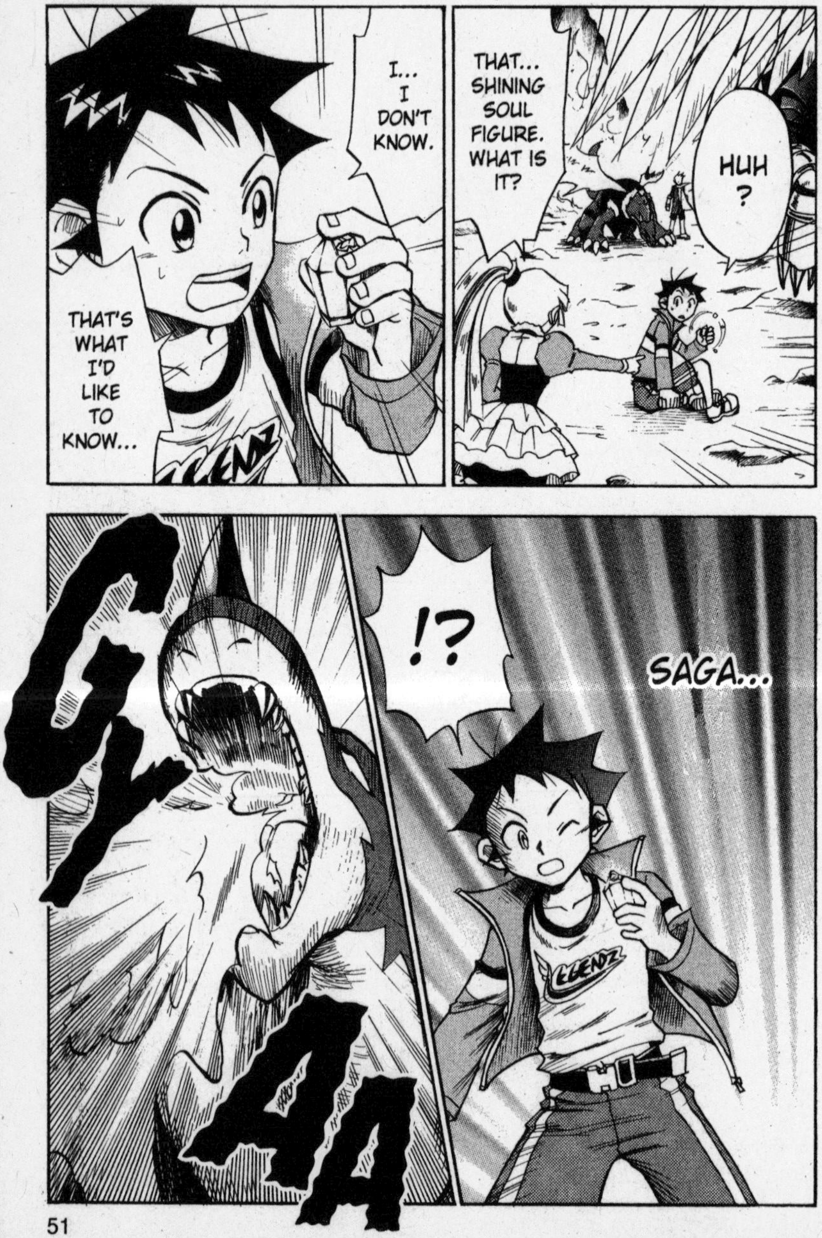
HUH?
THAT... SHINING SOUL FIGURE. WHAT IS IT?
I... I DON'T KNOW.
THAT'S WHAT I'D LIKE TO KNOW...
SAGA...
!?
GYAA

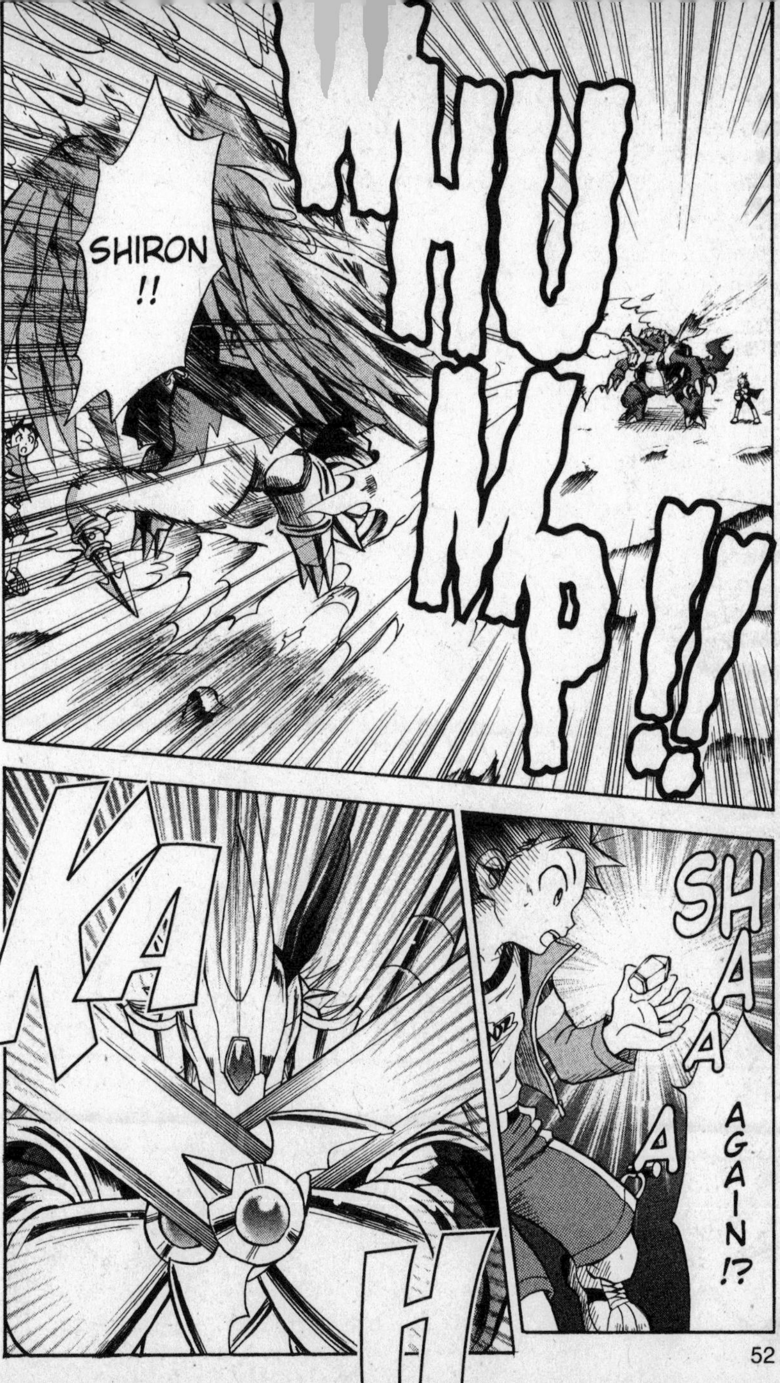
WHUMP!!
SHIRON!!
SHAAAA
AGAIN!?
KAAH

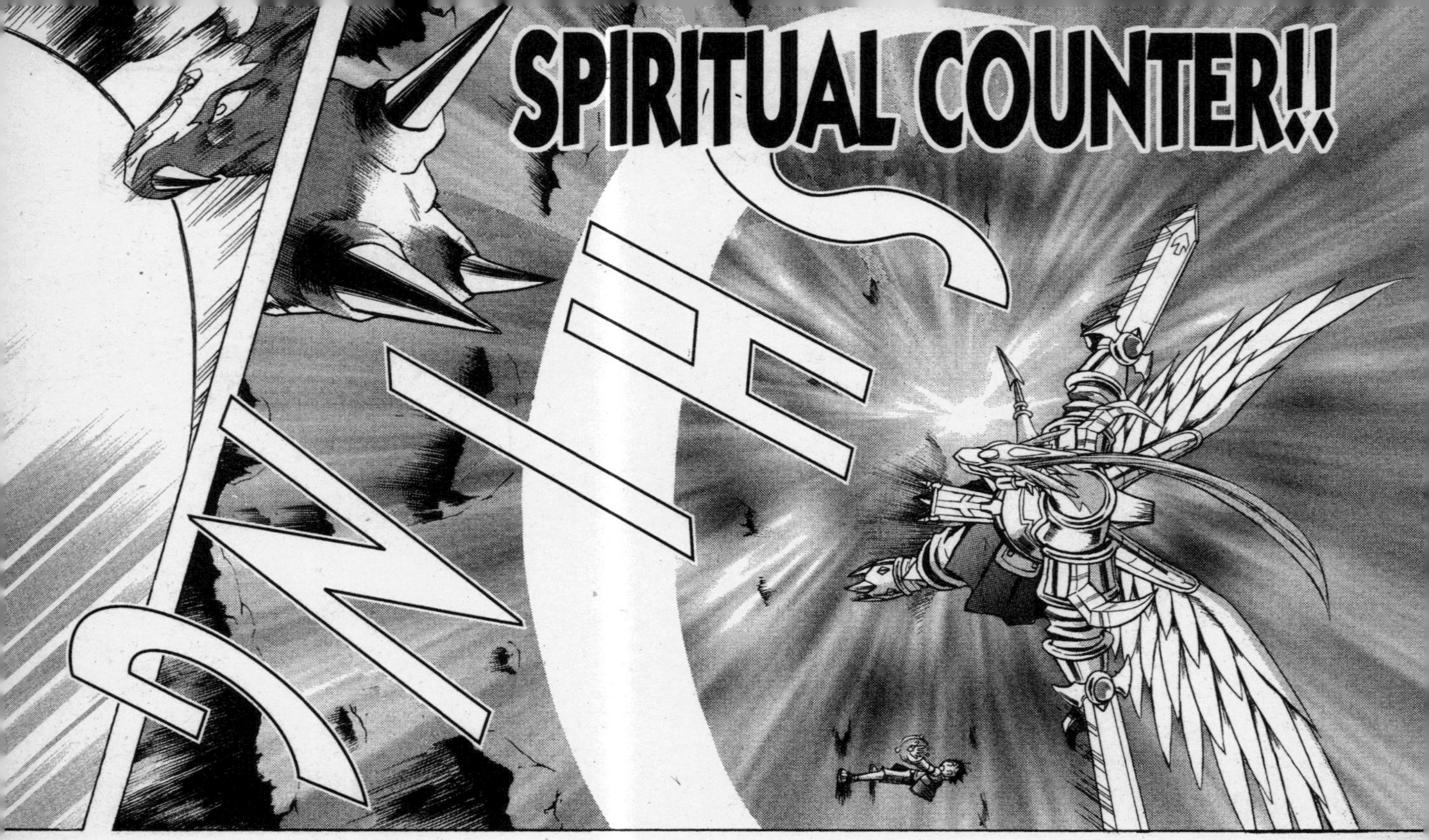
SPIRITUAL COUNTER!!
SHING

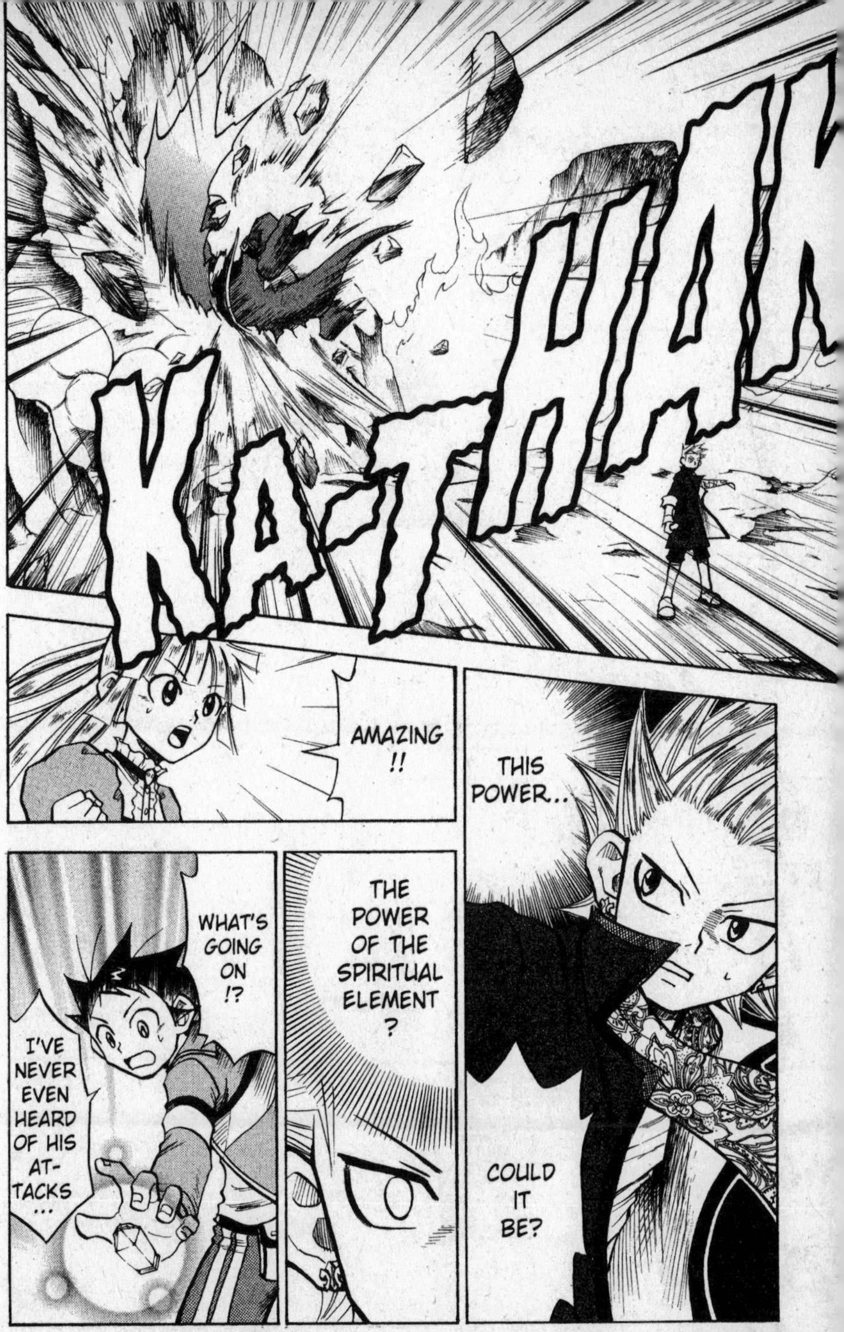
KA-THAK
THIS POWER...
COULD IT BE?
AMAZING!!
THE POWER OF THE SPIRITUAL ELEMENT?
WHAT'S GOING ON!?
I'VE NEVER EVEN HEARD OF HIS AT-TACKS...

READ THIS WAY

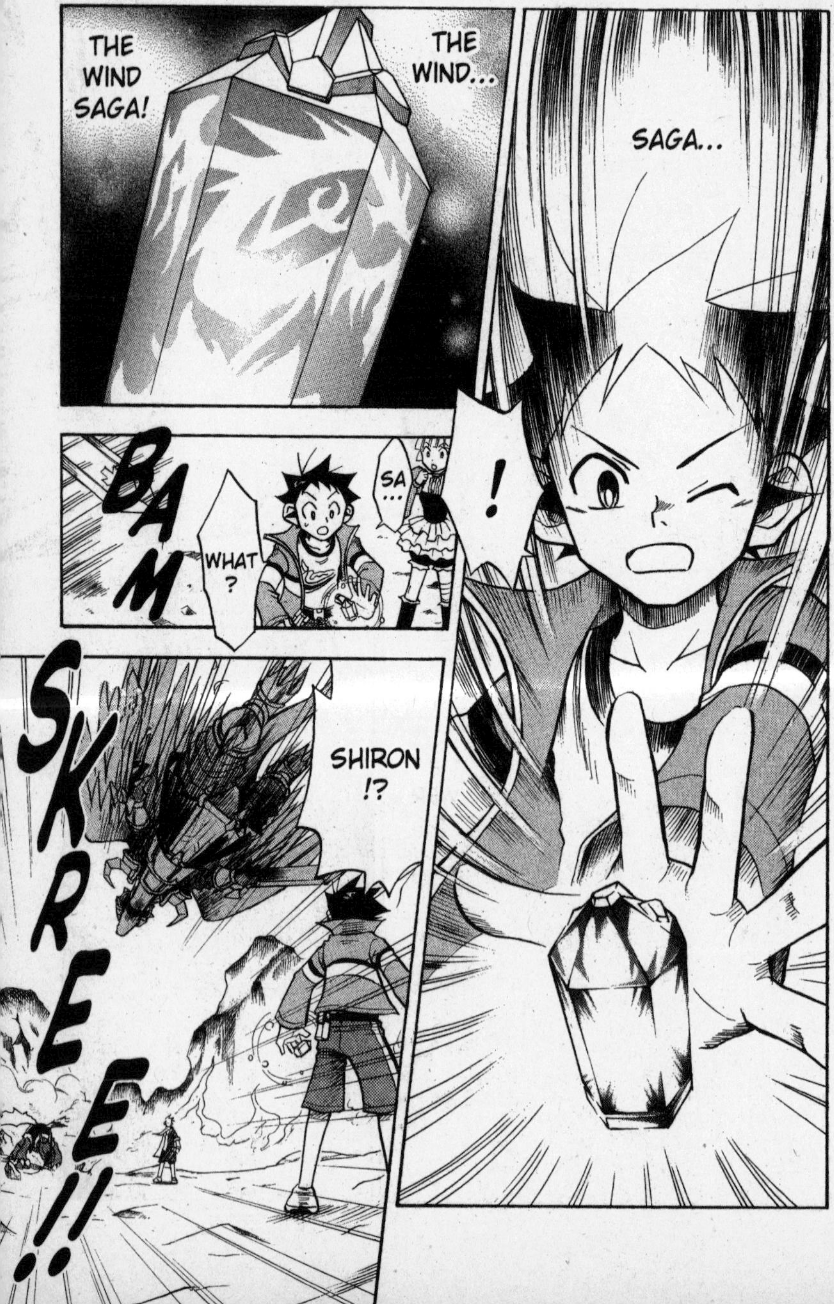
THE WIND...
SAGA...
THE WIND SAGA!
!
SA...
WHAT?
BAM
SHIRON!?
SKREE!!

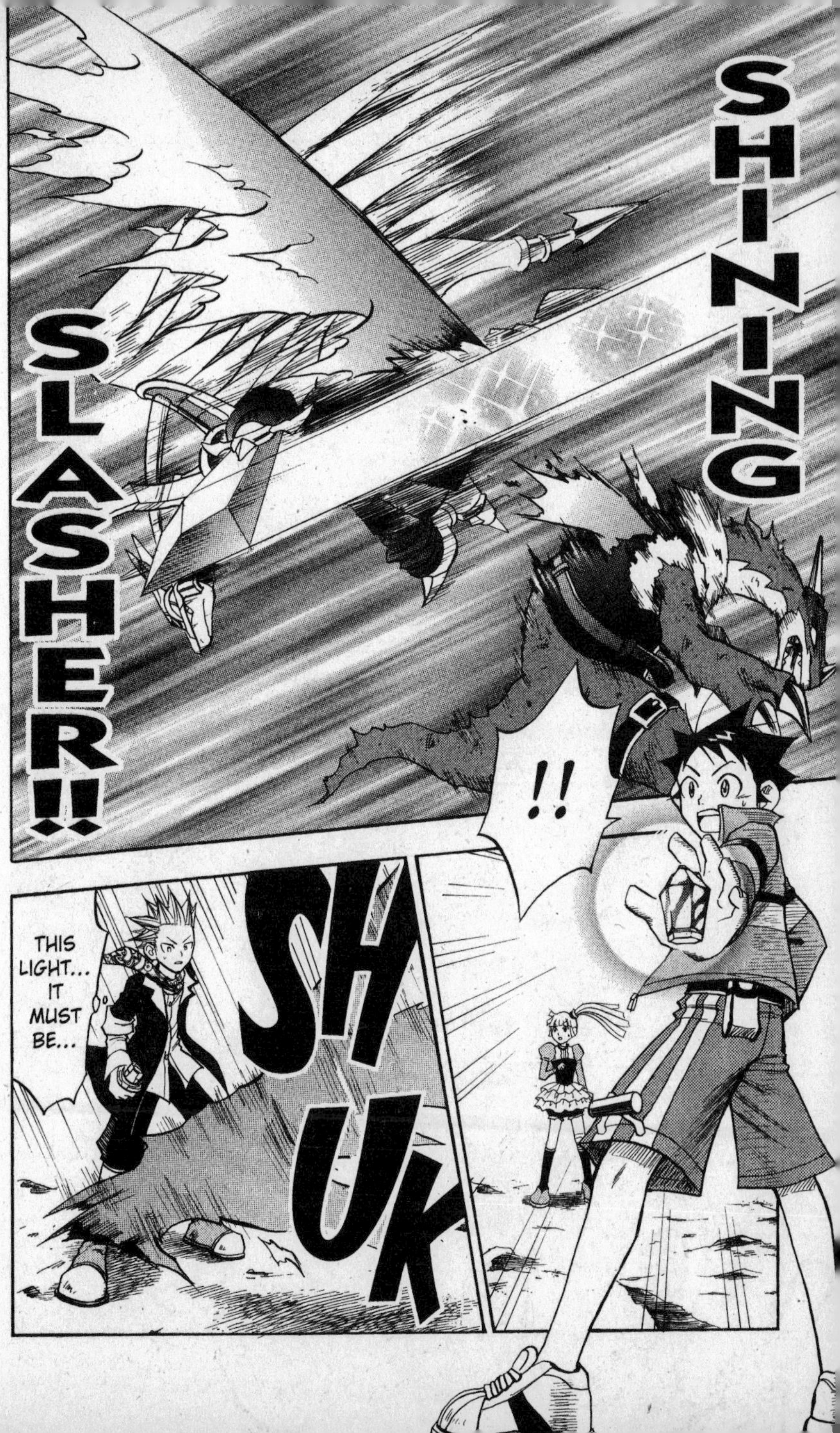
SHINING
SLASHER!!
!!
SHUK
THIS LIGHT... IT MUST BE...

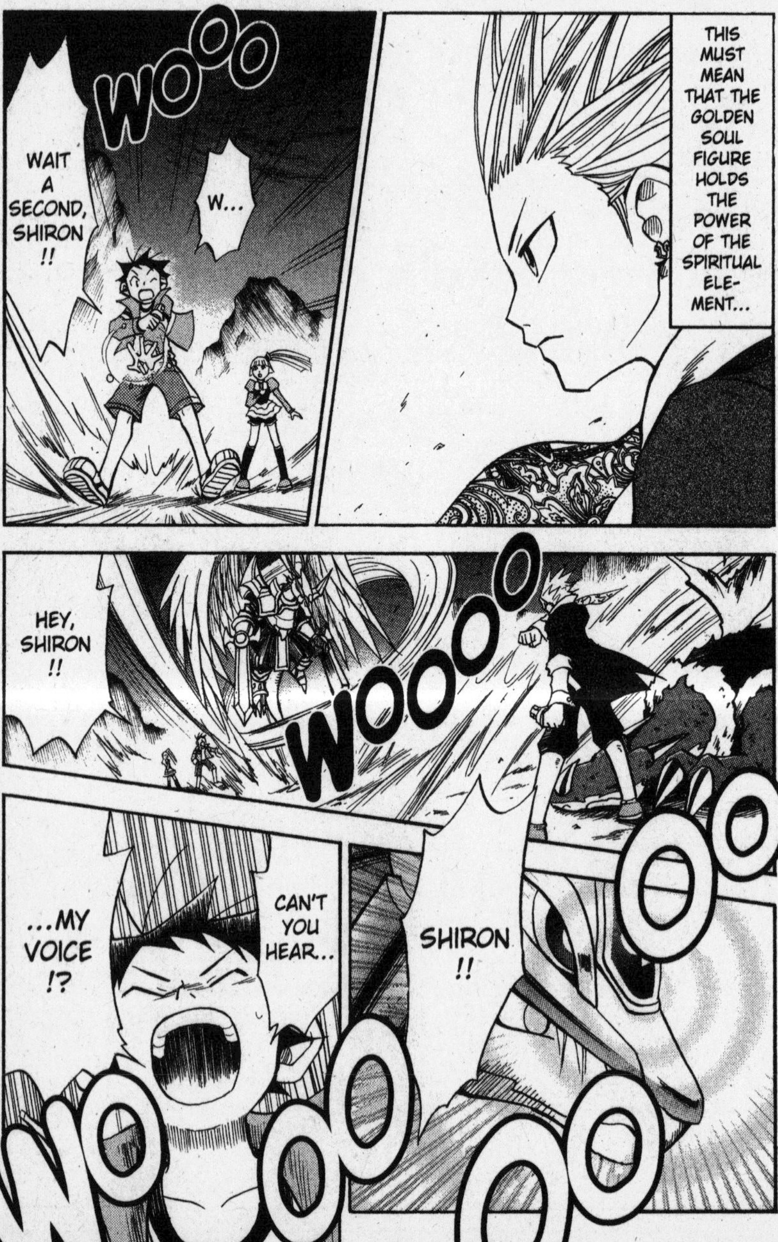
THIS MUST MEAN THAT THE GOLDEN SOUL FIGURE HOLDS THE POWER OF THE SPIRITUAL ELE-MENT...
WOOO
W...
WAIT A SECOND, SHIRON!!
WOOOOO
HEY, SHIRON!!
SHIRON!!
CAN'T YOU HEAR...
...MY VOICE!?
WOOOOOOOOO

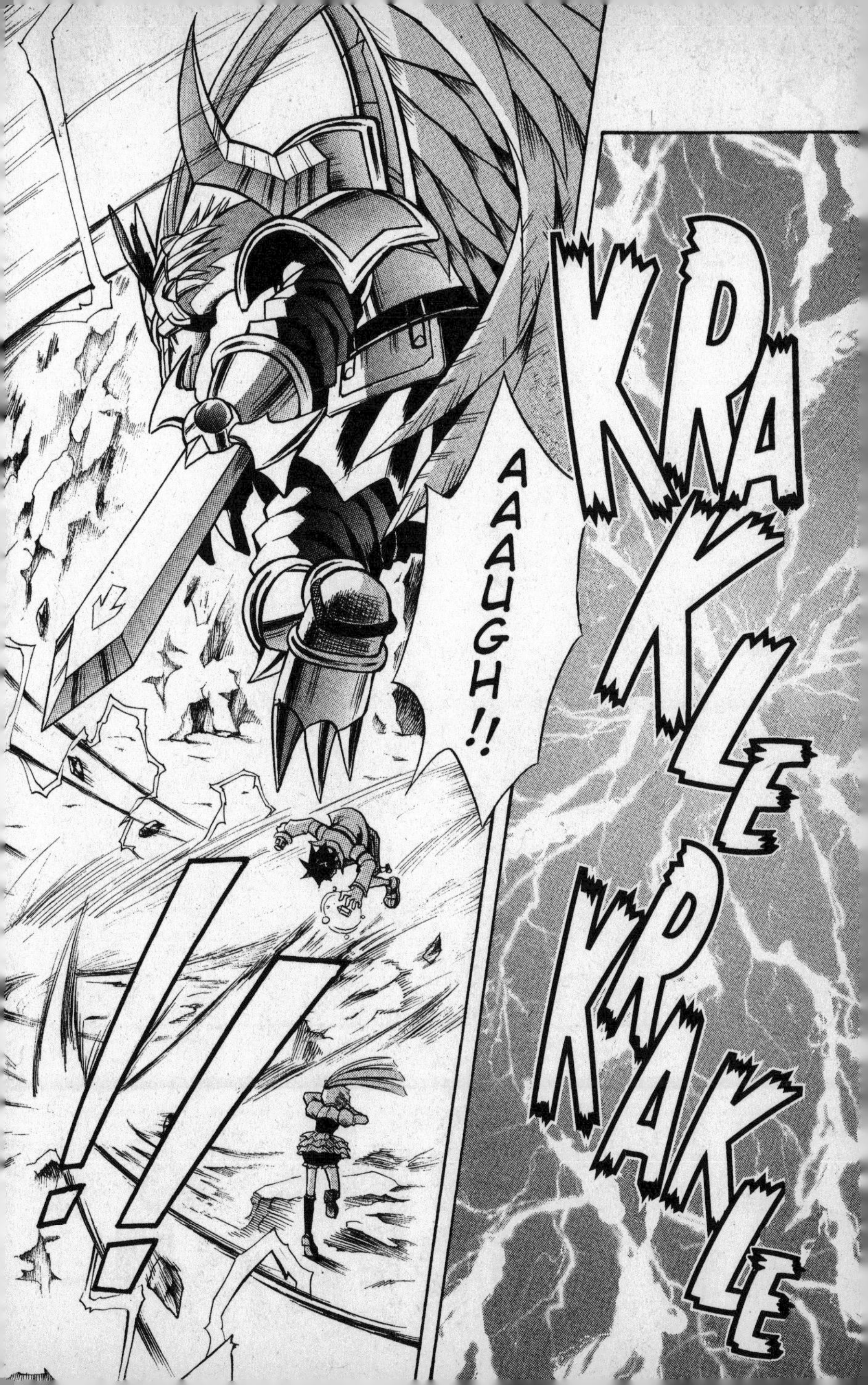
KRAKLE KRAKLE
AAAUGH!!
!!

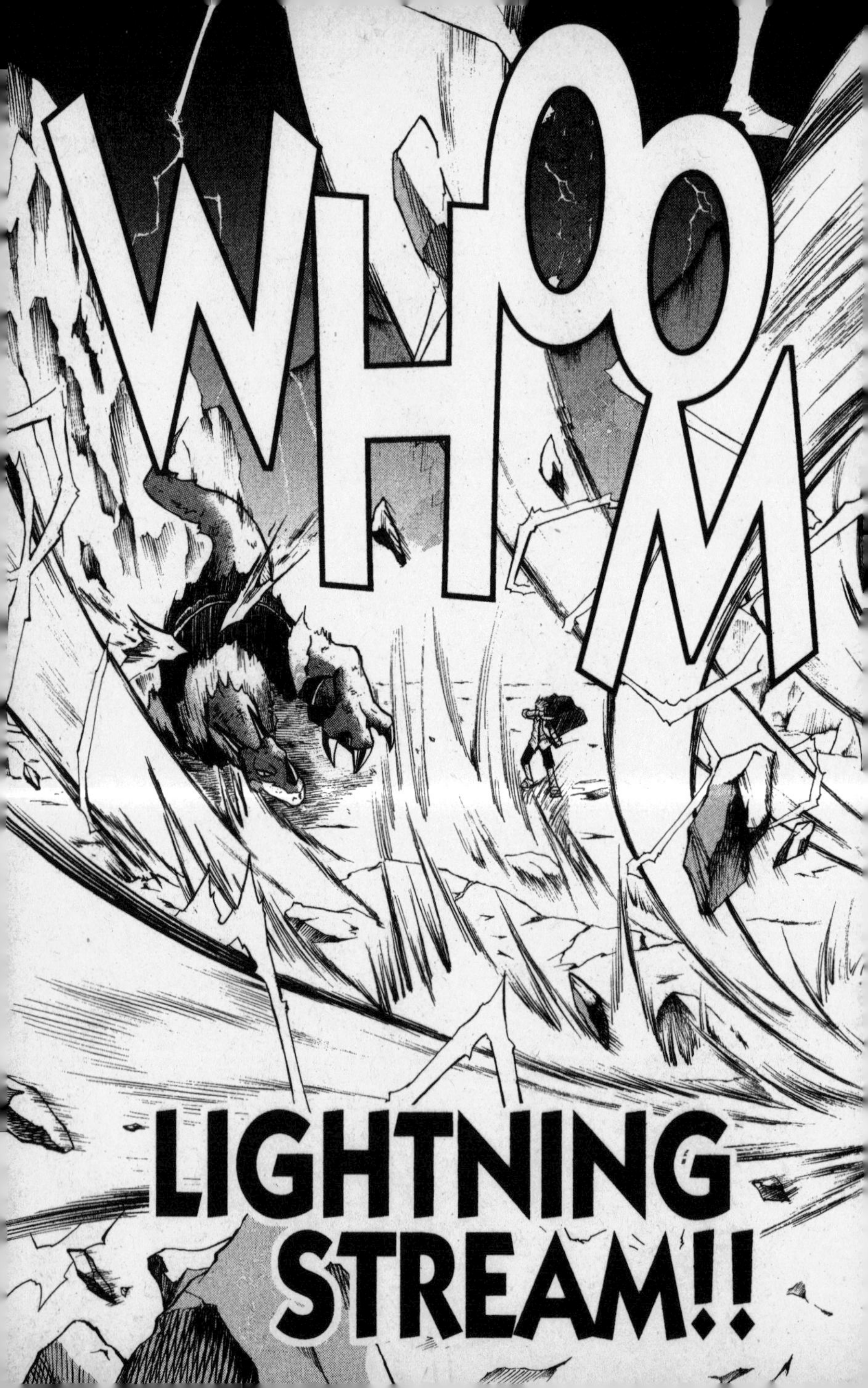
WHOOM
LIGHTNING STREAM!!

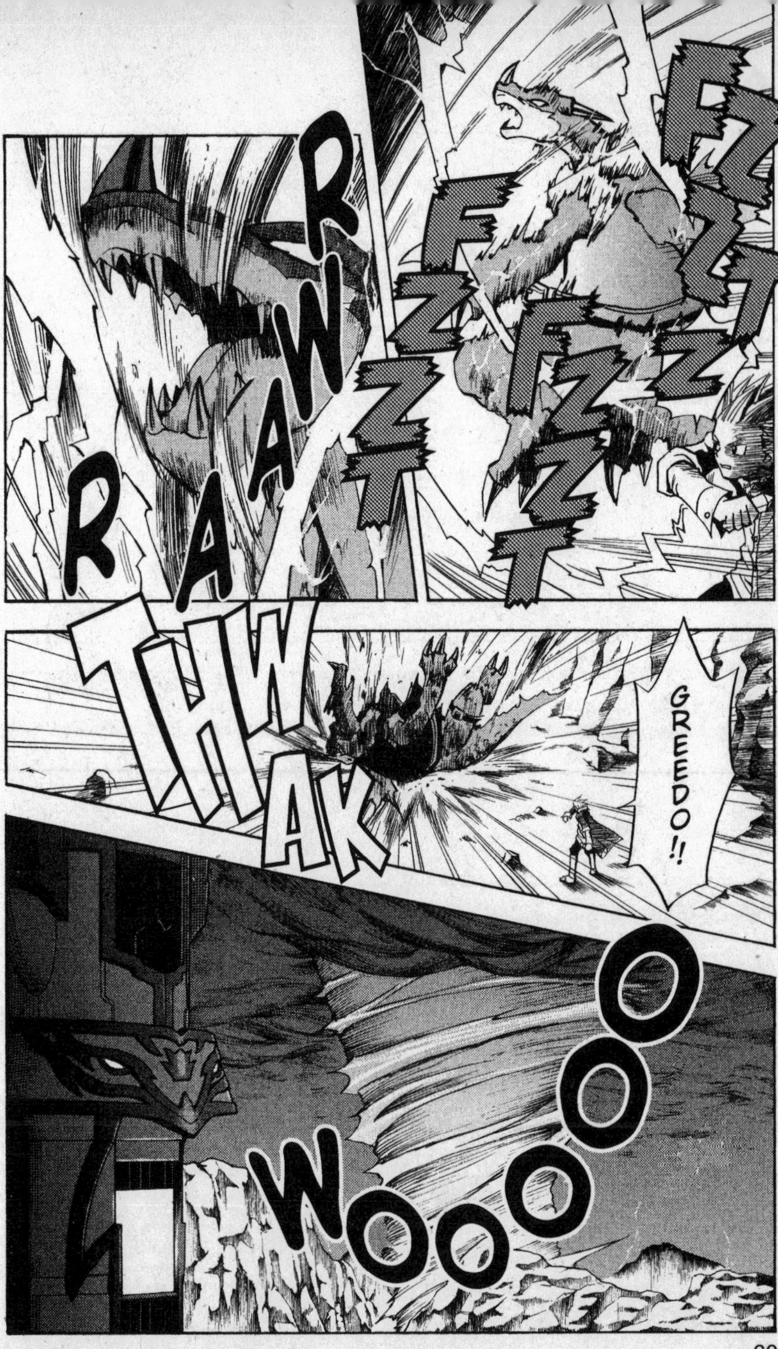
FZZT
FZZZT
FZZT
RAAWR
GREEDO!!
THWAK
WOOOOOO

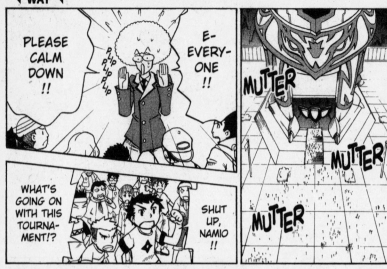

PLEASE
CALM
DOWN
!!

E-
EVERY-
ONE
!!

FLIP
FLIP
FLIP

MUTTER

MUTTER

MUTTER

WHAT'S
GOING ON
WITH THIS
TOURNA-
MENT!?

SHUT
UP,
NAMIO
!!

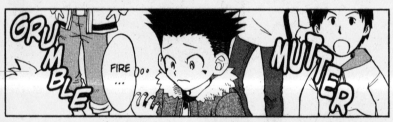

GRUMBLE

FIRE
...

MUTTER

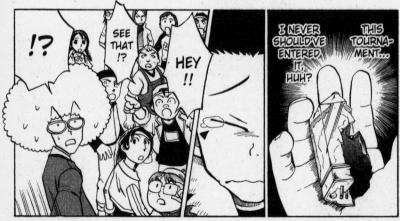

!?

SEE
THAT
!?

HEY
!!

I NEVER
SHOULD'VE
ENTERED
IT, HUH?

THIS
TOURNA-
MENT...

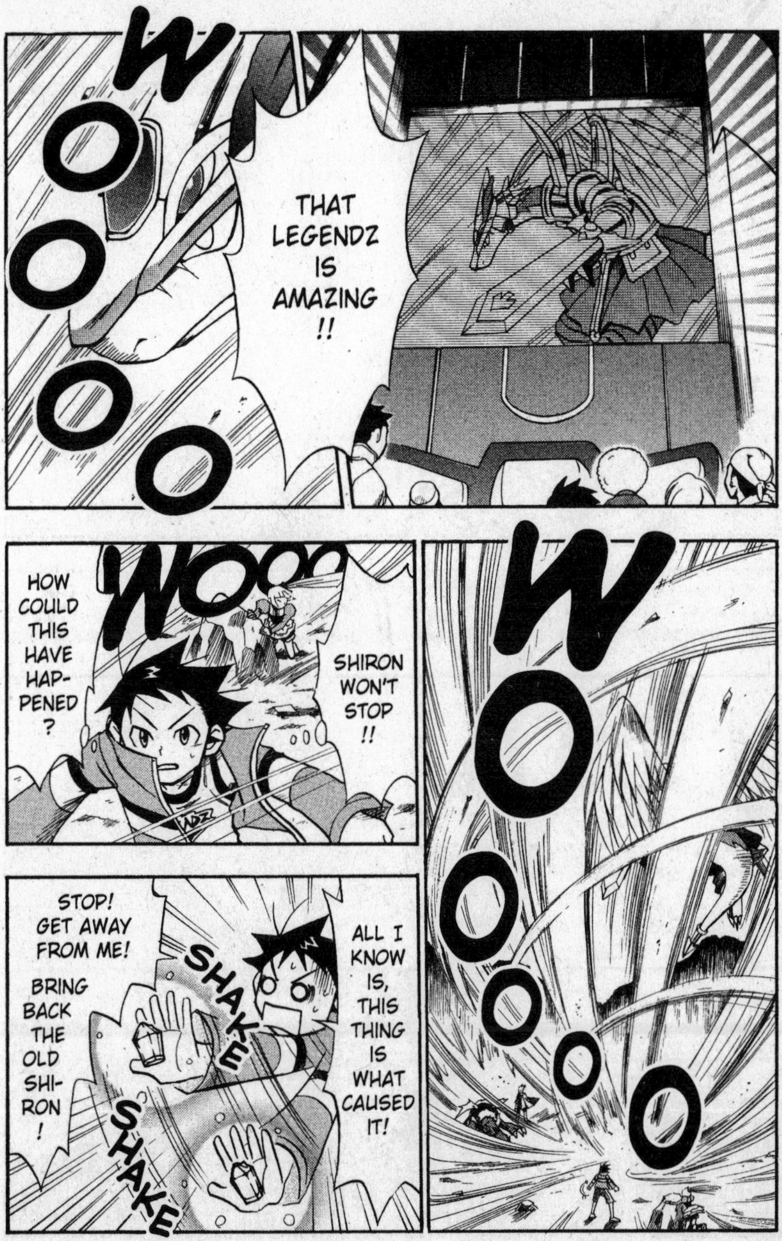
WOOOOO
THAT LEGENDZ IS AMAZING!!
WOOOOOOO
WOOO
SHIRON WON'T STOP!!
HOW COULD THIS HAVE HAP-PENED?
ALL I KNOW IS, THIS THING IS WHAT CAUSED IT!
SHAKE
SHAKE
STOP! GET AWAY FROM ME!
BRING BACK THE OLD SHI-RON!

READ THIS WAY

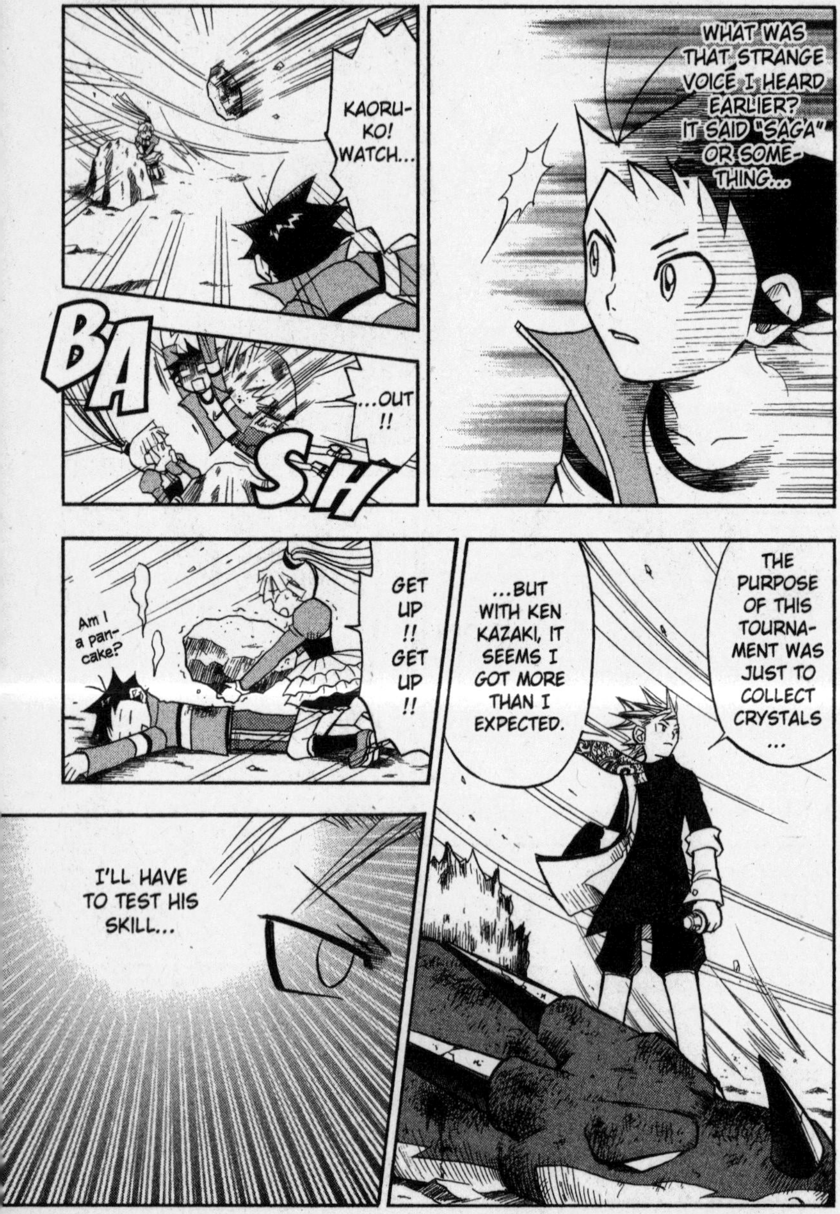
WHAT WAS THAT STRANGE VOICE I HEARD EARLIER? IT SAID "SAGA" OR SOME-THING...
KAORU-KO! WATCH...
BA
SH
...OUT !!
THE PURPOSE OF THIS TOURNA-MENT WAS JUST TO COLLECT CRYSTALS ...
...BUT WITH KEN KAZAKI, IT SEEMS I GOT MORE THAN I EXPECTED.
GET UP !! GET UP !!
Am I a pan-cake?
I'LL HAVE TO TEST HIS SKILL...

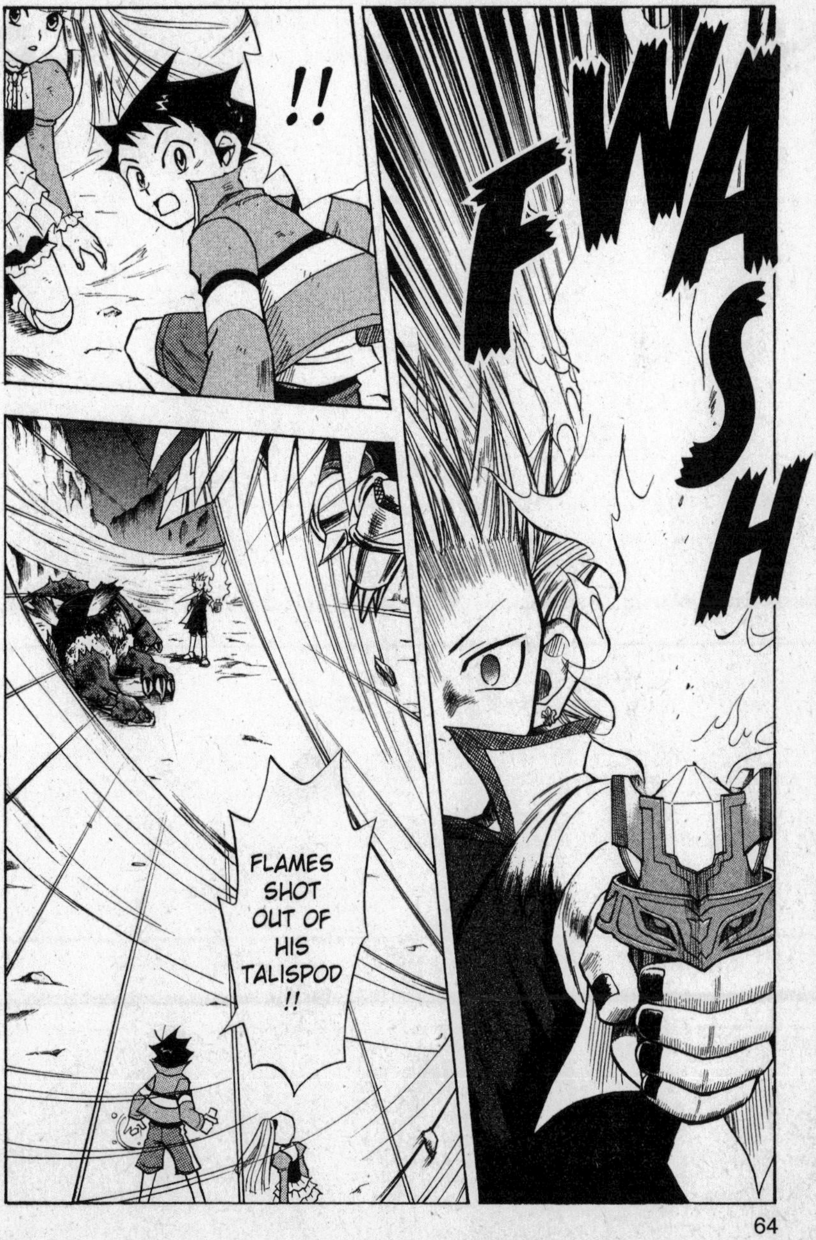
FWASH
!!
FLAMES SHOT OUT OF HIS TALISPOD !!

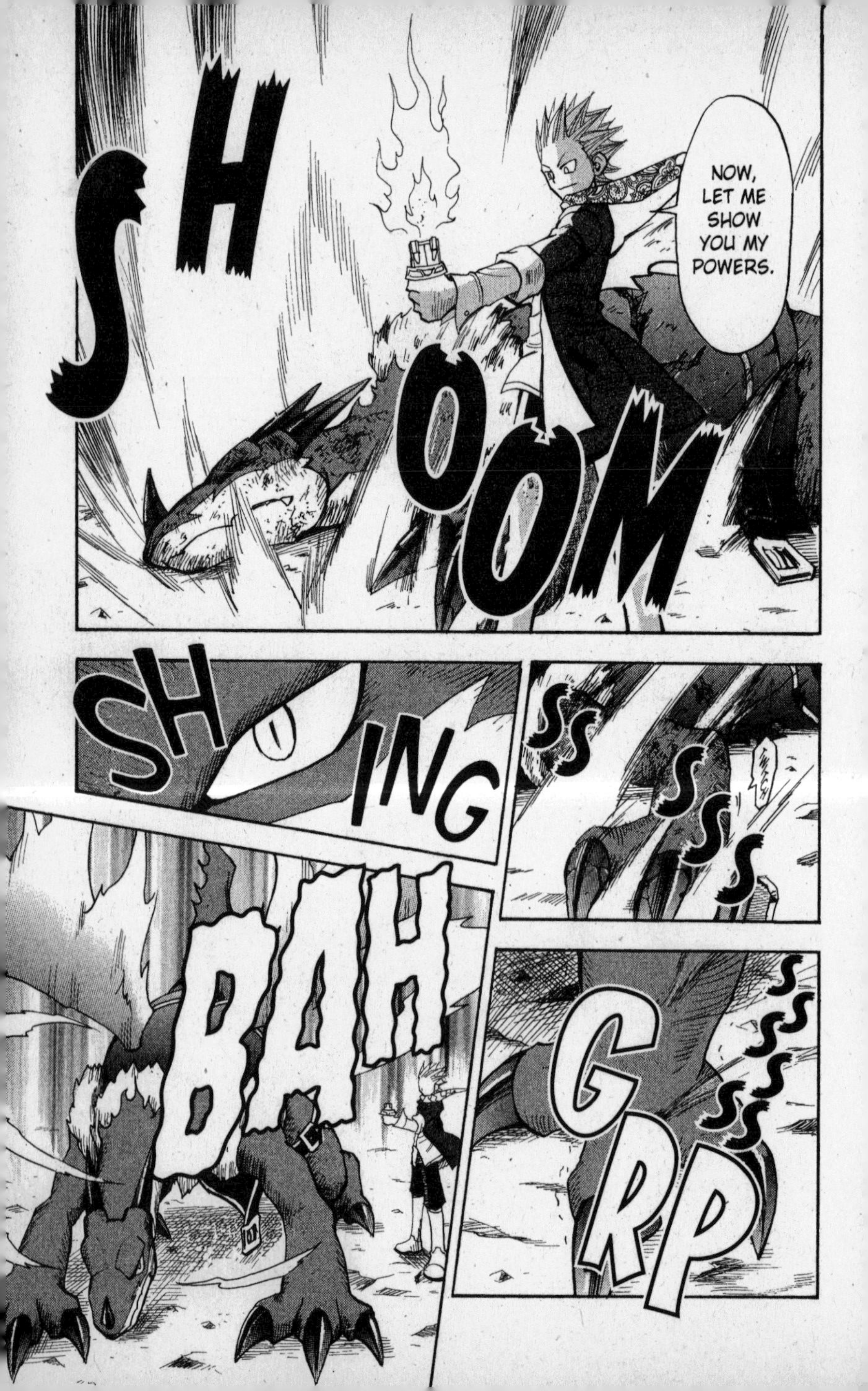
NOW, LET ME SHOW YOU MY POWERS.
SHOOM
SSSSS
TWITCH
SHING
GRP
SSSSS
BAH

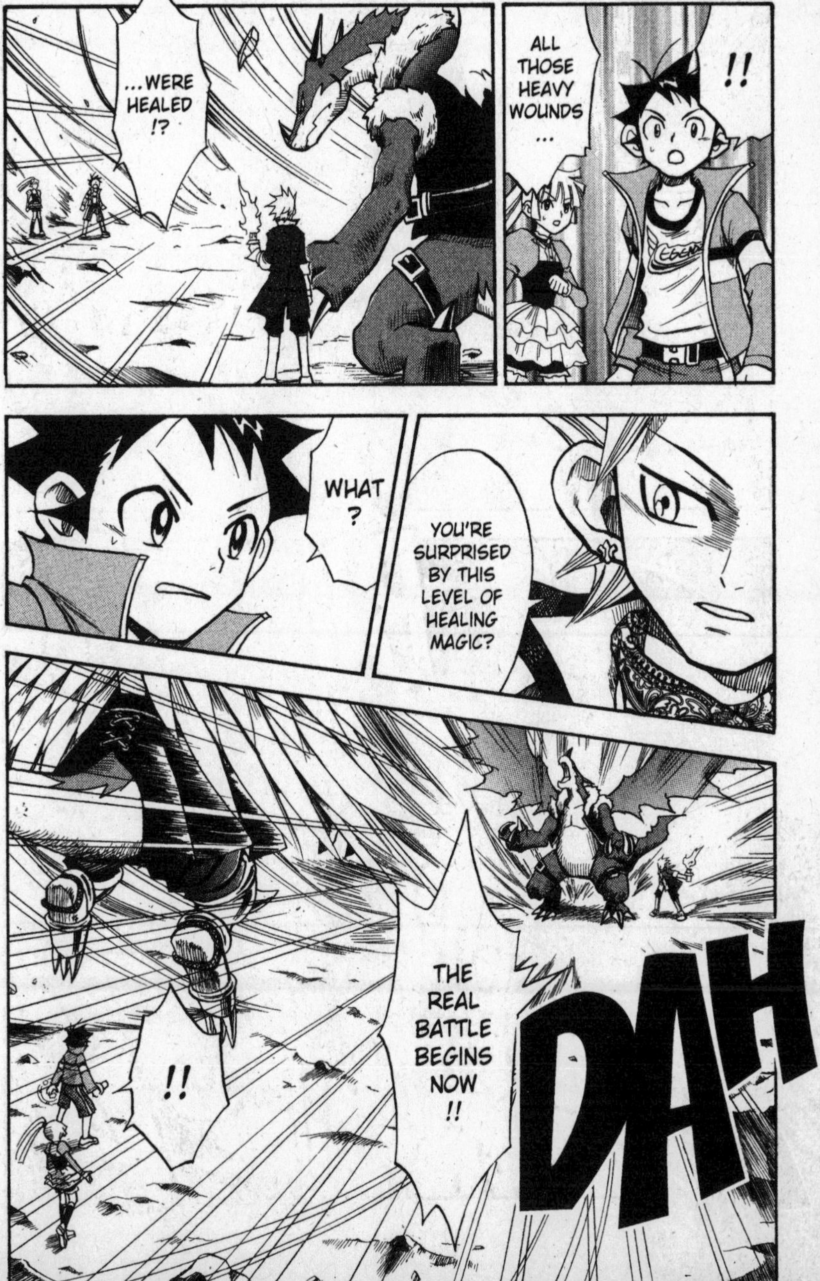
!!
ALL THOSE HEAVY WOUNDS ...
...WERE HEALED !?
YOU'RE SURPRISED BY THIS LEVEL OF HEALING MAGIC?
WHAT ?
THE REAL BATTLE BEGINS NOW !!
DAH
!!

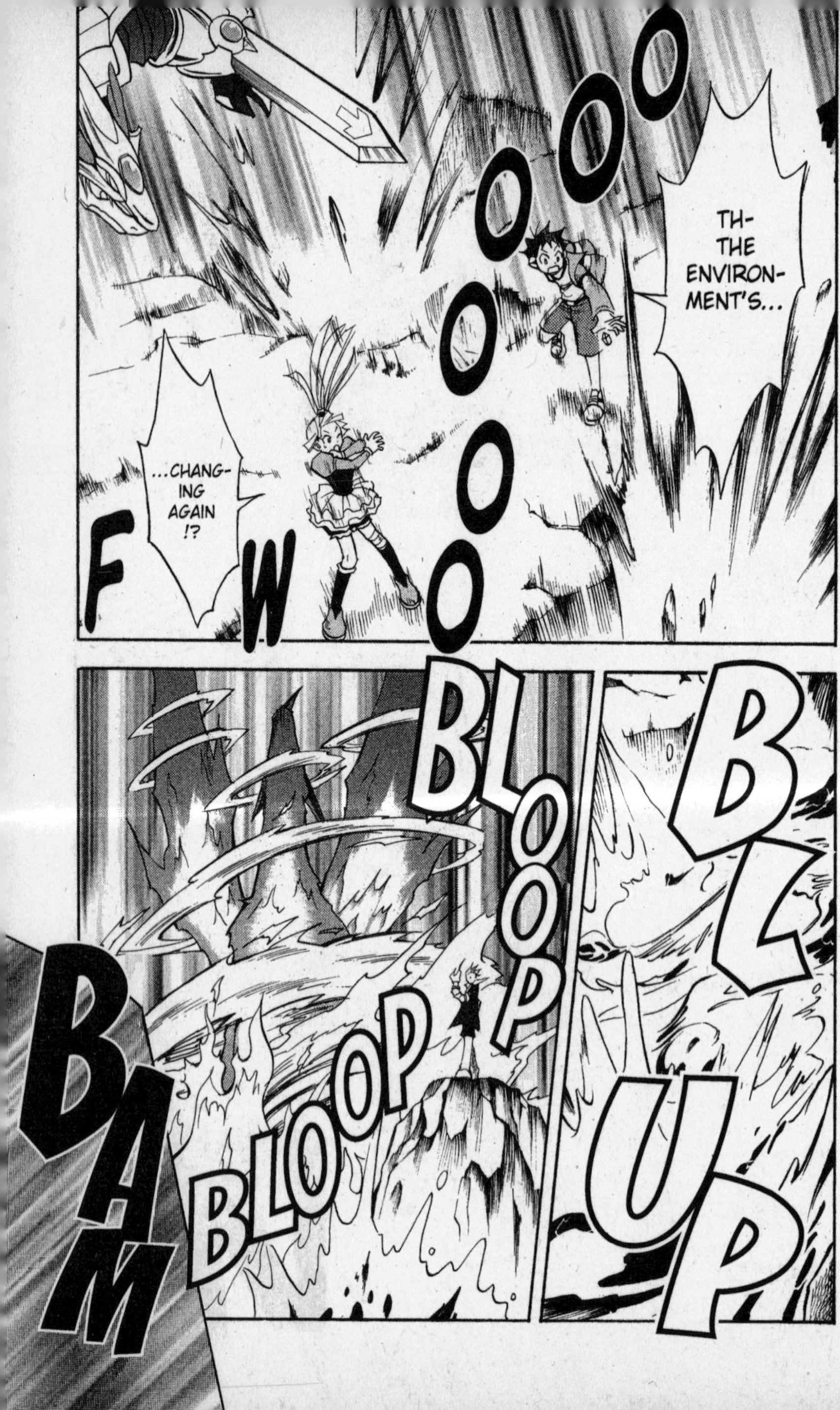
TH- THE ENVIRONMENT'S...
...CHANGING AGAIN!?
FWOOOOOOO
BLUP
BLOOP
BLOOP
BAM

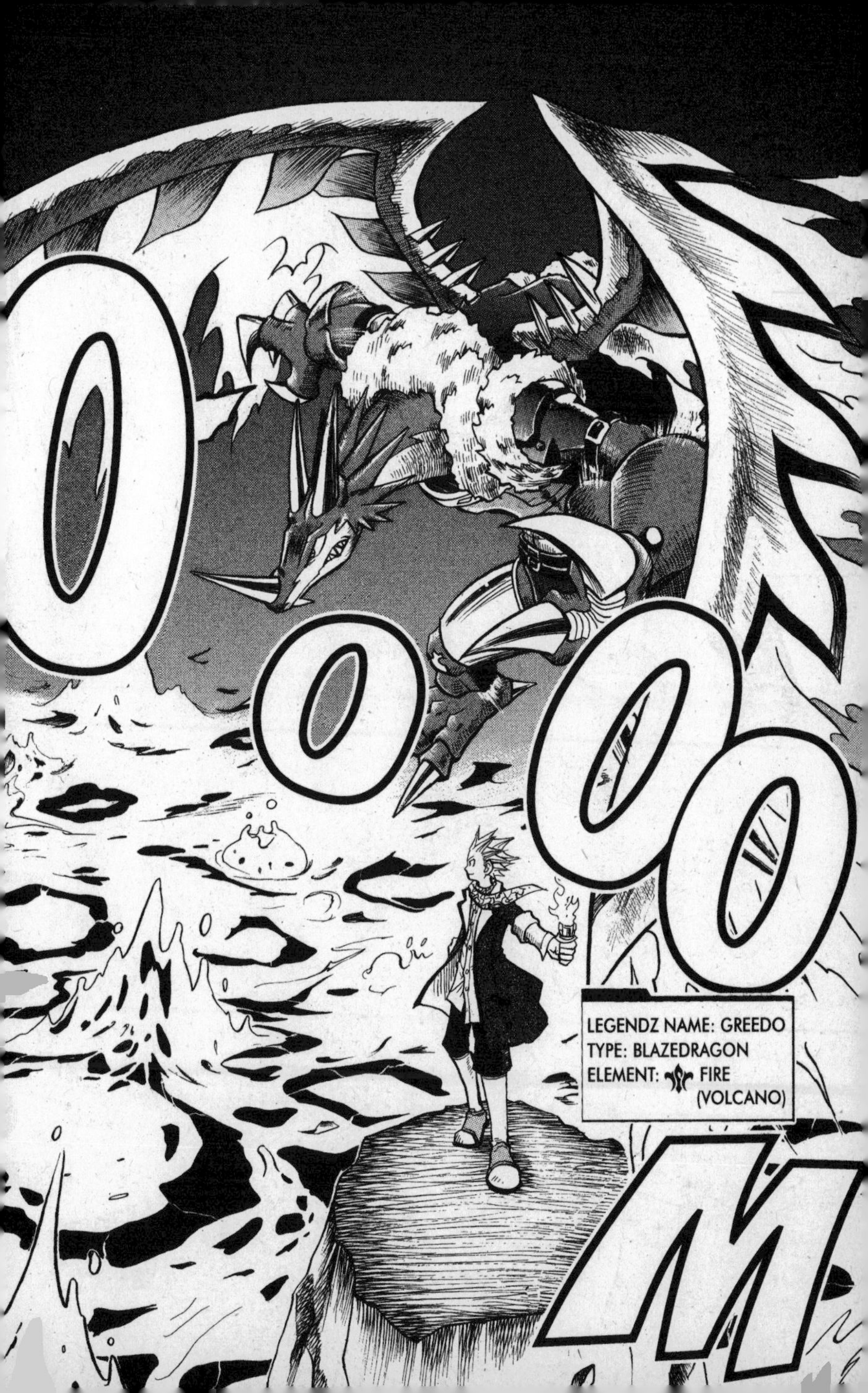

OOOOOM
LEGENDZ NAME: GREEDO
TYPE: BLAZEDRAGON
ELEMENT: FIRE (VOLCANO)

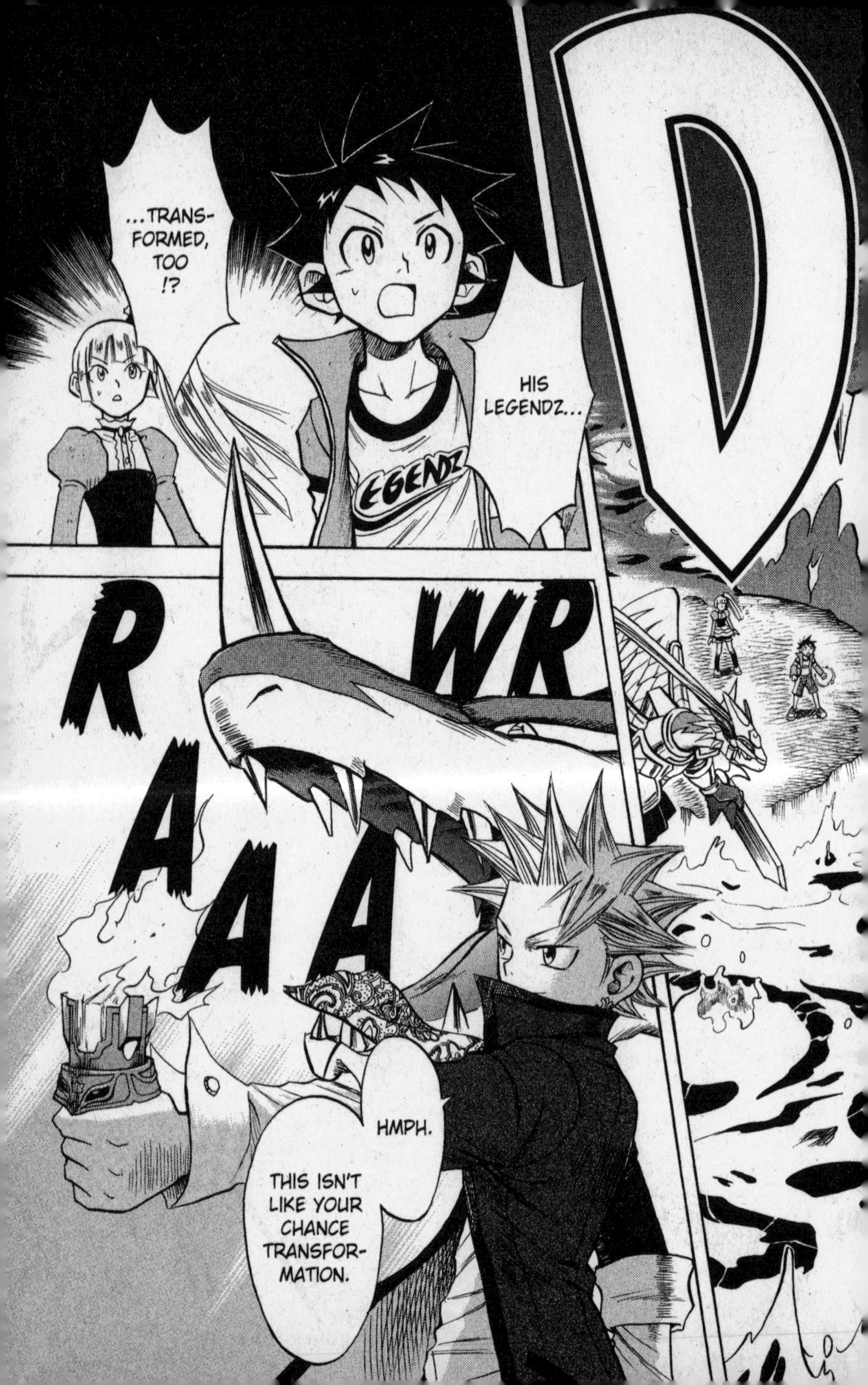
D
HIS LEGENDZ...
...TRANS-FORMED, TOO !?
RAAAWR
HMPH.
THIS ISN'T LIKE YOUR CHANCE TRANSFOR-MATION.

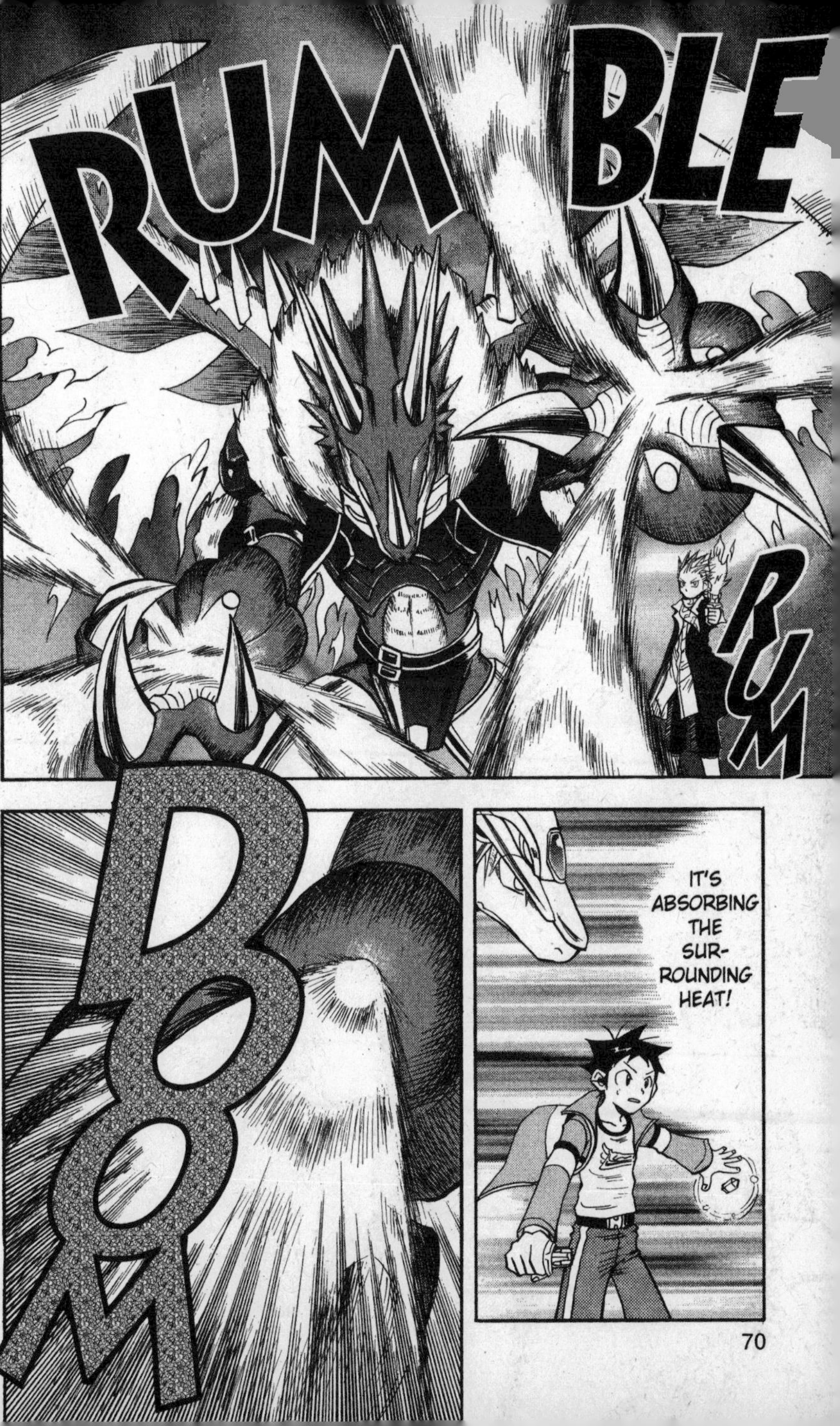
RUMBLE
RUM
IT'S ABSORBING THE SUR-ROUNDING HEAT!
BOOM

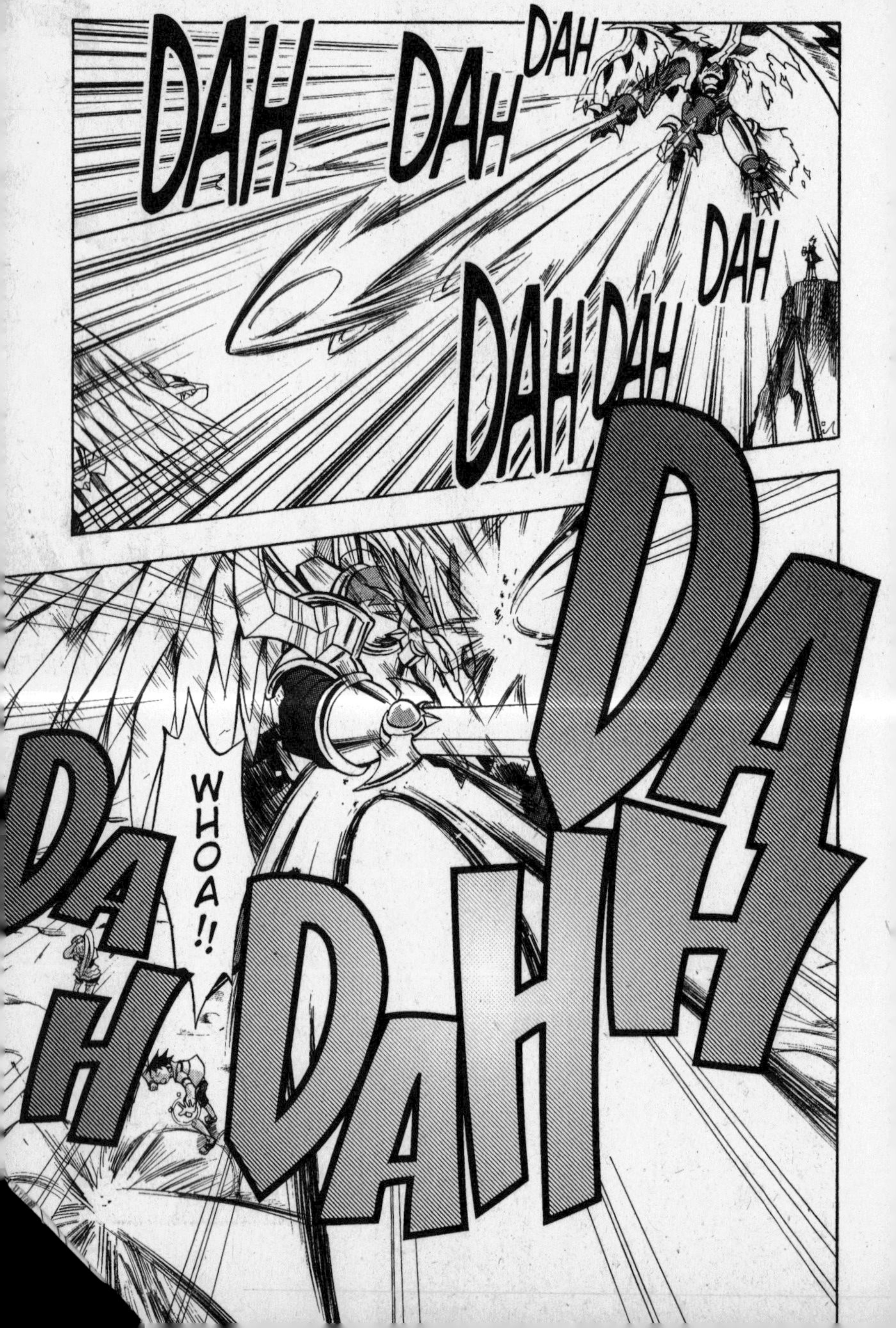
DAH DAH DAH
DAH DAH DAH
DAH
WHOA!!
DAH
DAH

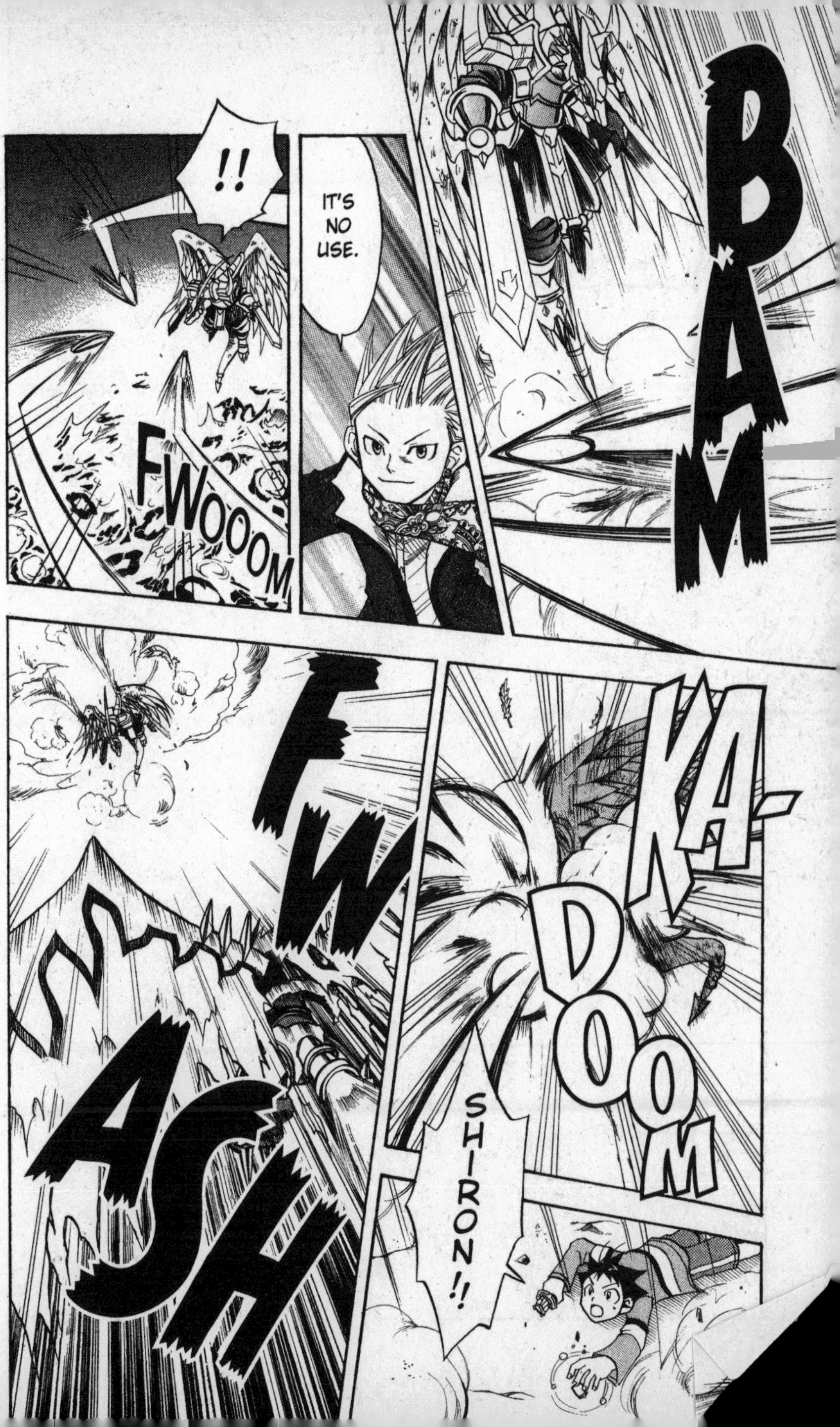
BAM
IT'S NO USE.
!!
FWOOOM
KA-DOOOM
SHIRON!!
FWASH

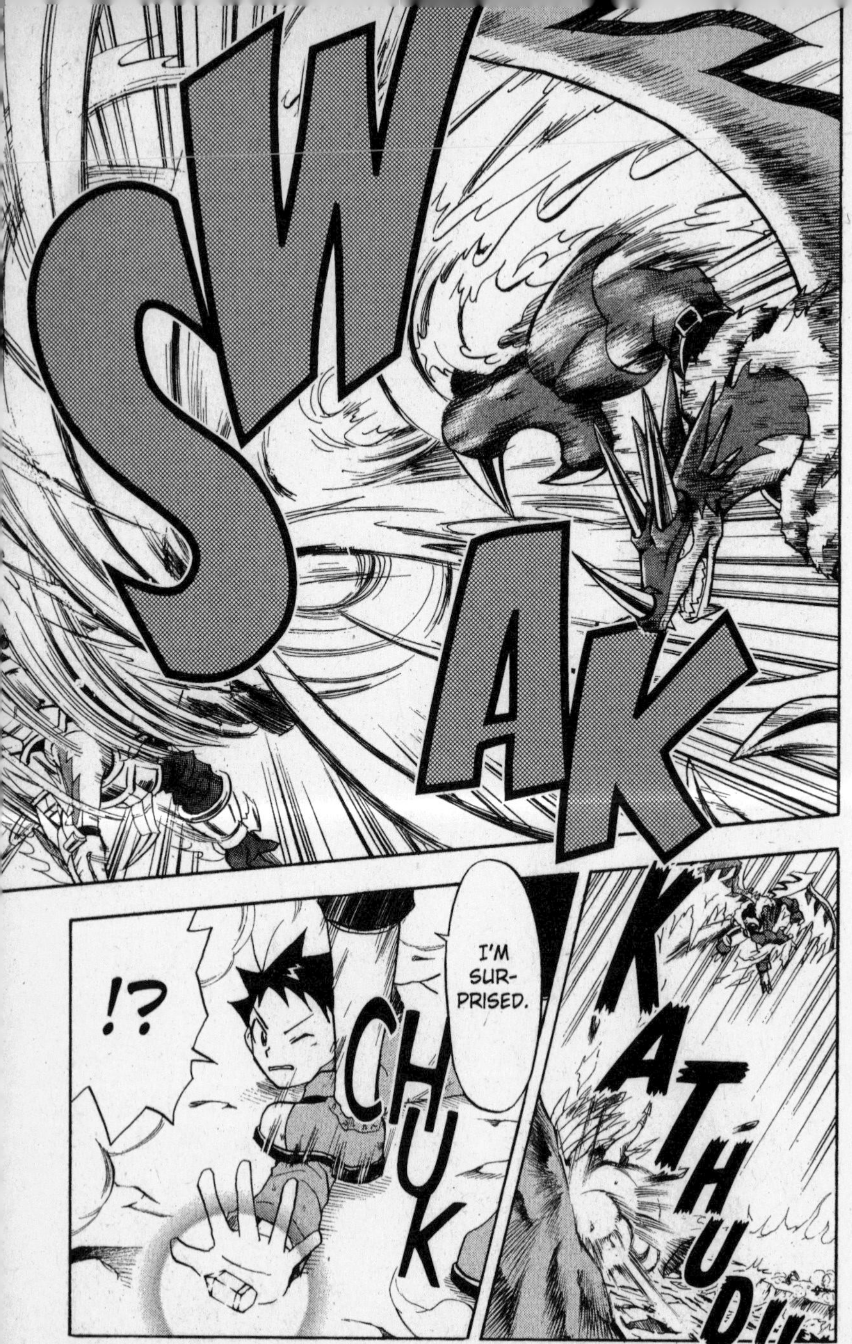
SWAK
KATHUD!!
I'M SURPRISED.
CHUK
!?

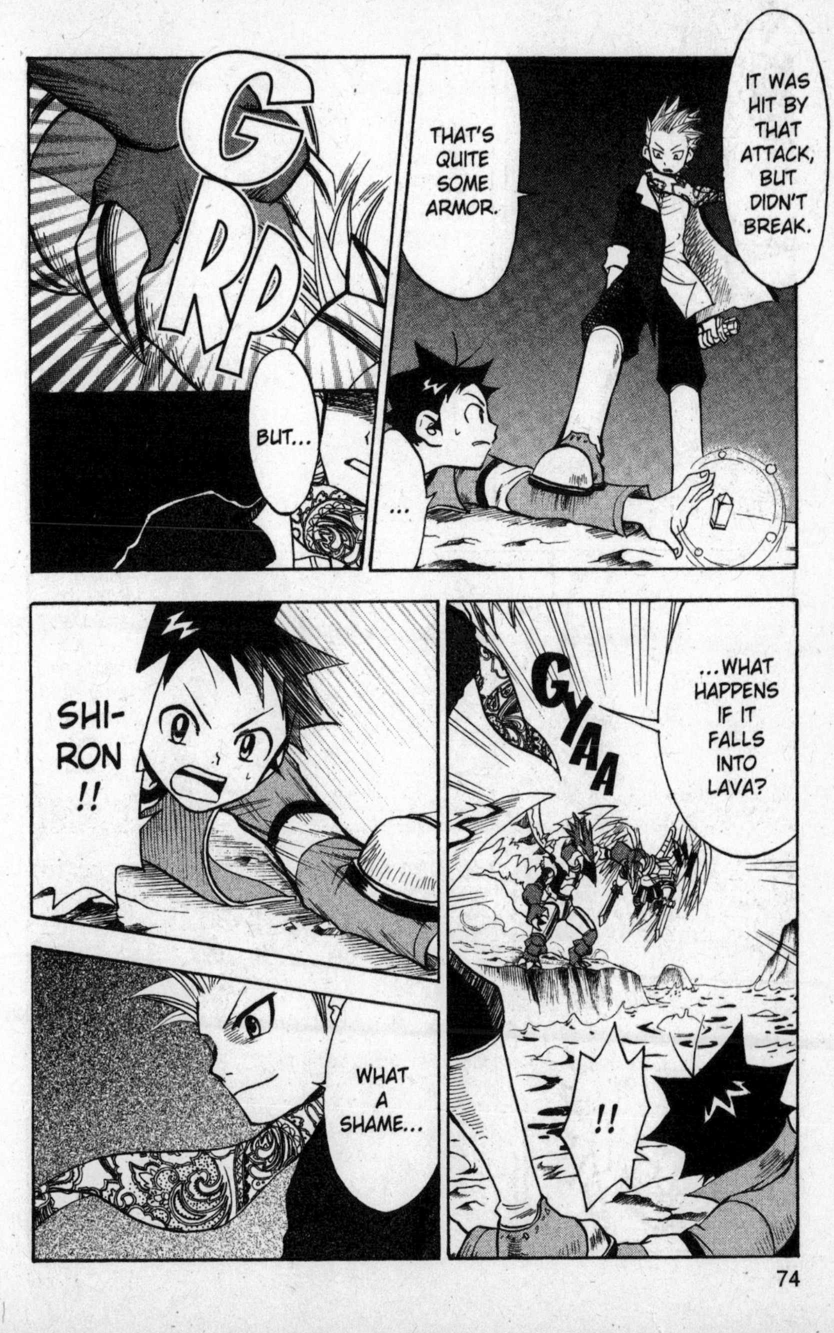
IT WAS HIT BY THAT ATTACK, BUT DIDN'T BREAK.
THAT'S QUITE SOME ARMOR.
...
GRRP
BUT...
...WHAT HAPPENS IF IT FALLS INTO LAVA?
GYAAA
!!
SHI-RON!!
WHAT A SHAME...

READ THIS WAY

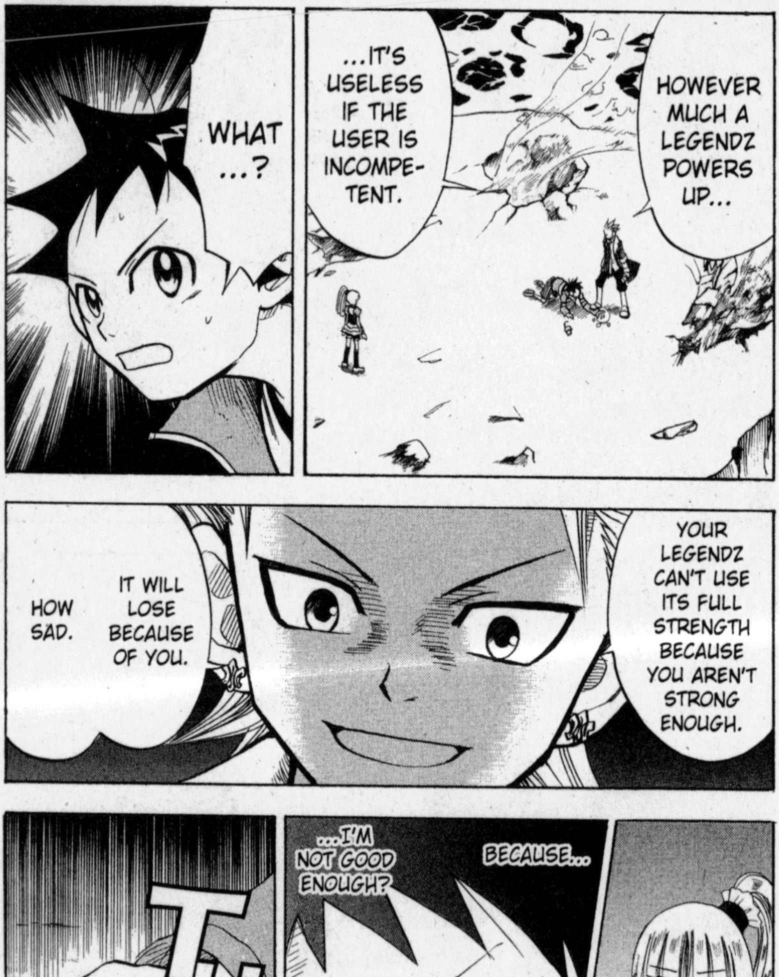
HOWEVER MUCH A LEGENDZ POWERS UP...
...IT'S USELESS IF THE USER IS INCOMPETENT.
WHAT ...?
YOUR LEGENDZ CAN'T USE ITS FULL STRENGTH BECAUSE YOU AREN'T STRONG ENOUGH.
IT WILL LOSE BECAUSE OF YOU.
HOW SAD.
BECAUSE...
...I'M NOT GOOD ENOUGH?
TUK...

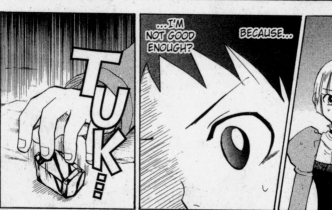

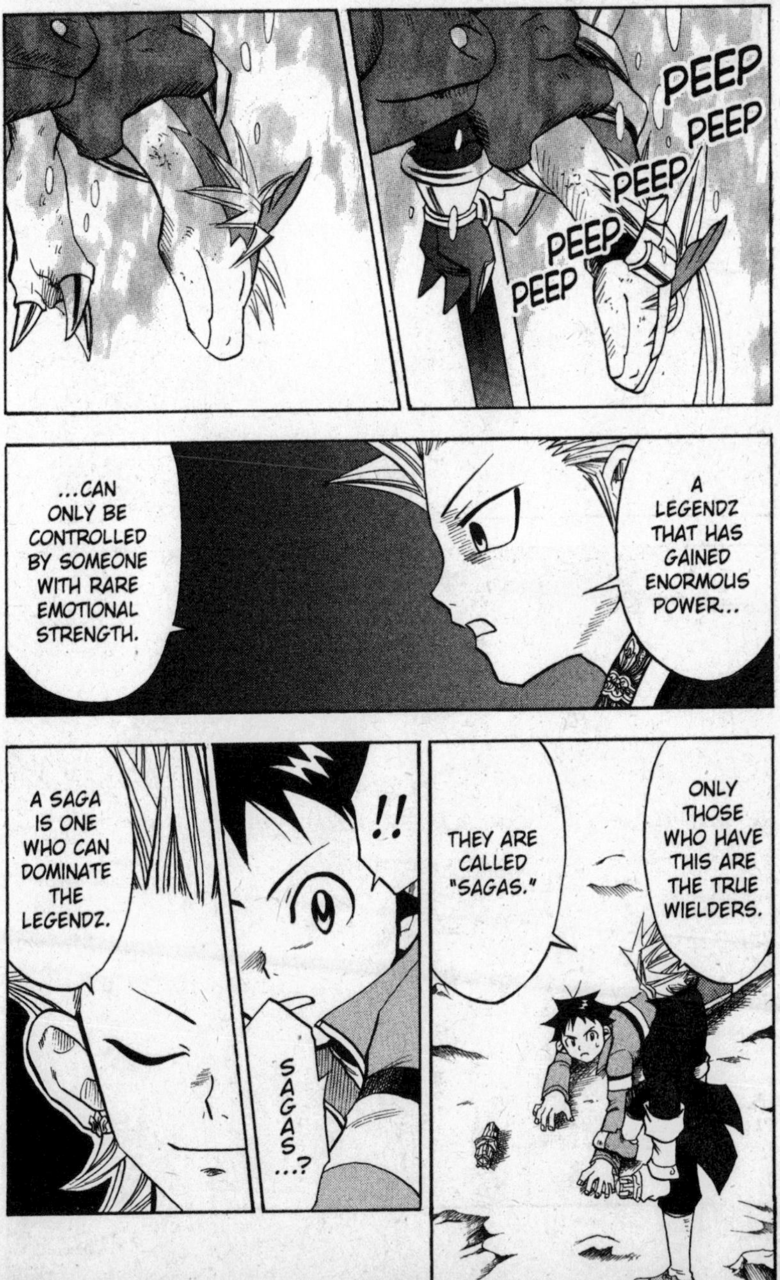
PEEP
PEEP
PEEP
PEEP
PEEP
A LEGENDZ THAT HAS GAINED ENORMOUS POWER...
...CAN ONLY BE CONTROLLED BY SOMEONE WITH RARE EMOTIONAL STRENGTH.
ONLY THOSE WHO HAVE THIS ARE THE TRUE WIELDERS.
THEY ARE CALLED "SAGAS."
!!
SAGAS...?
A SAGA IS ONE WHO CAN DOMINATE THE LEGENDZ.

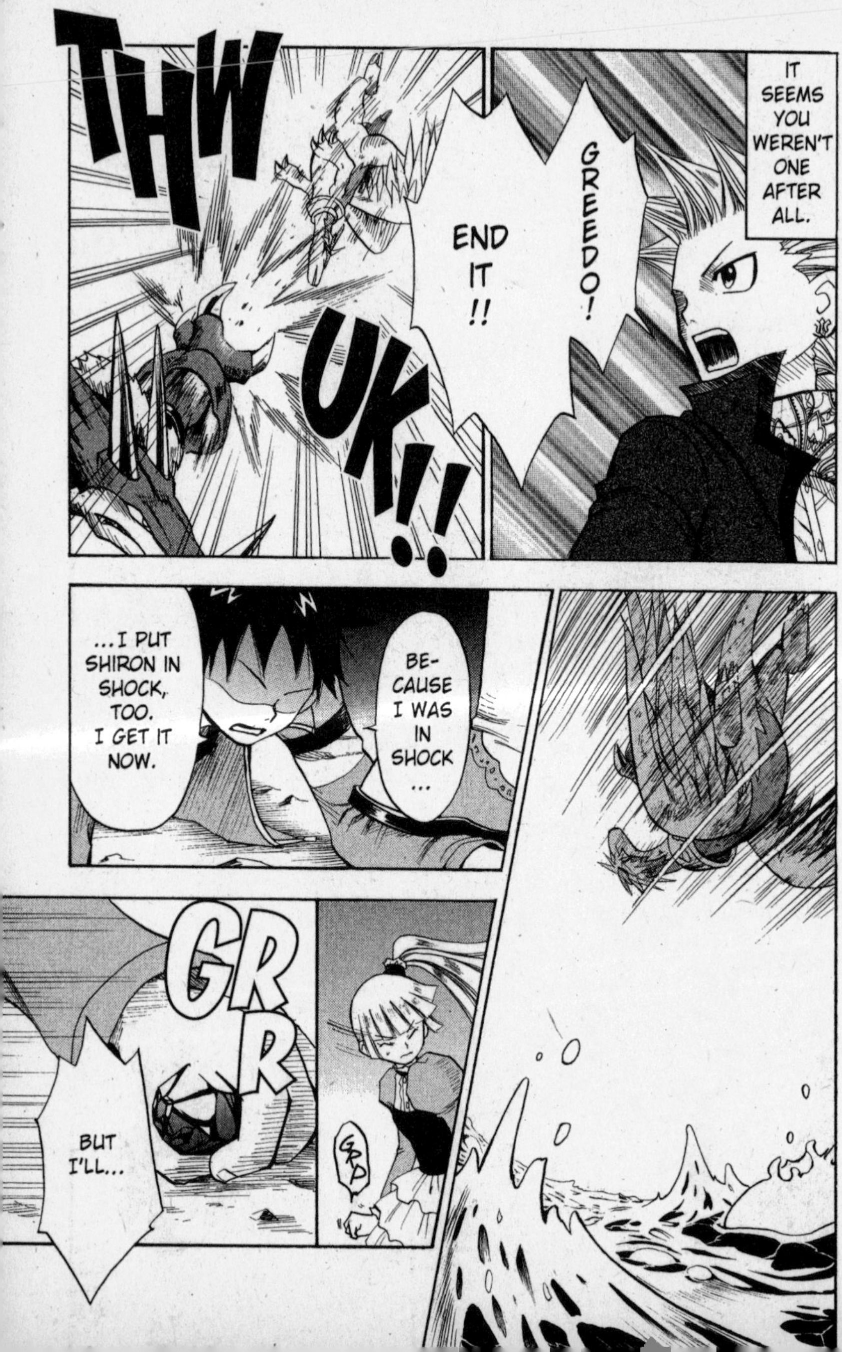
IT SEEMS YOU WEREN'T ONE AFTER ALL.
GREEDO!
END IT!!
THWUK!!
BE- CAUSE I WAS IN SHOCK...
...I PUT SHIRON IN SHOCK, TOO. I GET IT NOW.
GRP
GRR
BUT I'LL...

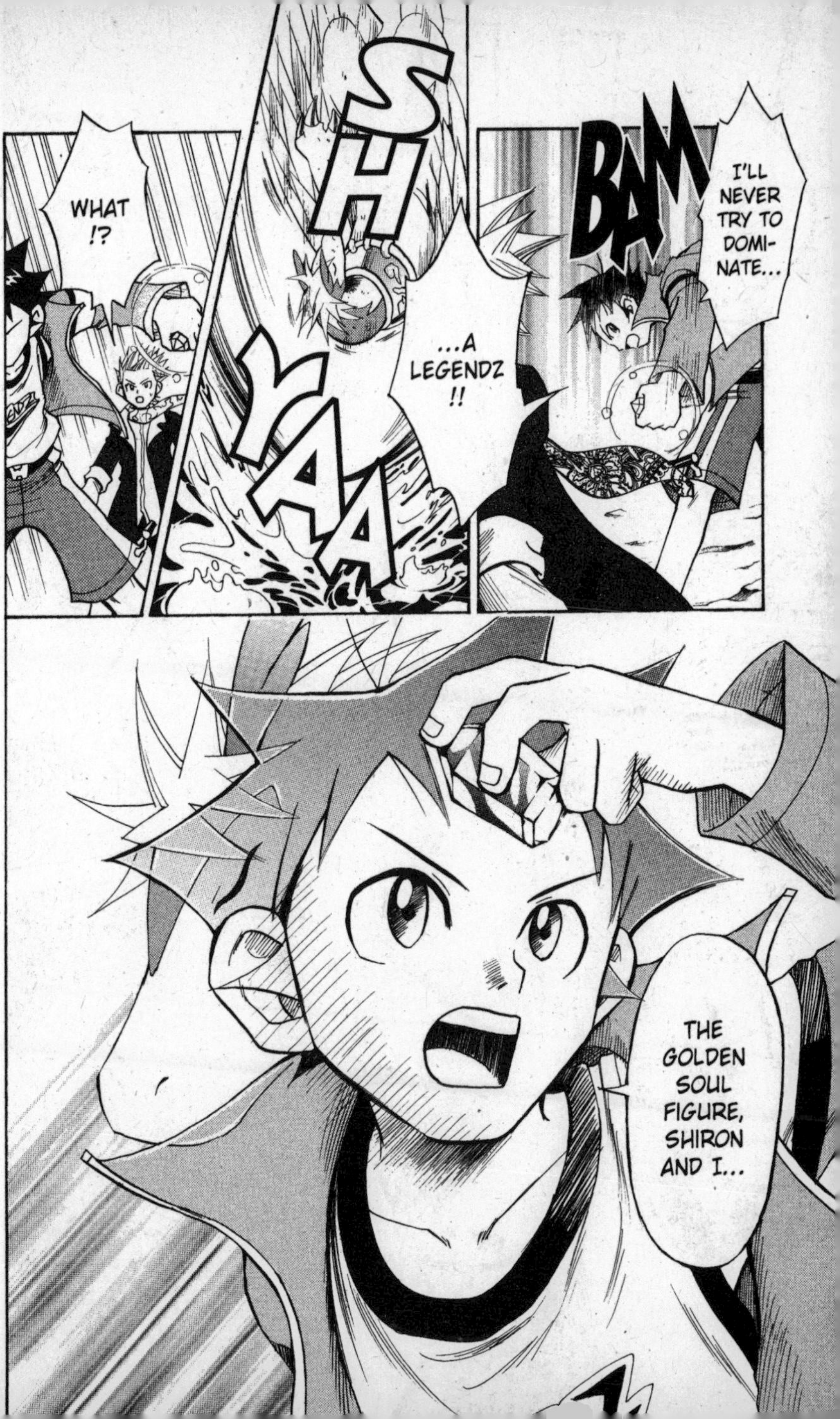
BAM
I'LL NEVER TRY TO DOMI-NATE...
SH
YAAA
...A LEGENDZ!!
WHAT!?
THE GOLDEN SOUL FIGURE, SHIRON AND I...

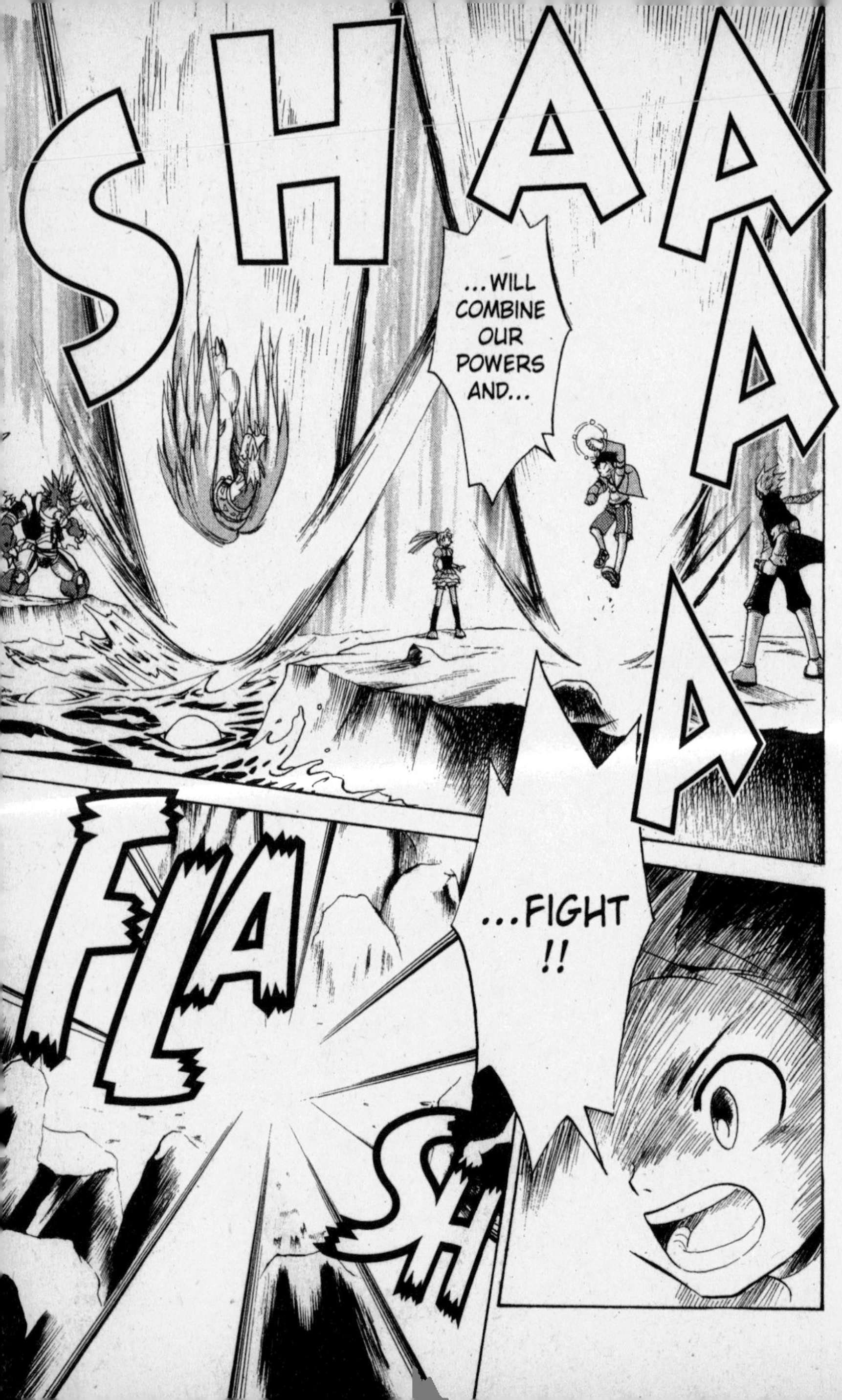
SHAAAA
...WILL COMBINE OUR POWERS AND...
FLASH
...FIGHT !!

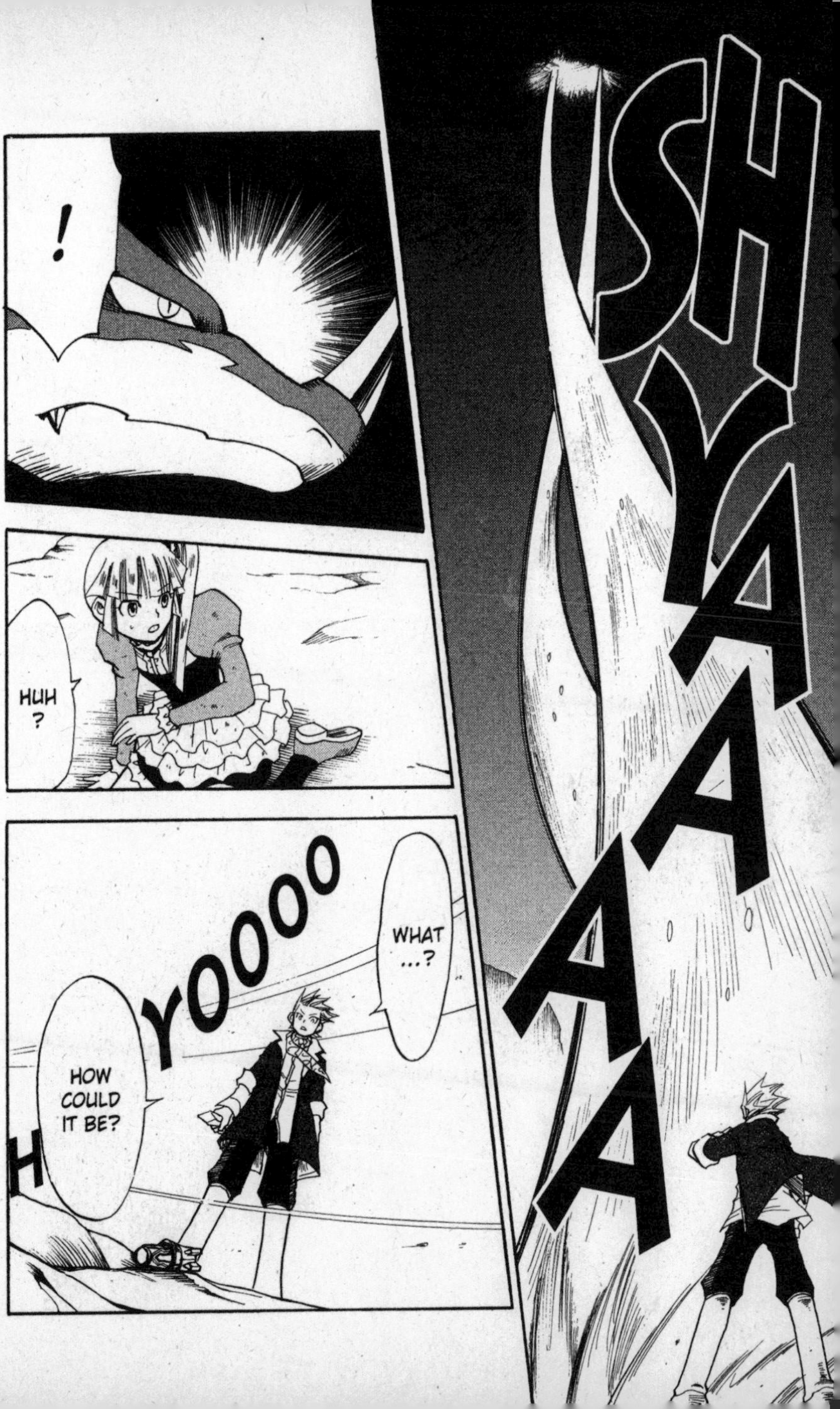

SHYAAAA
!
HUH ?
WHAT ...?
HYOOOO
HOW COULD IT BE?

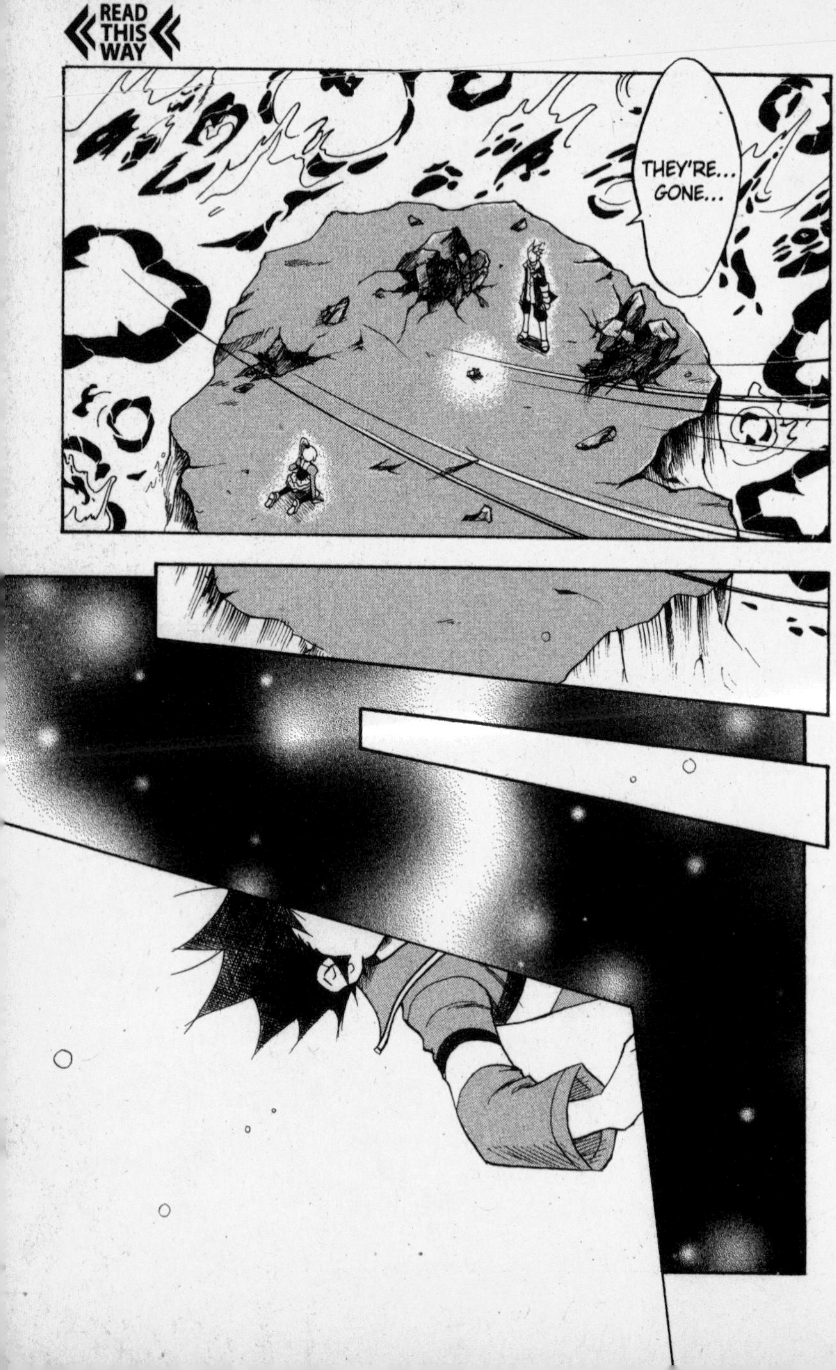
READ THIS WAY
THEY'RE... GONE...

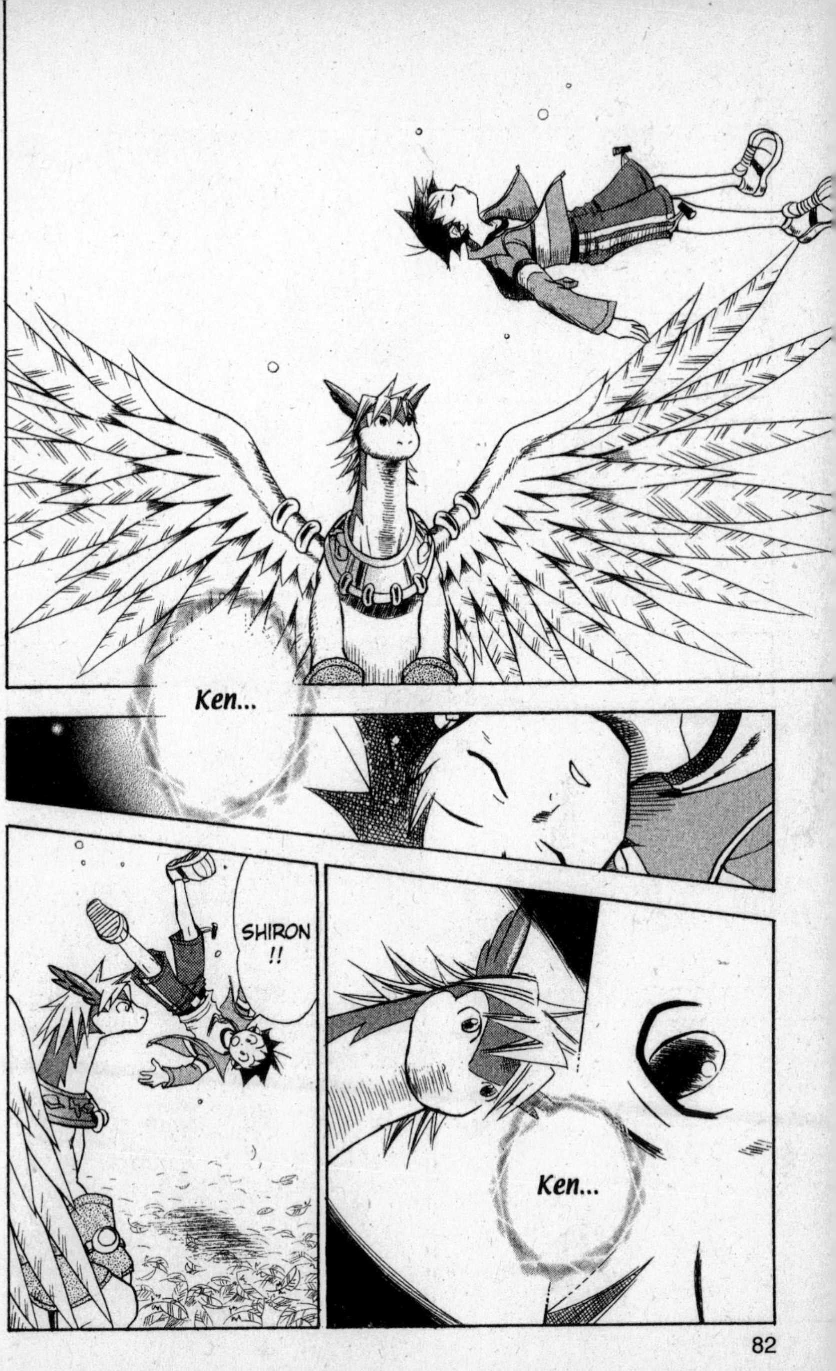
Ken...
Ken...
SHIRON !!

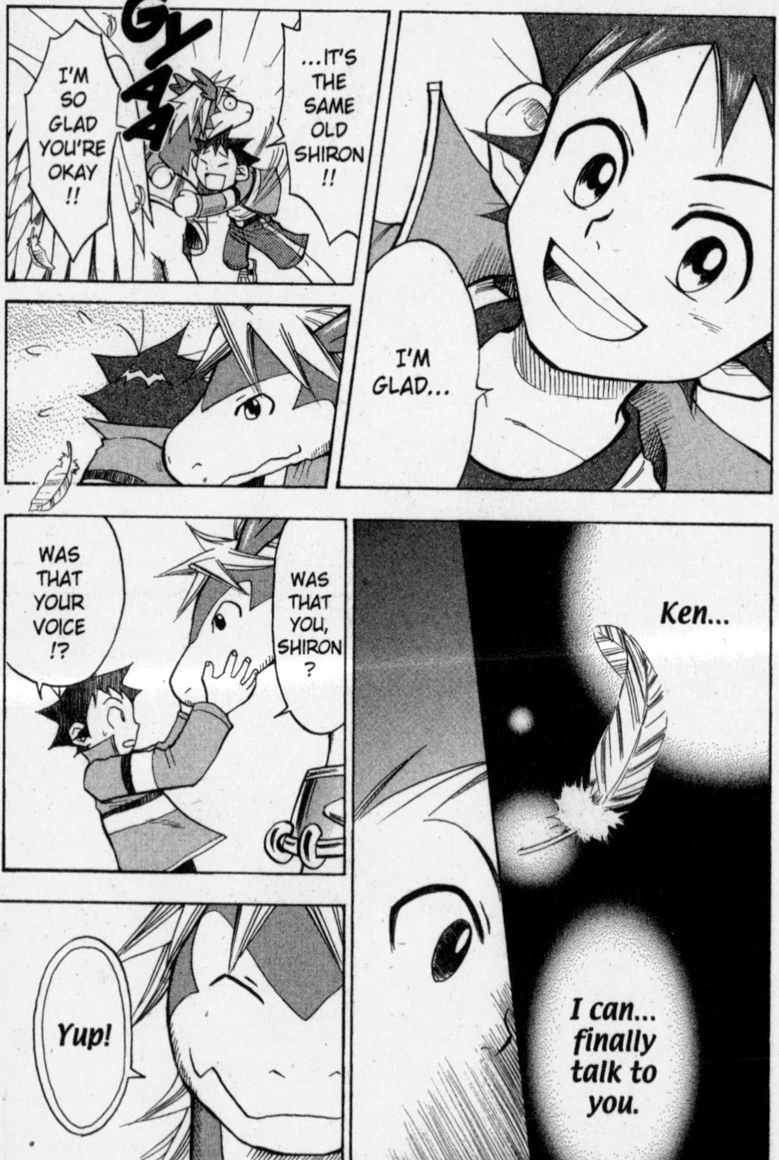
I'M GLAD...
...IT'S THE SAME OLD SHIRON!!
GYAA
I'M SO GLAD YOU'RE OKAY!!
Ken...
I can... finally talk to you.
WAS THAT YOU, SHIRON?
WAS THAT YOUR VOICE!?
Yup!

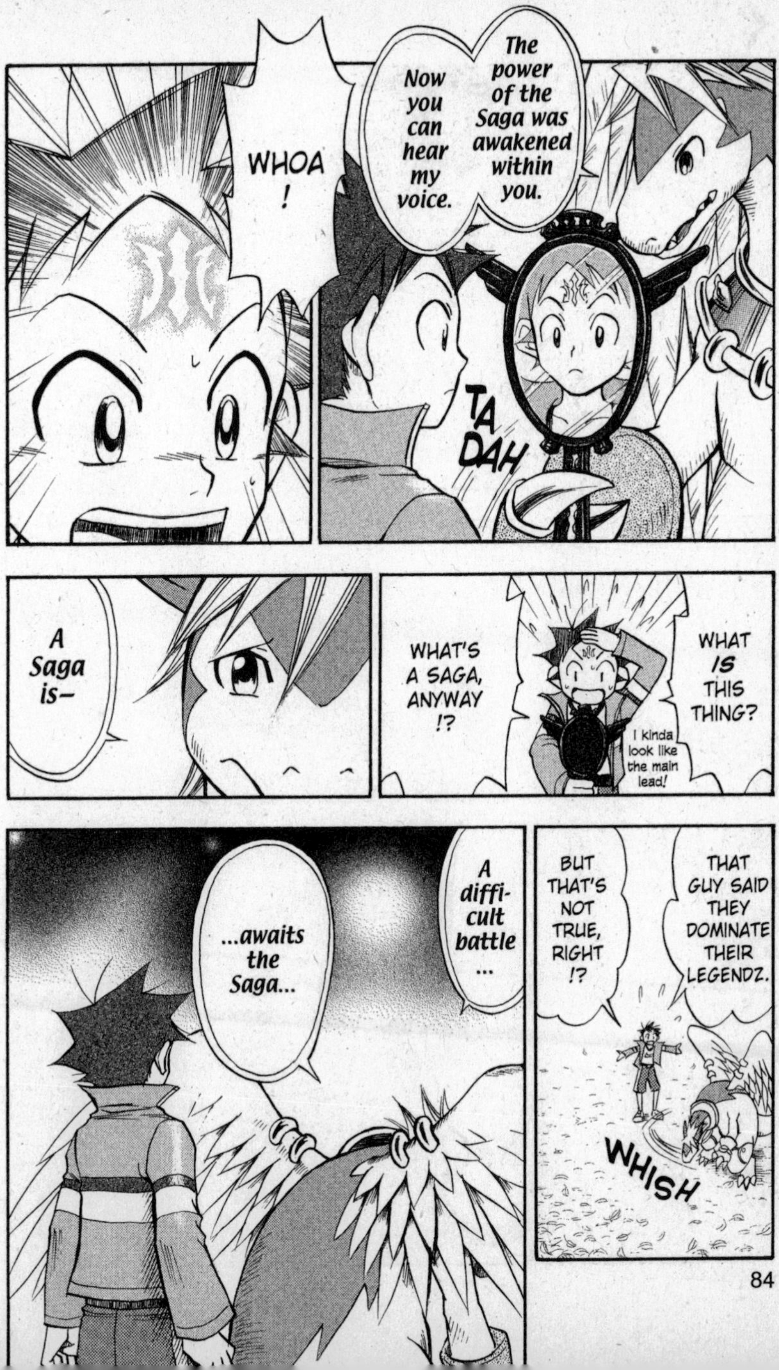
The power of the Saga was awakened within you.
Now you can hear my voice.
TA DAH
WHOA!
WHAT IS THIS THING?
WHAT'S A SAGA, ANYWAY!?
I kinda look like the main lead!
A Saga is–
THAT GUY SAID THEY DOMINATE THEIR LEGENDZ.
BUT THAT'S NOT TRUE, RIGHT!?
WHISH
A difficult battle...
...awaits the Saga...

READ THIS WAY

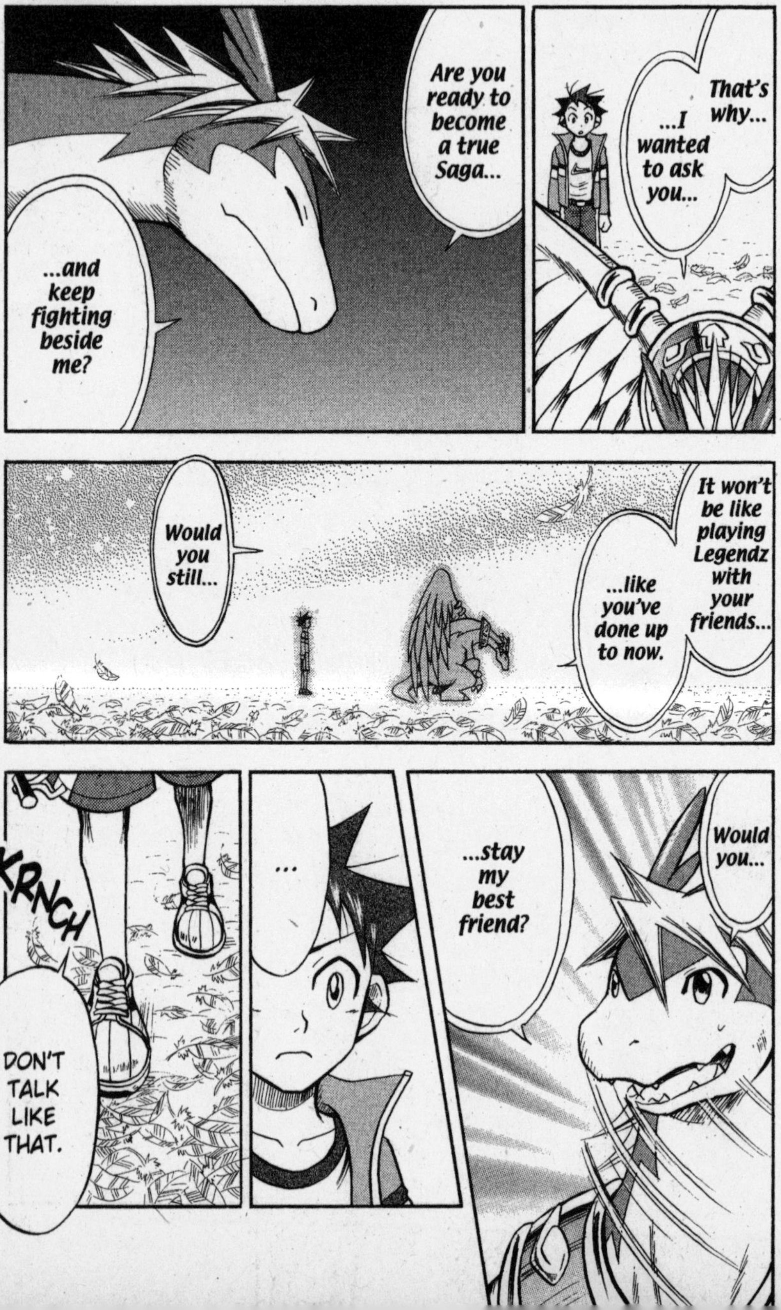
That's why...
...I wanted to ask you...
Are you ready to become a true Saga...
...and keep fighting beside me?
It won't be like playing Legendz with your friends...
...like you've done up to now.
Would you still...
Would you...
...stay my best friend?
...
KRNCH
DON'T TALK LIKE THAT.

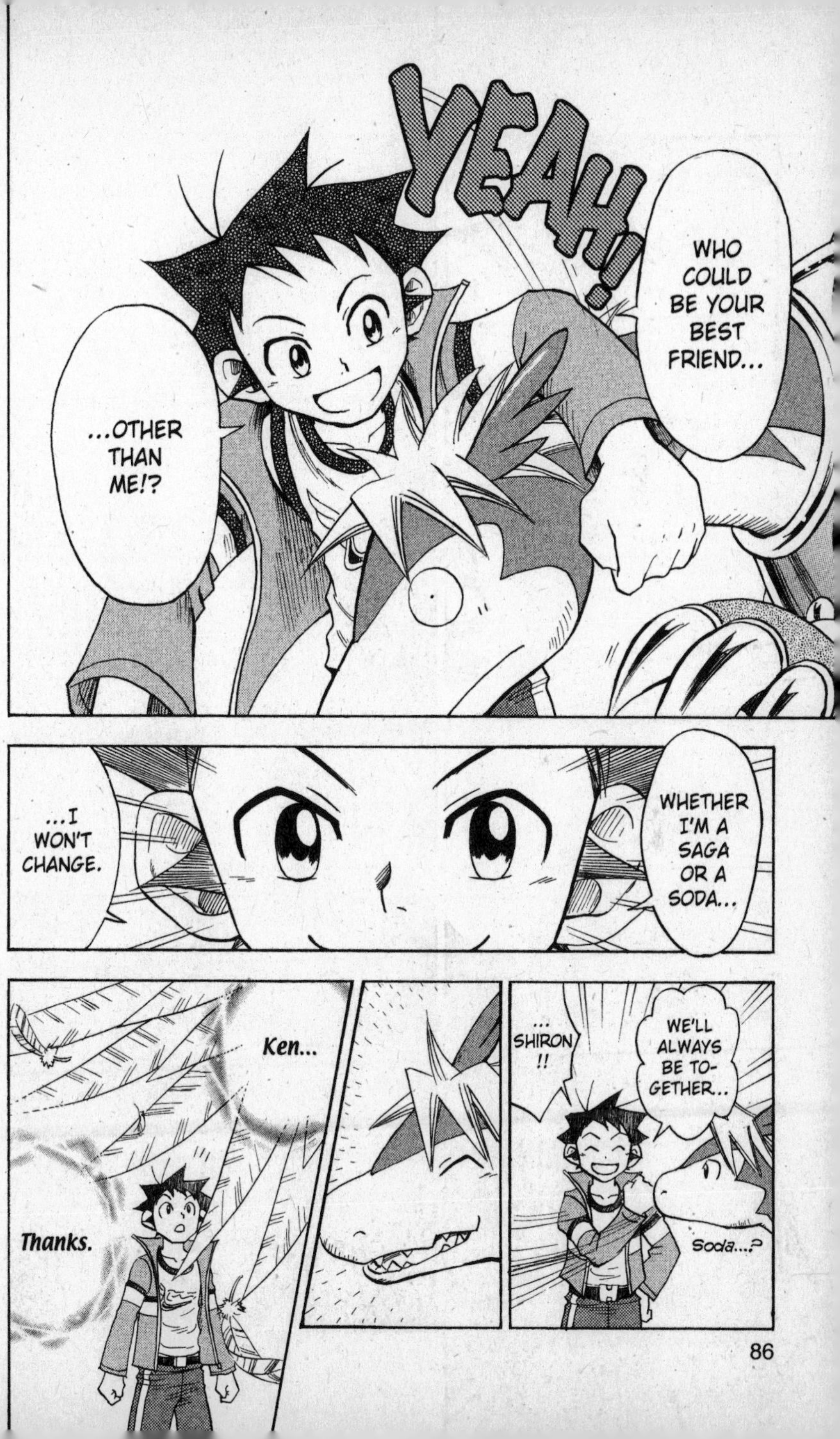
YEAH!
WHO COULD BE YOUR BEST FRIEND...
...OTHER THAN ME!?
WHETHER I'M A SAGA OR A SODA...
...I WON'T CHANGE.
WE'LL ALWAYS BE TO-GETHER...
...SHIRON!!
Soda...?
Ken...
Thanks.

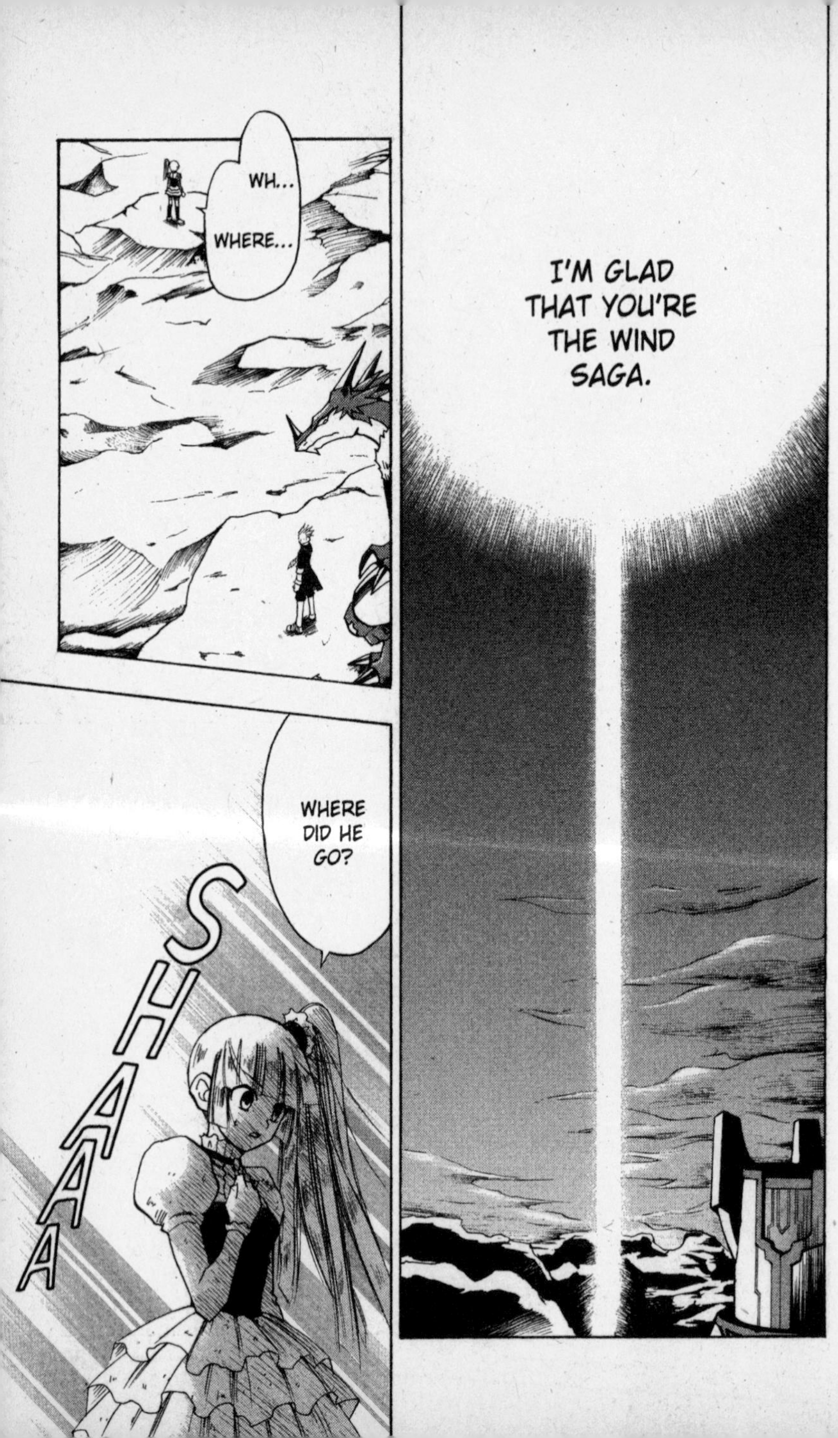
I'M GLAD THAT YOU'RE THE WIND SAGA.
WH...
WHERE...
WHERE DID HE GO?
SHAAAAA

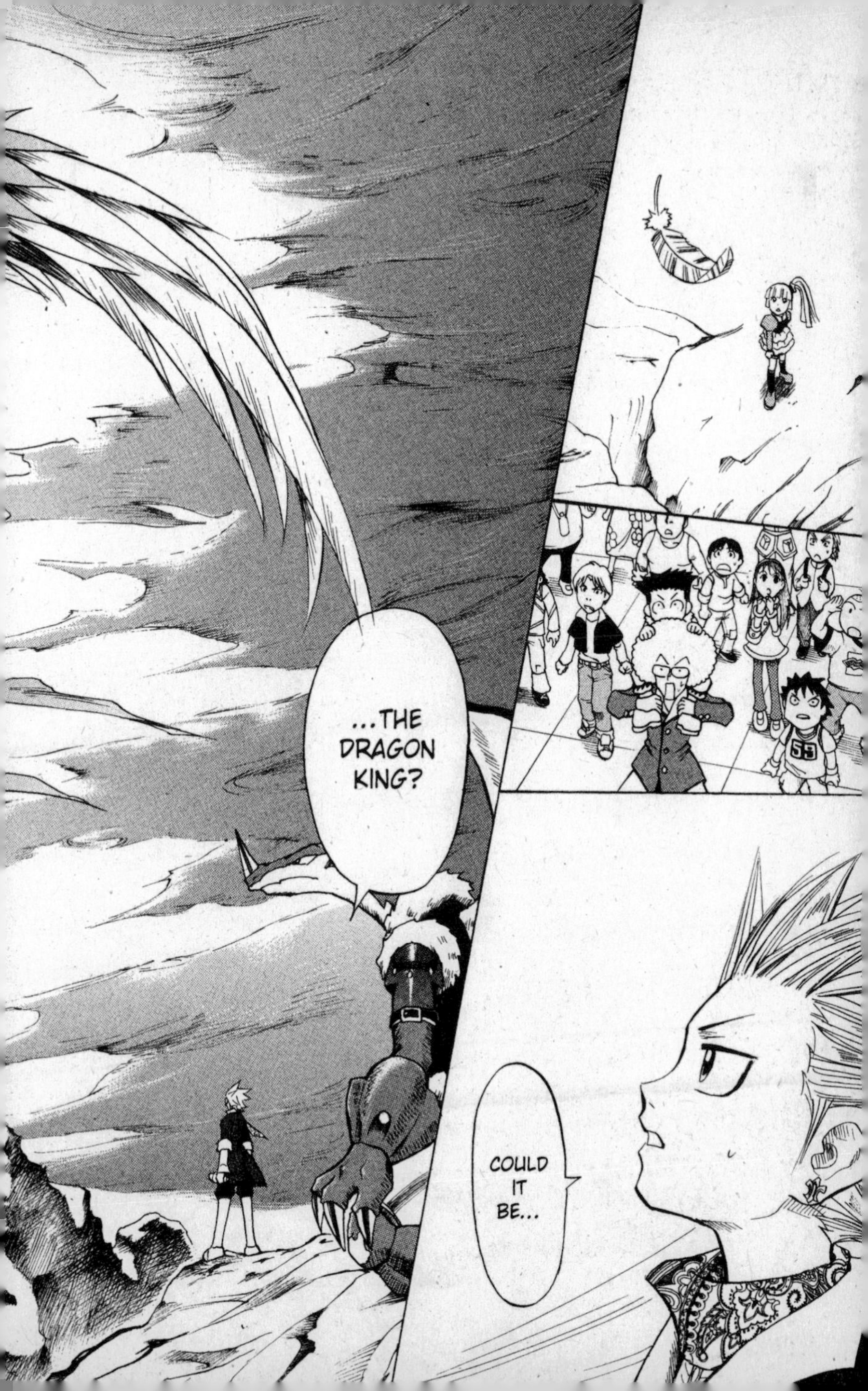
COULD IT BE...
...THE DRAGON KING?

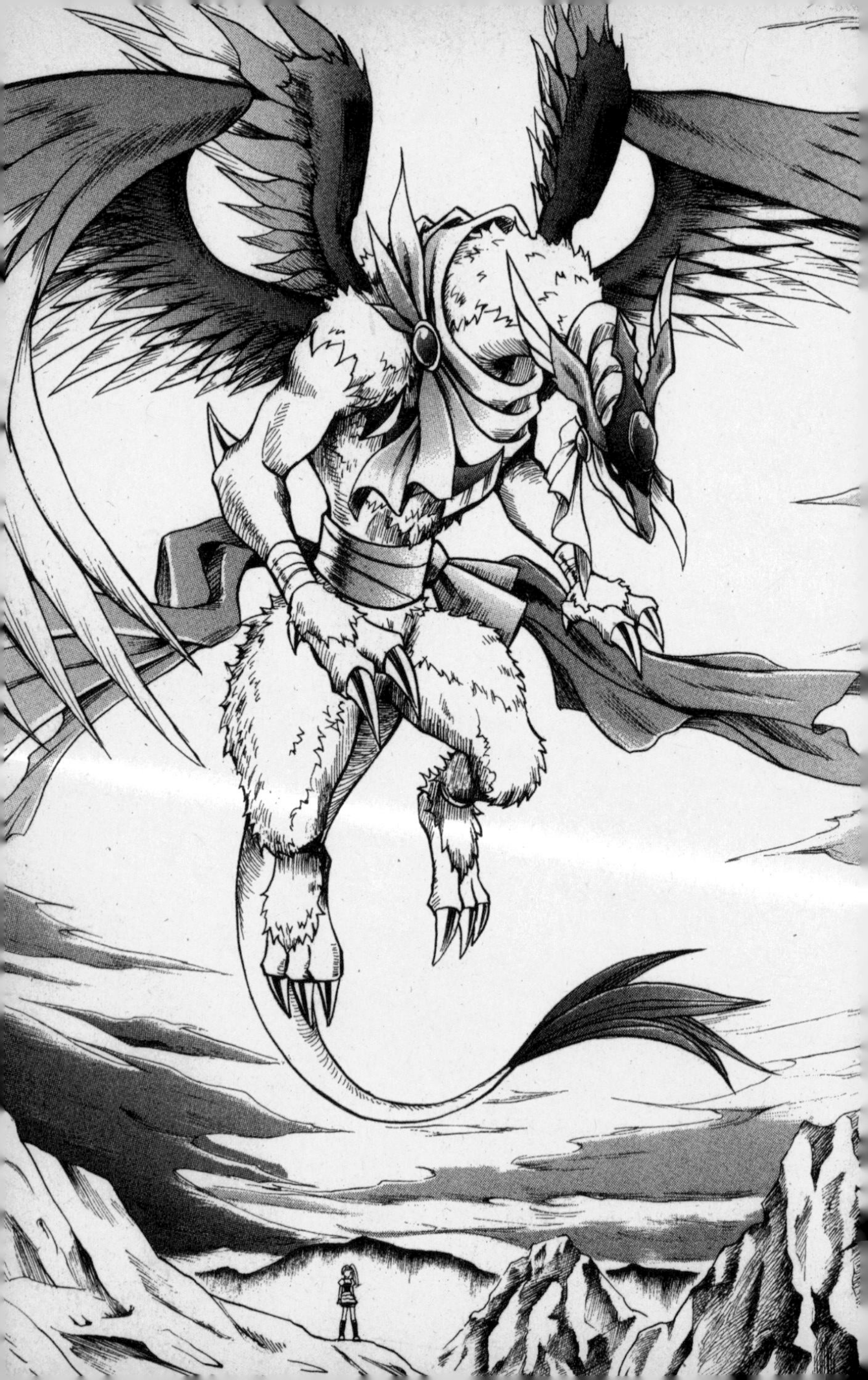

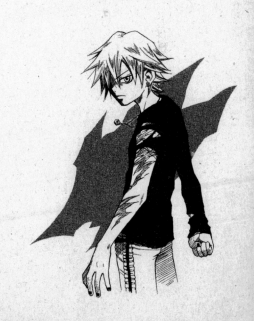

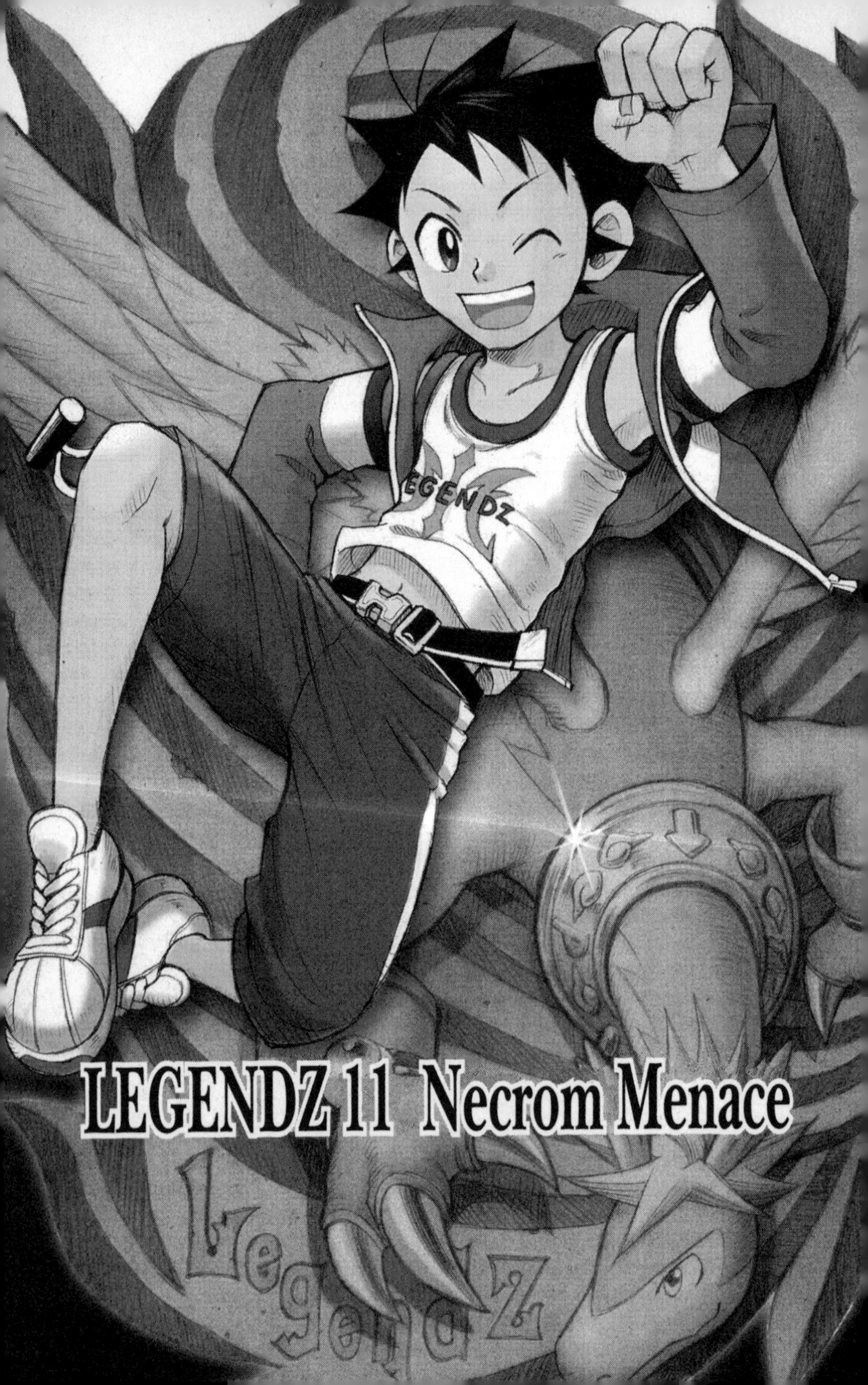
LEGENDZ
Legendz

LEGENDZ 11 Necrom Menace

LEGENDZ COLLECTION

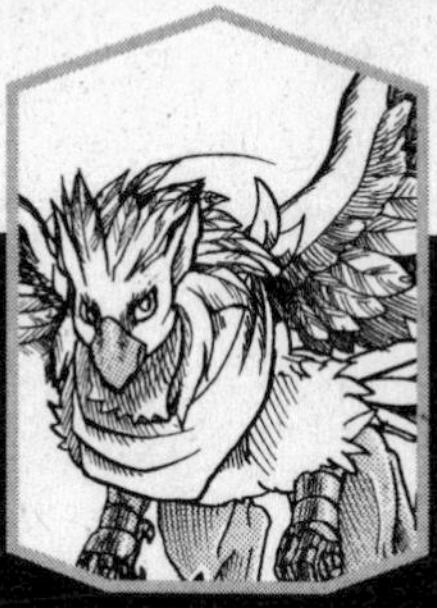

ELEMENT: WIND (TORNADO)
TYPE: HIPPOGRIFF
HIT POINTS: 540
FAVORITE ATTACK: BACK-DRAFTER, LIGHTBLIST

LEGENDZ NAME:TOREEN
SAGA: UNKNOWN

A GENTLE-HEARTED WIND SPIRIT. BUT WHEN CORNERED, IT WILL FIGHT TO THE DEATH WITH ITS POWERFUL COUNTERATTACKS.

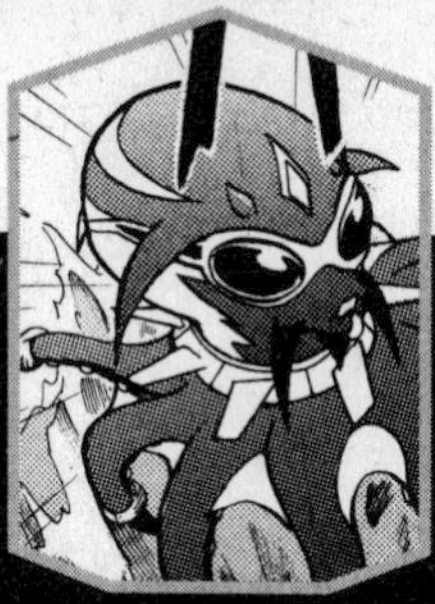

ELEMENT: WATER (STORM)
TYPE: MAZE OCTOPUS
HIT POINTS: 700
FAVORITE ATTACK: DANCE-QUARIUM, EIGHT BIND

LEGENDZ NAME: TAKOKO
SAGA: UNKNOWN

A GIANT SQUID FEARED AS THE DEMON OF THE SEAS. FAVORS WATER BATTLES AND USES ITS EIGHT LEGS FOR ITS VARIOUS ATTACKS.

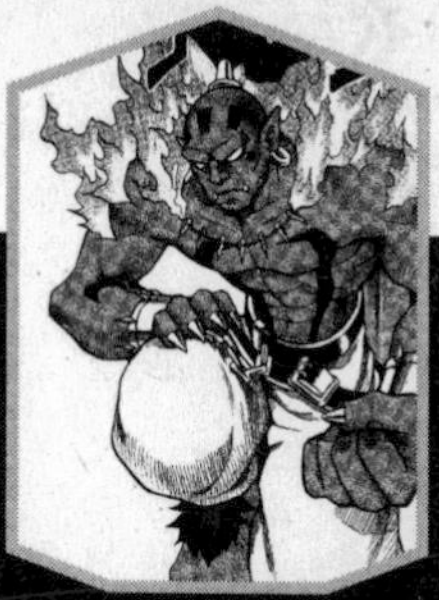

ELEMENT: FIRE (VOLCANO)
TYPE: IFREET
HIT POINTS: 890
FAVORITE ATTACK: SANDFRADE, BURN DISASTER

LEGENDZ NAME: GALAGA
SAGA: UNKNOWN

THIS FLAME DEMON SPIRIT WRAPS ITSELF IN FIRE AND GOES ON A RAMPAGE. VERY HARD TO CONTROL, BECAUSE IT WANTS TO BURN EVERYTHING TO ASH.

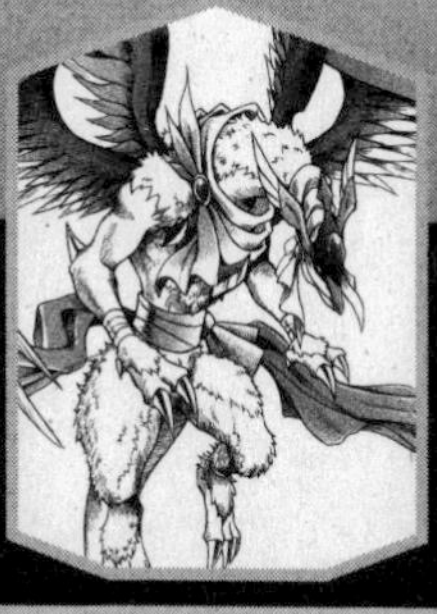

ELEMENT: WIND (TORNADO)
TYPE: TORNADO KINGDRAGON
HIT POINTS: 9000
FAVORITE ATTACK: KING WING TORNADO, RISING BREIGA

LEGENDZ NAME: SHIRON
SAGA: KEN KAZAKI

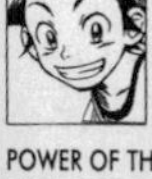

THE WIND ELEMENT LEGENDZ'S ULTIMATE FORM, WHICH SHIRON EVOLVED INTO BECAUSE KEN AWOKE TO THE POWER OF THE SAGA. THIS POWER IS SHROUDED IN MYSTERY.

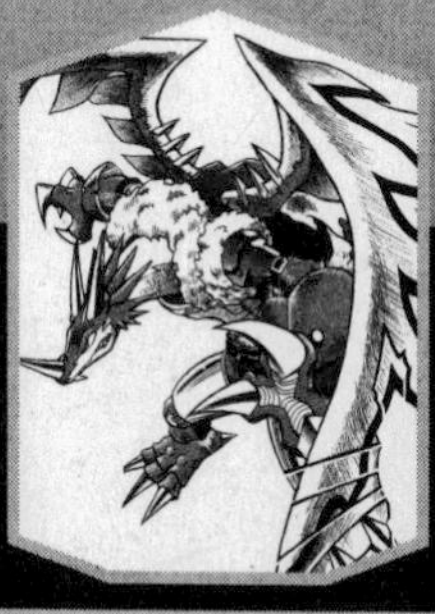

ELEMENT: FIRE (VOLCANO)
TYPE: COMMAND BLAZEDRAGON
HIT POINTS: 3550
FAVORITE ATTACK: VOLKBURN, DEATH HEAT

LEGENDZ NAME: GREEDO
SAGA: LEO ENGOKUIN

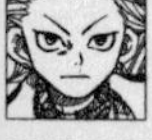

GREEDO'S ADVANCED FORM, THANKS TO LEO'S POWER. BECAUSE OF LEO'S TRAINING, ITS MAGICAL ATTACK POWER HAS DEVELOPED TO ITS FULLEST.

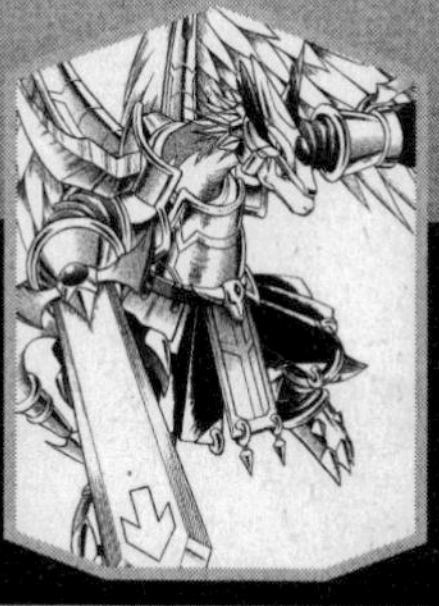

ELEMENT: WIND (TORNADO)
TYPE: SPIRITUAL WINDRAGON
HIT POINTS: 2700
FAVORITE ATTACK: LIGHTNING STREAM, SHINING SLASHER

LEGENDZ NAME: SHIRON
SAGA: KEN KAZAKI

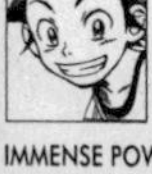

SHIRON WEARS THE "ARMOR OF LIGHT" CREATED BY THE SIX GREAT DRAGON KINGS. BECAUSE OF THE IMMENSE POWER IT ATTAINED, KEN COULDN'T MAINTAIN CONTROL.

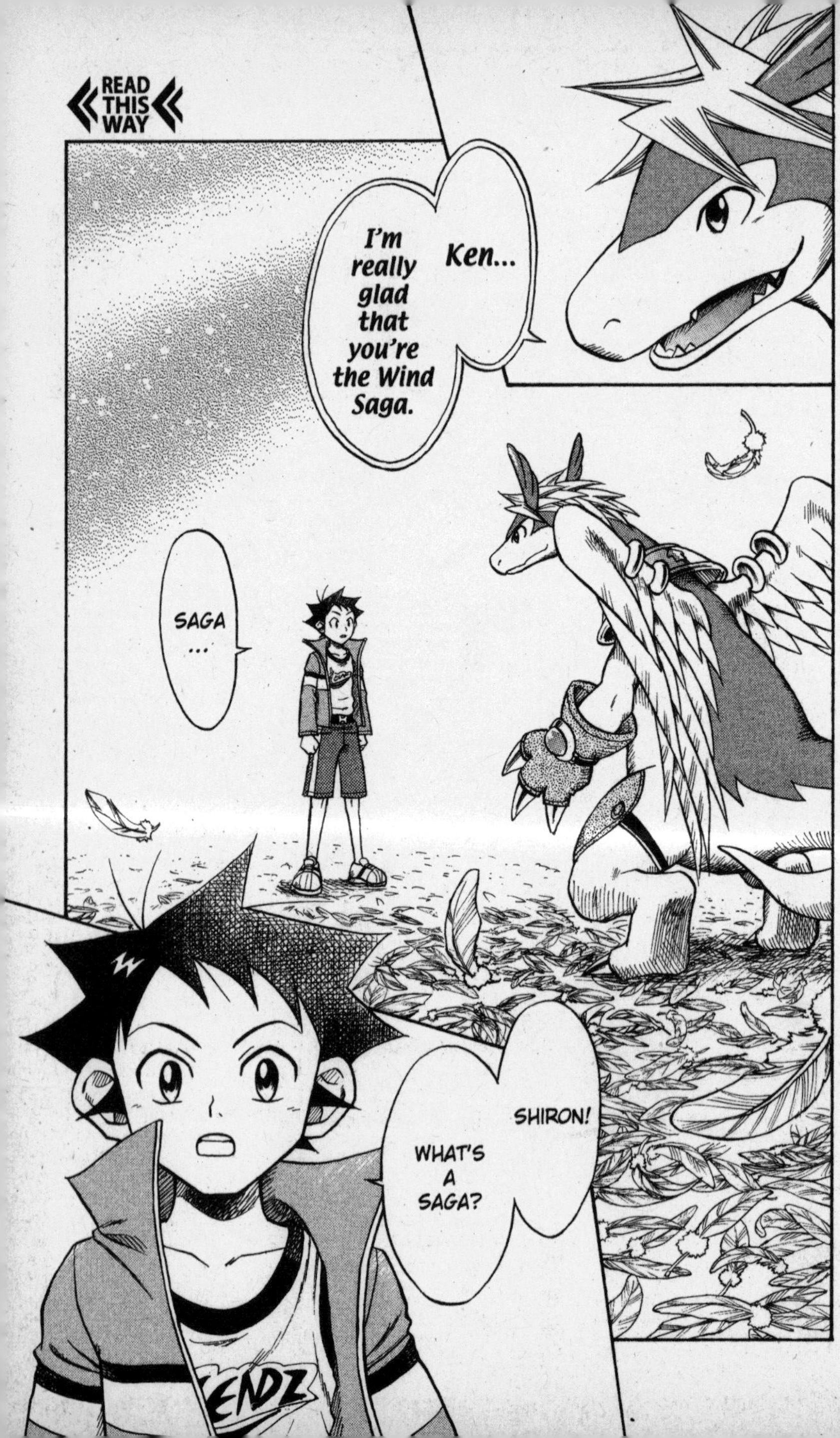
READ THIS WAY
Ken...
I'm really glad that you're the Wind Saga.
SAGA ...
SHIRON!
WHAT'S A SAGA?

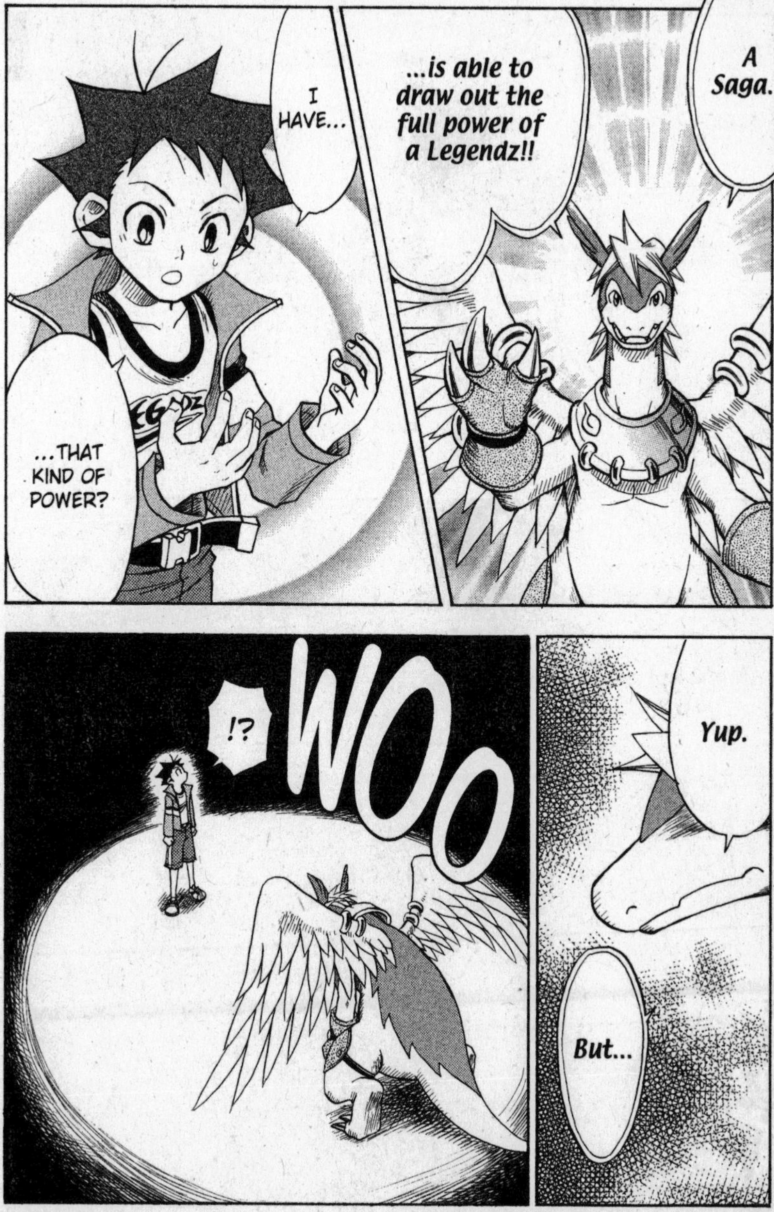
A Saga...
...is able to draw out the full power of a Legendz!!
I HAVE...
...THAT KIND OF POWER?
Yup.
But...
!?
WOO

READ THIS WAY

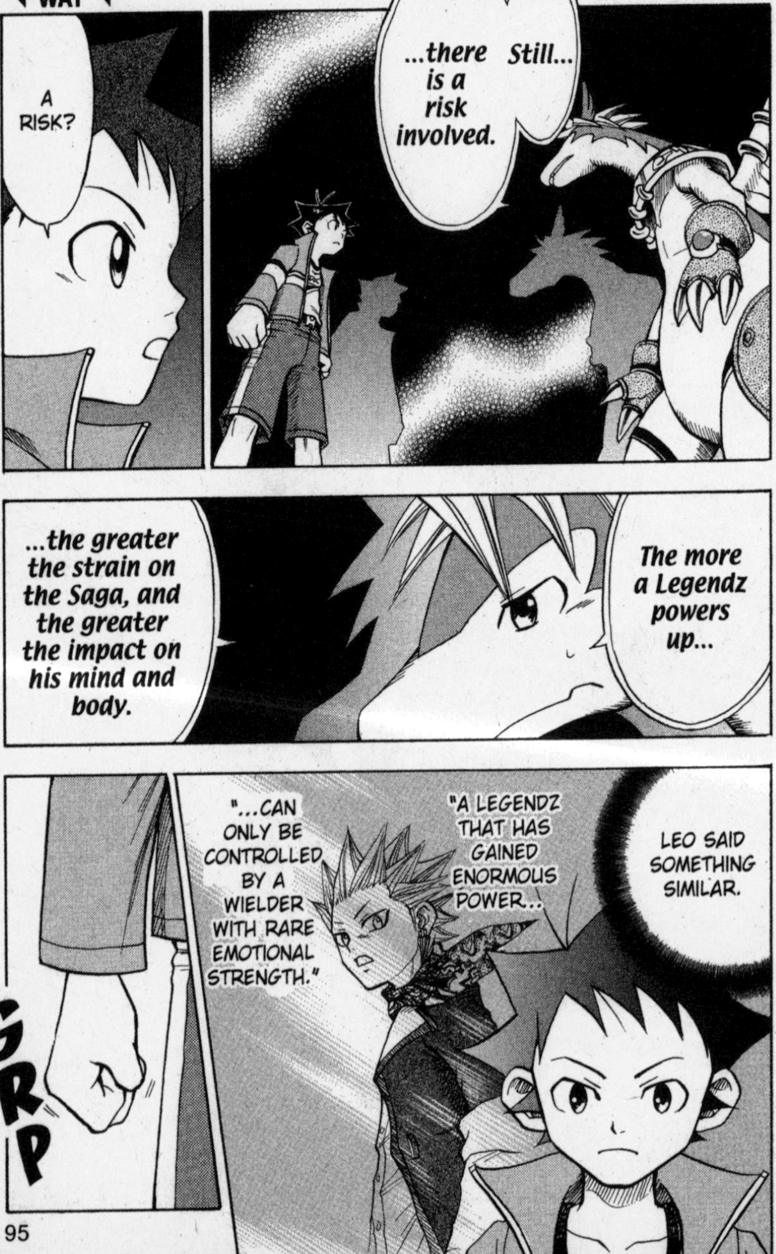
Still... ...there is a risk involved.
A RISK?
The more a Legendz powers up...
...the greater the strain on the Saga, and the greater the impact on his mind and body.
LEO SAID SOMETHING SIMILAR.
"A LEGENDZ THAT HAS GAINED ENORMOUS POWER...
"...CAN ONLY BE CONTROLLED BY A WIELDER WITH RARE EMOTIONAL STRENGTH."
GRP

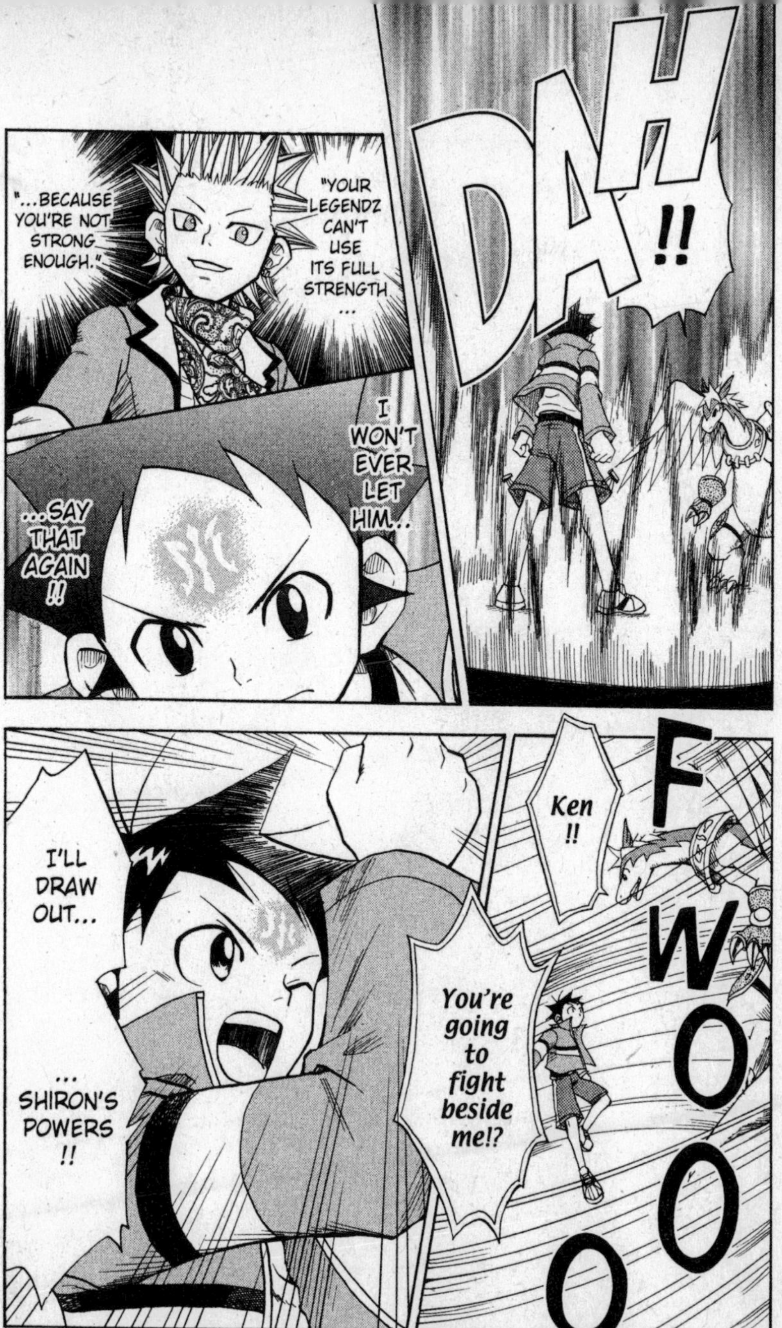
DAH!!
"YOUR LEGENDZ CAN'T USE ITS FULL STRENGTH ...
"...BECAUSE YOU'RE NOT STRONG ENOUGH."
I WON'T EVER LET HIM...
...SAY THAT AGAIN!!
FWOOOOO
Ken!!
You're going to fight beside me!?
I'LL DRAW OUT...
... SHIRON'S POWERS!!

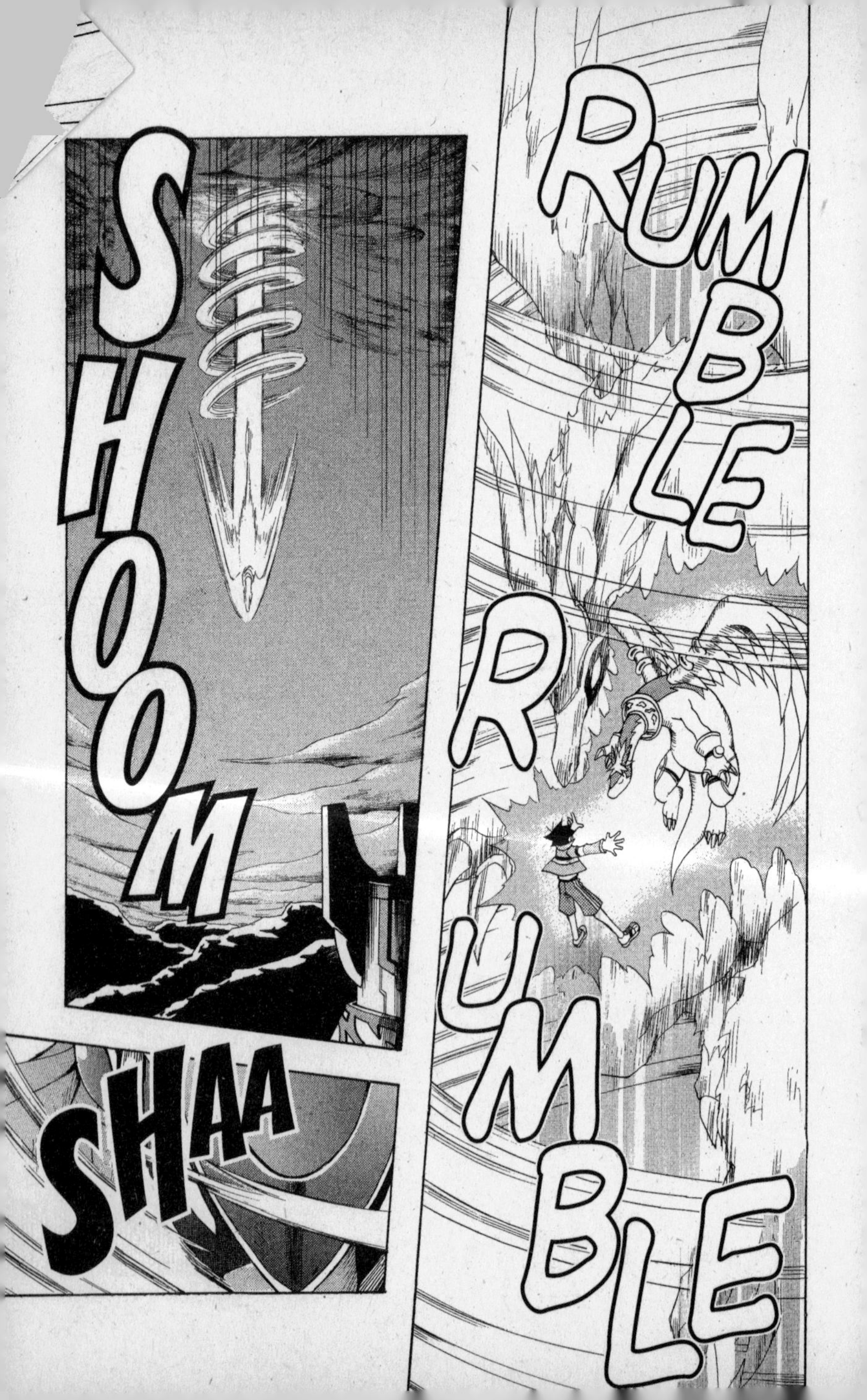
RUMBLE
RUMBLE
SHOOM
SHAA

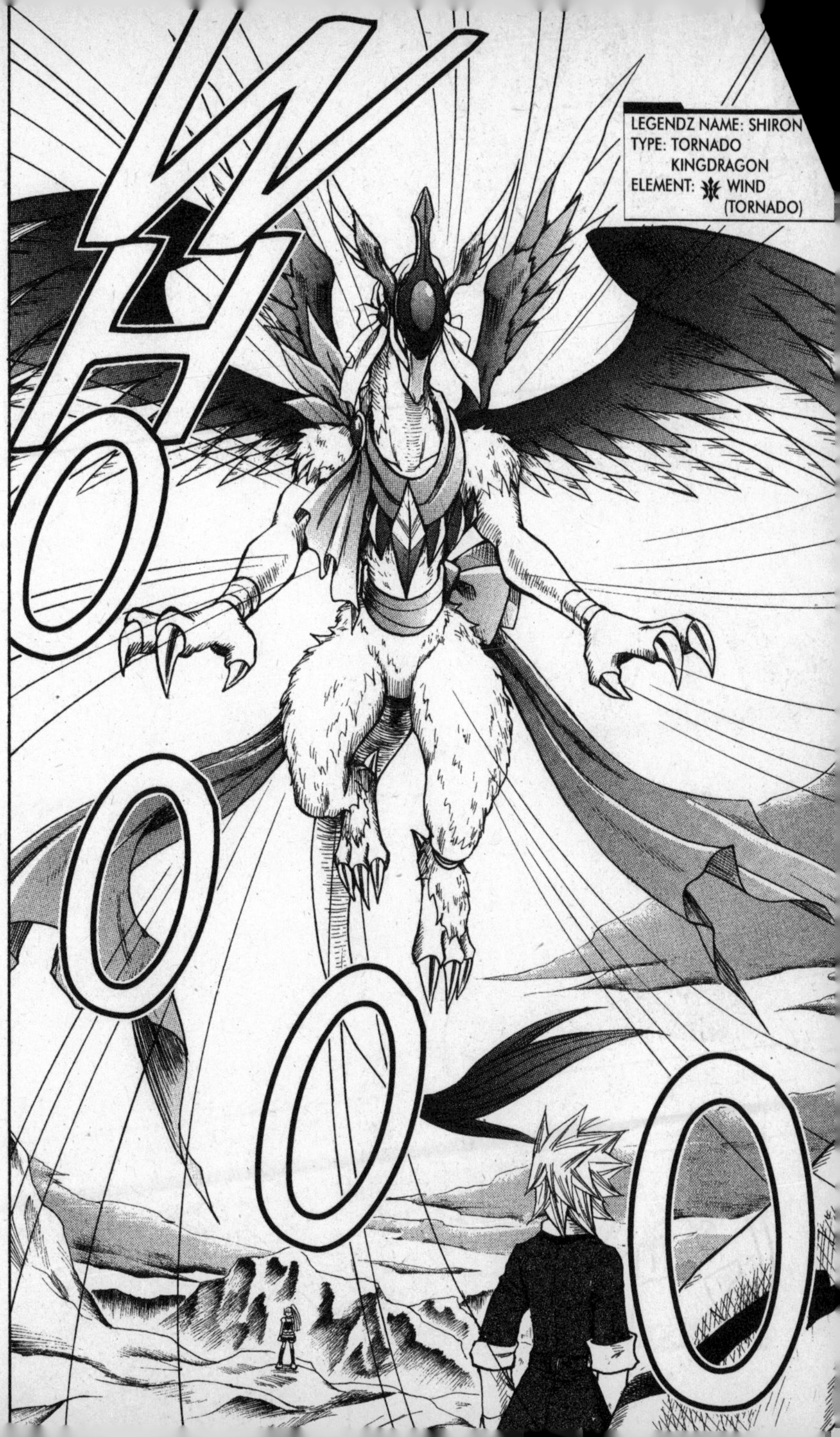
LEGENDZ NAME: SHIRON
TYPE: TORNADO KINGDRAGON
ELEMENT: WIND (TORNADO)
WHOOOO

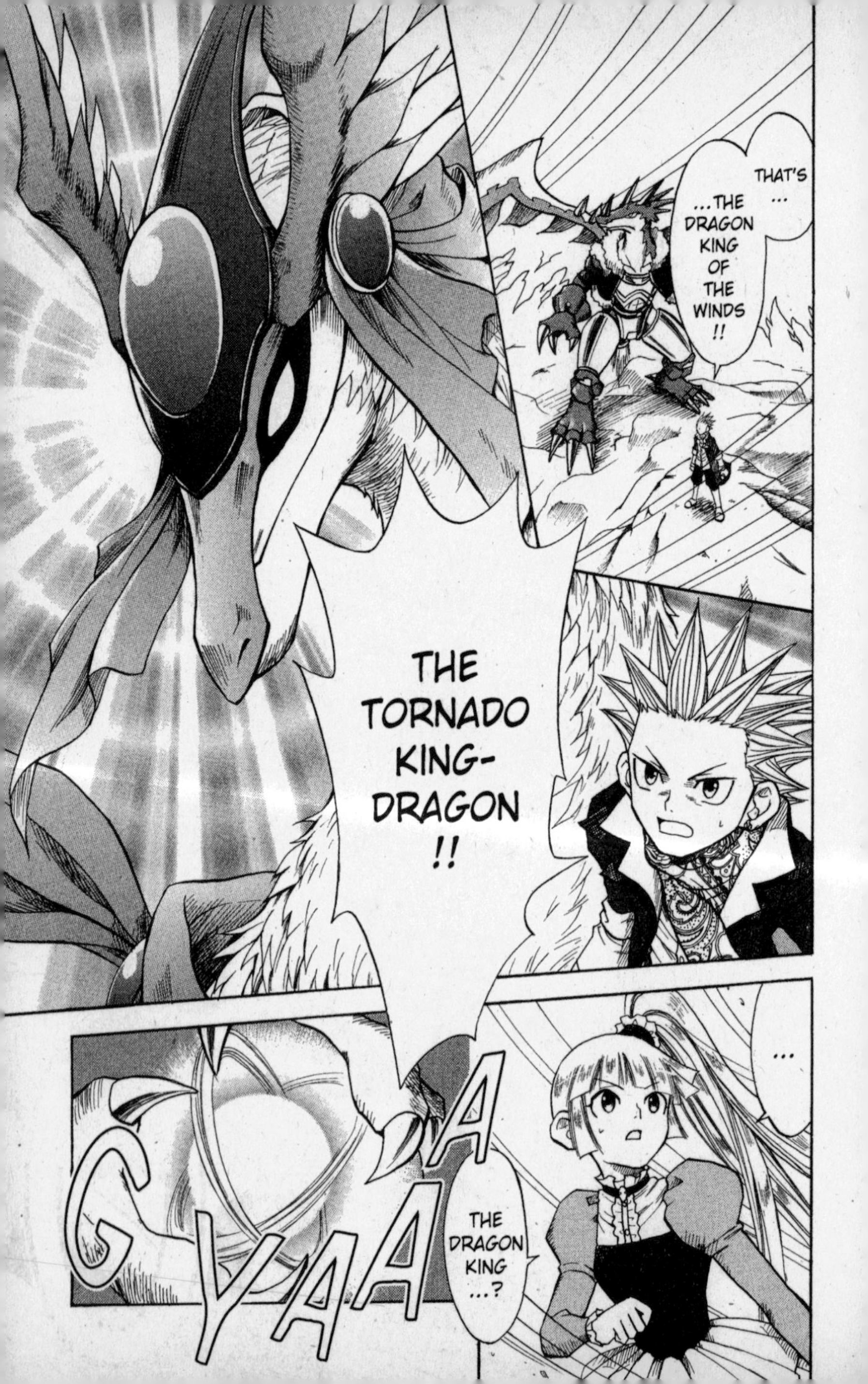
THAT'S ...
...THE DRAGON KING OF THE WINDS !!
THE TORNADO KING-DRAGON !!
...
THE DRAGON KING ...?
GYAAA

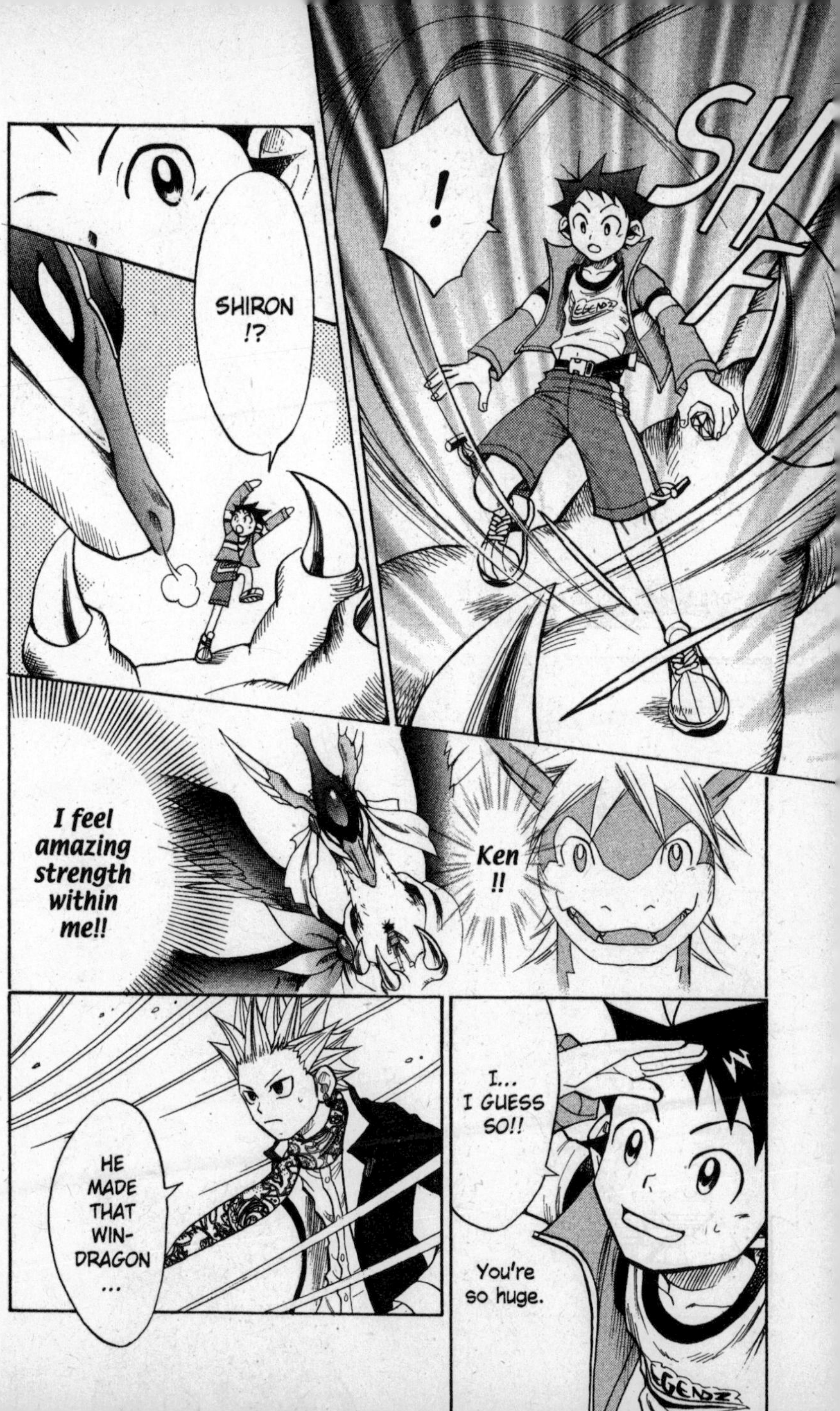
!
SHF
SHIRON !?
Ken !!
I feel amazing strength within me!!
I... I GUESS SO!!
You're so huge.
HE MADE THAT WIN-DRAGON ...

READ THIS WAY

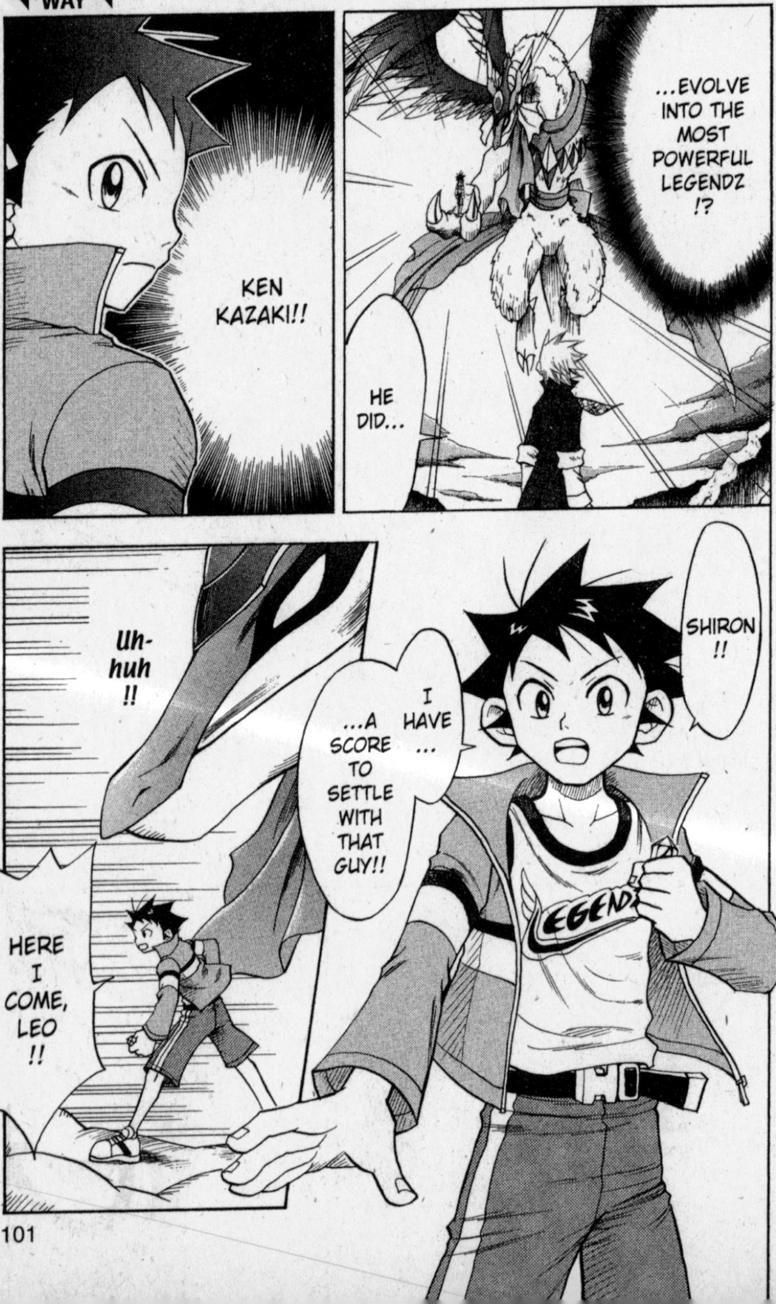
...EVOLVE INTO THE MOST POWERFUL LEGENDZ !?
HE DID...
KEN KAZAKI!!
SHIRON !!
I HAVE ...
...A SCORE TO SETTLE WITH THAT GUY!!
Uh-huh !!
HERE I COME, LEO !!

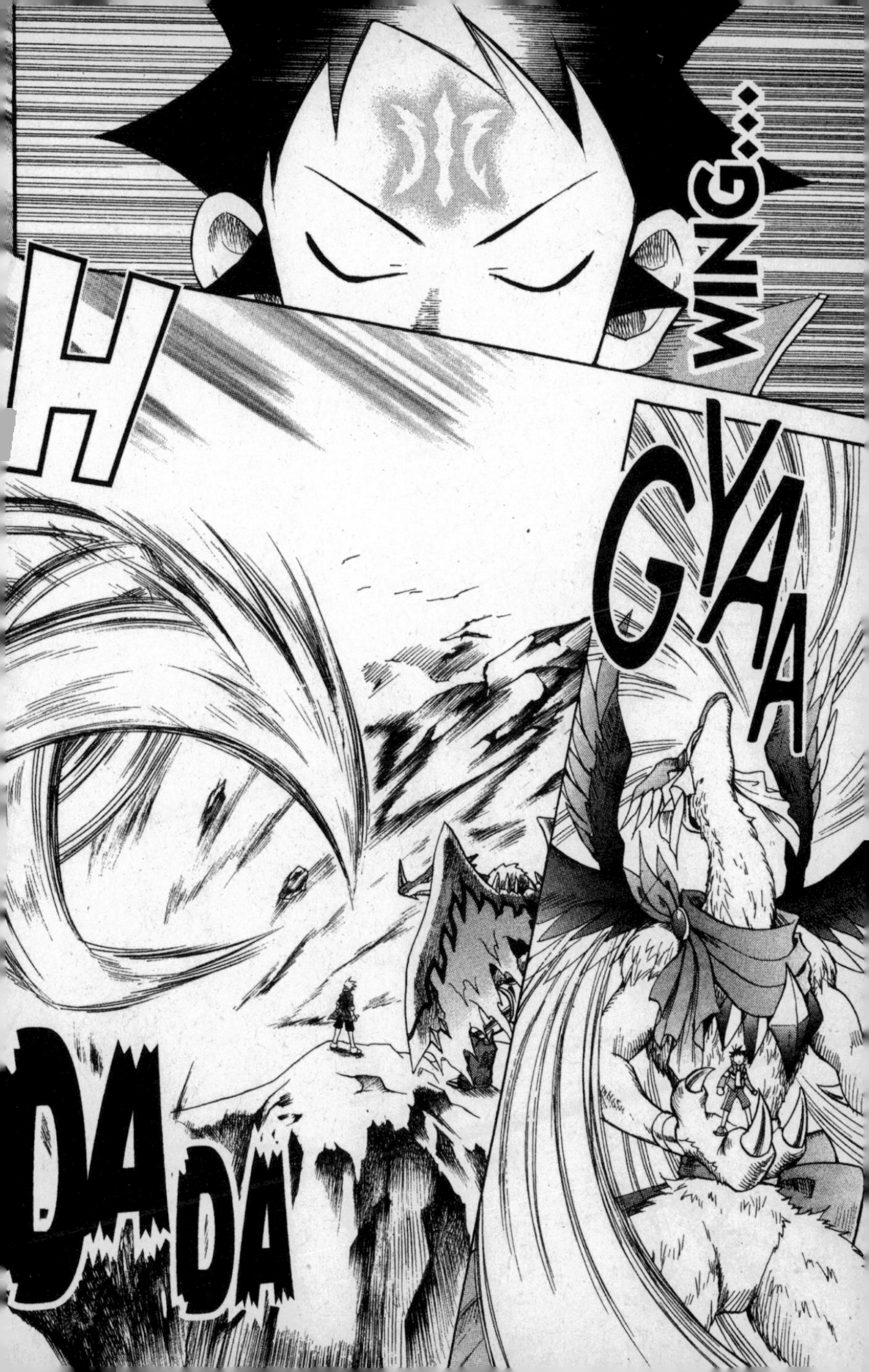
WING...
H
GYAAA
DADA

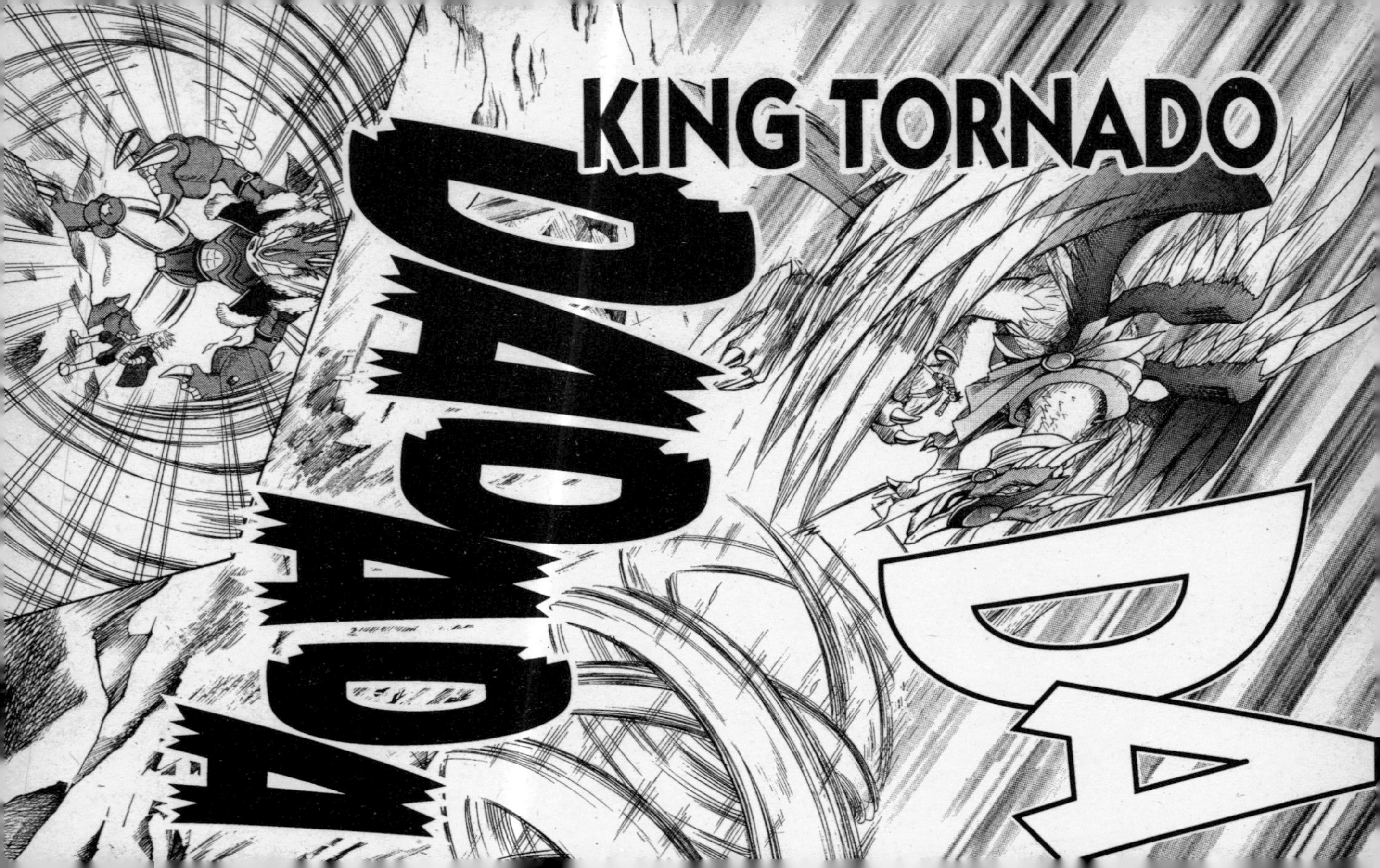
DA
KING TORNADO
DADADADA

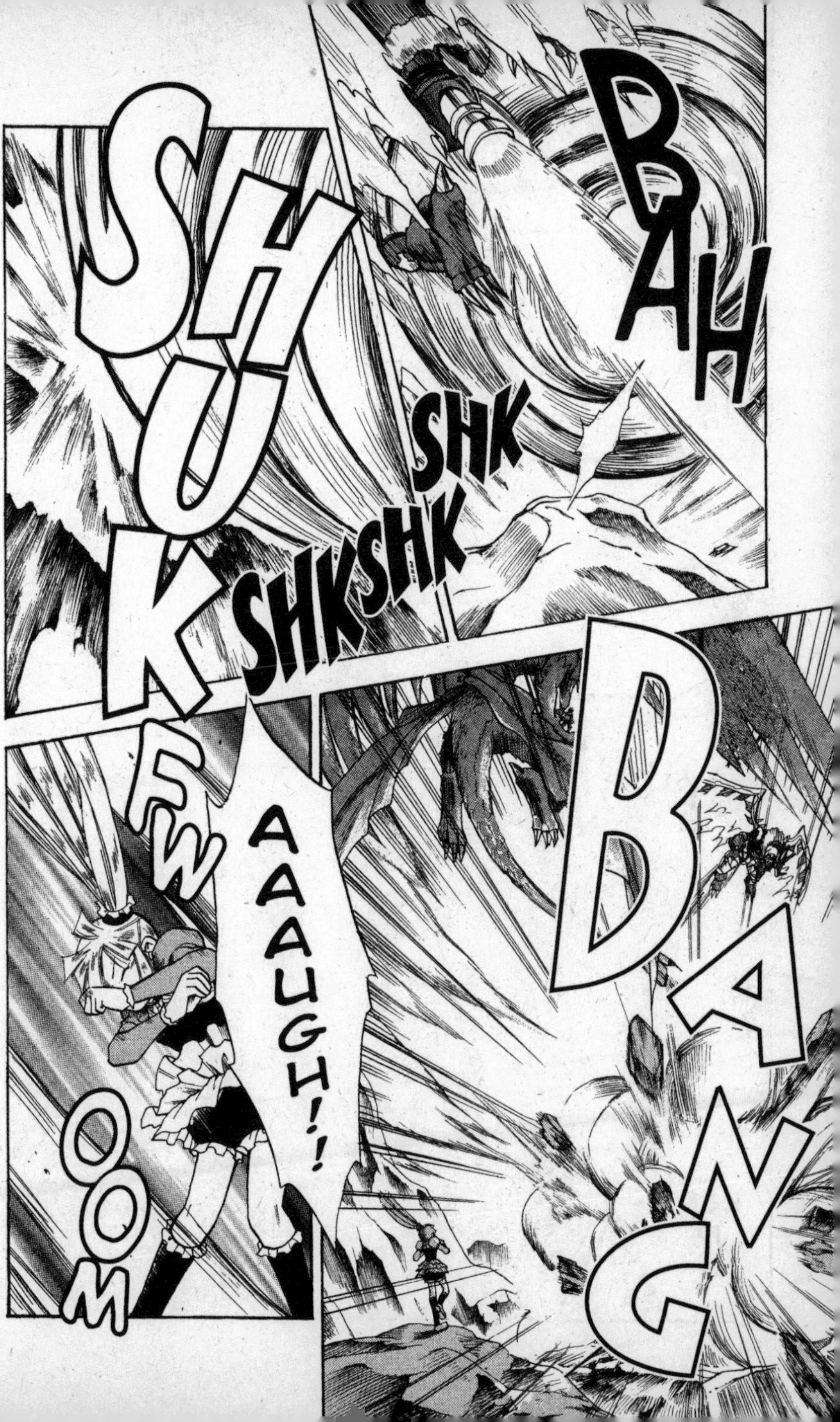
BAH
SHK
SHKSHK
SHUK
BANG
AAAUGH!!
FWOOM

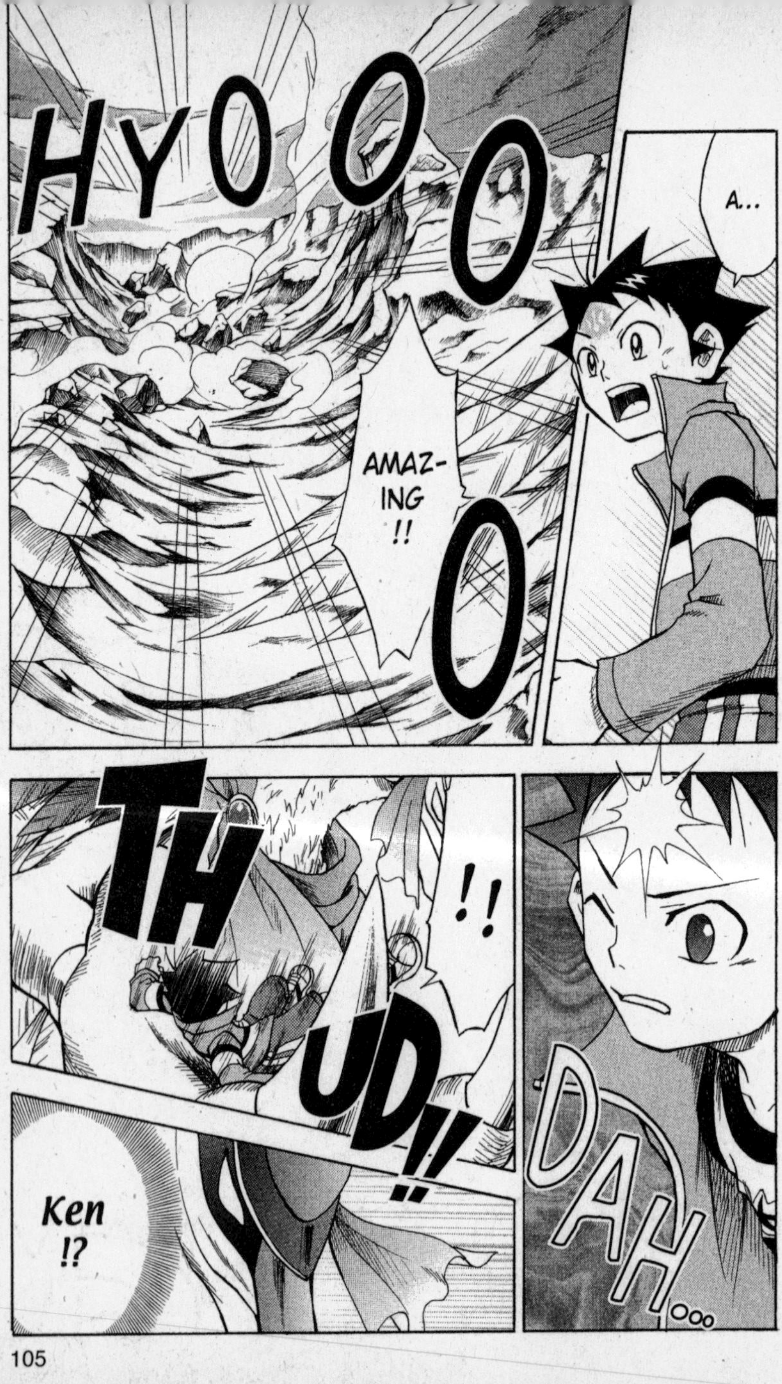
A...
HYOOOOO
AMAZING !!
DAH...
THUD!!
!!
Ken !?

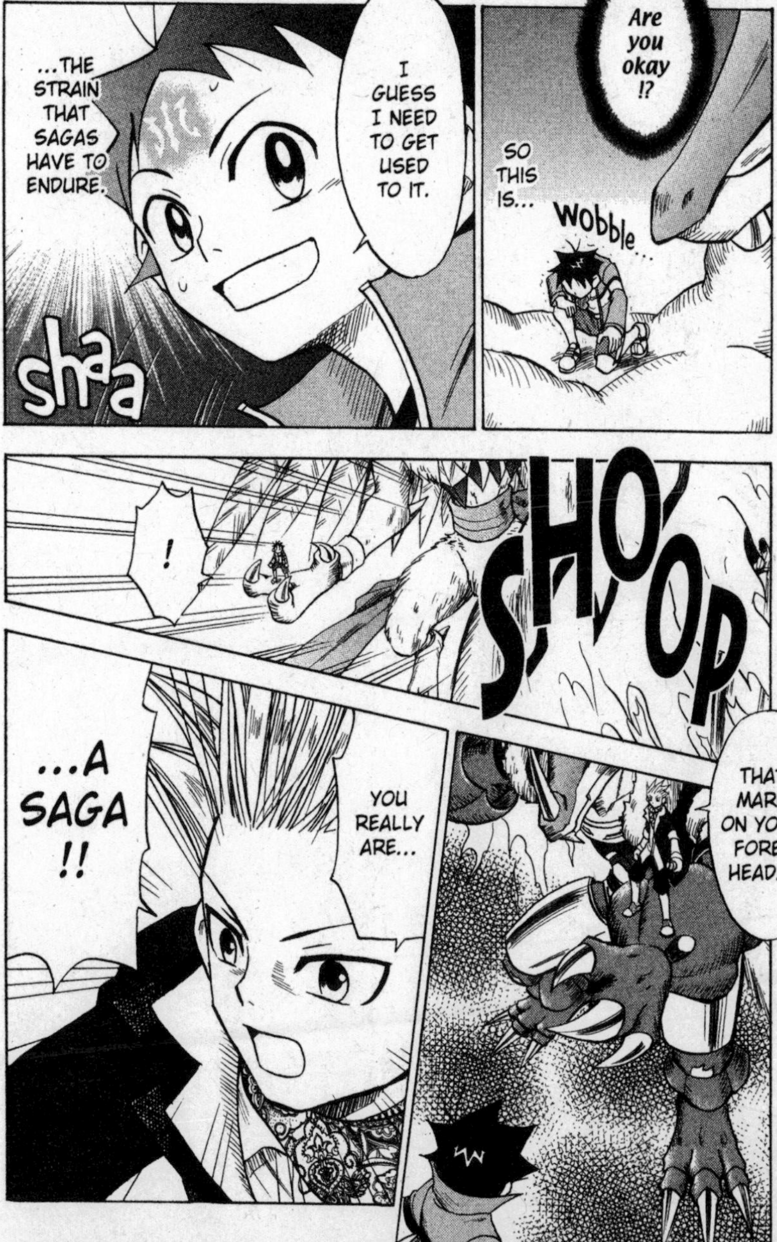
Are you okay !?
SO THIS IS...
wobble...
I GUESS I NEED TO GET USED TO IT.
...THE STRAIN THAT SAGAS HAVE TO ENDURE.
shaa
SHOOOP
!
THAT MARK ON YOUR FORE-HEAD...
YOU REALLY ARE...
...A SAGA !!

READ THIS WAY

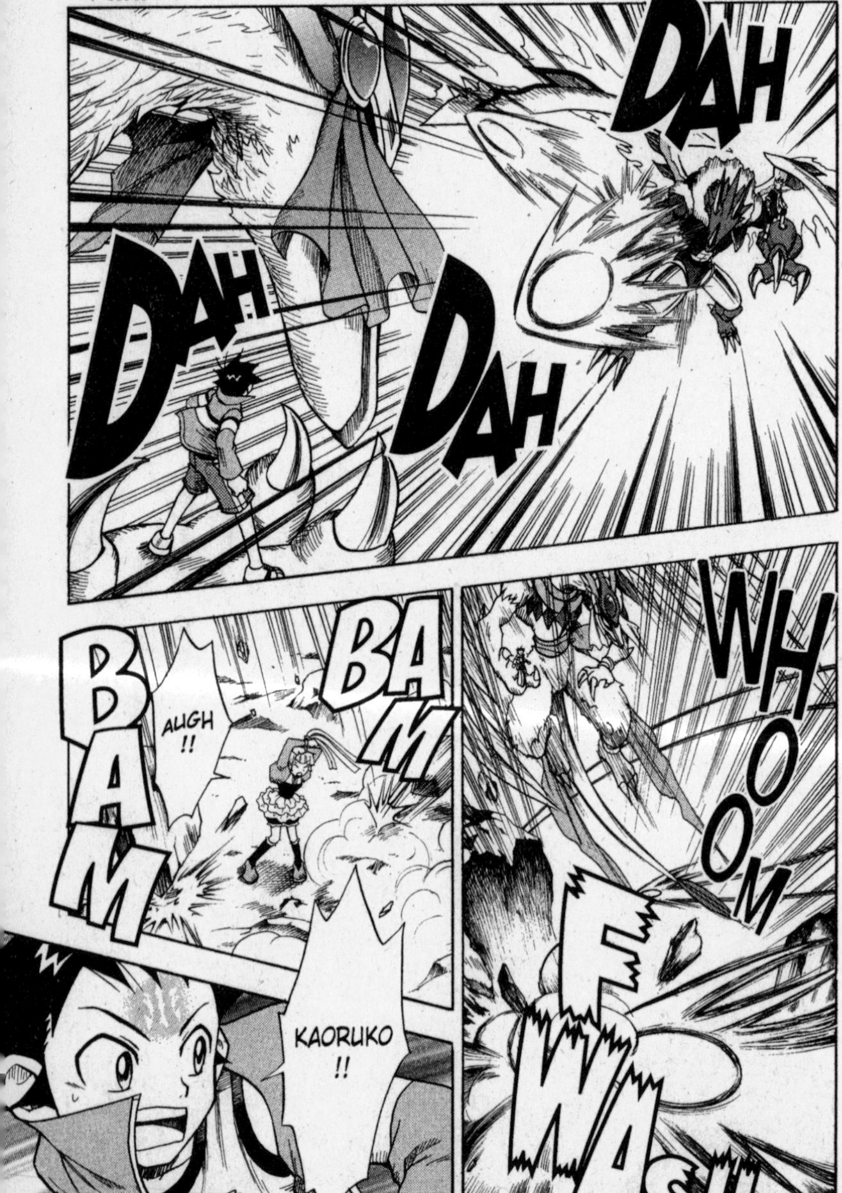
DAH
DAH
DAH
WHOOOM
FWASH
BAM
BAM
AUGH !!
KAORUKO !!

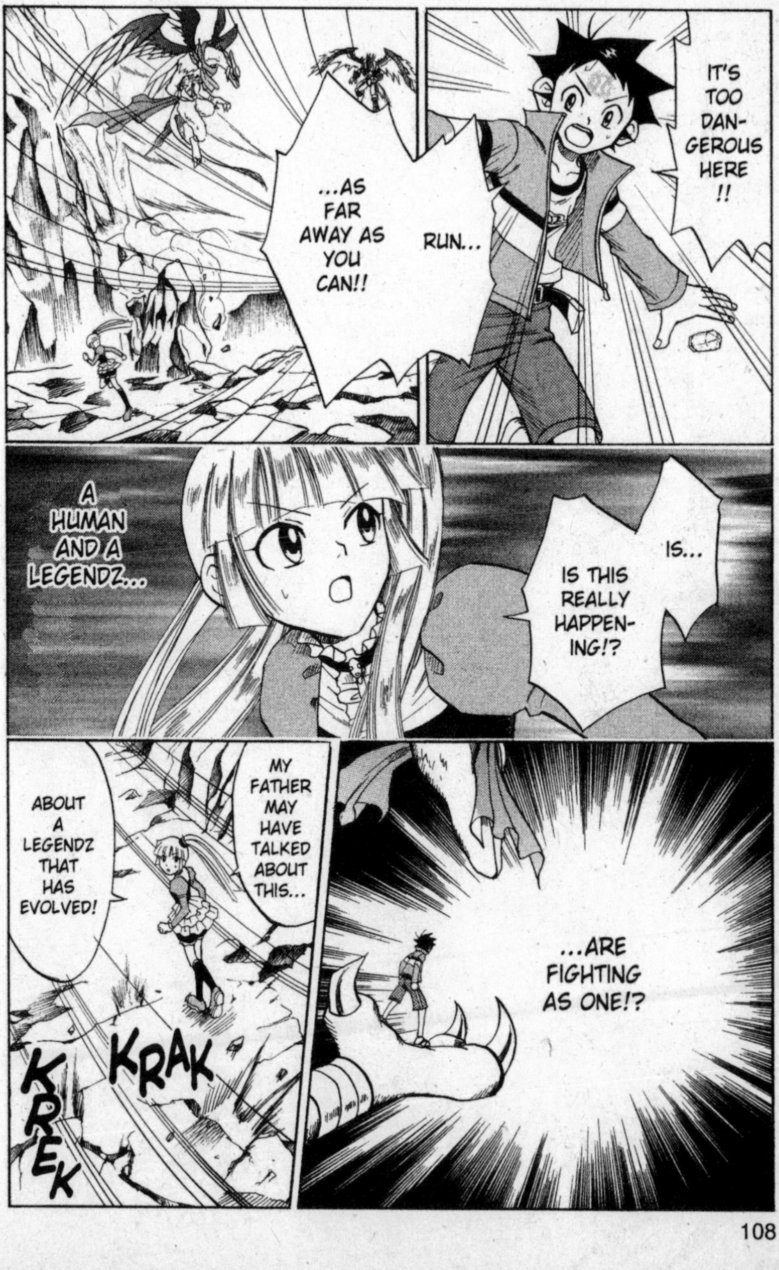
IT'S TOO DANGEROUS HERE!!
RUN...
...AS FAR AWAY AS YOU CAN!!
IS...
IS THIS REALLY HAPPENING!?
A HUMAN AND A LEGENDZ...
...ARE FIGHTING AS ONE!?
MY FATHER MAY HAVE TALKED ABOUT THIS...
ABOUT A LEGENDZ THAT HAS EVOLVED!
KRAK
KREK

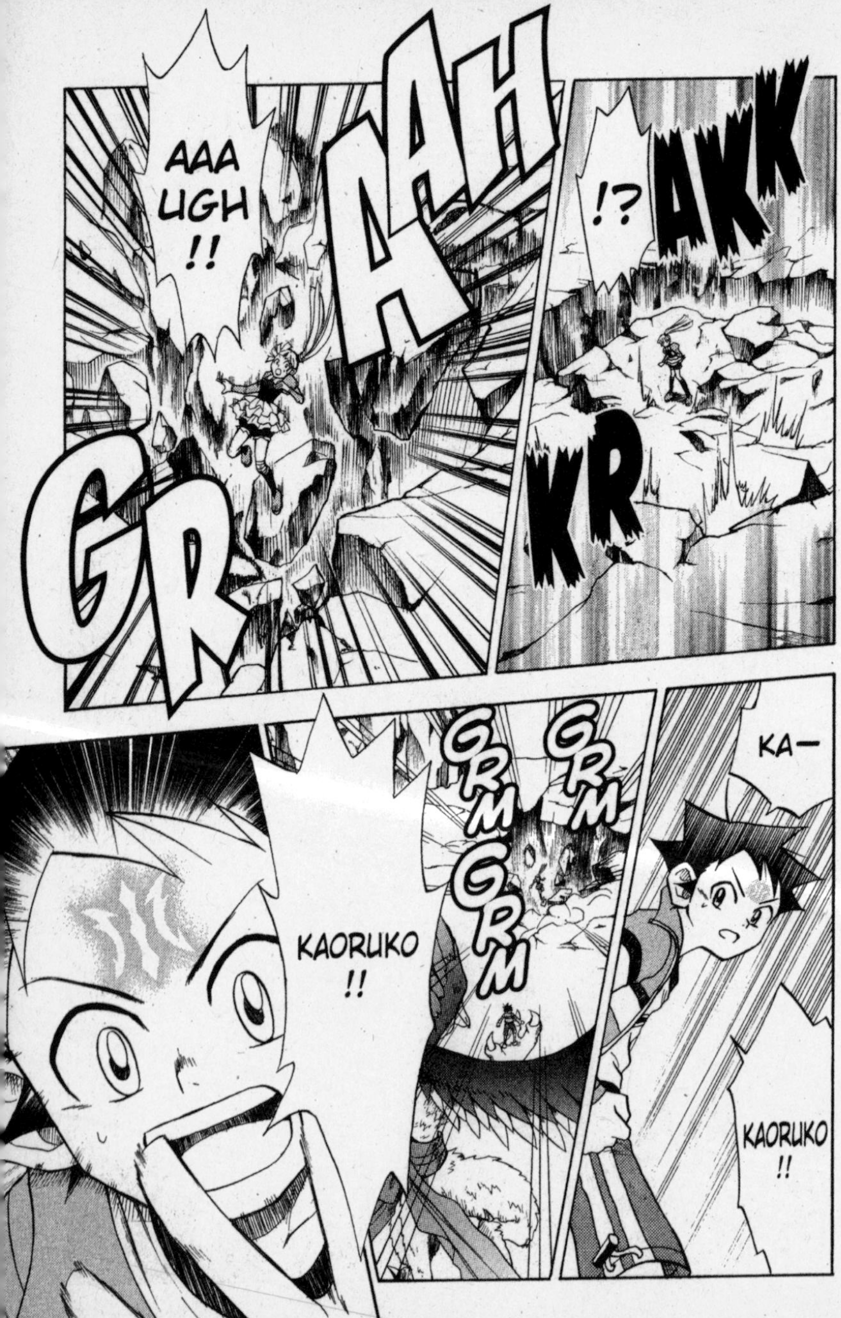
!?
AKK
KR
AAA UGH !!
AH
GR
KA—
KAORUKO !!
GRM GRM
GRM GRM
KAORUKO !!

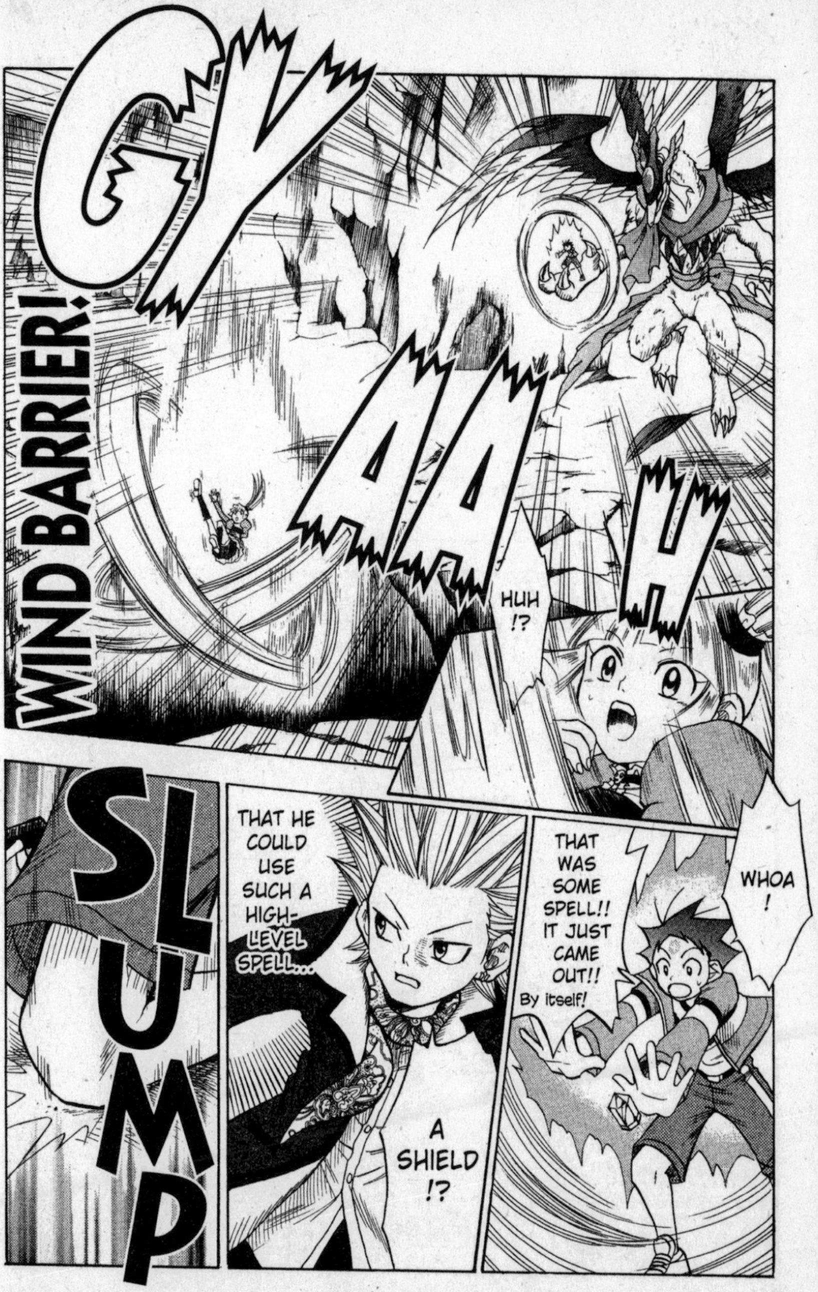
GYAAAH
HUH!?
WIND BARRIER!
WHOA!
THAT WAS SOME SPELL!! IT JUST CAME OUT!!
By itself!
THAT HE COULD USE SUCH A HIGH-LEVEL SPELL...
A SHIELD!?
SLUMP

READ THIS WAY

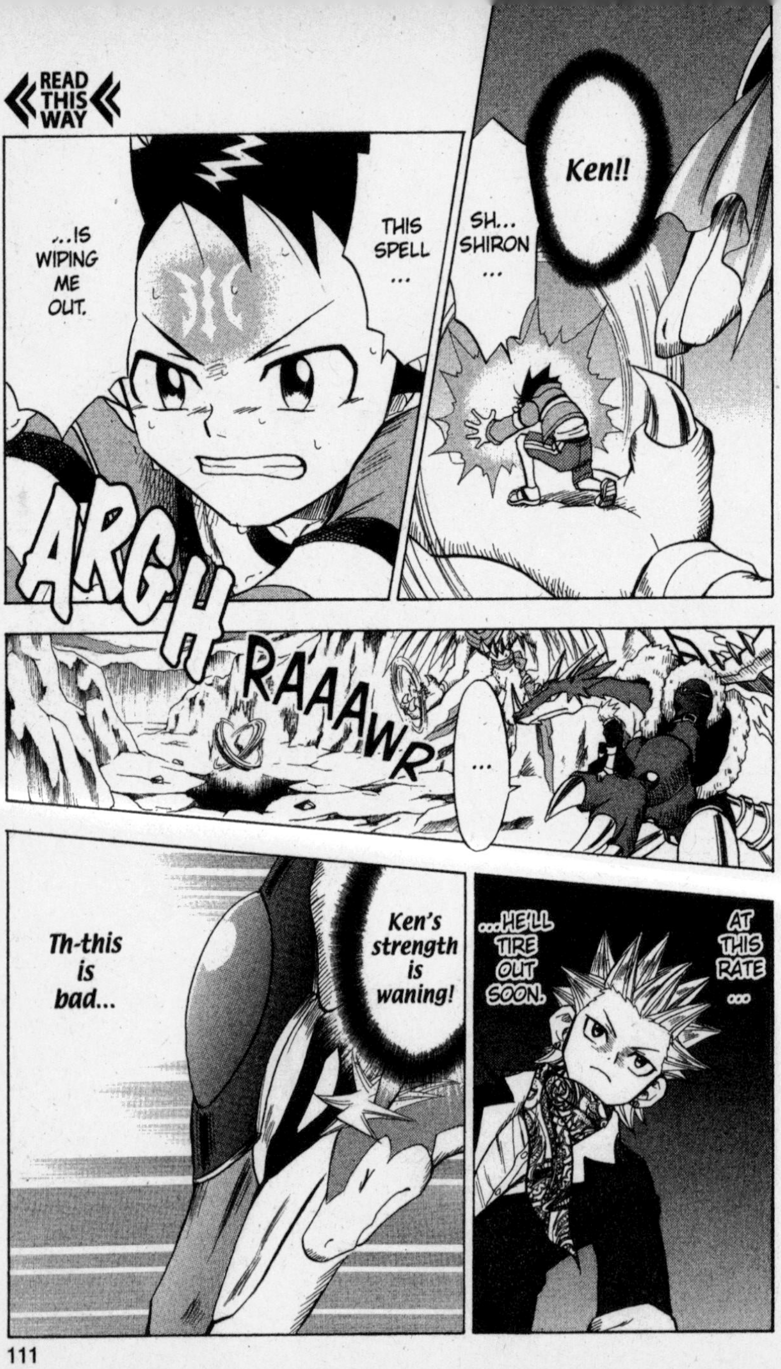
Ken!!
SH... SHIRON ...
THIS SPELL ...
...IS WIPING ME OUT.
ARGH
RAAAWR
...
AT THIS RATE ...
...HE'LL TIRE OUT SOON.
Ken's strength is waning!
Th-this is bad...

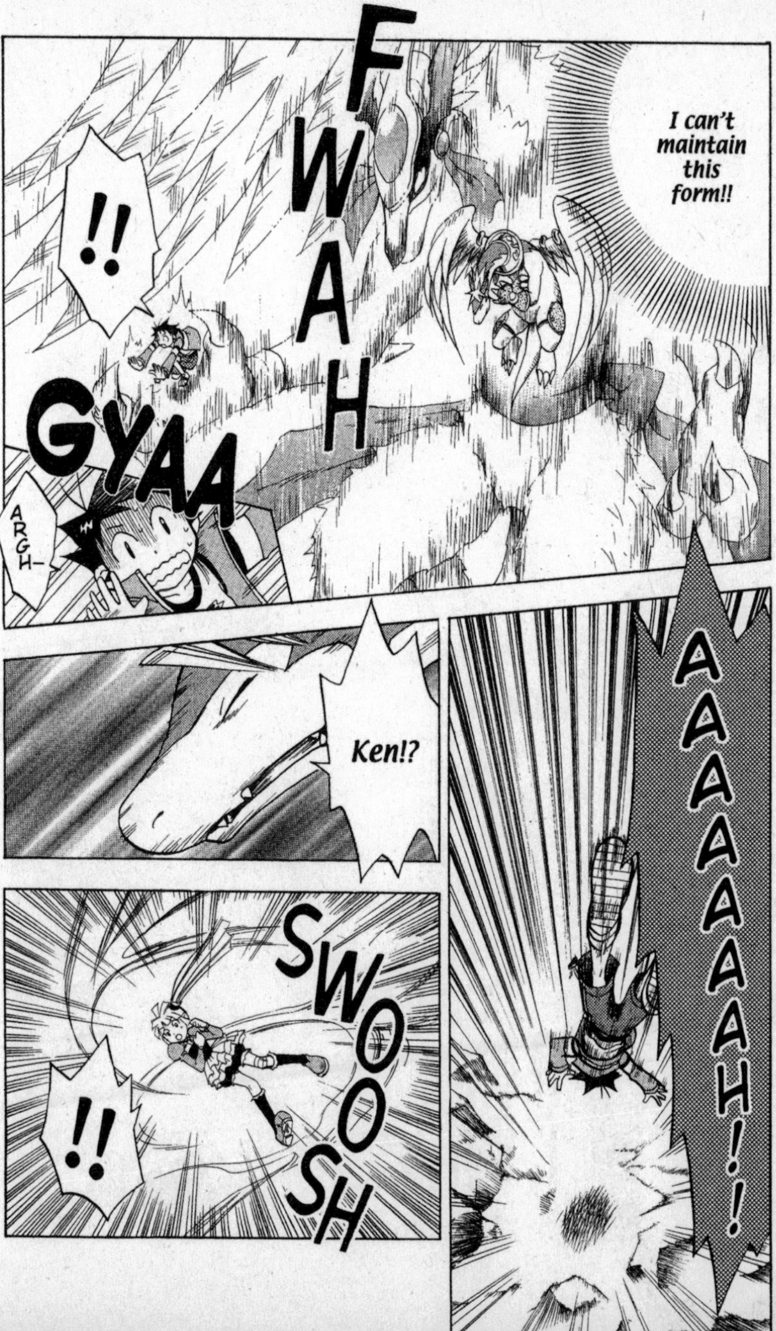
I can't maintain this form!!
FWAH
!!
GYAA
ARGH–
AAAAAAAH!!
Ken!?
SWOOSH
!!

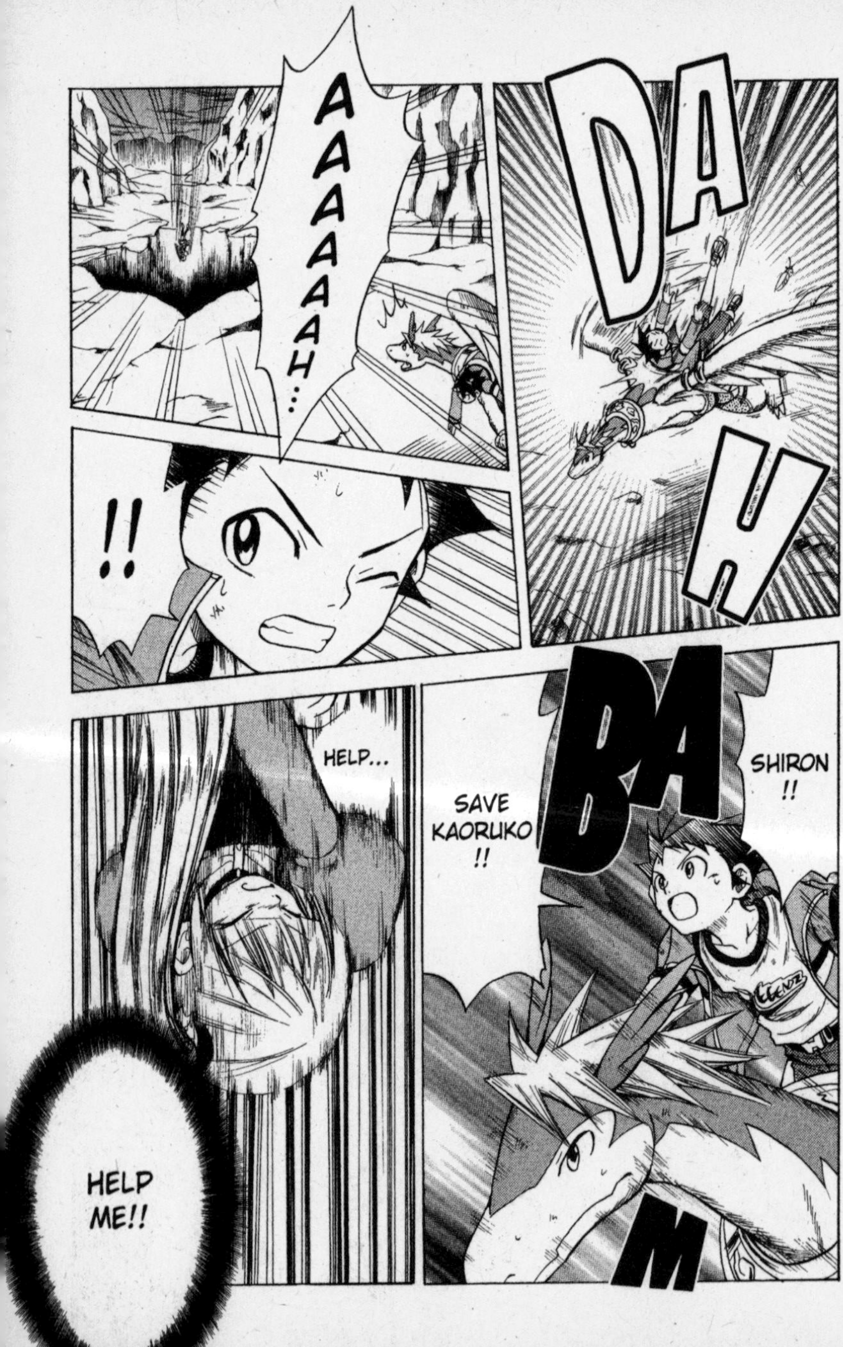
DA
H
AAAAAAH...
!!
BA
M
SHIRON !!
SAVE KAORUKO !!
HELP...
HELP ME!!

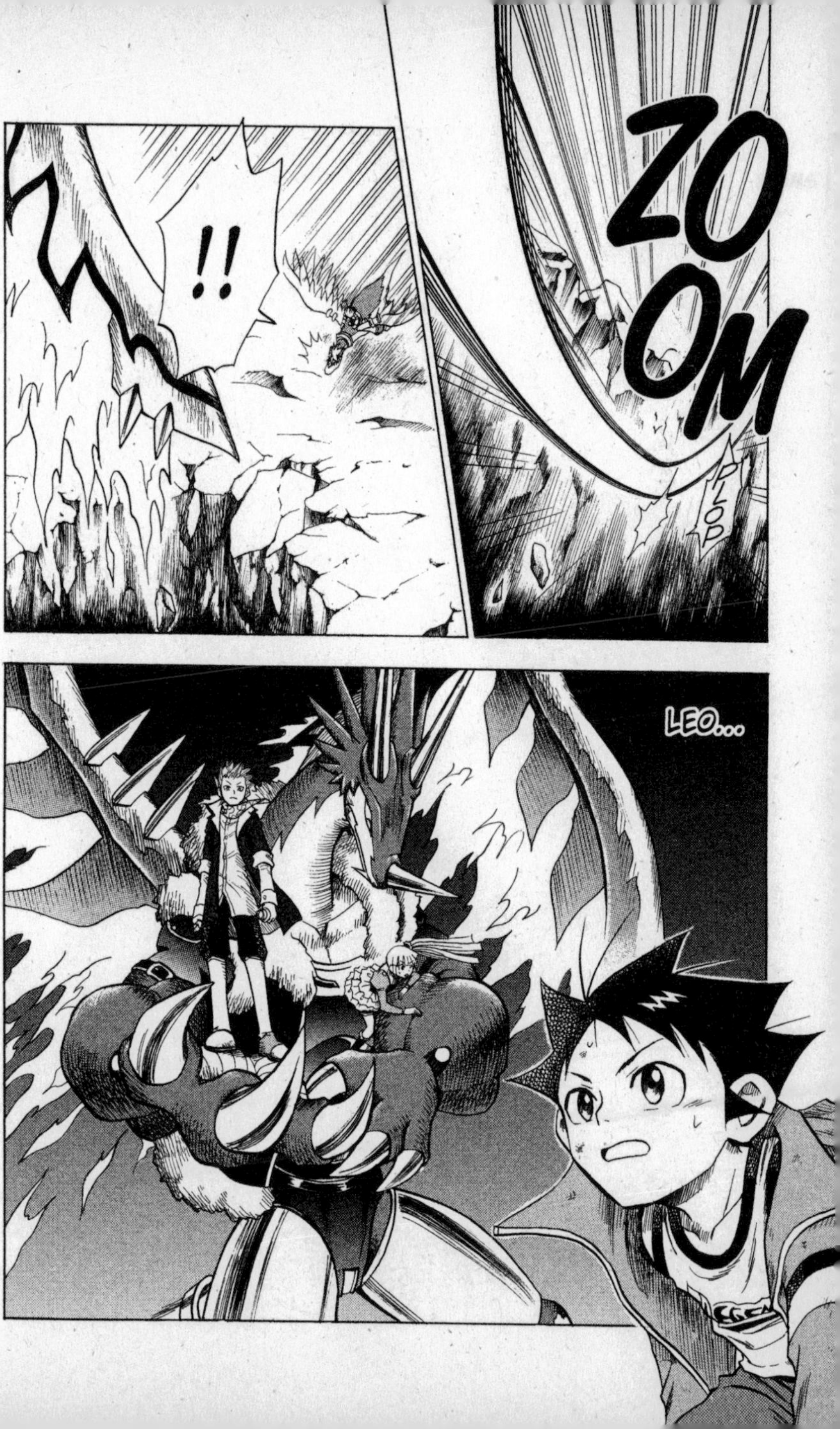
ZOOM
PLOP
!!
LEO...

READ THIS WAY

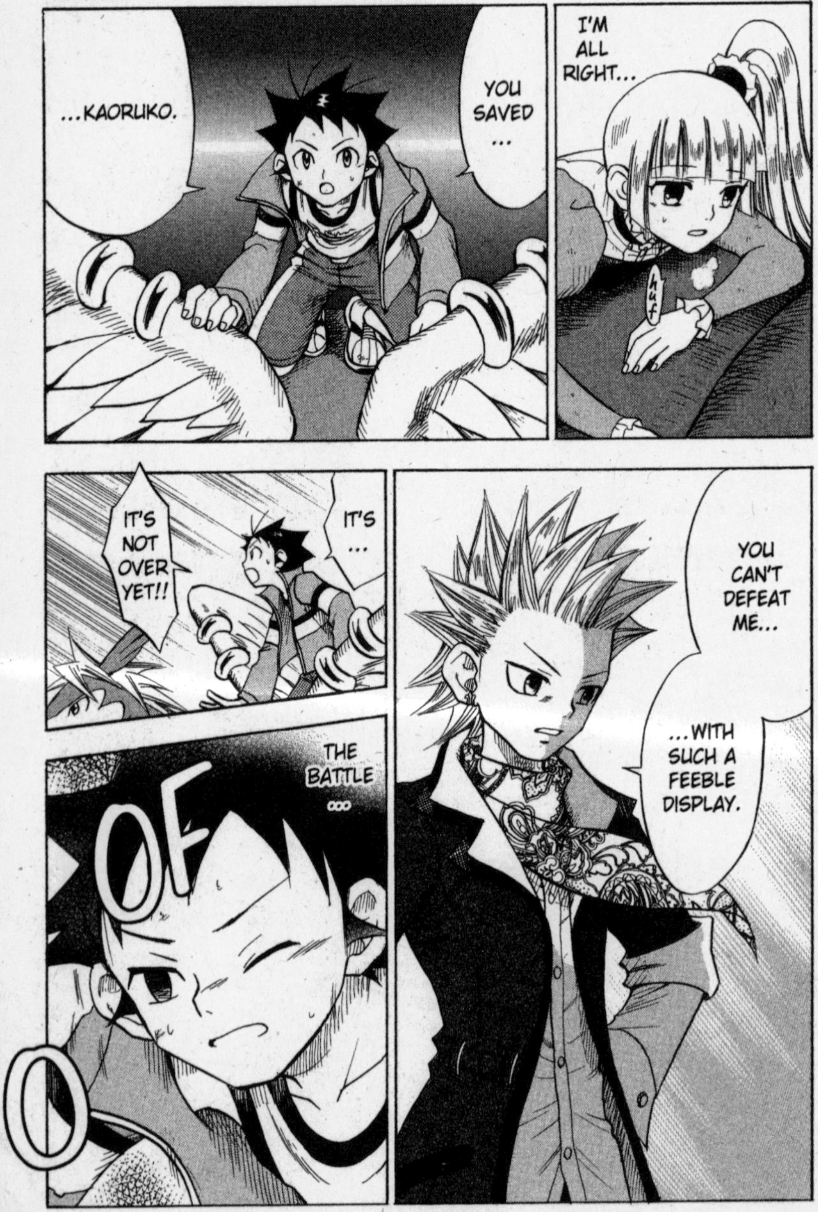

I'M ALL RIGHT...
huf
YOU SAVED ...
...KAORUKO.
YOU CAN'T DEFEAT ME...
...WITH SUCH A FEEBLE DISPLAY.
IT'S ...
IT'S NOT OVER YET!!
THE BATTLE ...
OF
O

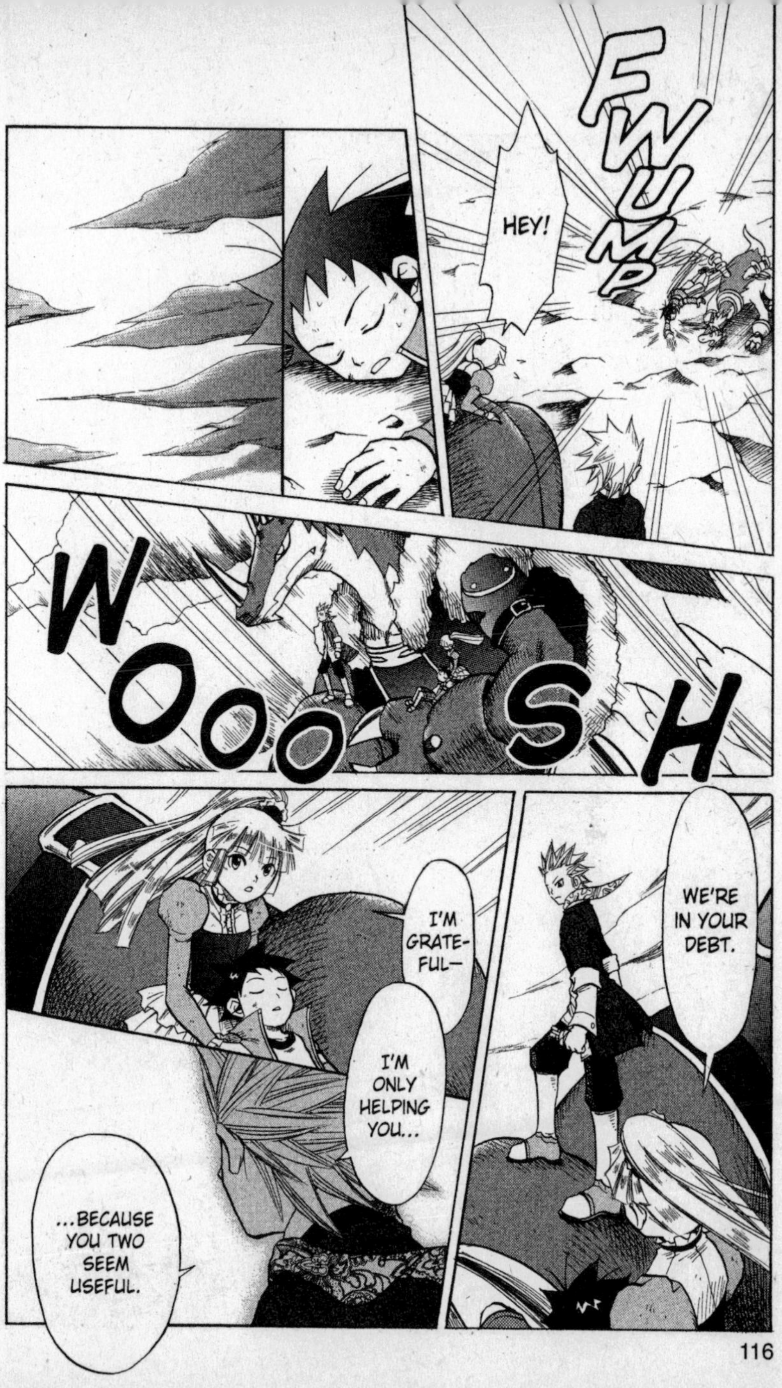
FWUMP
HEY!
WOOOSH
WE'RE IN YOUR DEBT.
I'M GRATEFUL—
I'M ONLY HELPING YOU...
...BECAUSE YOU TWO SEEM USEFUL.

READ THIS WAY

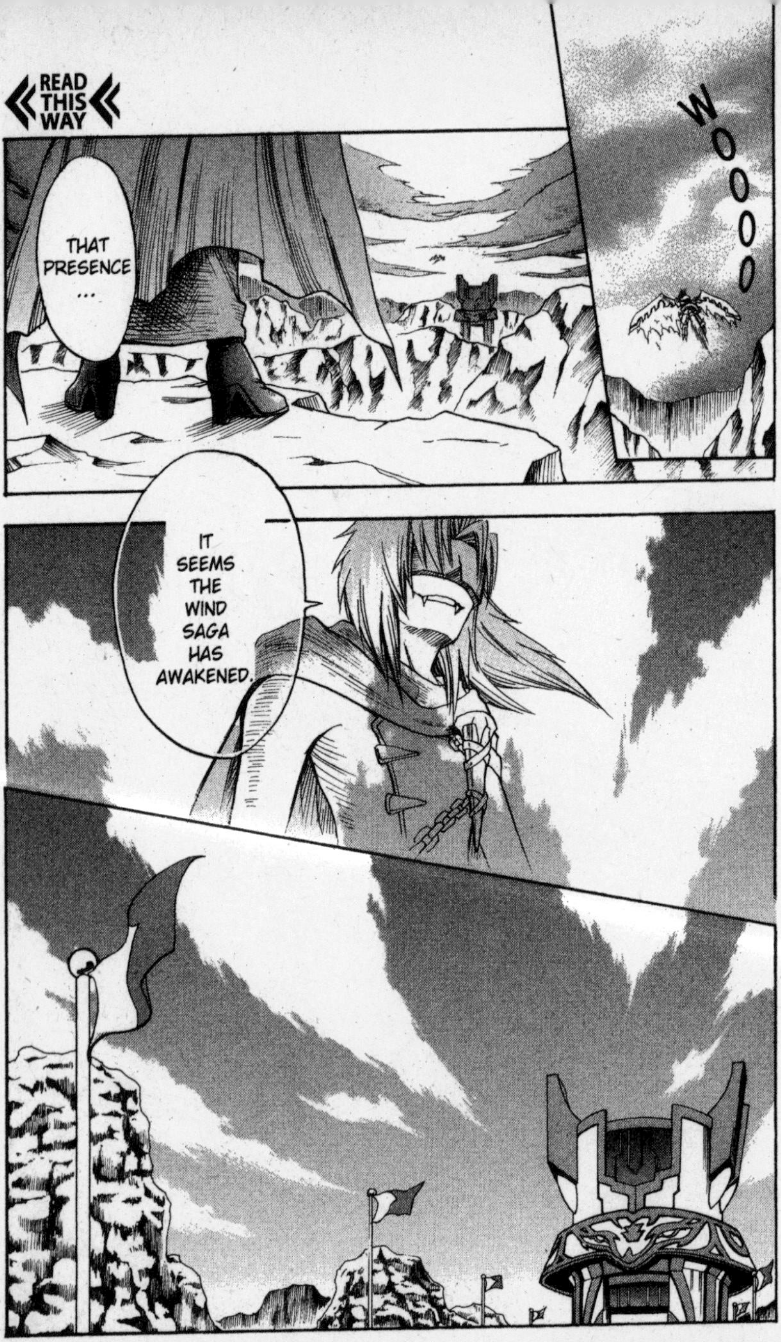

WOOOO
THAT PRESENCE ...
IT SEEMS THE WIND SAGA HAS AWAKENED.

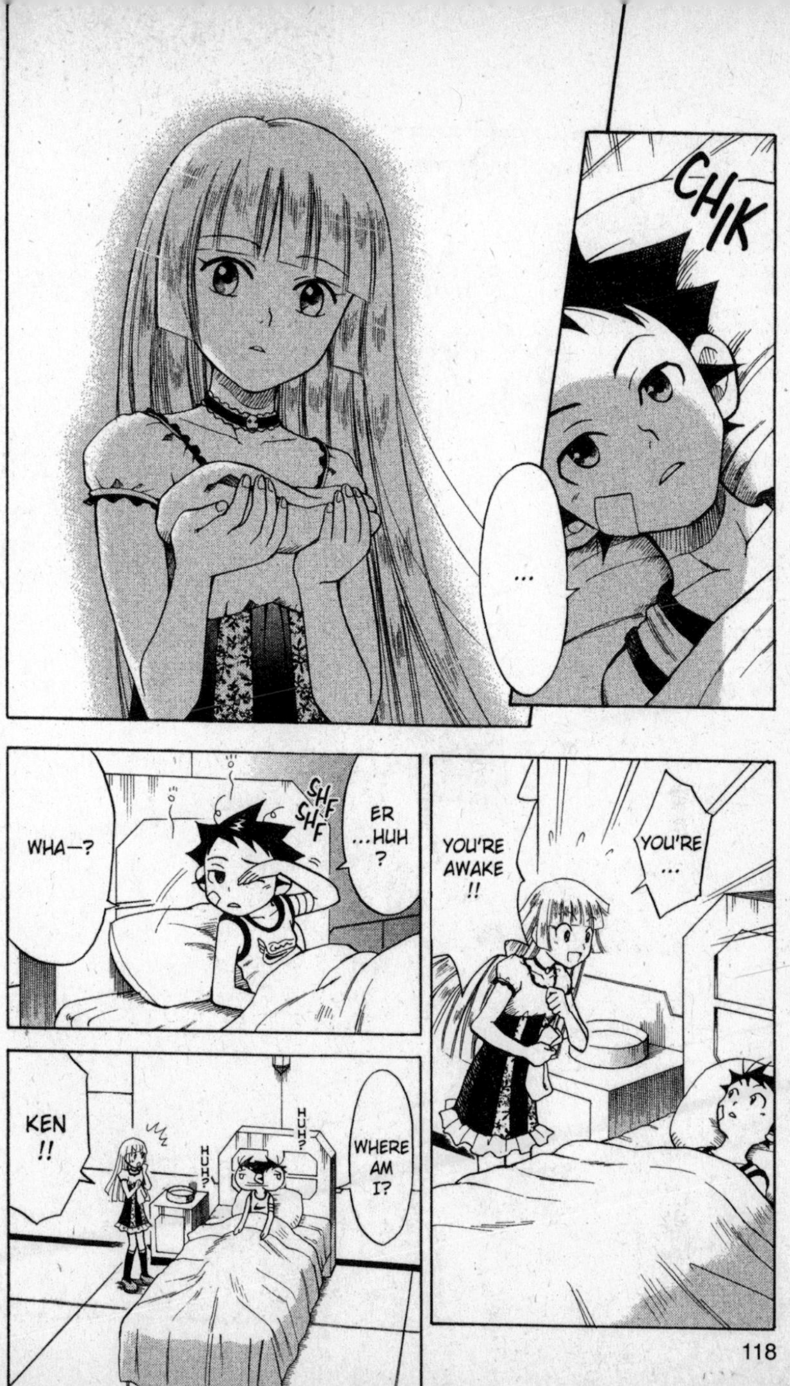
CHIK
...
YOU'RE ...
YOU'RE AWAKE !!
SHF SHF
ER ...HUH ?
WHA—?
WHERE AM I?
HUH?
HUH?
KEN !!

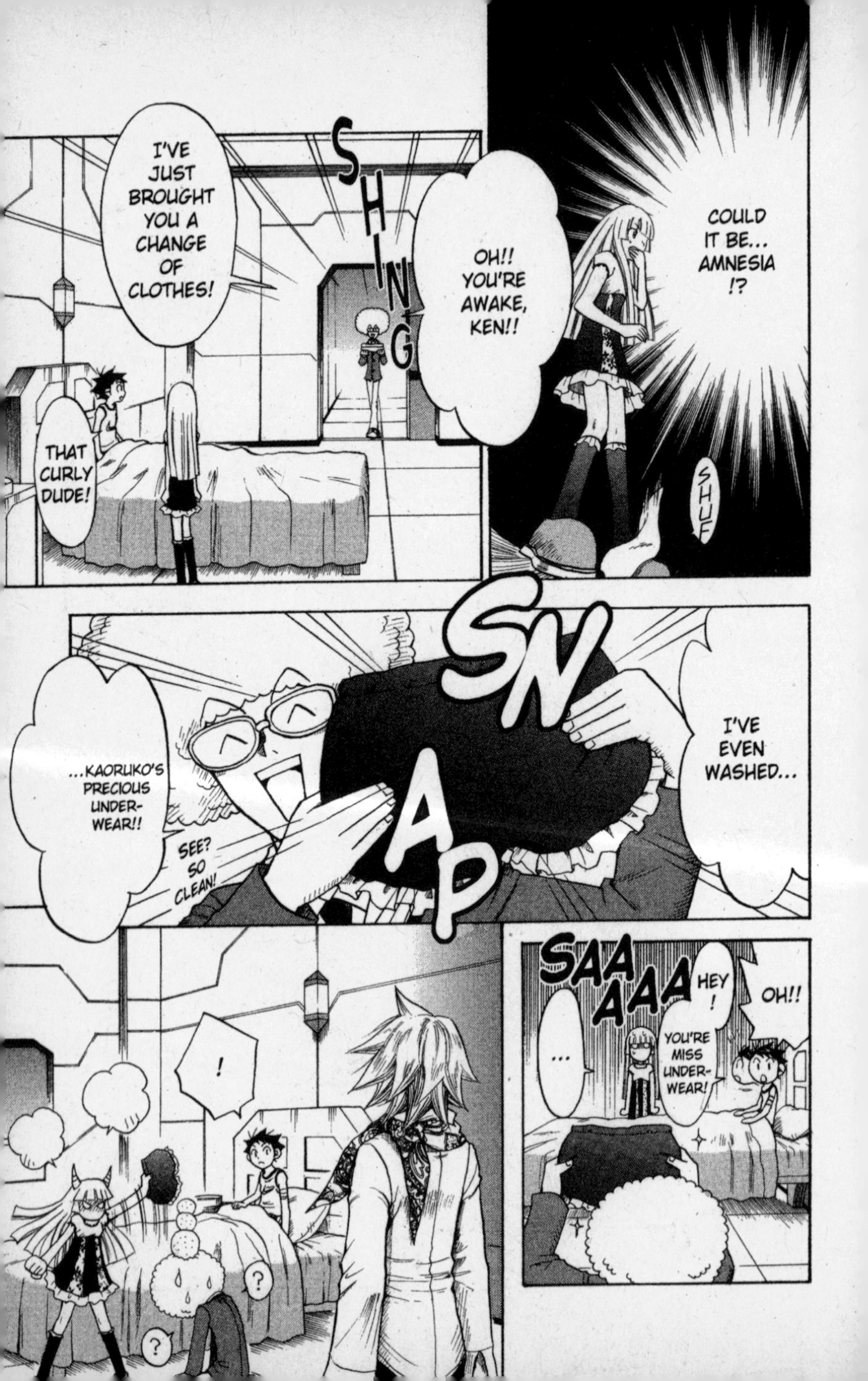
COULD IT BE... AMNESIA !?
SHUF
OH!! YOU'RE AWAKE, KEN!!
SHING
I'VE JUST BROUGHT YOU A CHANGE OF CLOTHES!
THAT CURLY DUDE!
I'VE EVEN WASHED...
SNAP
...KAORUKO'S PRECIOUS UNDER-WEAR!!
SEE? SO CLEAN!
OH!!
HEY!
YOU'RE MISS UNDER-WEAR!
SAAAAAA
...
!
?
?

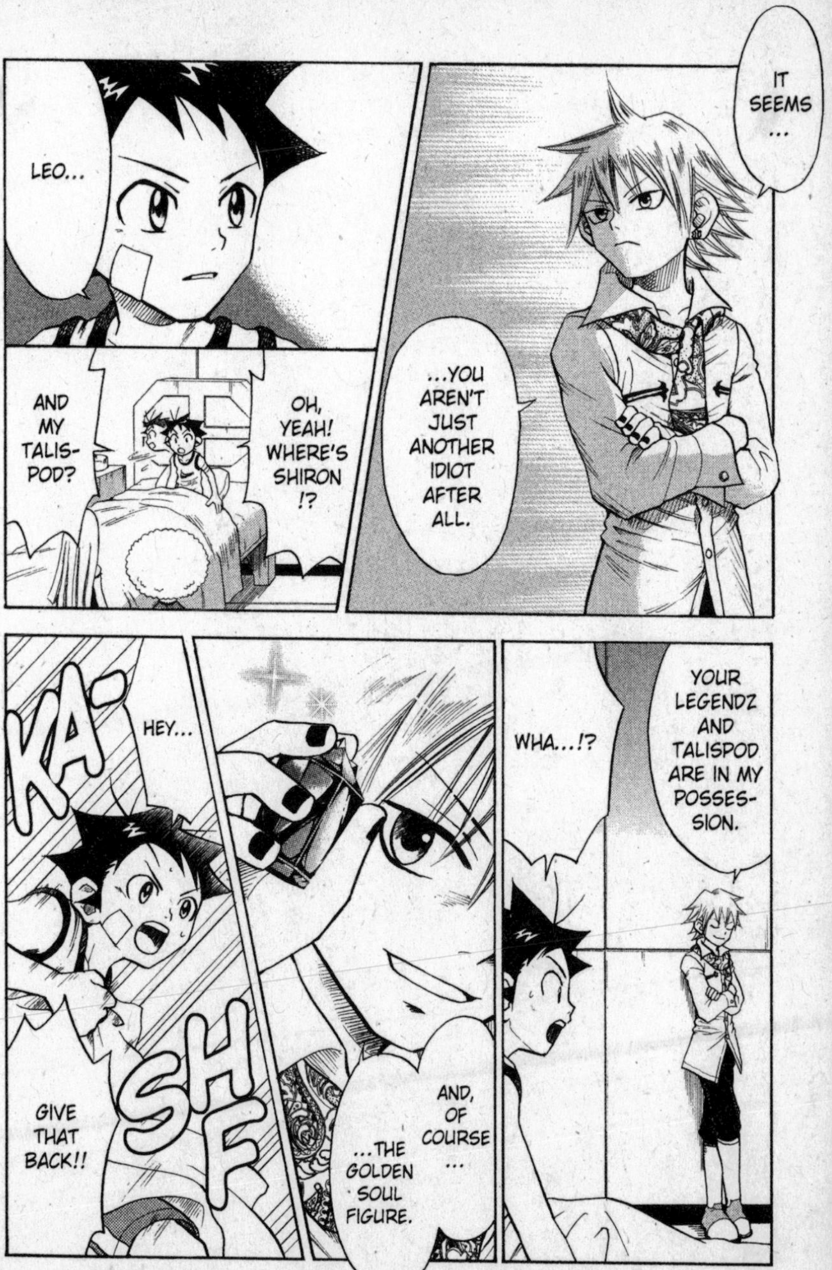
IT SEEMS...
...YOU AREN'T JUST ANOTHER IDIOT AFTER ALL.
LEO...
OH, YEAH! WHERE'S SHIRON!?
AND MY TALIS-POD?
YOUR LEGENDZ AND TALISPOD ARE IN MY POSSES-SION.
WHA...!?
AND, OF COURSE...
...THE GOLDEN SOUL FIGURE.
HEY...
KA-SHF
GIVE THAT BACK!!

READ THIS WAY

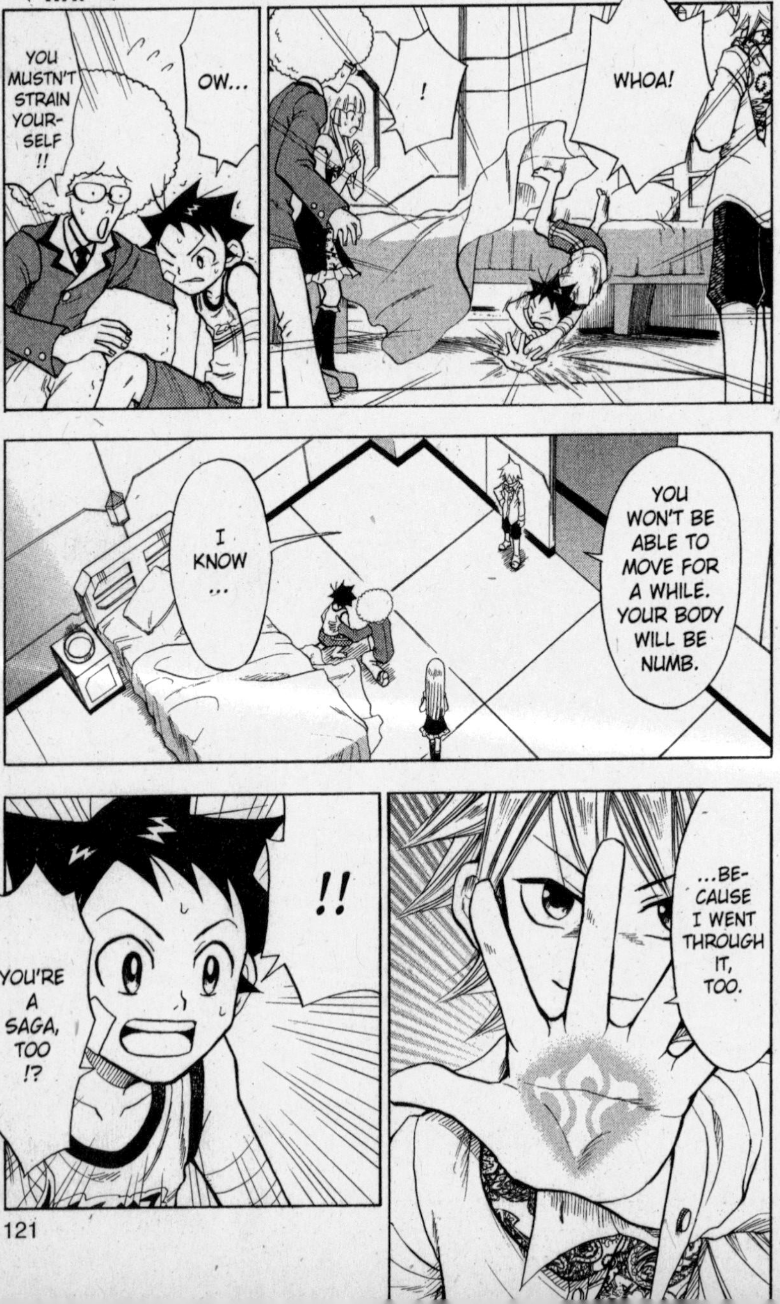
WHOA!
!
OW...
YOU MUSTN'T STRAIN YOURSELF !!
YOU WON'T BE ABLE TO MOVE FOR A WHILE. YOUR BODY WILL BE NUMB.
I KNOW ...
...BECAUSE I WENT THROUGH IT, TOO.
!!
YOU'RE A SAGA, TOO !?

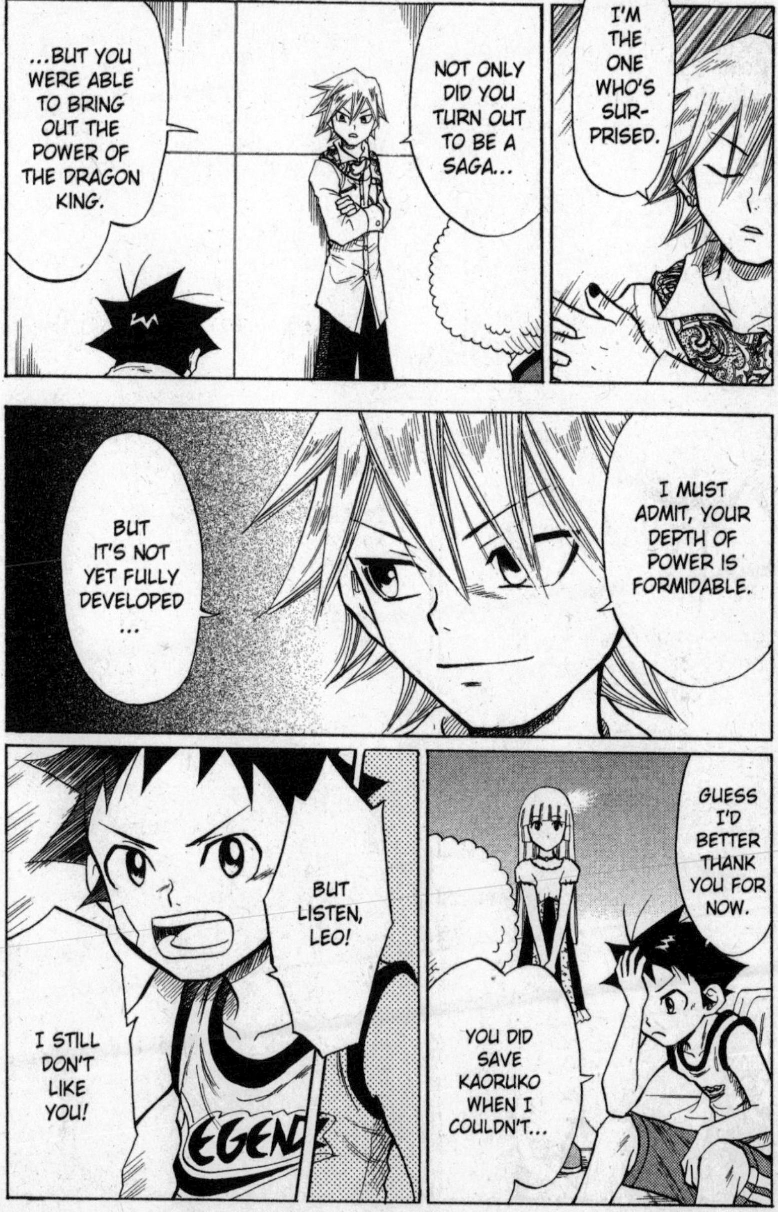
I'M THE ONE WHO'S SUR-PRISED.
NOT ONLY DID YOU TURN OUT TO BE A SAGA...
...BUT YOU WERE ABLE TO BRING OUT THE POWER OF THE DRAGON KING.
I MUST ADMIT, YOUR DEPTH OF POWER IS FORMIDABLE.
BUT IT'S NOT YET FULLY DEVELOPED ...
GUESS I'D BETTER THANK YOU FOR NOW.
YOU DID SAVE KAORUKO WHEN I COULDN'T...
BUT LISTEN, LEO!
I STILL DON'T LIKE YOU!
EGEND

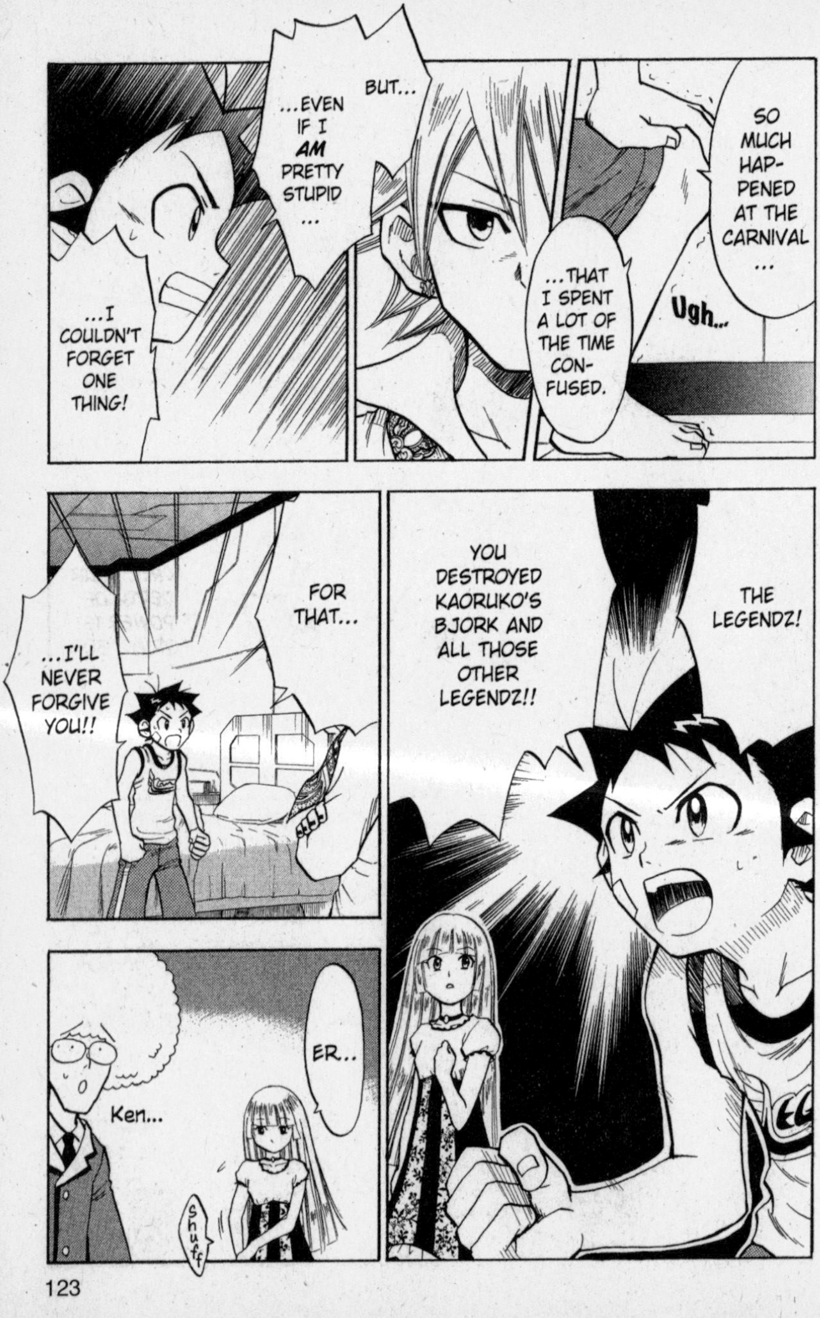
SO MUCH HAPPENED AT THE CARNIVAL...
Ugh...
...THAT I SPENT A LOT OF THE TIME CONFUSED.
BUT...
...EVEN IF I **AM** PRETTY STUPID...
...I COULDN'T FORGET ONE THING!
THE LEGENDZ!
YOU DESTROYED KAORUKO'S BJORK AND ALL THOSE OTHER LEGENDZ!!
FOR THAT...
...I'LL NEVER FORGIVE YOU!!
ER...
Ken...
Shuff

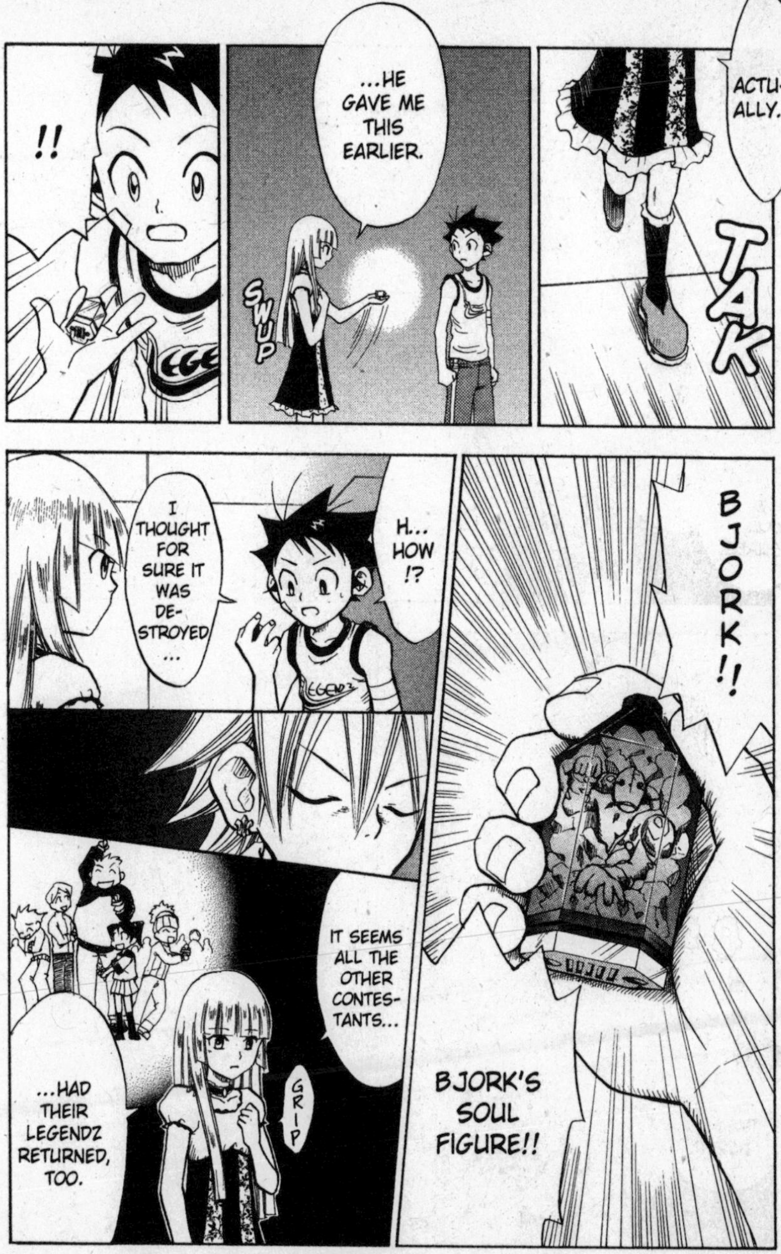
ACTU-ALLY...
TAK
...HE GAVE ME THIS EARLIER.
SWUP
!!
BJORK!!
BJORK'S SOUL FIGURE!!
H... HOW !?
I THOUGHT FOR SURE IT WAS DE-STROYED ...
IT SEEMS ALL THE OTHER CONTES-TANTS...
GRIP
...HAD THEIR LEGENDZ RETURNED, TOO.

READ THIS WAY

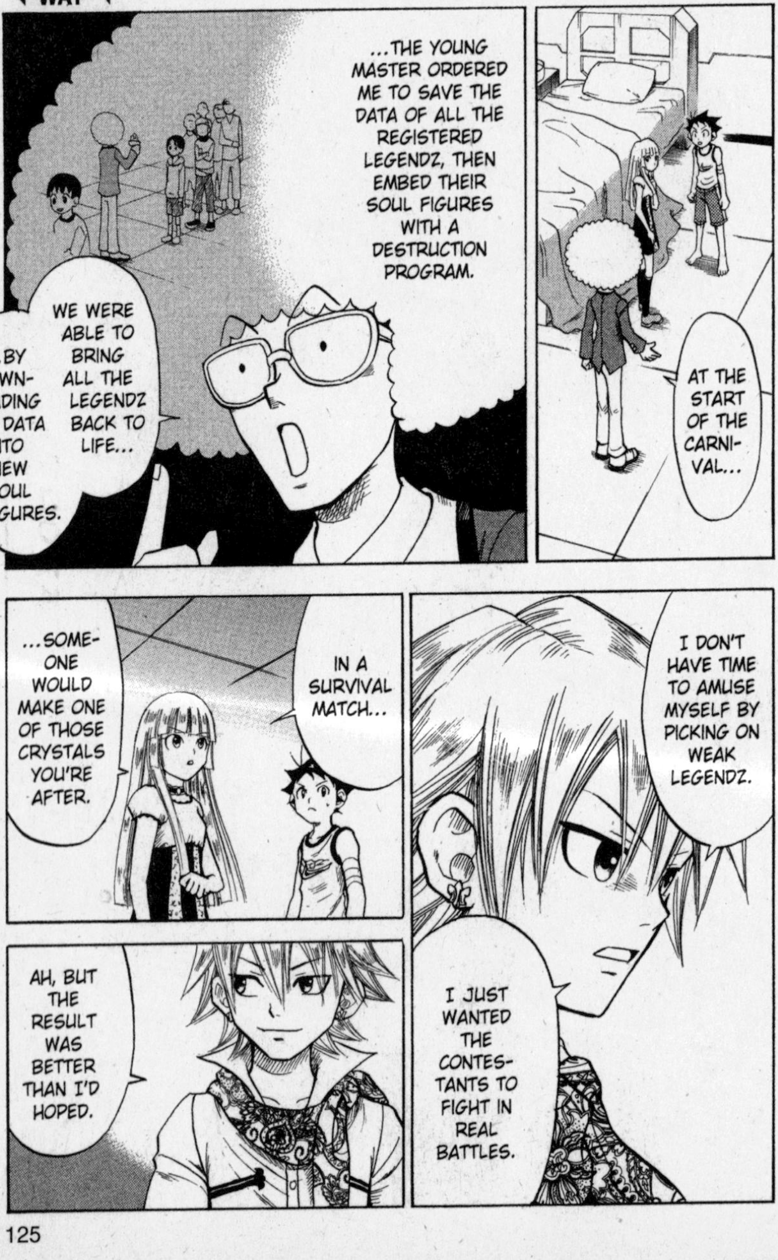
AT THE START OF THE CARNIVAL...
...THE YOUNG MASTER ORDERED ME TO SAVE THE DATA OF ALL THE REGISTERED LEGENDZ, THEN EMBED THEIR SOUL FIGURES WITH A DESTRUCTION PROGRAM.
WE WERE ABLE TO BRING ALL THE LEGENDZ BACK TO LIFE...
...BY DOWNLOADING THE DATA INTO NEW SOUL FIGURES.
I DON'T HAVE TIME TO AMUSE MYSELF BY PICKING ON WEAK LEGENDZ.
I JUST WANTED THE CONTESTANTS TO FIGHT IN REAL BATTLES.
IN A SURVIVAL MATCH...
...SOMEONE WOULD MAKE ONE OF THOSE CRYSTALS YOU'RE AFTER.
AH, BUT THE RESULT WAS BETTER THAN I'D HOPED.

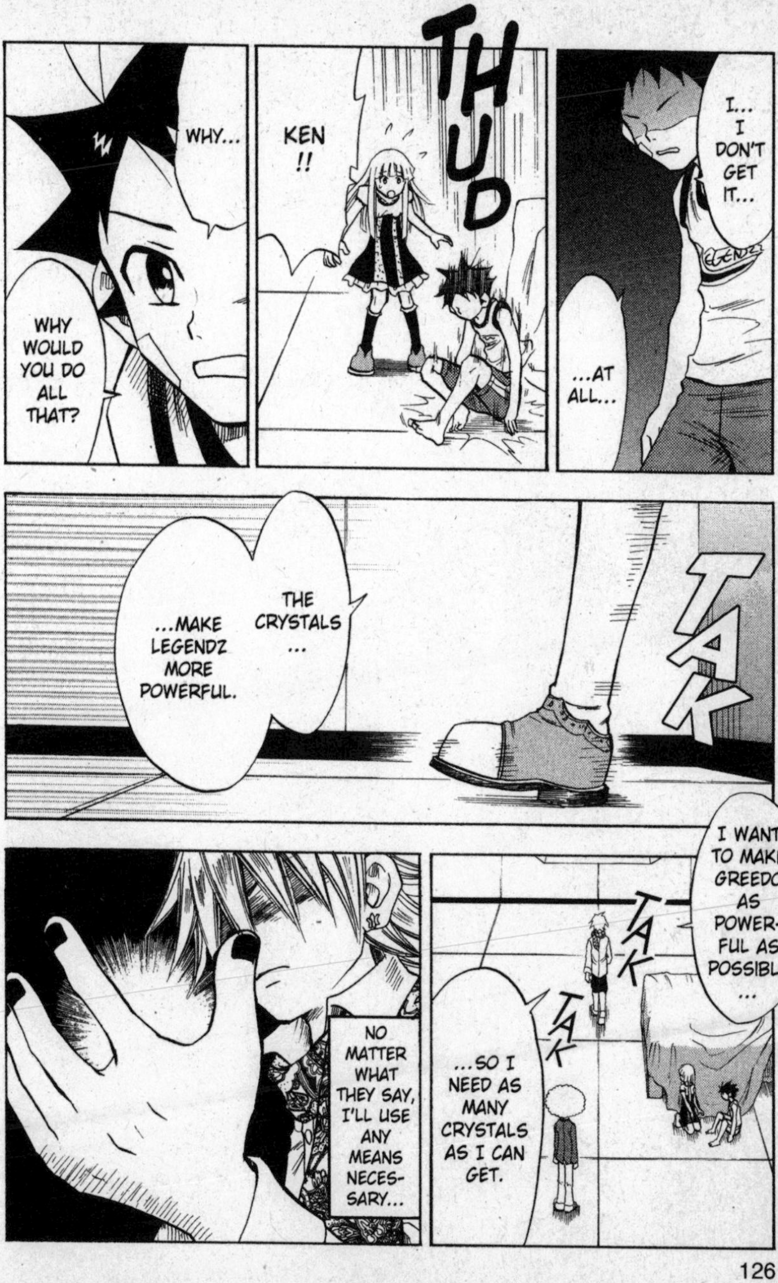
I... I DON'T GET IT...
...AT ALL...
THUD
KEN !!
WHY...
WHY WOULD YOU DO ALL THAT?
TAK
THE CRYSTALS ...
...MAKE LEGENDZ MORE POWERFUL.
I WANT TO MAKE GREEDO AS POWER-FUL AS POSSIBLE ...
TAK
TAK
...SO I NEED AS MANY CRYSTALS AS I CAN GET.
NO MATTER WHAT THEY SAY, I'LL USE ANY MEANS NECES-SARY...

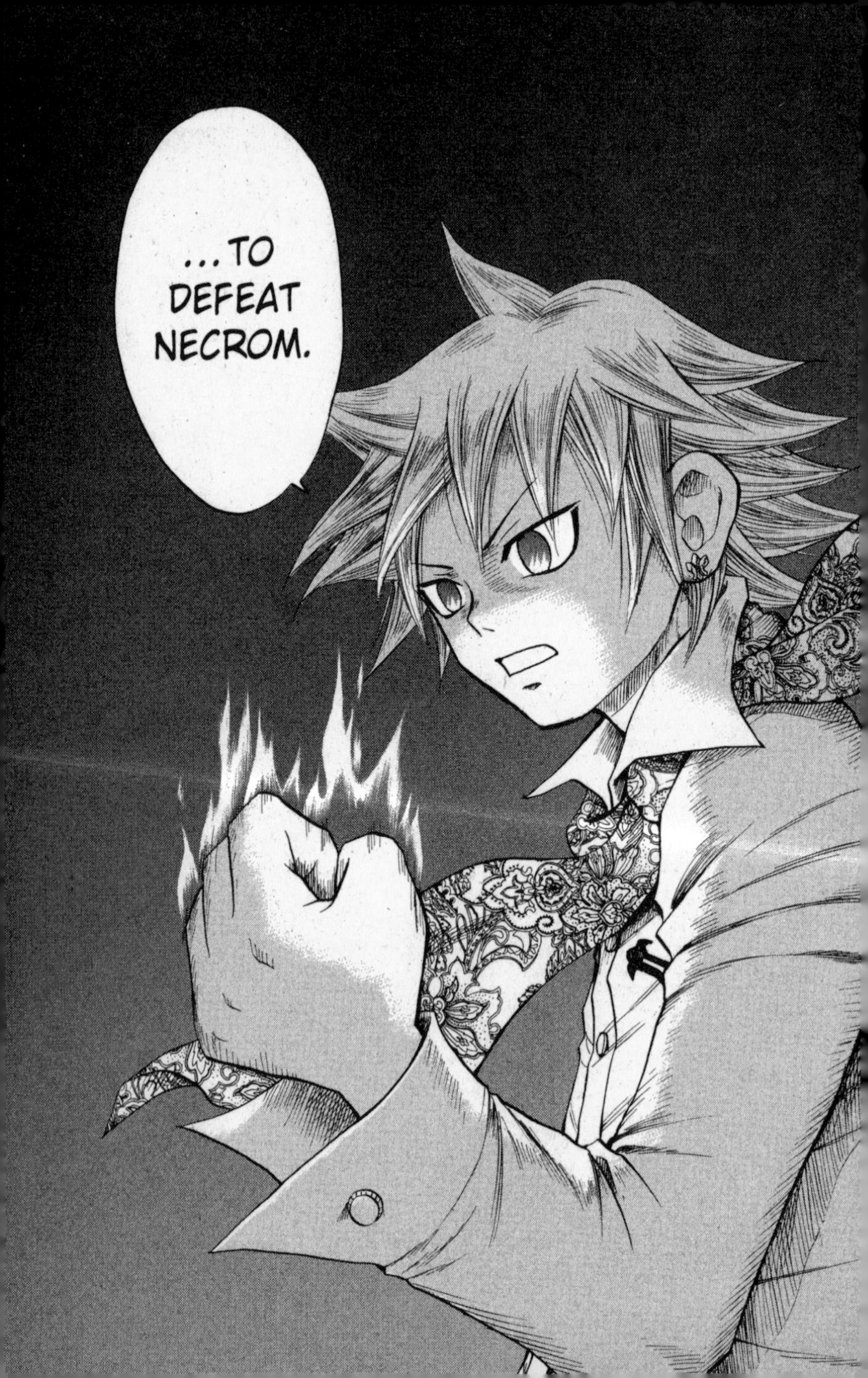
...TO DEFEAT NECROM.

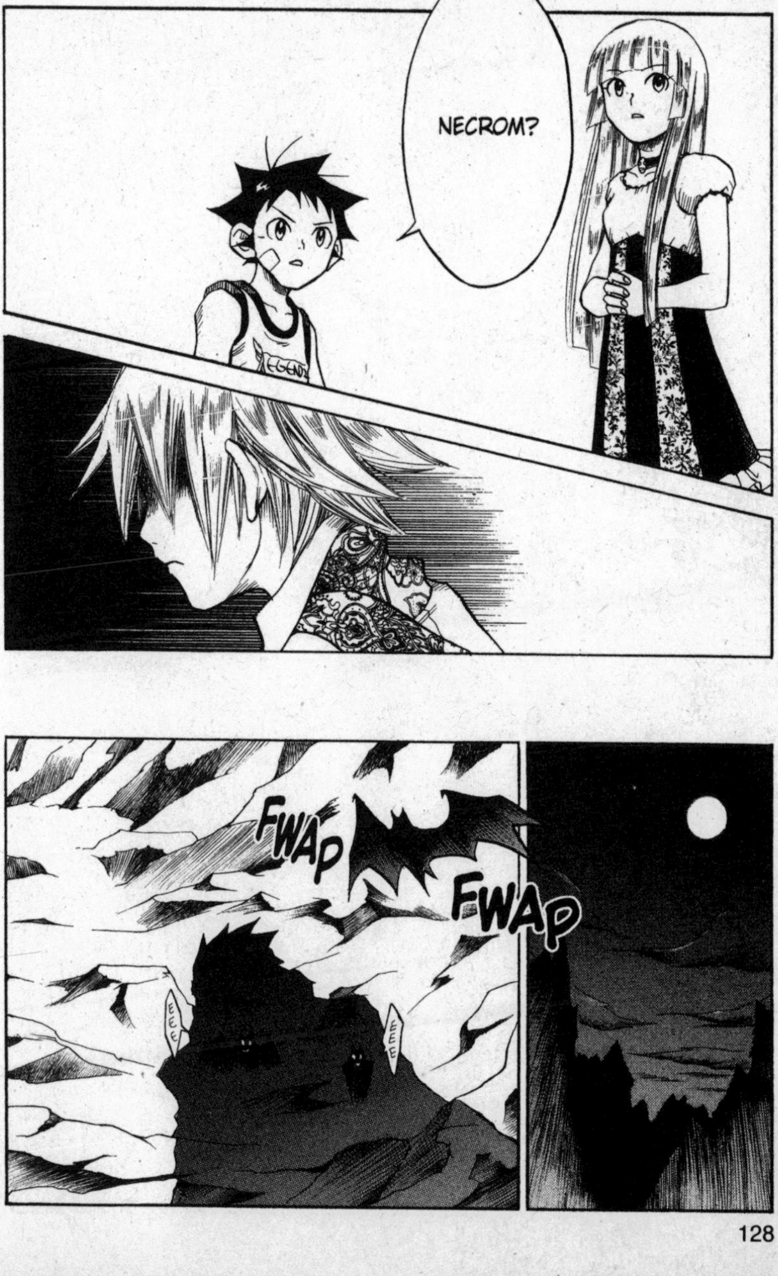
NECROM?
FWAP
FWAP
EEE
EEE

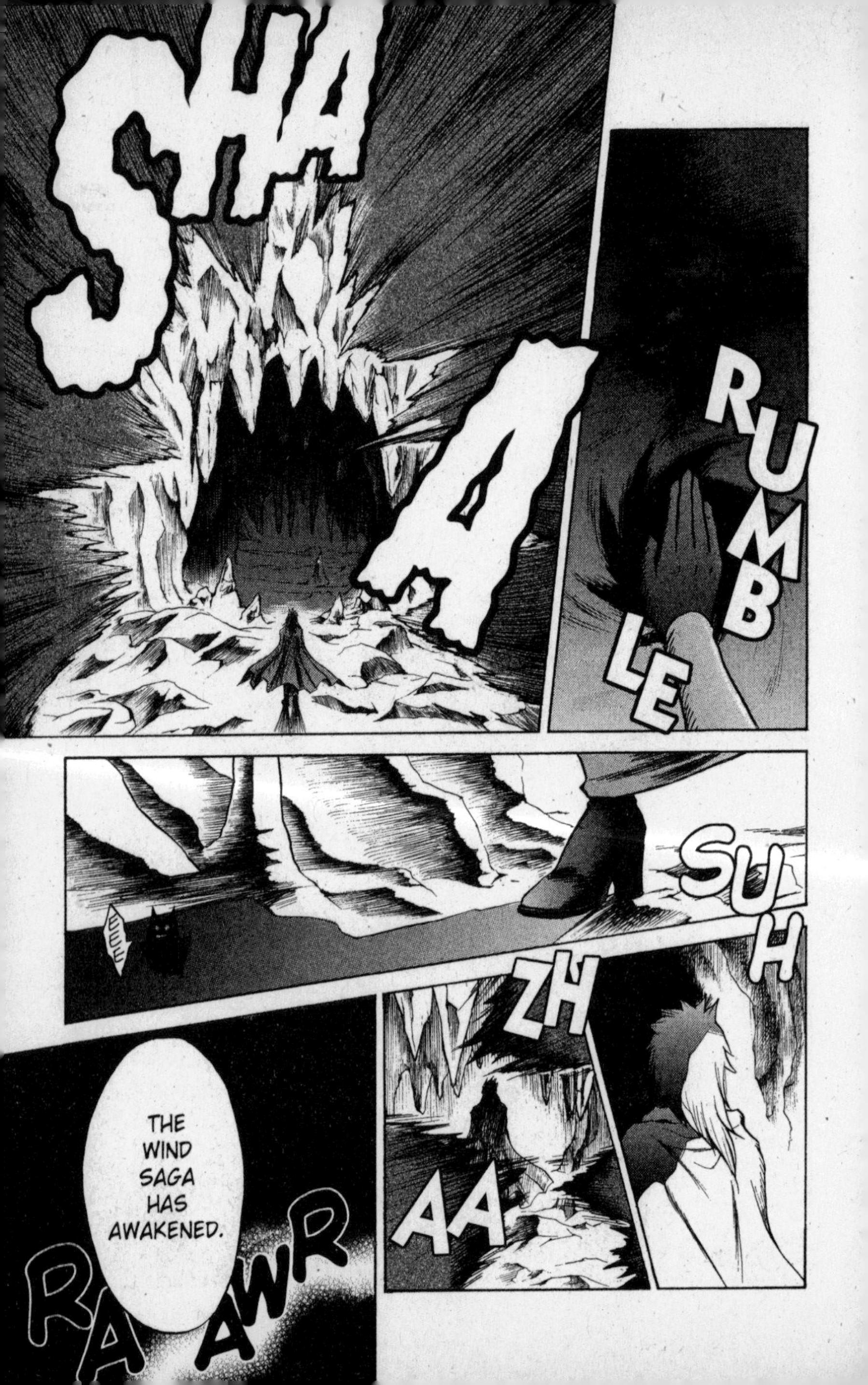
RUMBLE
SHAA
SUH
EEE
ZH
AA
THE WIND SAGA HAS AWAKENED.
RAAWR

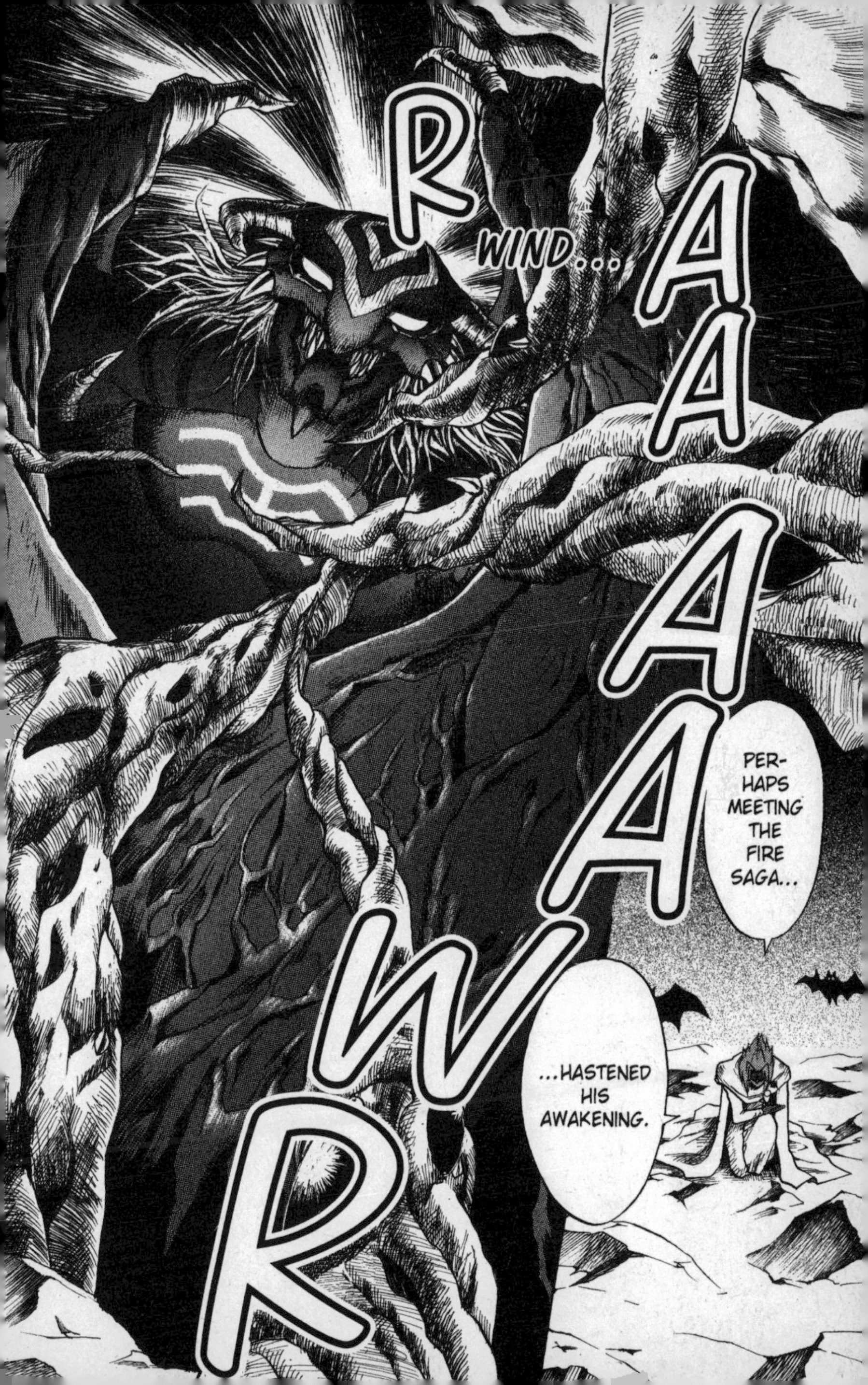
RAAAAAWR
WIND...
PER-HAPS MEETING THE FIRE SAGA...
...HASTENED HIS AWAKENING.

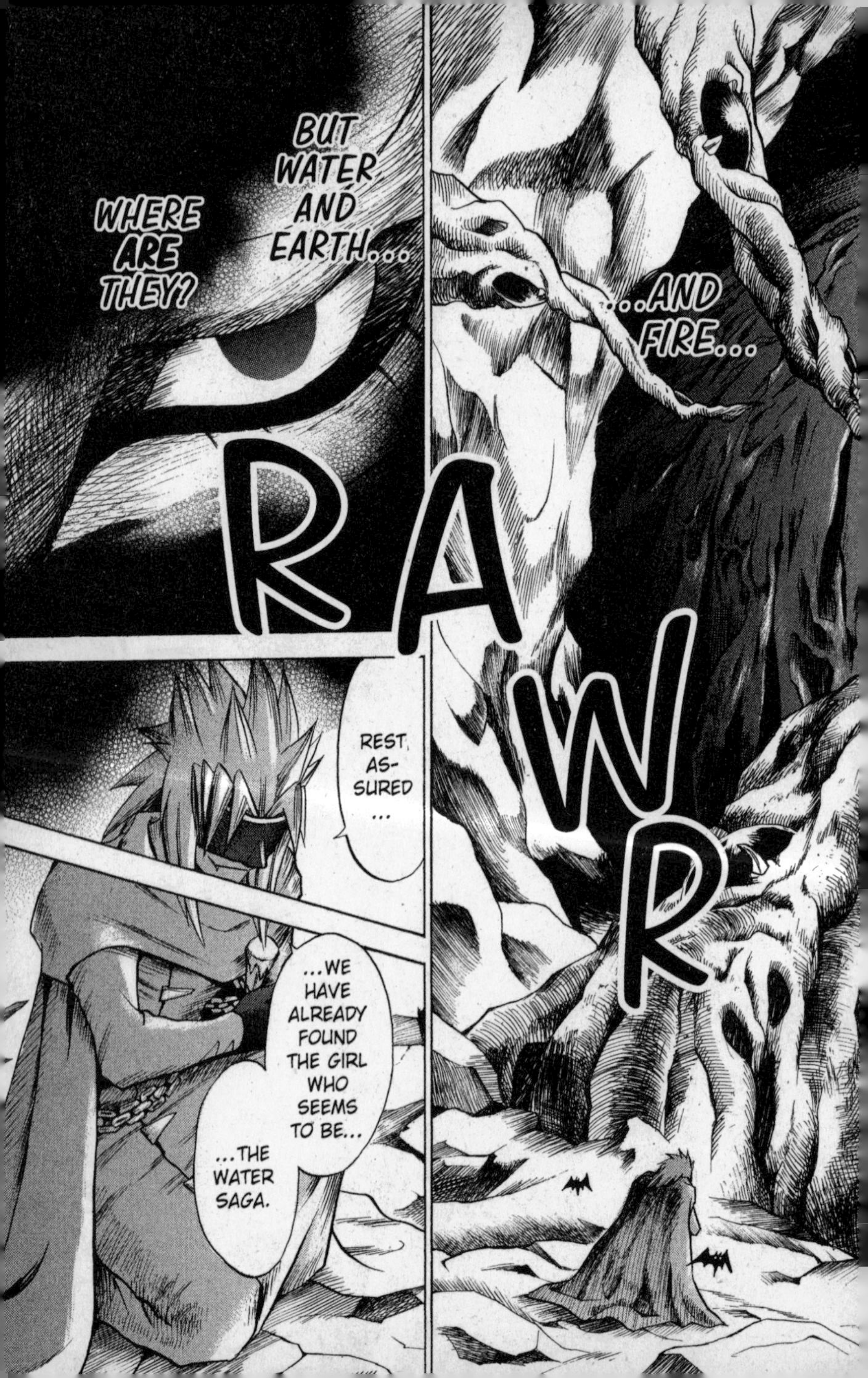
BUT WATER AND EARTH...
...AND FIRE...
WHERE ARE THEY?
RAWR
REST ASSURED...
...WE HAVE ALREADY FOUND THE GIRL WHO SEEMS TO BE...
...THE WATER SAGA.

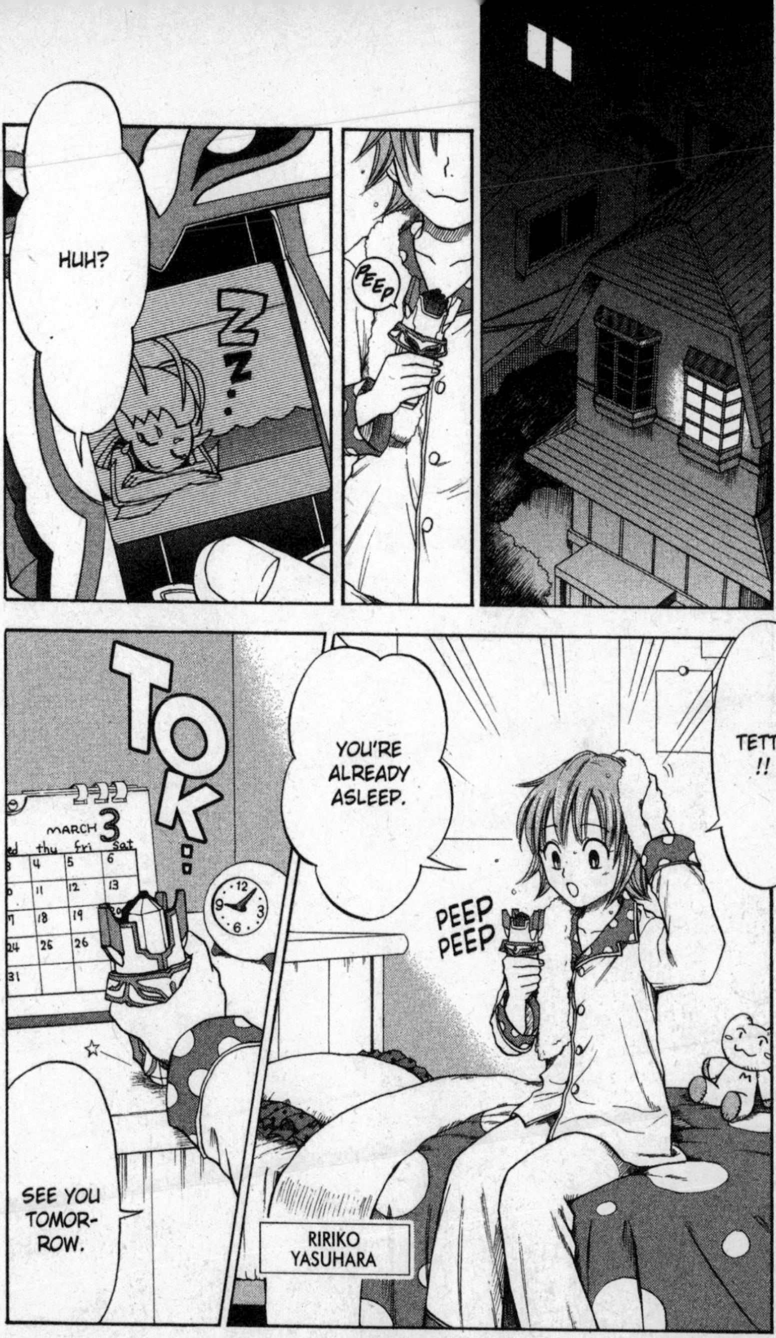
PEEP
HUH?
ZZZ..
TETTY !!
YOU'RE ALREADY ASLEEP.
PEEP PEEP
RIRIKO YASUHARA
TOK..
SEE YOU TOMOR-ROW.

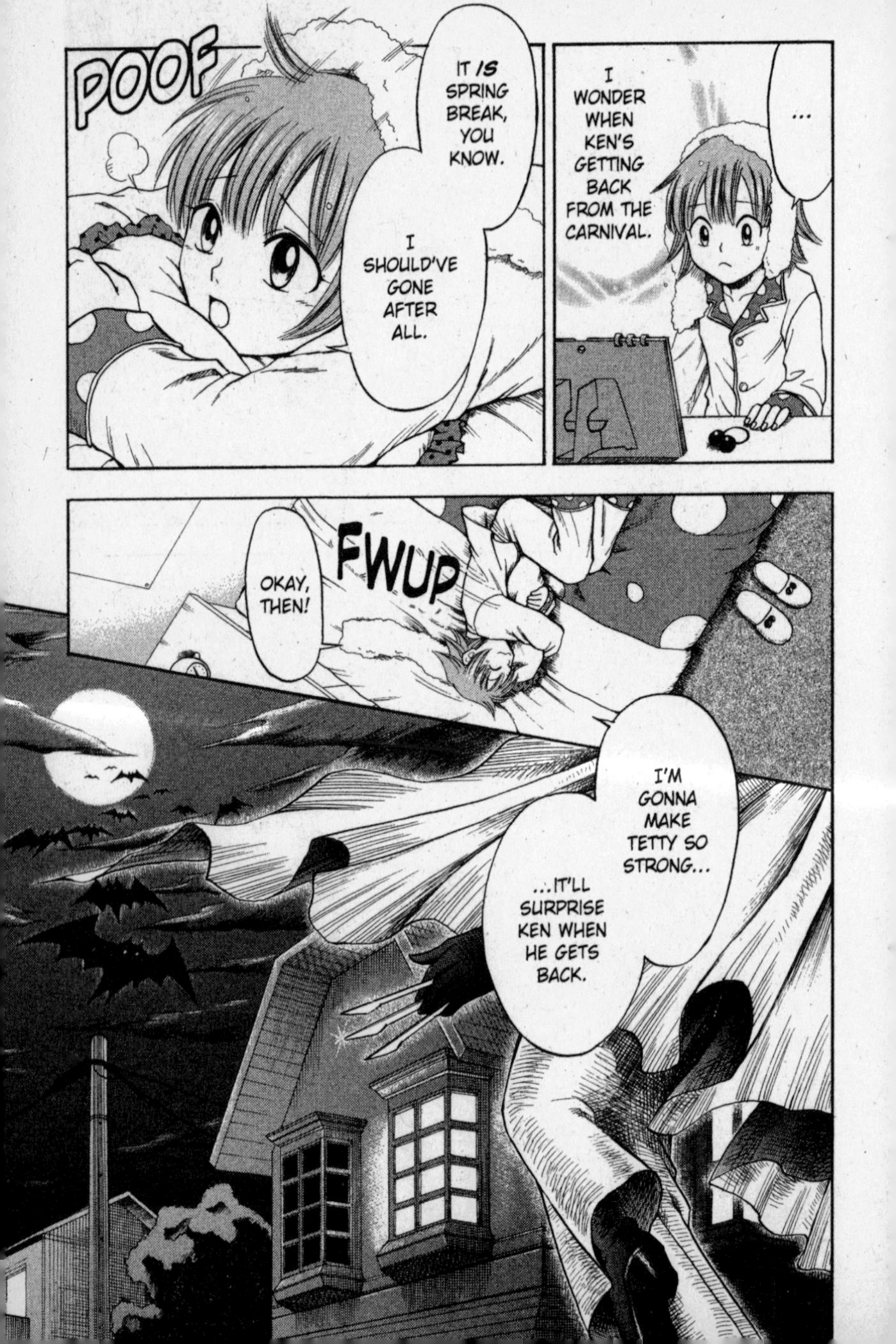
...
I WONDER WHEN KEN'S GETTING BACK FROM THE CARNIVAL.
POOF
IT *IS* SPRING BREAK, YOU KNOW.
I SHOULD'VE GONE AFTER ALL.
FWUP
OKAY, THEN!
I'M GONNA MAKE TETTY SO STRONG...
...IT'LL SURPRISE KEN WHEN HE GETS BACK.

LEGENDZ COLLECTION

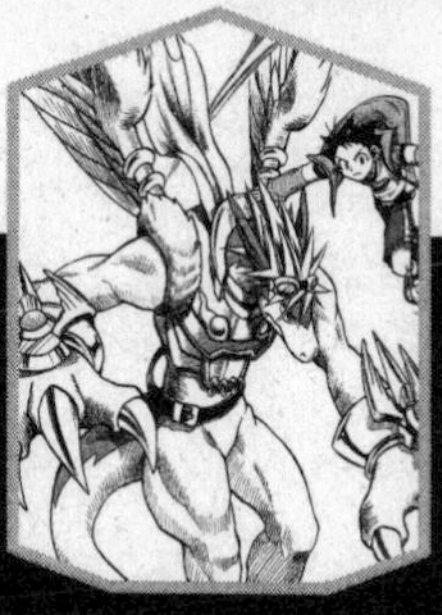

ELEMENT: WIND (TORNADO)
TYPE: WINDRAGON BERSERK MODE
HIT POINTS: 2500
FAVORITE ATTACK: NEO WING TORNADO

LEGENDZ NAME: SHIRON
SAGA: KEN KAZAKI

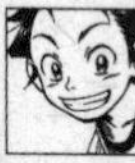

KEN'S ANGER AMPLIFIED SHIRON'S BASIC ABILITIES AND CAUSED HIM TO TAKE THIS FORM. ITS COUNTERATTACKS HAVE BEEN STRENGTHENED, MAKING IT ABLE TO WITHSTAND ALMOST ANY ATTACK.

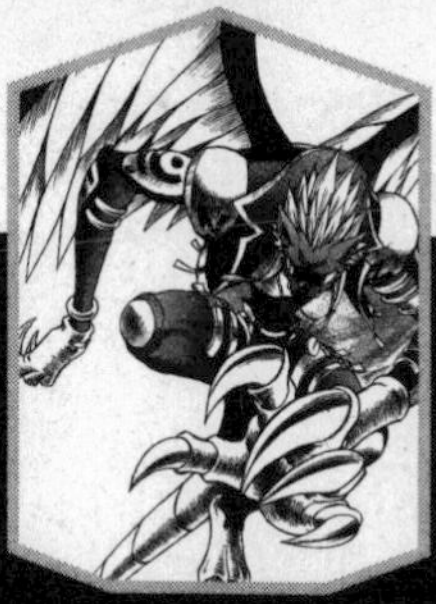

ELEMENT: DARKNESS (NECROM)
TYPE: GARGOYLE
HIT POINTS: 2070
FAVORITE ATTACK: METEO-DARDOS, SHIFT ZONE

LEGENDZ NAME: GOODENRICH
SAGA: UNKNOWN

IT ONCE BELONGED TO A DIFFERENT ELEMENT, BUT HAS DEGENERATED INTO A NECROM LEGENDZ. CAN CONTROL STONE STATUES AND TURN ITS ENEMIES INTO STONE. LOVES TO TOY WITH ITS ENEMIES IN BATTLE.

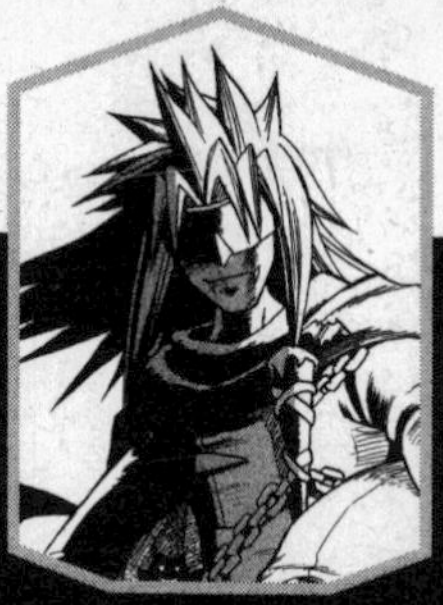

ELEMENT: DARKNESS (NECROM)
TYPE: VAMPIRE
HIT POINTS: 2190
FAVORITE ATTACK: ROSE DAL-DOM, SHIFT ZONE

LEGENDZ NAME: FANG D. ZEPPELIN
SAGA: UNKNOWN

A TERRIFYING VAMPIRE THAT USES ITS HIGH INTELLIGENCE TO TRAP ITS ENEMIES. HAS THE ABILITY TO CONTROL THE SPACE AROUND IT. AS A DISCIPLE OF THE LICH, IT SEEKS TO BRING ABOUT THE AGE OF NECROM (DARKNESS).

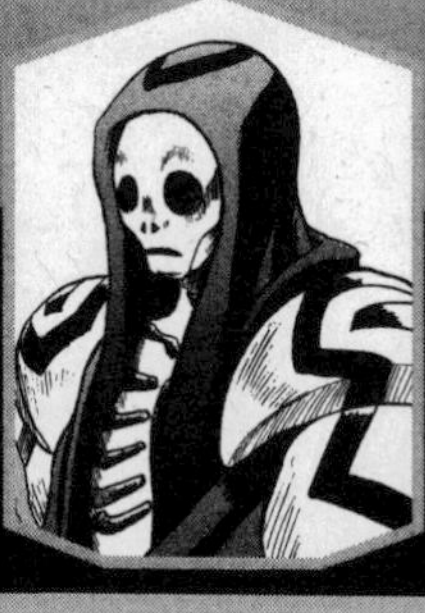

ELEMENT: DARKNESS (NECROM)
TYPE: LICH
HIT POINTS: 5000
FAVORITE ATTACK: HARDES-DARDOS, LOST TIME

LEGENDZ NAME: ZONO
SAGA: UNKNOWN

AN EVIL WIZARD LEGENDZ CONTRACTED BY NECROM. IT SEEKS THE POWER OF THE SAGAS FOR THE REBIRTH OF JABBERWOCK.

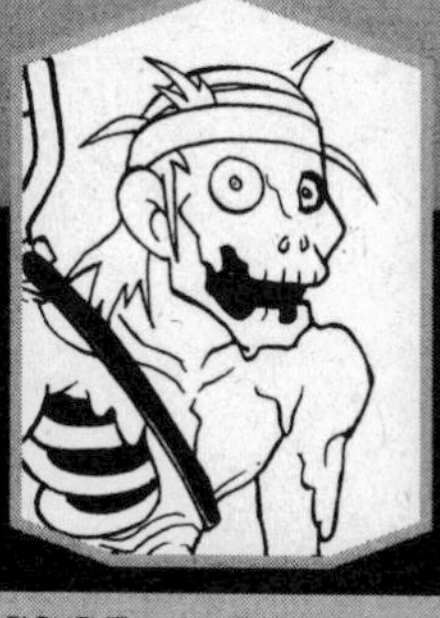

ELEMENT: DARKNESS (NECROM)
TYPE: ZOMBIE
HIT POINTS: 1500
FAVORITE ATTACK: MELTDAG-RUM, ROTTEN TOUCH

LEGENDZ NAME: UNKNOWN
SAGA: UNKNOWN

A DISGUSTING DARK LEGENDZ CREATED WHEN AN EVIL SPIRIT CONTROLS A DEAD BODY. HARD TO KILL DUE TO ITS HIGH LEVEL OF HIT POINTS.

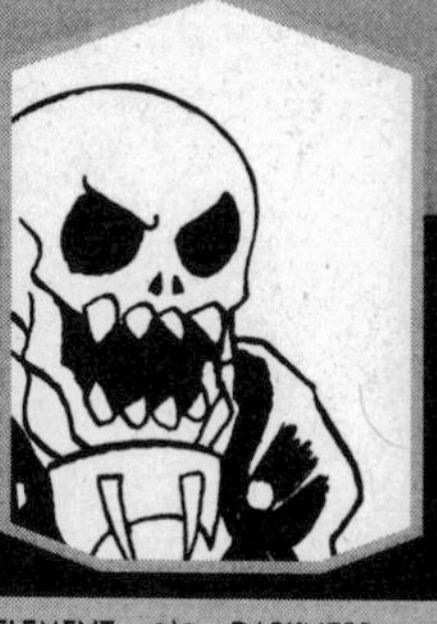

ELEMENT: DARKNESS (NECROM)
TYPE: SKELETON
HIT POINTS: 1320
FAVORITE ATTACK: CANNON DARK, NECROM PIT

LEGENDZ NAME: UNKNOWN
SAGA: UNKNOWN

THESE SPIRITS OF WARRIORS BEARING ANGER AND HATRED HAVE BEEN TURNED INTO SKELETON WARRIORS BY NECROM. BECAUSE THEY WERE ONCE LIVING WARRIORS, THEY ARE STRONG BOTH INDIVIDUALLY AND IN GROUPS.

« READ THIS WAY «

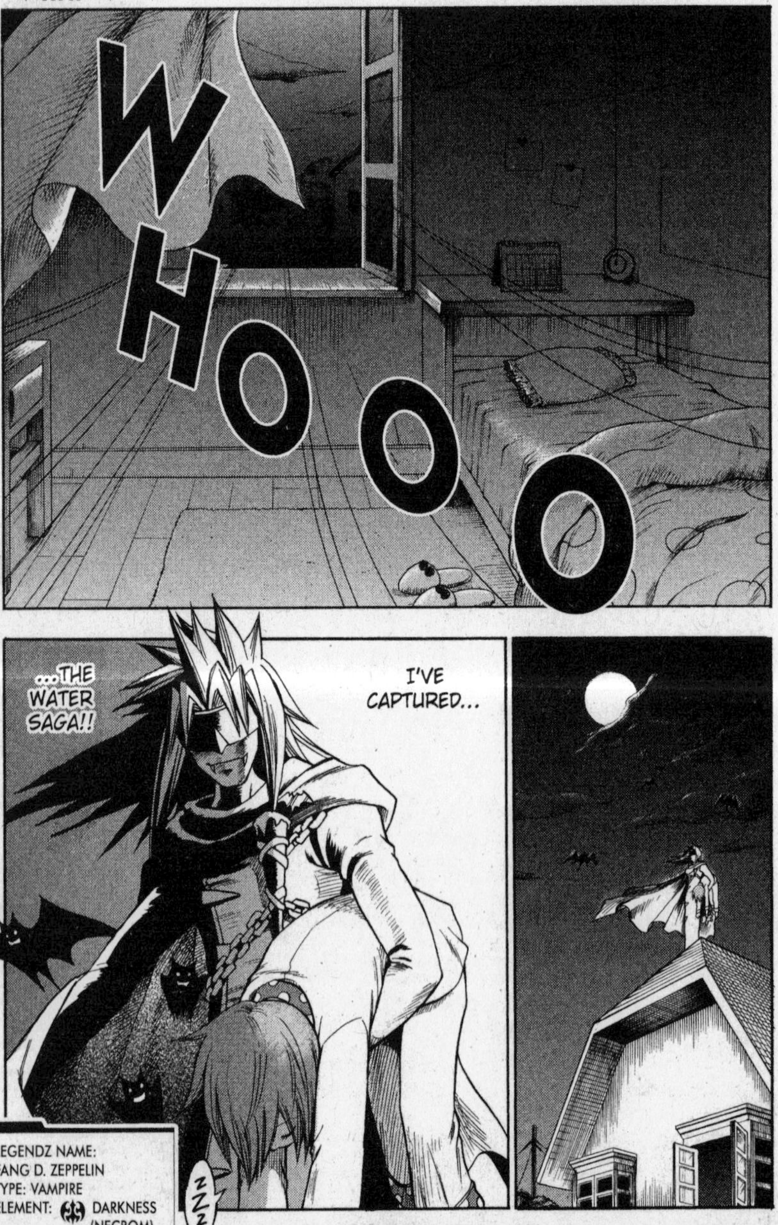
WHOOOO
I'VE CAPTURED...
...THE WATER SAGA!!
KEE
ZZZ
LEGENDZ NAME: FANG D. ZEPPELIN
TYPE: VAMPIRE
ELEMENT: DARKNESS (NECROM)

LEGENDZ 12 Crossing Force

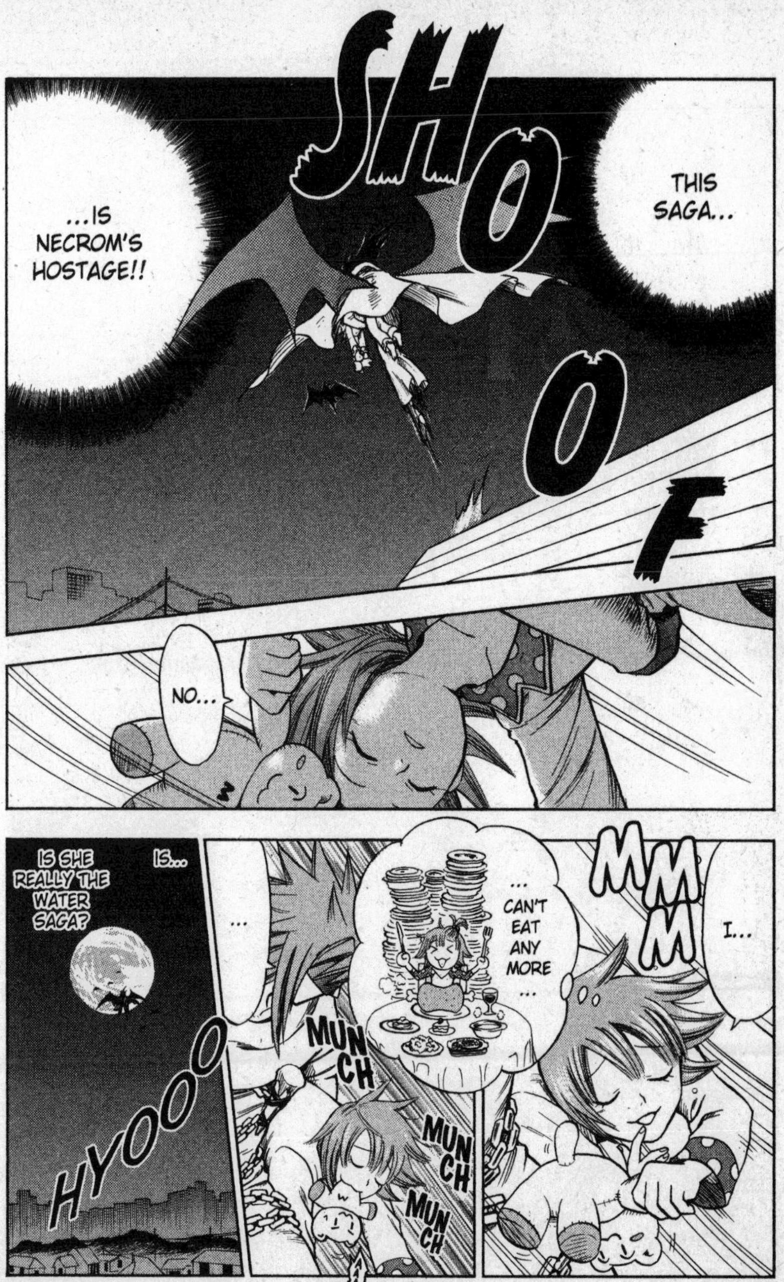
SHOOOF
THIS SAGA...
...IS NECROM'S HOSTAGE!!
NO...
MMM
I...
... CAN'T EAT ANY MORE ...
...
MUNCH
MUNCH
MUNCH
IS...
IS SHE REALLY THE WATER SAGA?
HYOOOO

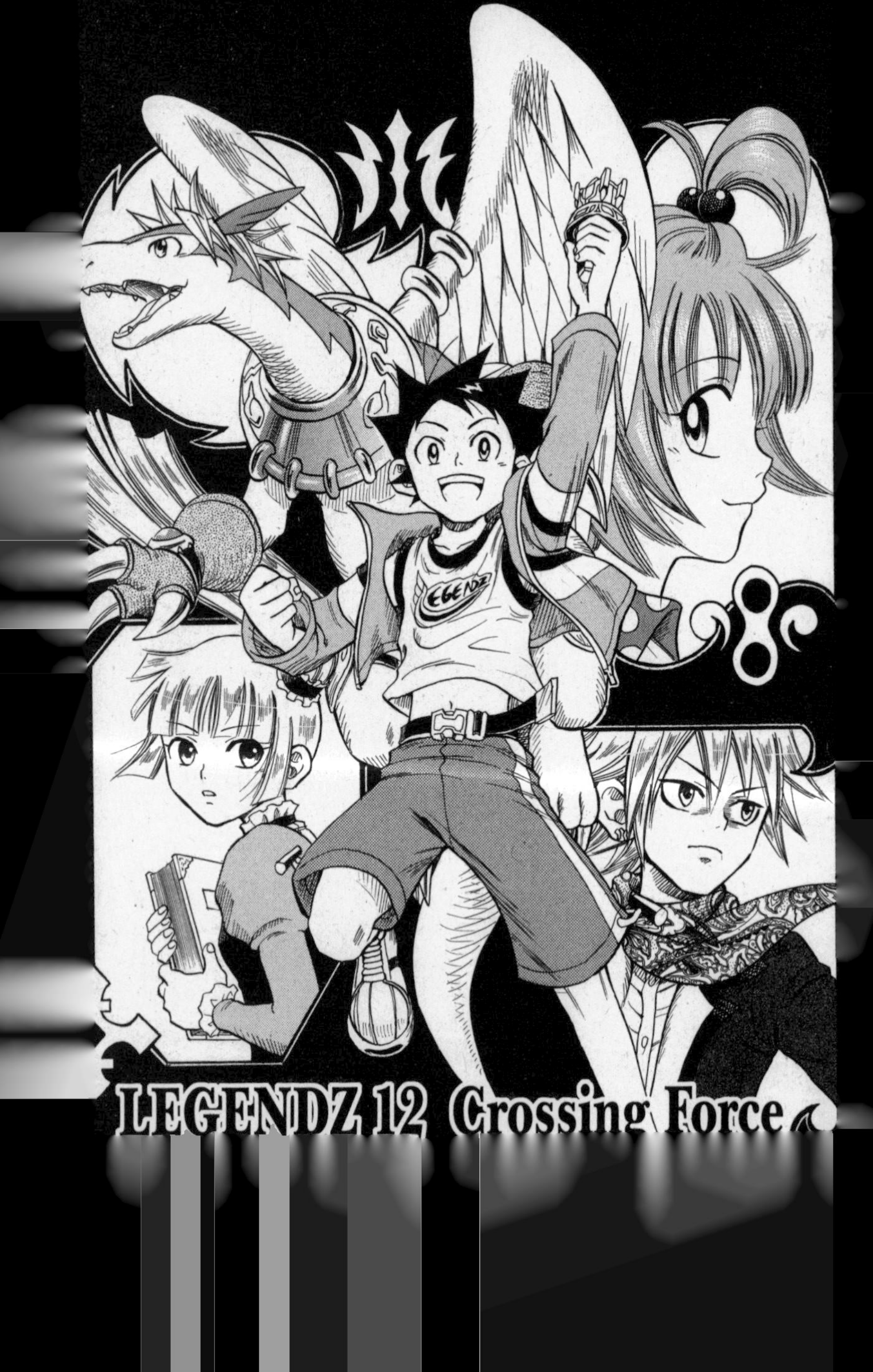
EGENDZ

LEGENDZ 12 Crossing Force

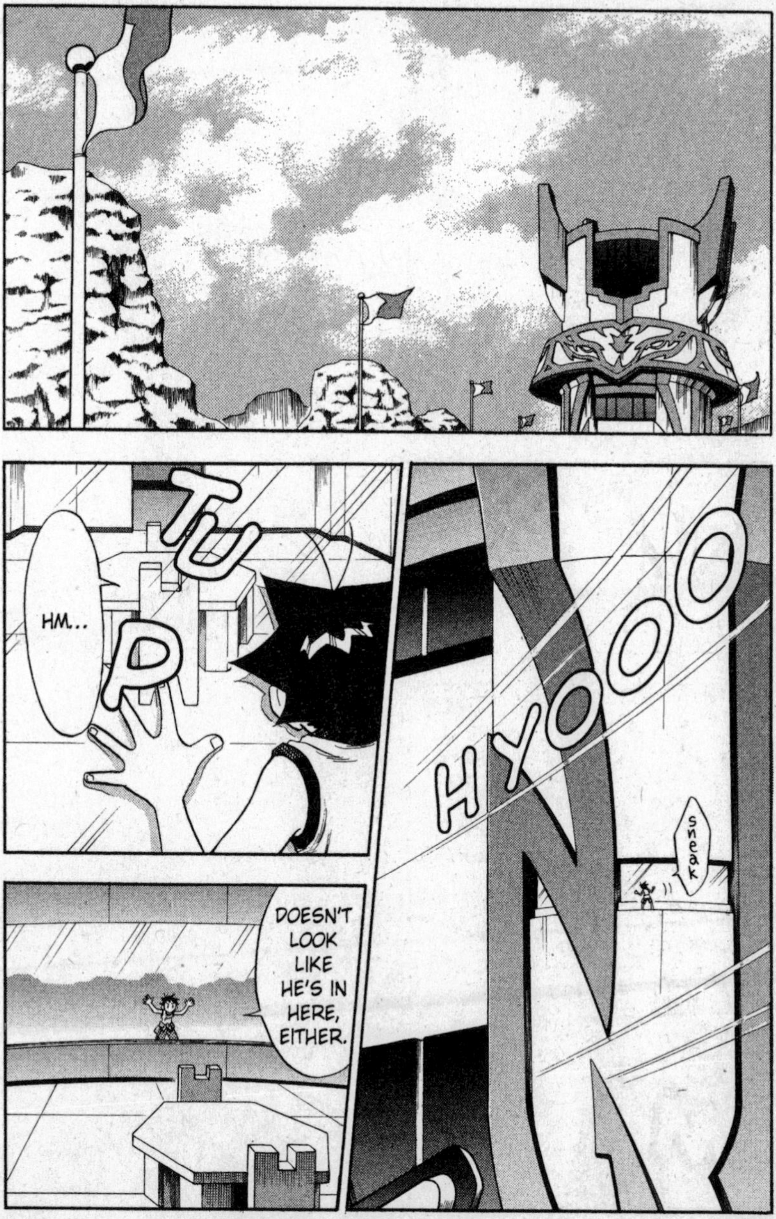
HYOOO
sneak
TUP
HM...
DOESN'T LOOK LIKE HE'S IN HERE, EITHER.

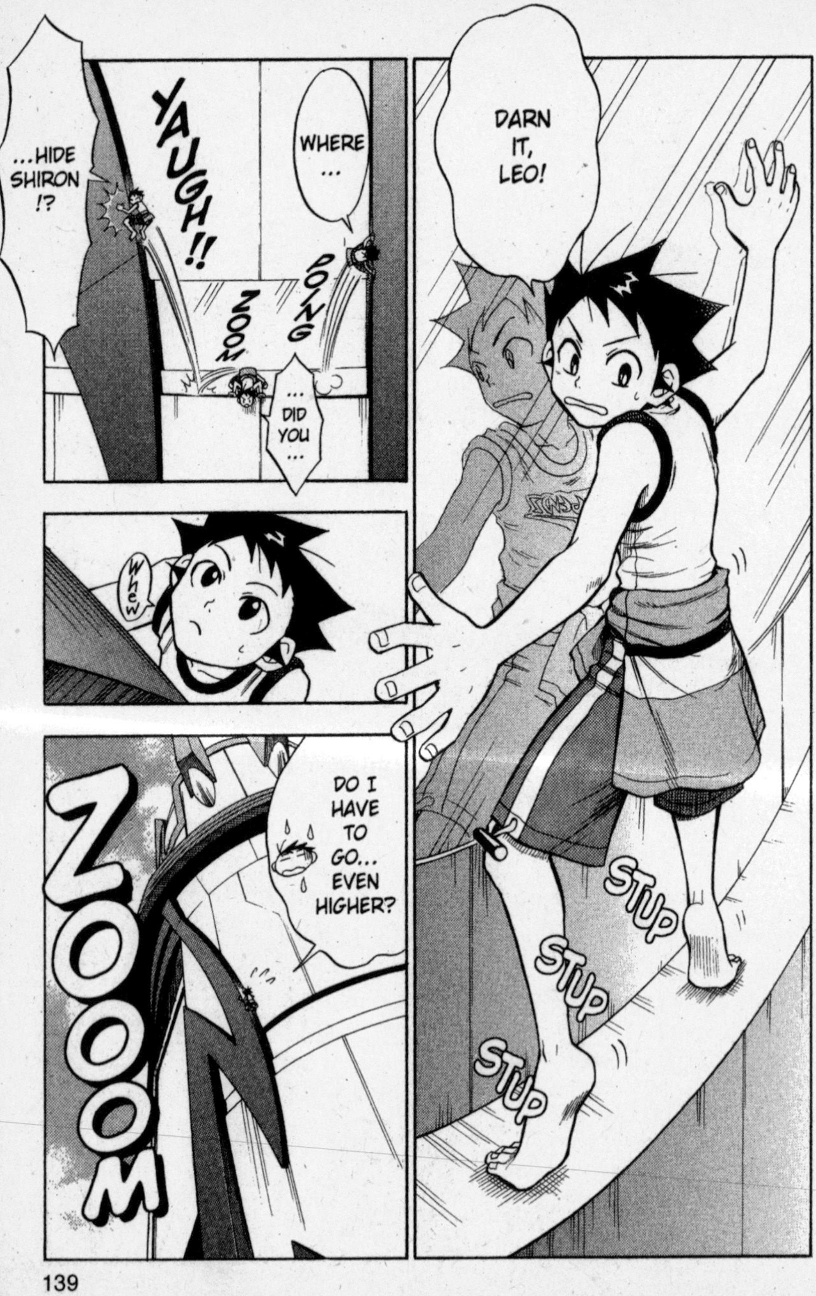
DARN IT, LEO!
STUP
STUP
STUP
WHERE ...
POING
... DID YOU ...
ZOOM
YAUGH!!
...HIDE SHIRON !?
Whew
DO I HAVE TO GO... EVEN HIGHER?
ZOOOOM

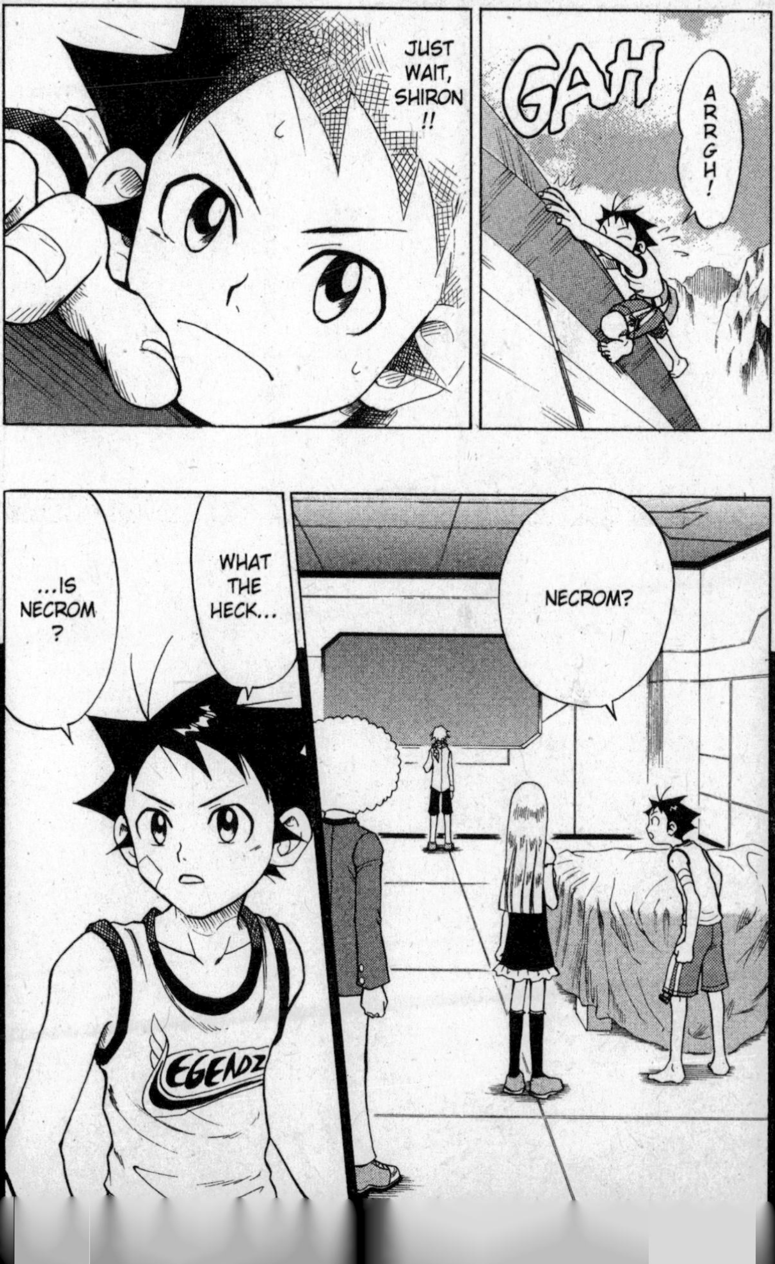
GAH
ARRGH!
JUST WAIT, SHIRON!!
NECROM?
WHAT THE HECK...
...IS NECROM?

READ THIS WAY

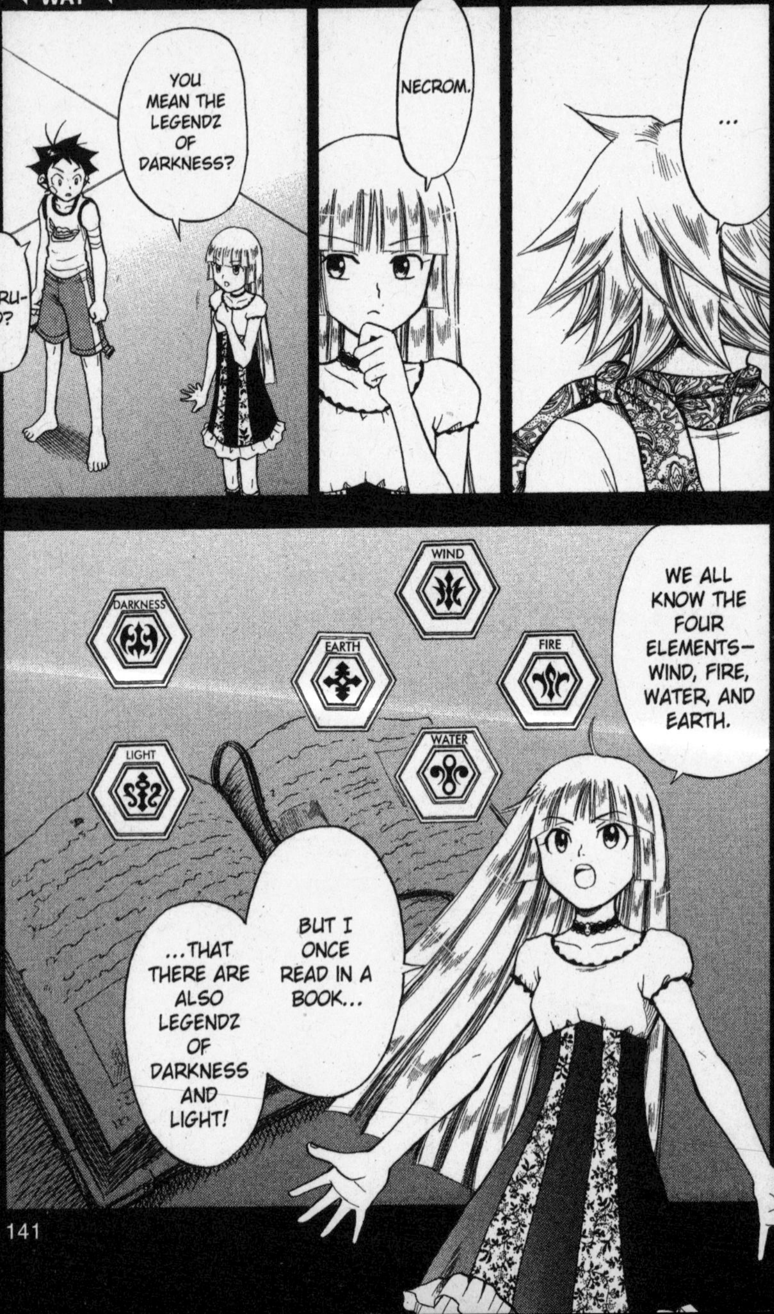
...
NECROM.
YOU MEAN THE LEGENDZ OF DARKNESS?
KAORU-KO?
WE ALL KNOW THE FOUR ELEMENTS—WIND, FIRE, WATER, AND EARTH.
WIND
FIRE
EARTH
DARKNESS
WATER
LIGHT
BUT I ONCE READ IN A BOOK...
...THAT THERE ARE ALSO LEGENDZ OF DARKNESS AND LIGHT!

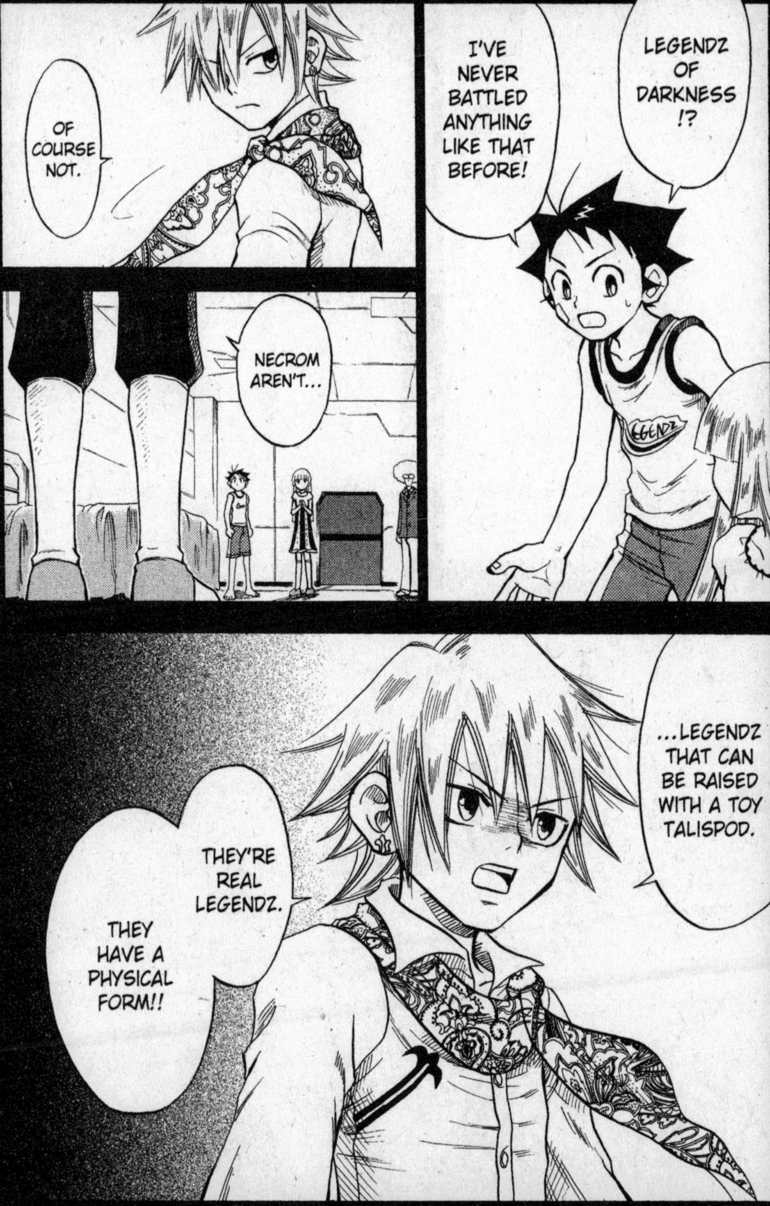
LEGENDZ OF DARKNESS !?
I'VE NEVER BATTLED ANYTHING LIKE THAT BEFORE!
OF COURSE NOT.
NECROM AREN'T...
...LEGENDZ THAT CAN BE RAISED WITH A TOY TALISPOD.
THEY'RE REAL LEGENDZ.
THEY HAVE A PHYSICAL FORM!!

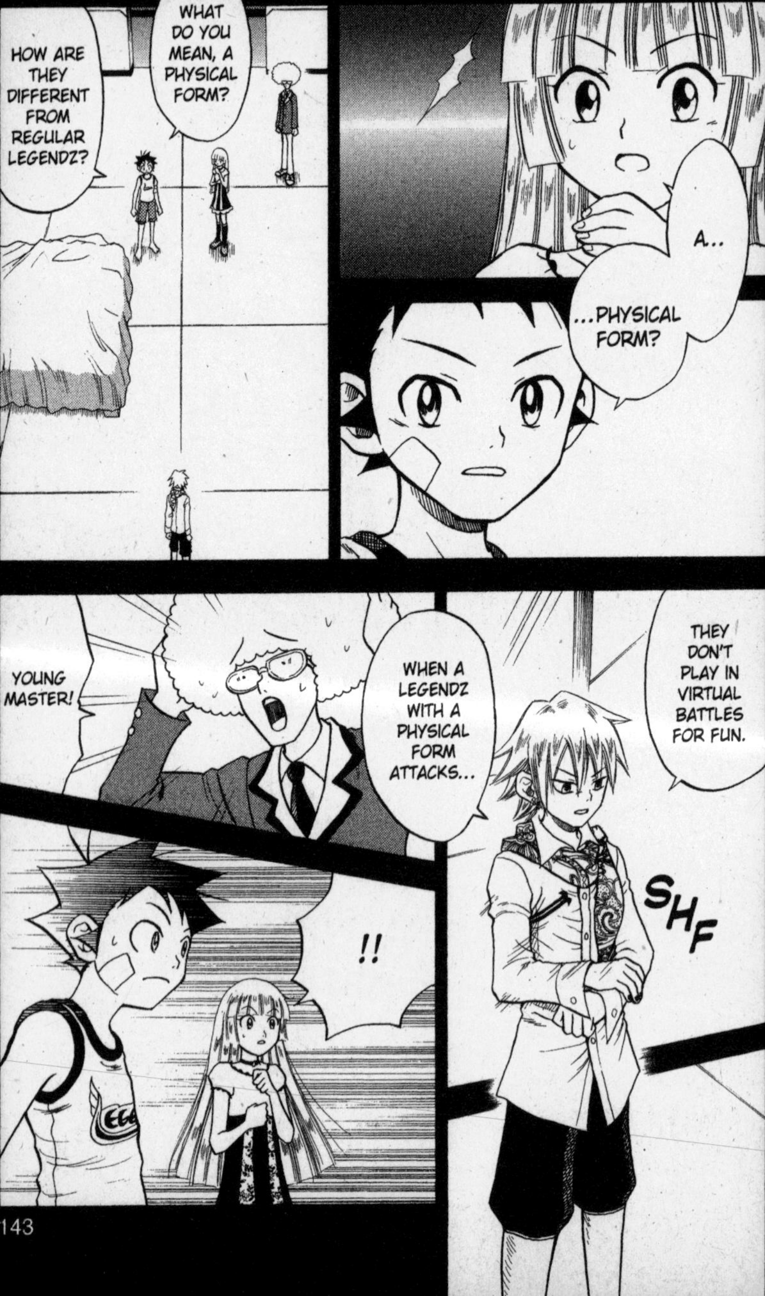
A...
...PHYSICAL FORM?
WHAT DO YOU MEAN, A PHYSICAL FORM?
HOW ARE THEY DIFFERENT FROM REGULAR LEGENDZ?
THEY DON'T PLAY IN VIRTUAL BATTLES FOR FUN.
SHF
WHEN A LEGENDZ WITH A PHYSICAL FORM ATTACKS...
YOUNG MASTER!
!!

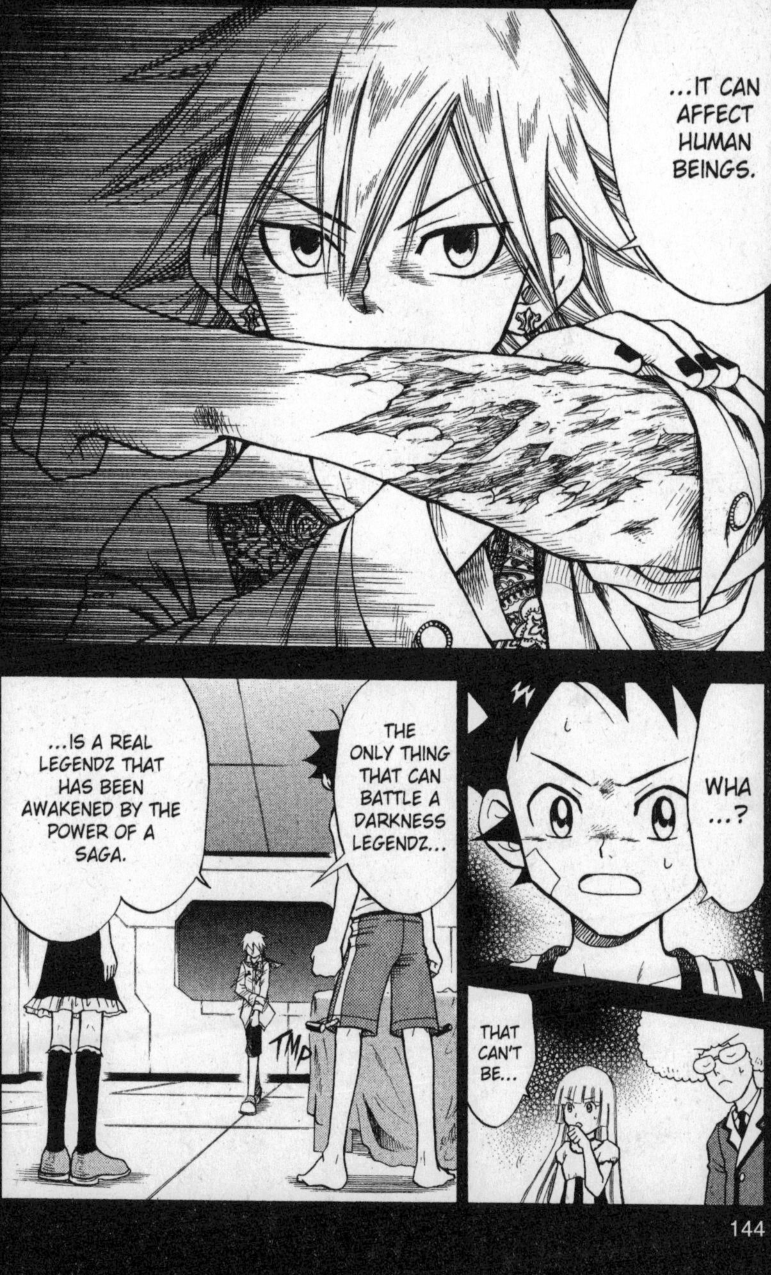
...IT CAN AFFECT HUMAN BEINGS.
WHA ...?
THAT CAN'T BE...
THE ONLY THING THAT CAN BATTLE A DARKNESS LEGENDZ...
...IS A REAL LEGENDZ THAT HAS BEEN AWAKENED BY THE POWER OF A SAGA.
TMP

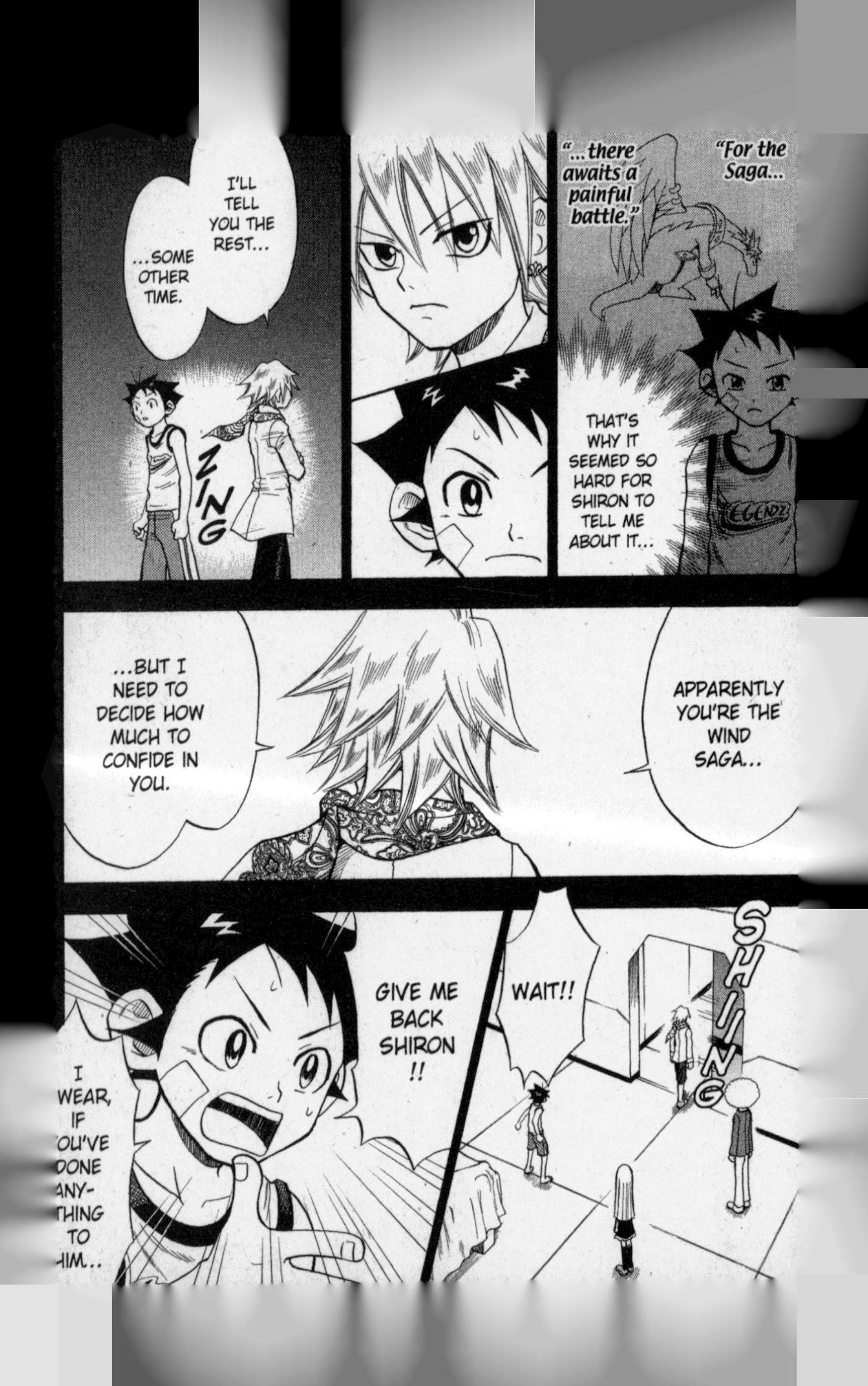
"For the Saga...
"...there awaits a painful battle."
THAT'S WHY IT SEEMED SO HARD FOR SHIRON TO TELL ME ABOUT IT...
I'LL TELL YOU THE REST...
...SOME OTHER TIME.
ZING
APPARENTLY YOU'RE THE WIND SAGA...
...BUT I NEED TO DECIDE HOW MUCH TO CONFIDE IN YOU.
SHING
WAIT!!
GIVE ME BACK SHIRON !!
I WEAR, IF OU'VE DONE ANY-THING TO HIM...

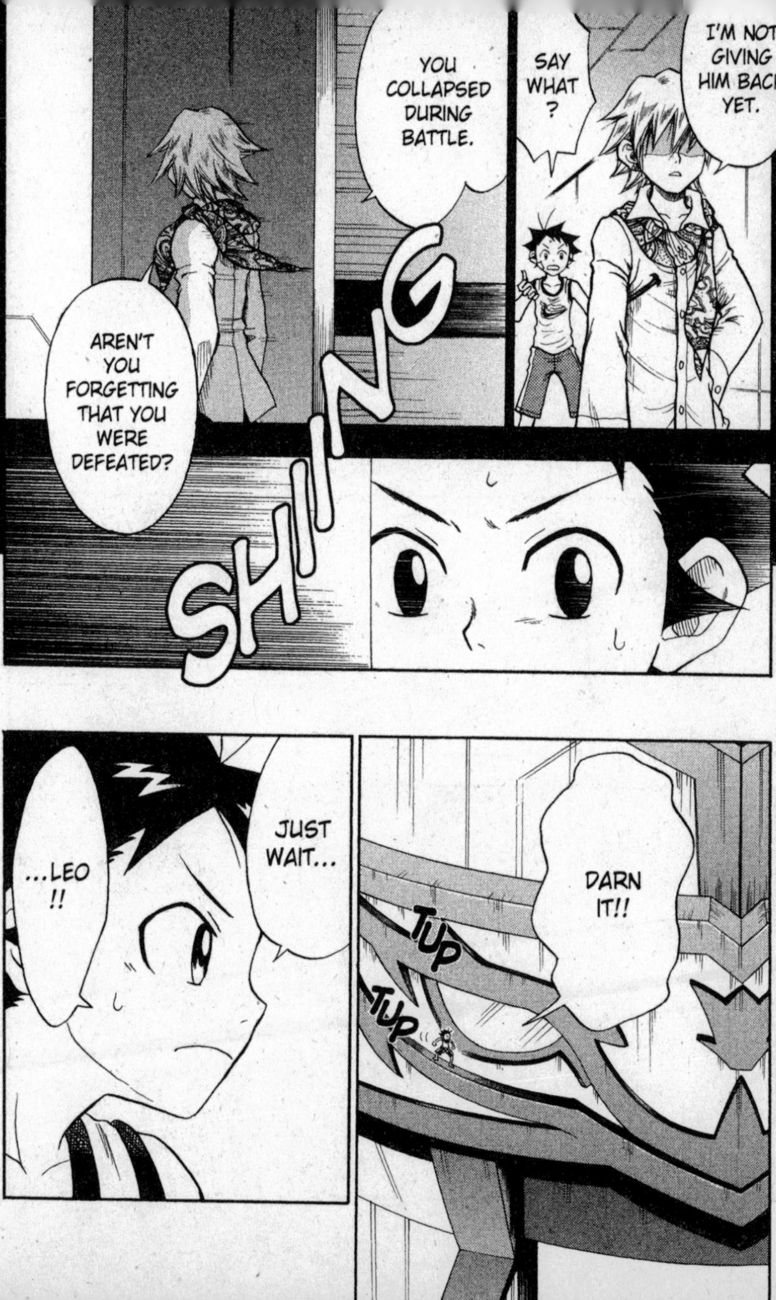
I'M NOT GIVING HIM BACK YET.
SAY WHAT?
YOU COLLAPSED DURING BATTLE.
AREN'T YOU FORGETTING THAT YOU WERE DEFEATED?
SHIIING
DARN IT!!
TUP
TUP
JUST WAIT...
...LEO!!

READ THIS WAY

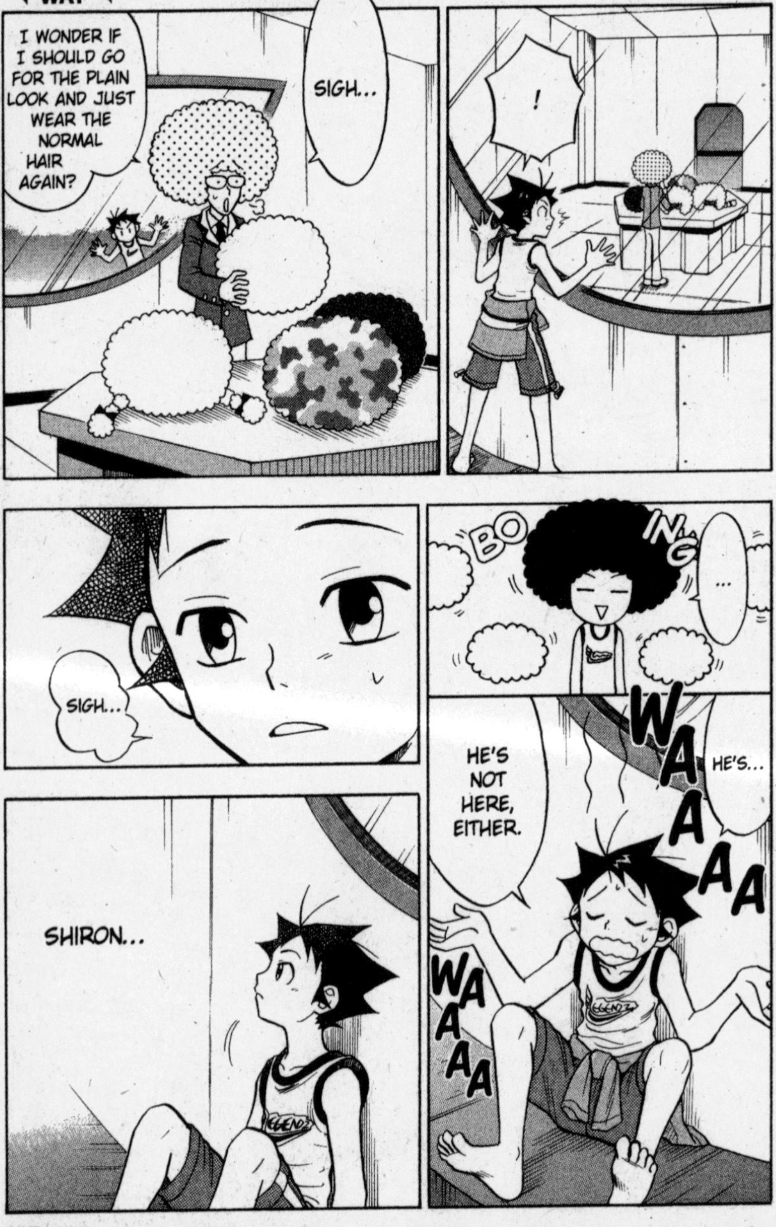
!
SIGH...
I WONDER IF I SHOULD GO FOR THE PLAIN LOOK AND JUST WEAR THE NORMAL HAIR AGAIN?
Courage, Namio, courage...
BOING
...
SIGH...
HE'S...
WAAAAA
HE'S NOT HERE, EITHER.
WAAAAA
SHIRON...

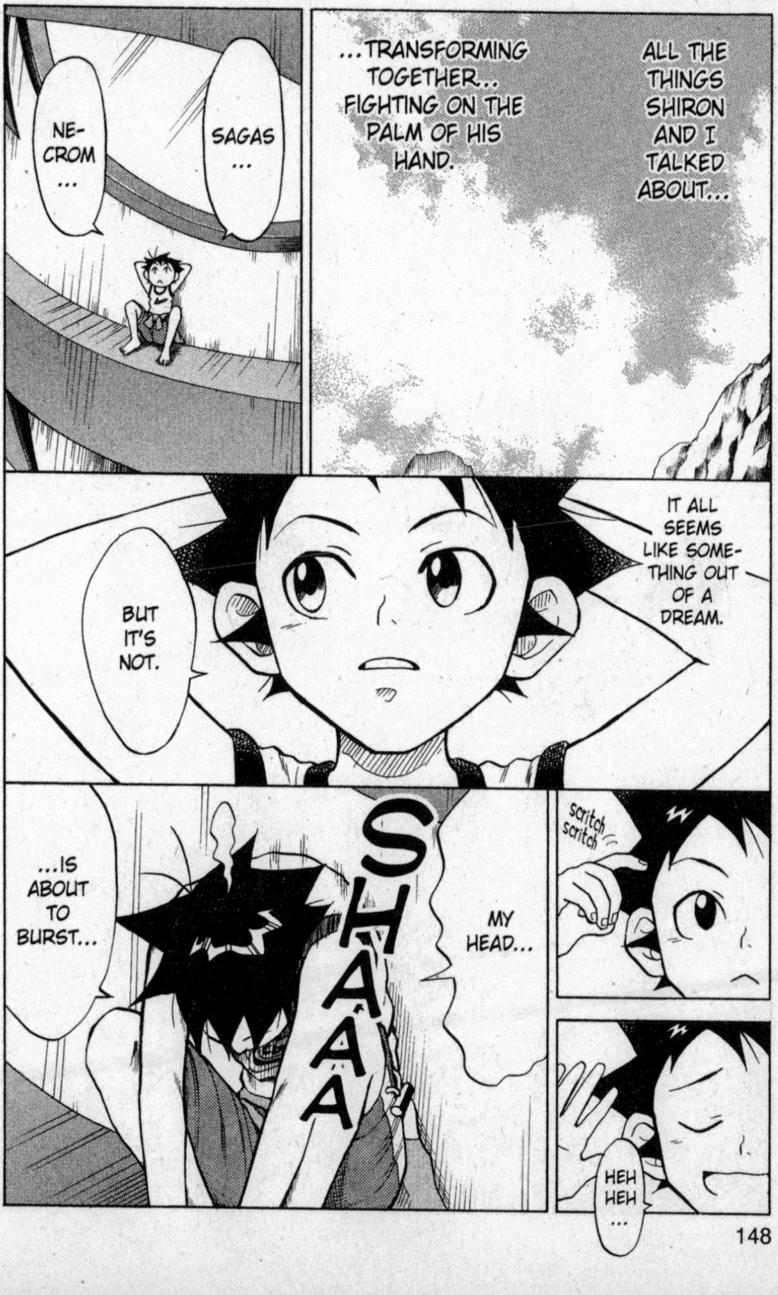
ALL THE THINGS SHIRON AND I TALKED ABOUT...
...TRANSFORMING TOGETHER... FIGHTING ON THE PALM OF HIS HAND.
SAGAS ...
NE-CROM ...
IT ALL SEEMS LIKE SOME-THING OUT OF A DREAM.
BUT IT'S NOT.
scritch scritch
HEH HEH ...
SHAAAA
MY HEAD...
...IS ABOUT TO BURST...

READ THIS WAY

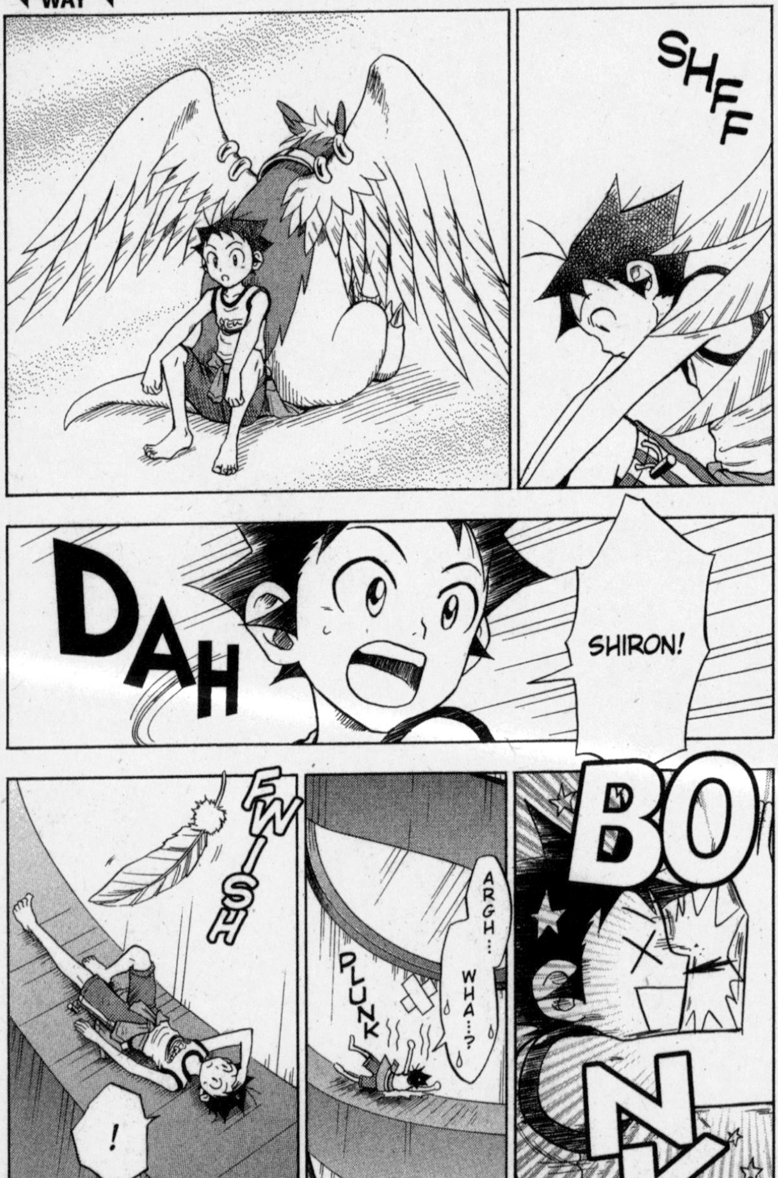
SHFF
SHIRON!
DAH
BONK
ARGH... WHA...?
PLUNK
FWISH
!

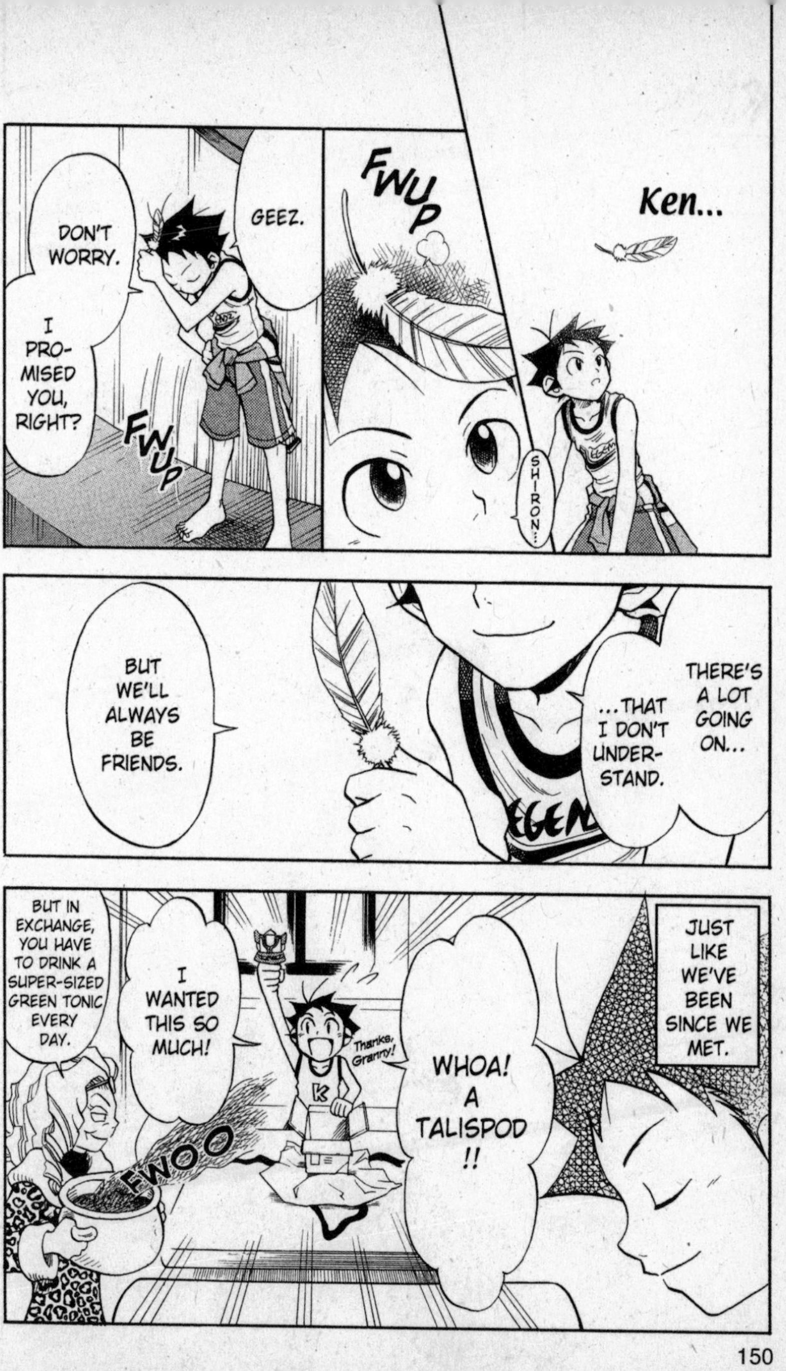
Ken...
SHIRON...
FWUP
GEEZ.
DON'T WORRY.
I PRO-MISED YOU, RIGHT?
FWUP
THERE'S A LOT GOING ON...
...THAT I DON'T UNDER-STAND.
BUT WE'LL ALWAYS BE FRIENDS.
JUST LIKE WE'VE BEEN SINCE WE MET.
WHOA! A TALISPOD !!
Thanks, Granny!
I WANTED THIS SO MUCH!
BUT IN EXCHANGE, YOU HAVE TO DRINK A SUPER-SIZED GREEN TONIC EVERY DAY.
FWOO

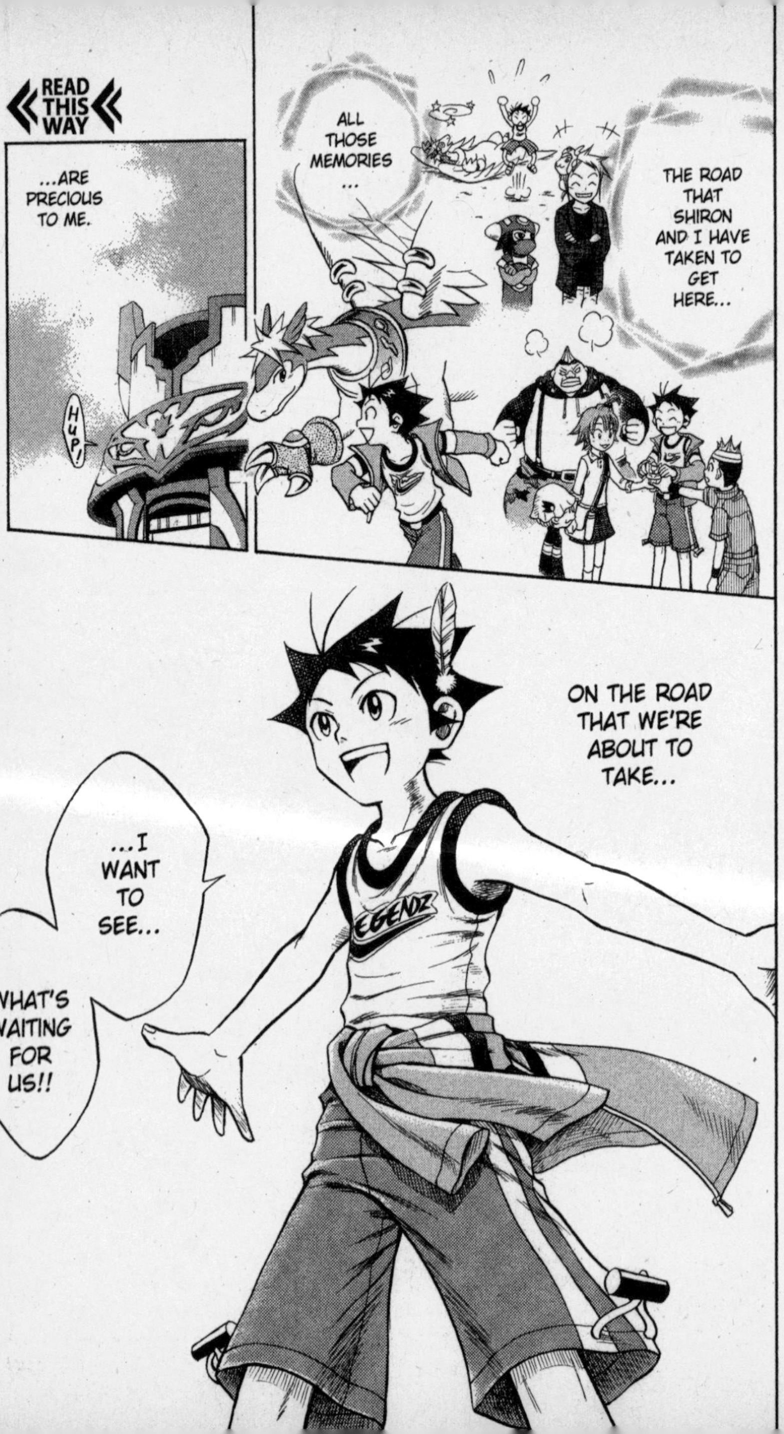
READ THIS WAY
THE ROAD THAT SHIRON AND I HAVE TAKEN TO GET HERE...
ALL THOSE MEMORIES...
...ARE PRECIOUS TO ME.
HUP!
ON THE ROAD THAT WE'RE ABOUT TO TAKE...
...I WANT TO SEE...
WHAT'S WAITING FOR US!!

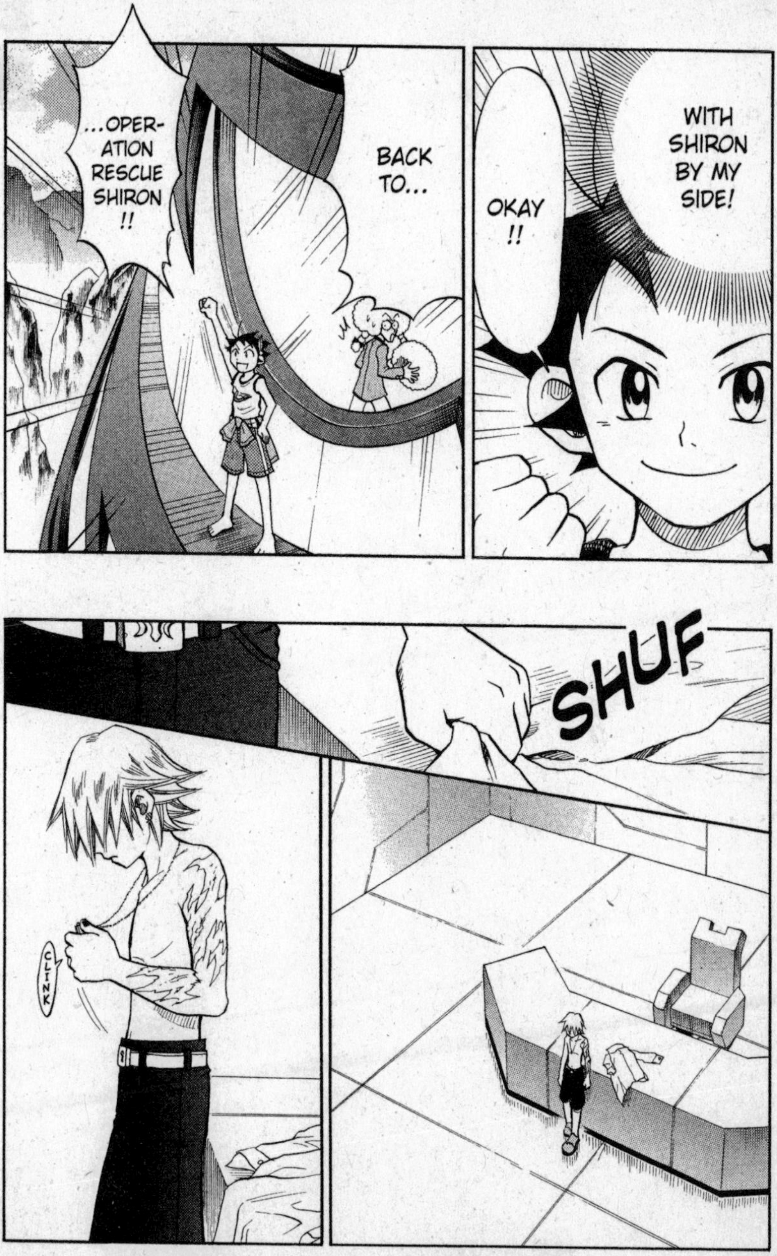
WITH SHIRON BY MY SIDE!
OKAY !!
BACK TO...
...OPERATION RESCUE SHIRON !!
SHUF
CLINK

READ THIS WAY

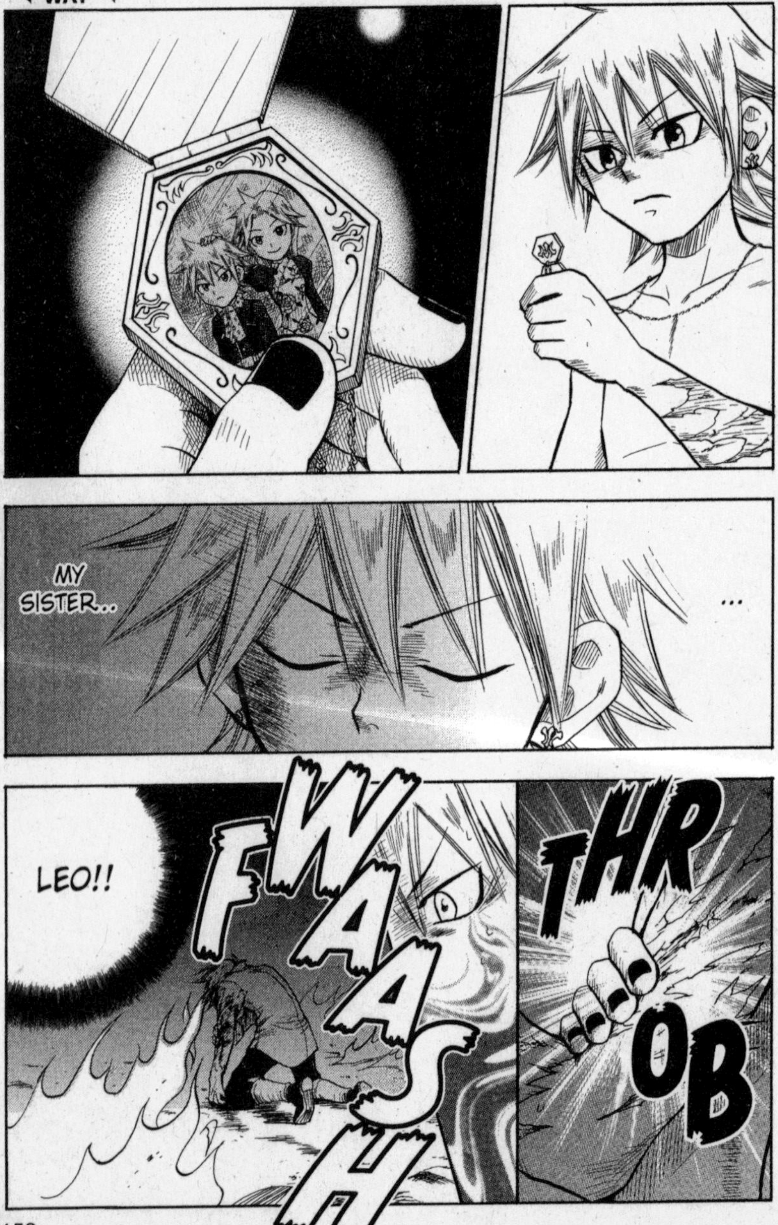
...
MY SISTER...
THROB
LEO!!
FWASH

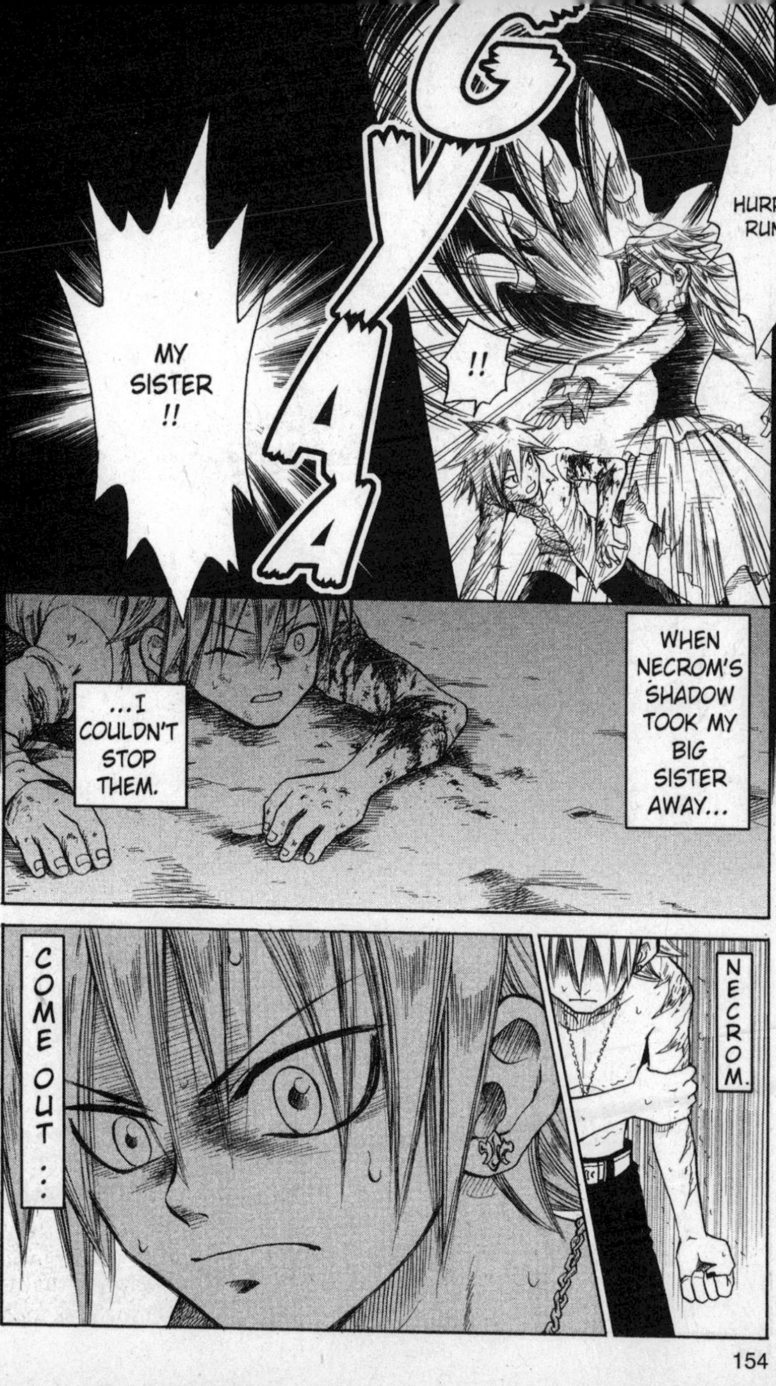
HURRY! RUN!
!!
GYAA
MY SISTER !!
WHEN NECROM'S SHADOW TOOK MY BIG SISTER AWAY...
...I COULDN'T STOP THEM.
NECROM.
COME OUT ...

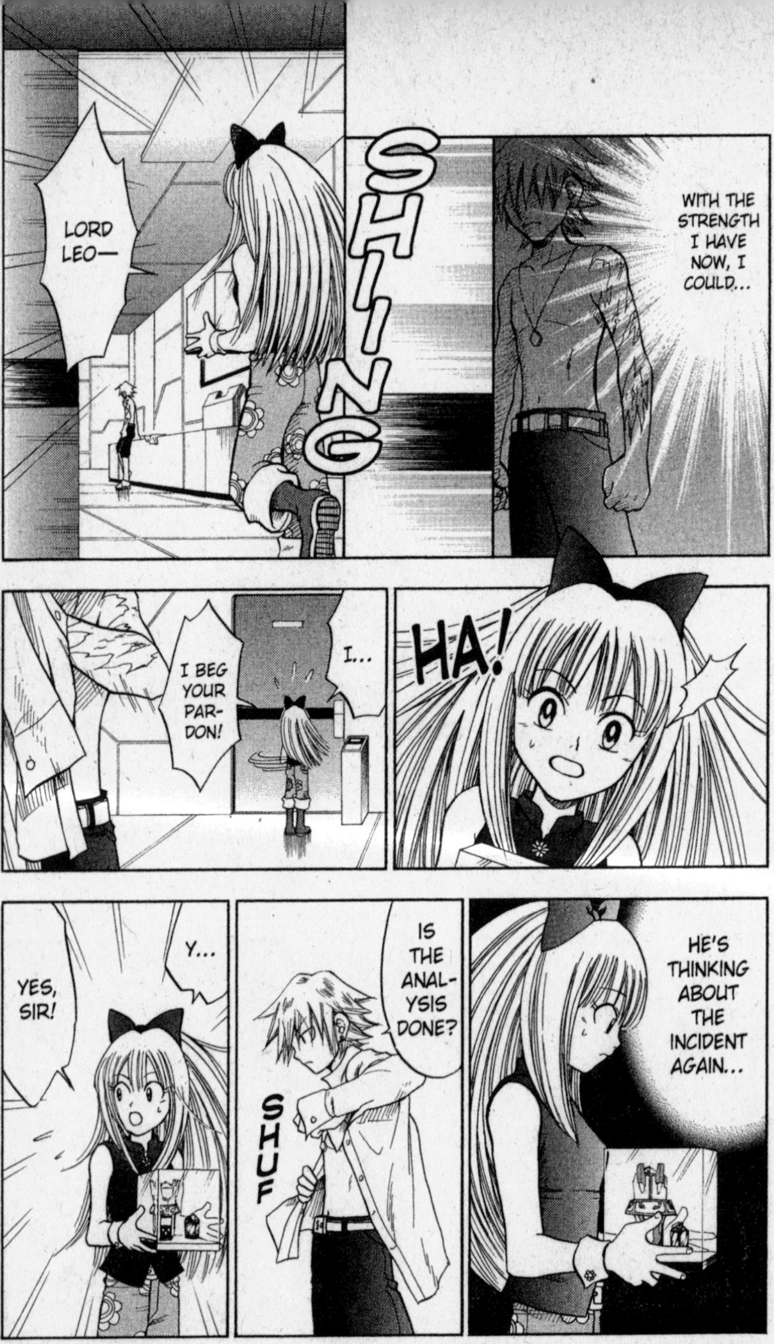

WITH THE STRENGTH I HAVE NOW, I COULD...
SHIING
LORD LEO—
HA!
I...
I BEG YOUR PARDON!
HE'S THINKING ABOUT THE INCIDENT AGAIN...
IS THE ANALYSIS DONE?
SHUF
Y...
YES, SIR!

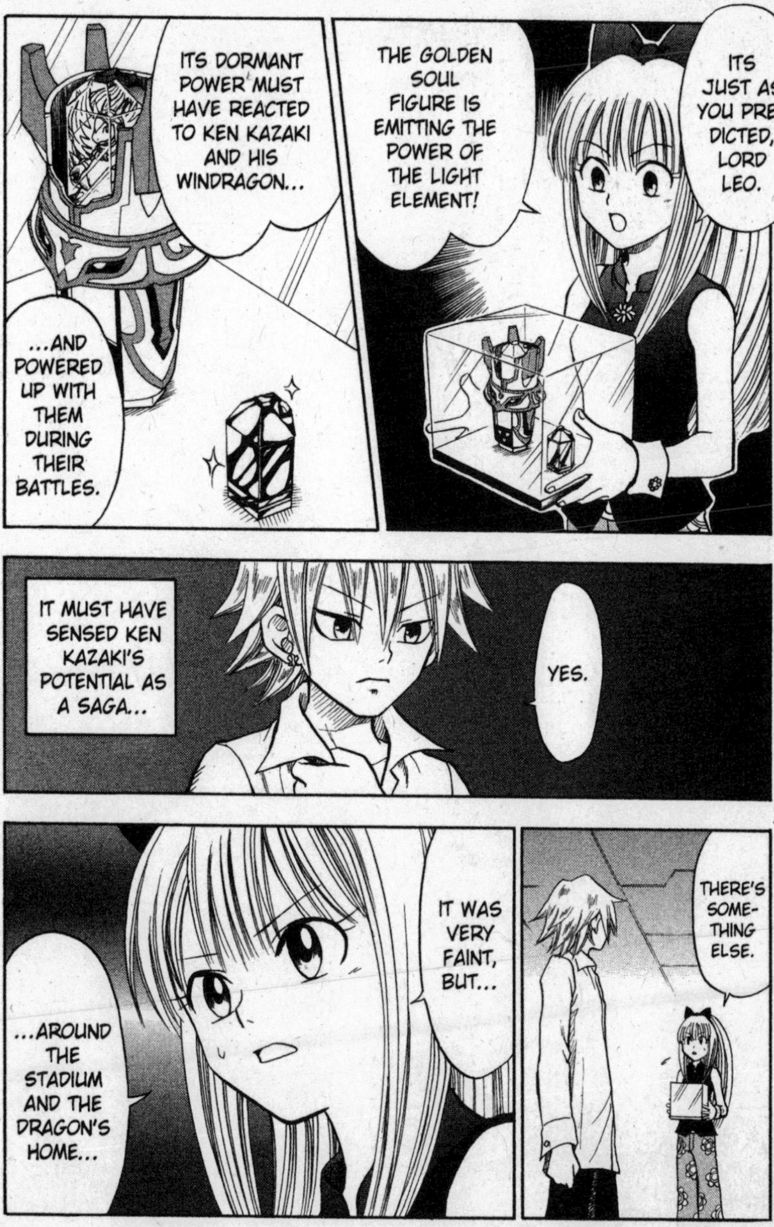

ITS JUST AS YOU PRE-DICTED, LORD LEO.
THE GOLDEN SOUL FIGURE IS EMITTING THE POWER OF THE LIGHT ELEMENT!
ITS DORMANT POWER MUST HAVE REACTED TO KEN KAZAKI AND HIS WINDRAGON...
...AND POWERED UP WITH THEM DURING THEIR BATTLES.
YES.
IT MUST HAVE SENSED KEN KAZAKI'S POTENTIAL AS A SAGA...
THERE'S SOME-THING ELSE.
IT WAS VERY FAINT, BUT...
...AROUND THE STADIUM AND THE DRAGON'S HOME...

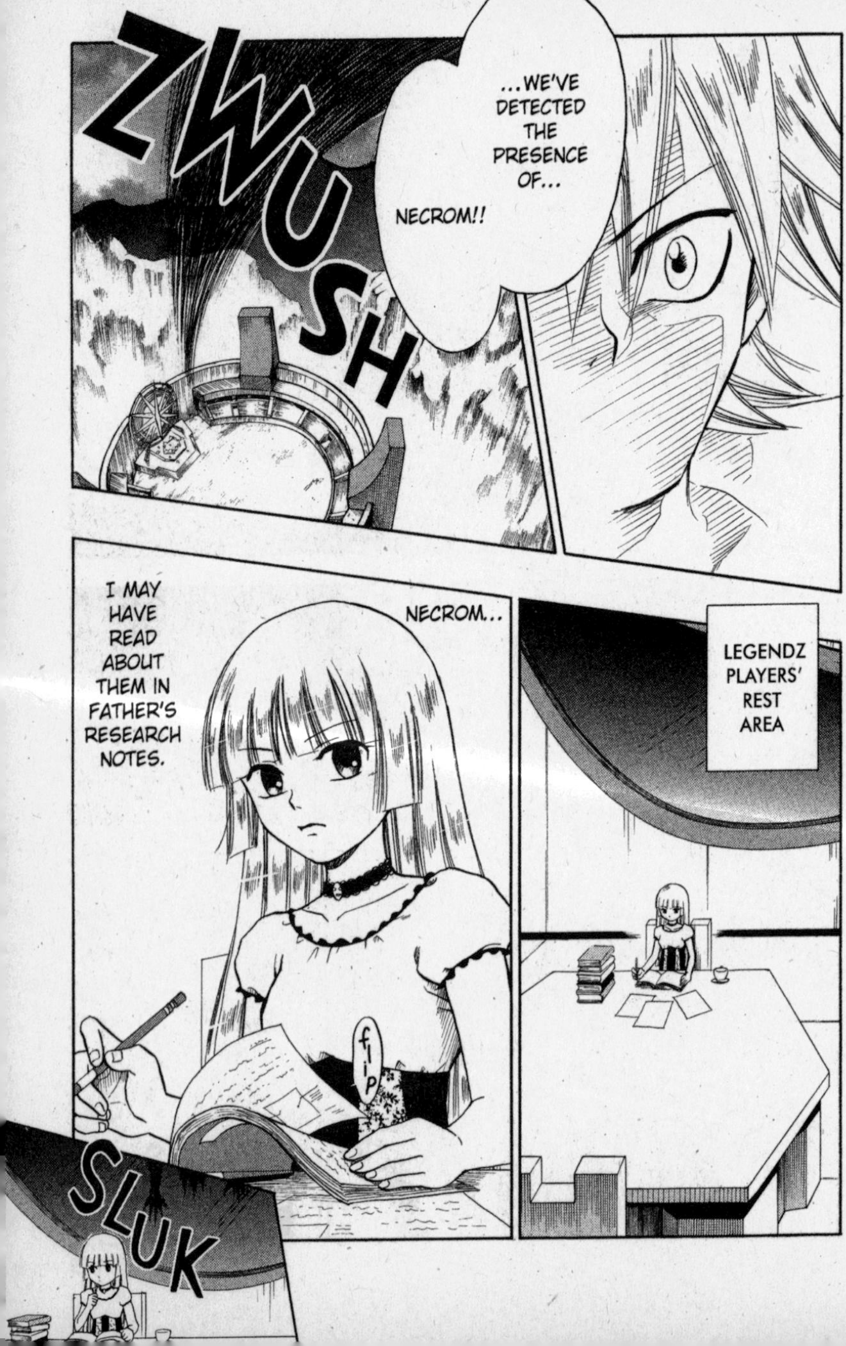
...WE'VE DETECTED THE PRESENCE OF...
NECROM!!
ZWUSH
LEGENDZ PLAYERS' REST AREA
NECROM...
I MAY HAVE READ ABOUT THEM IN FATHER'S RESEARCH NOTES.
flip
SLUK

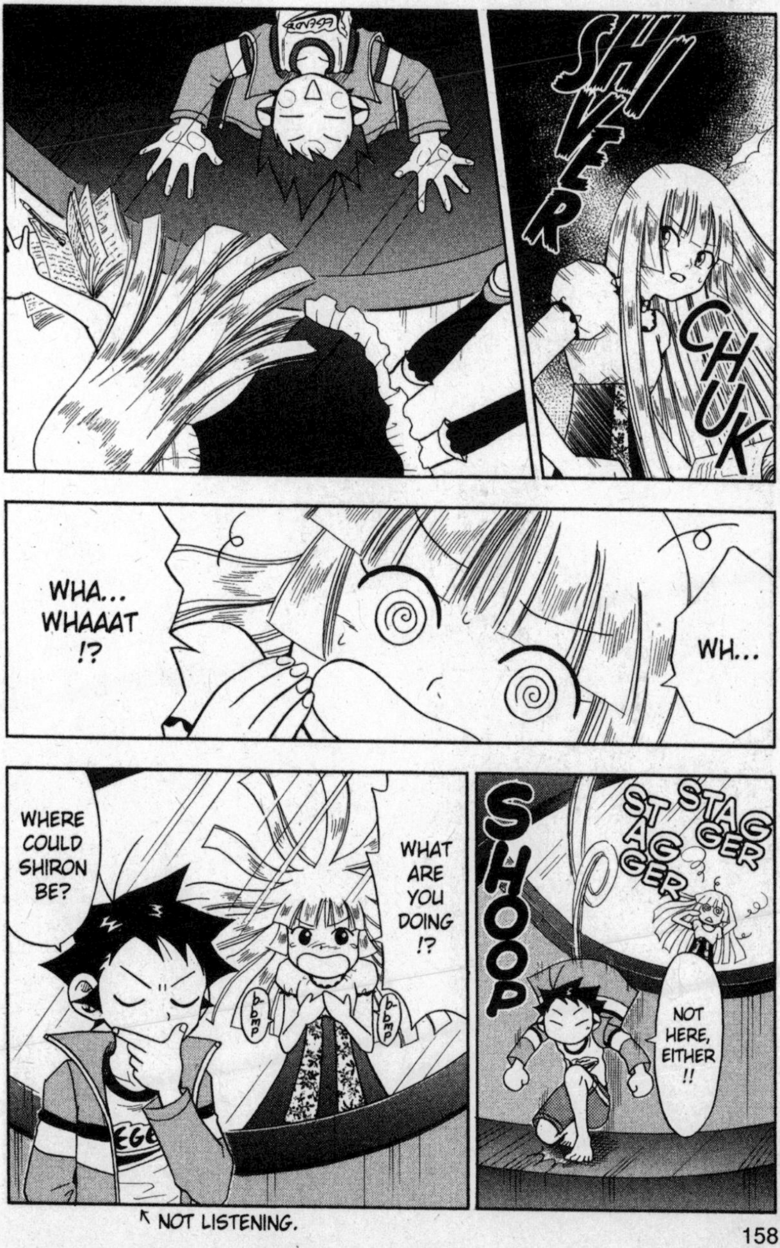
SHIVER
CHUK
WH...
WHA... WHAAAT !?
SHOOP
STAGGER STAGGER
NOT HERE, EITHER !!
WHAT ARE YOU DOING !?
b-bmp
b-bmp
WHERE COULD SHIRON BE?

↖ NOT LISTENING.

READ THIS WAY

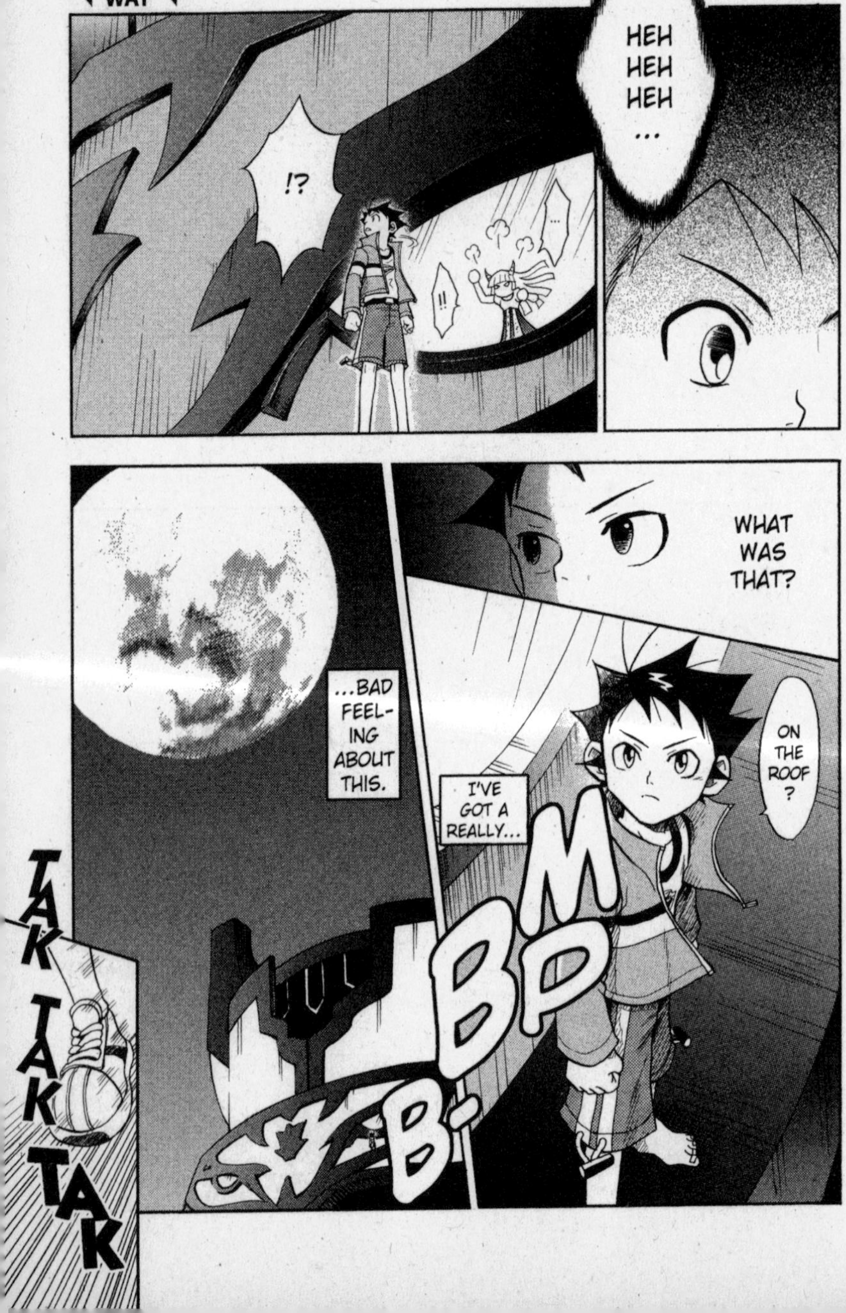
HEH HEH HEH …
…
!?
!!
WHAT WAS THAT?
ON THE ROOF ?
I'VE GOT A REALLY…
…BAD FEEL-ING ABOUT THIS.
BMP
B-
TAK TAK TAK TAK

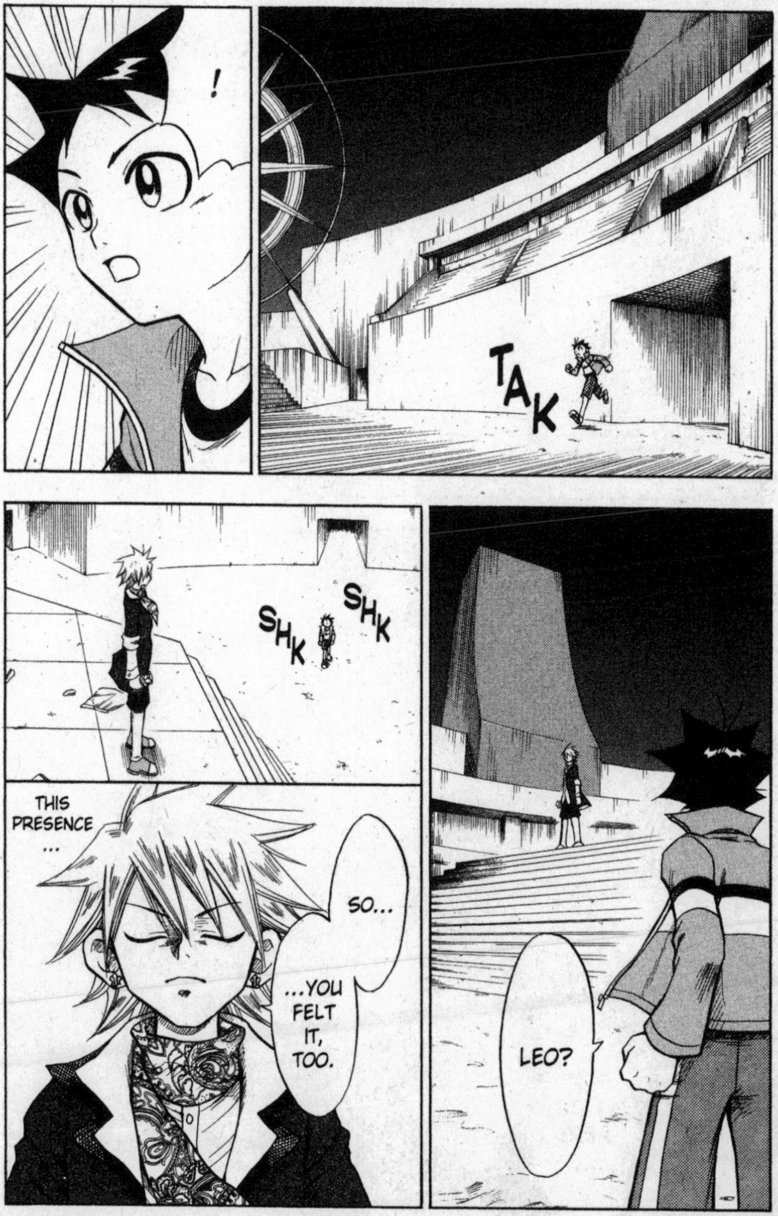
TAK
!
LEO?
SHK
SHK
THIS PRESENCE ...
SO...
...YOU FELT IT, TOO.

READ THIS WAY

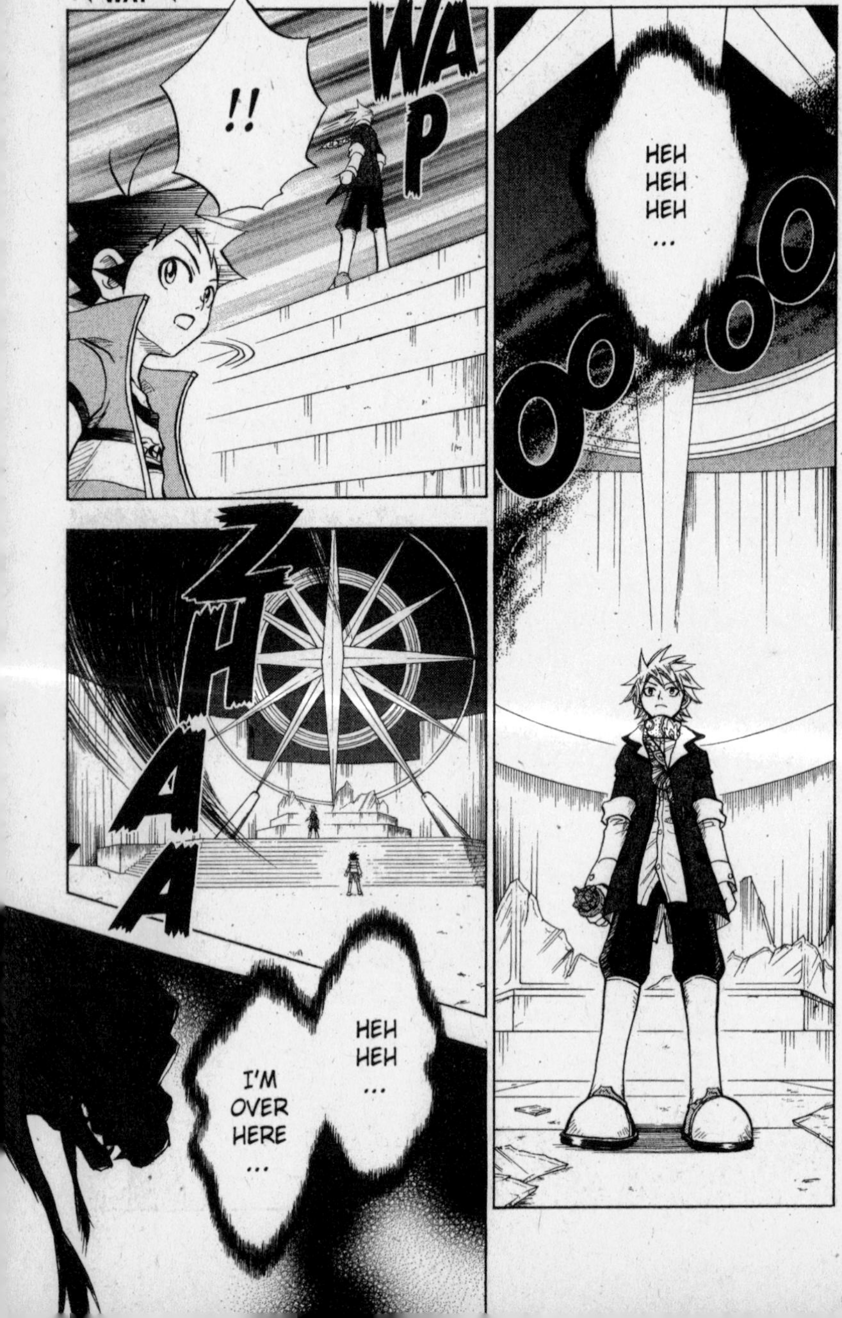
HEH HEH HEH ...
!!
WAP
ZHAA
HEH HEH ...
I'M OVER HERE ...

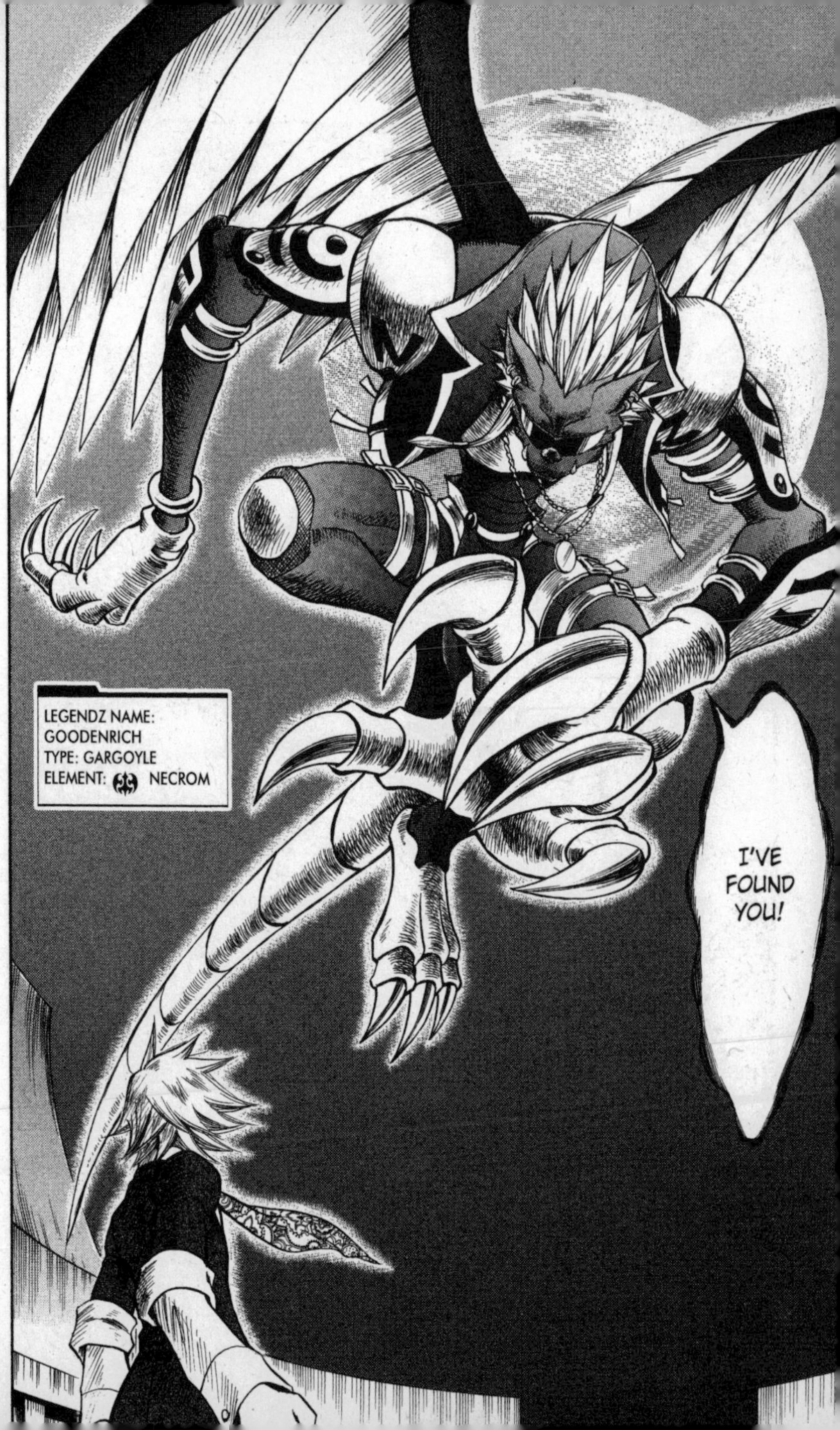
I'VE FOUND YOU!
LEGENDZ NAME: GOODENRICH
TYPE: GARGOYLE
ELEMENT: NECROM

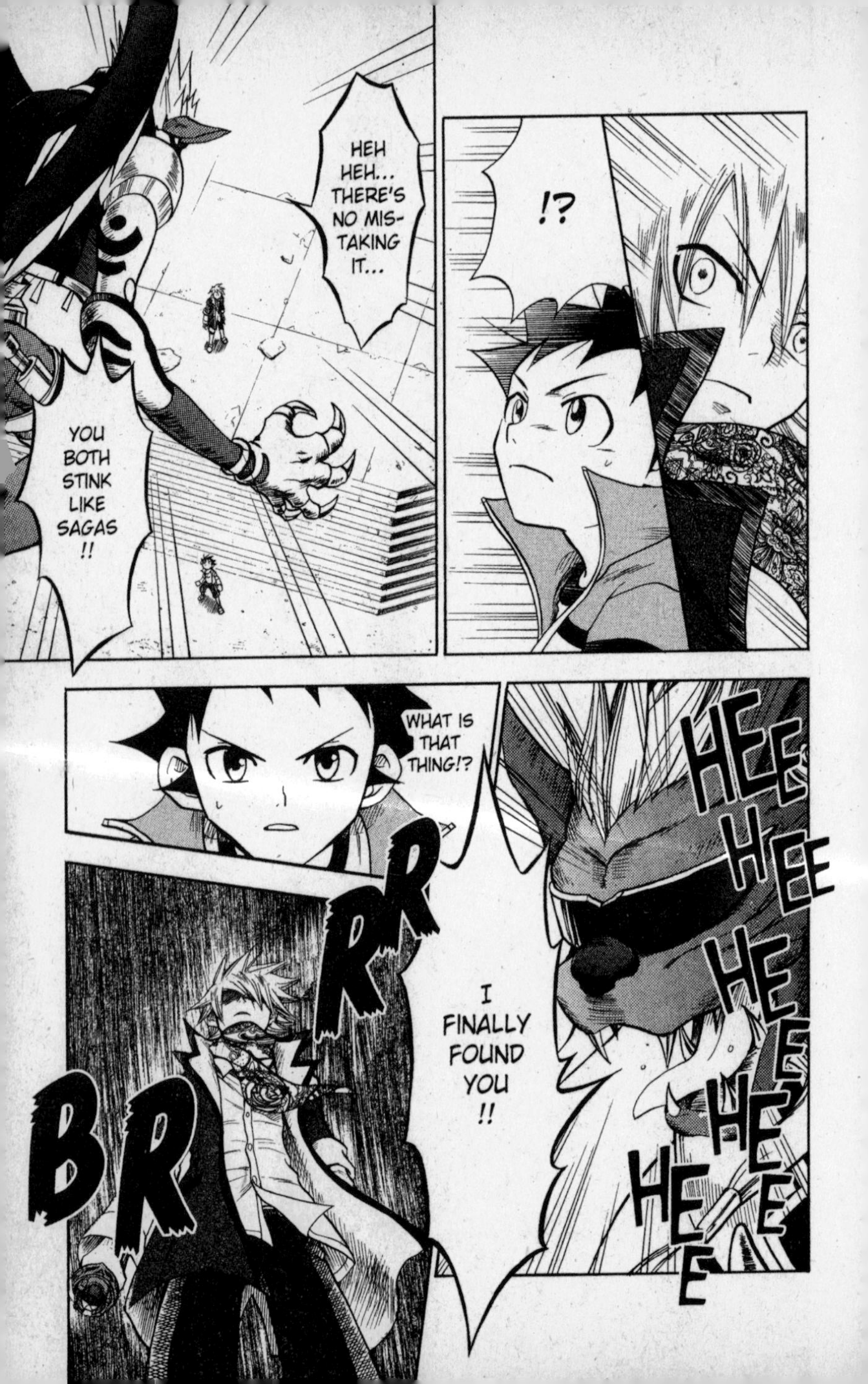
!?
HEH HEH... THERE'S NO MIS-TAKING IT...
YOU BOTH STINK LIKE SAGAS!!
HEE HEE HE HE HE HE HE HEE HE HE
WHAT IS THAT THING!?
BRRR
I FINALLY FOUND YOU!!

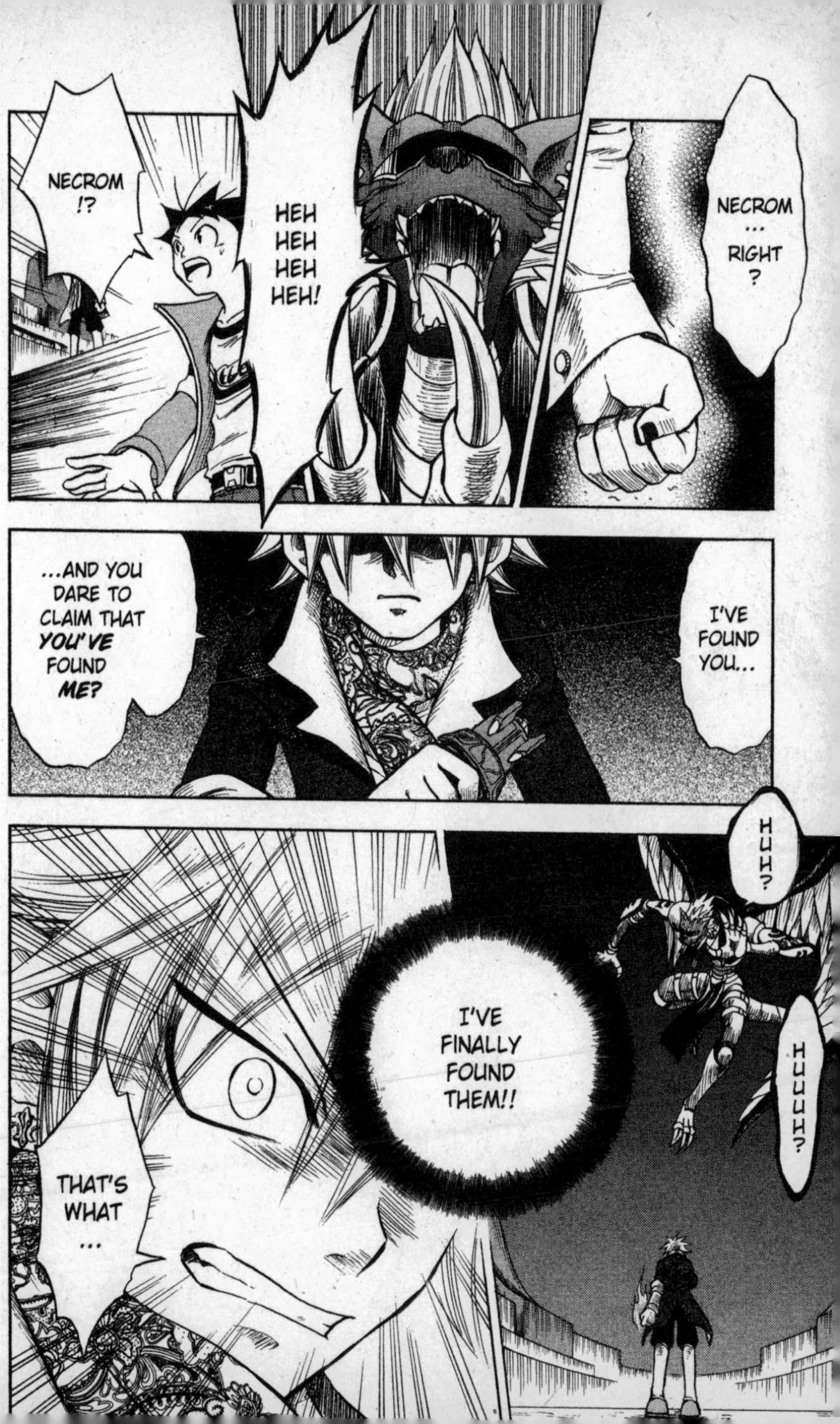
NECROM ... RIGHT?
NECROM !?
HEH HEH HEH HEH!
I'VE FOUND YOU...
...AND YOU DARE TO CLAIM THAT *YOU'VE* FOUND *ME?*
HUH?
HUUUH?
I'VE FINALLY FOUND THEM!!
THAT'S WHAT ...

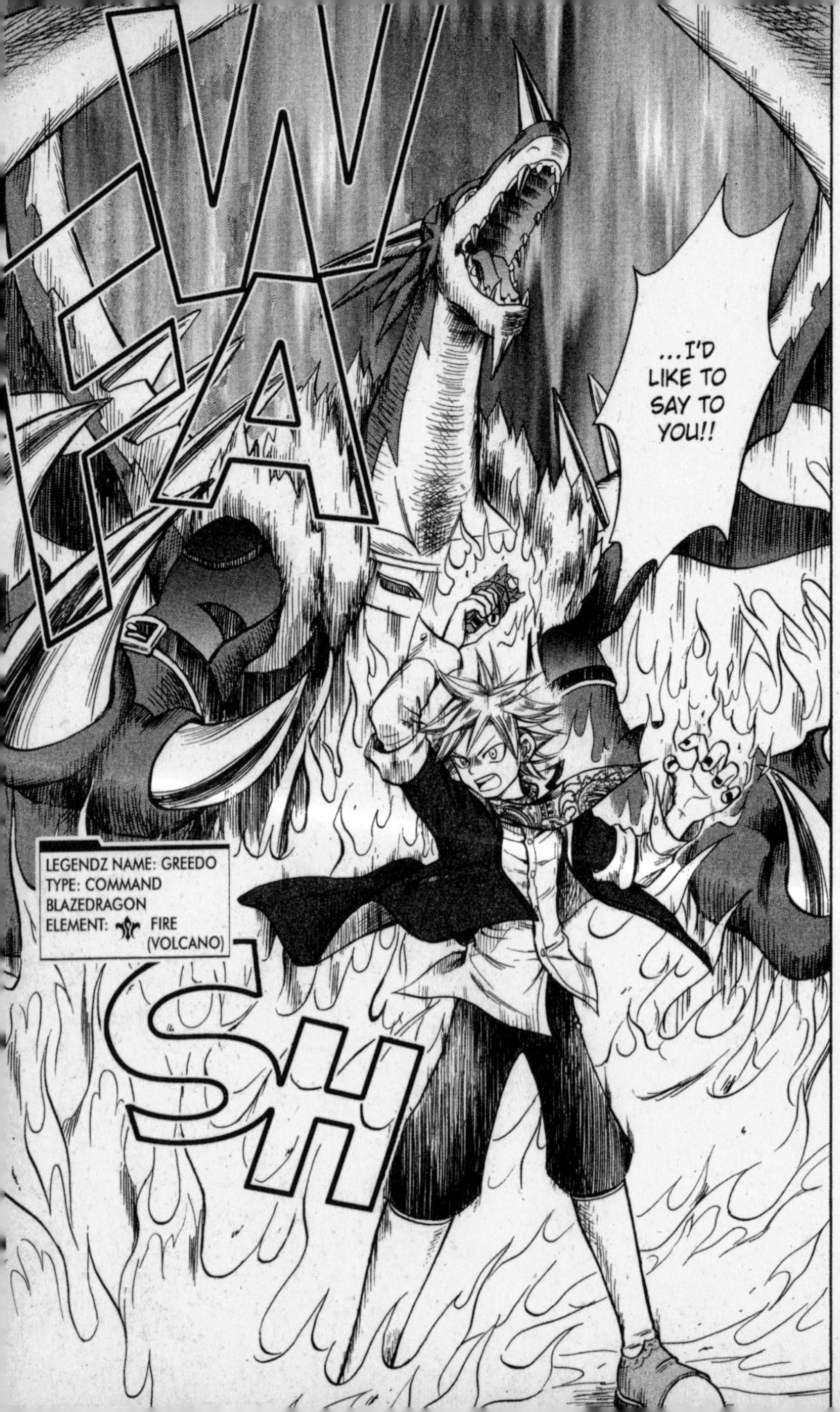
...I'D LIKE TO SAY TO YOU!!
LEGENDZ NAME: GREEDO
TYPE: COMMAND
BLAZEDRAGON
ELEMENT: FIRE
(VOLCANO)
SH

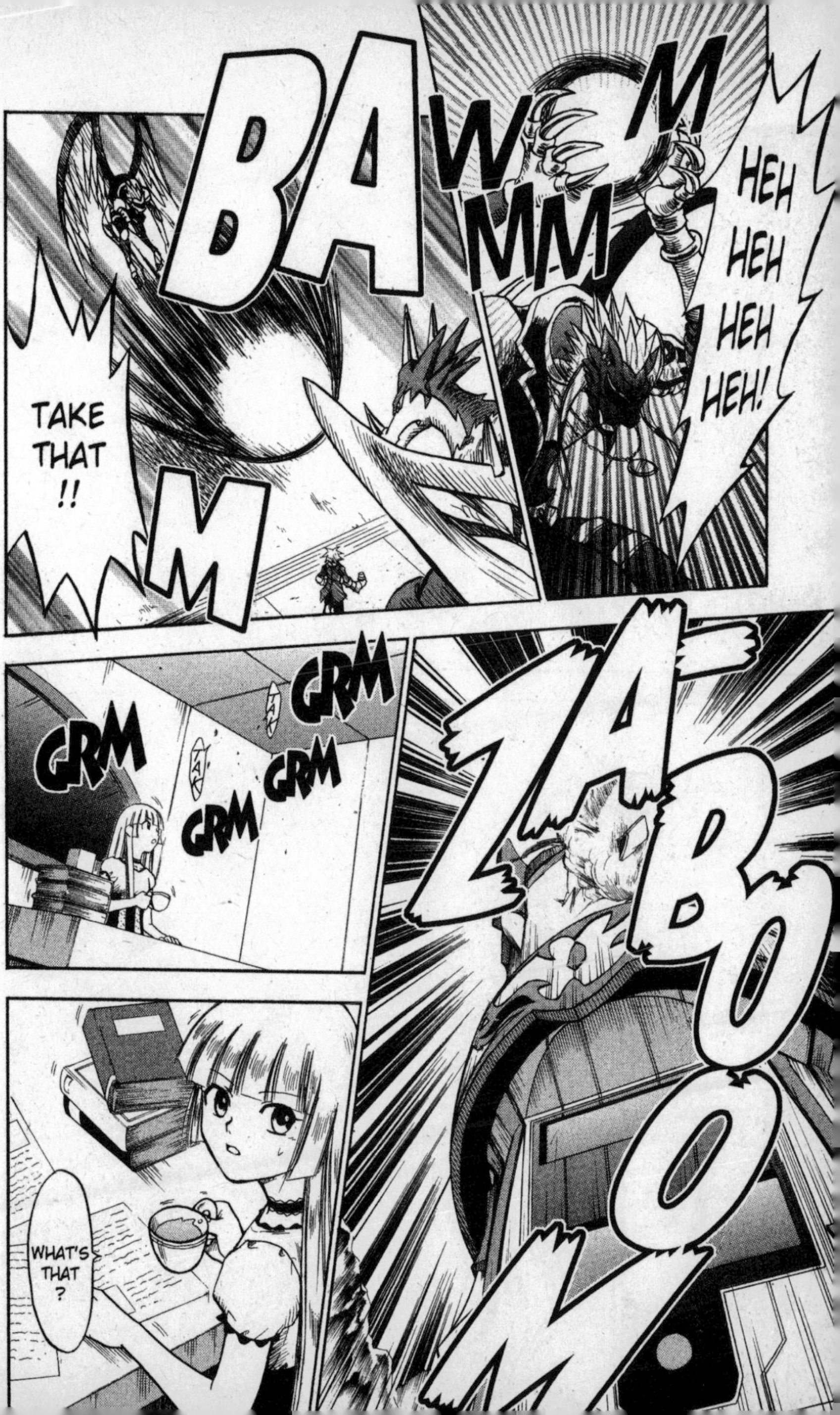
HEH HEH HEH HEH!
BAWMMMM
TAKE THAT !!
ZABOOM
GRM
GRM
GRM
GRM
TAK
TAK
WHAT'S THAT ?

READ THIS WAY

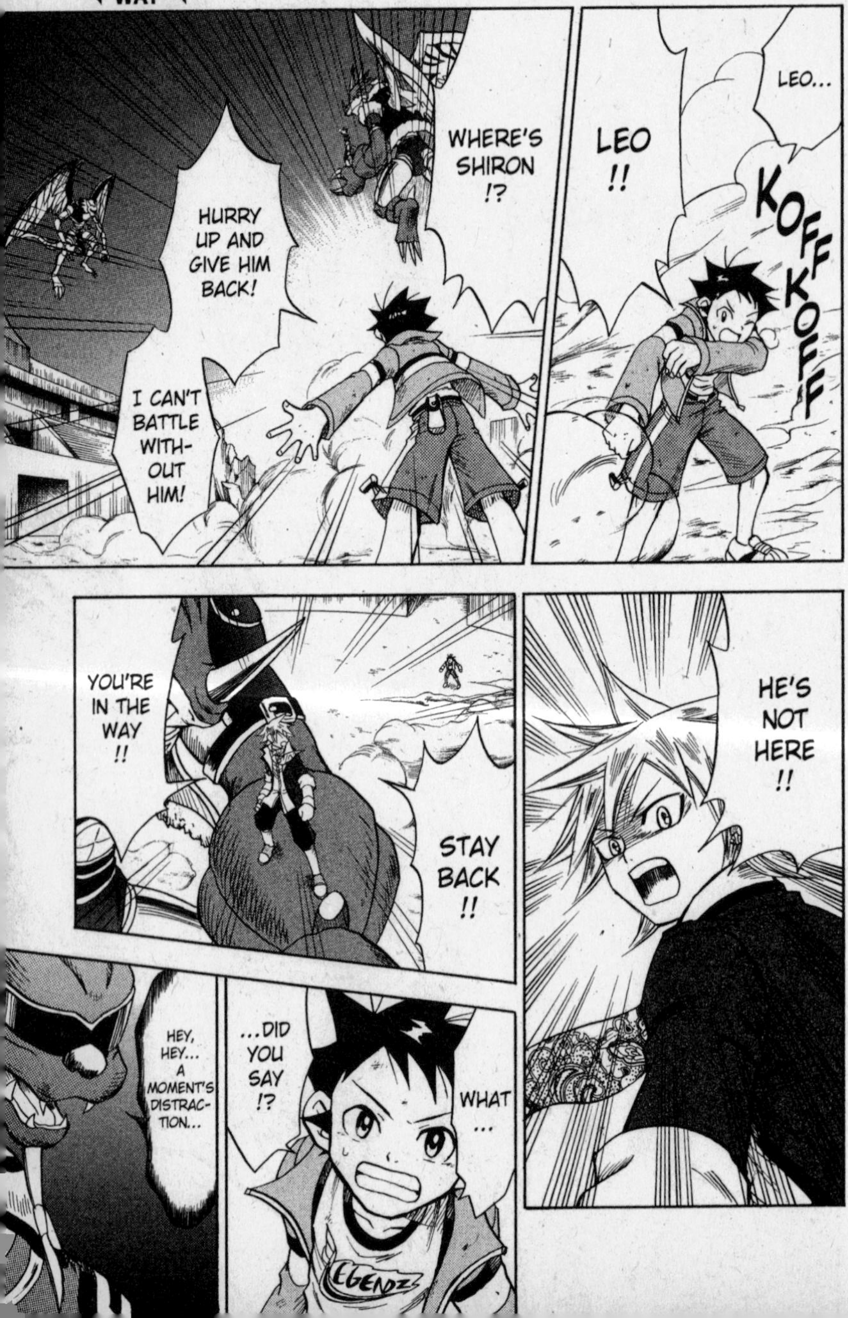
LEO...
KOFF KOFF KOFF
LEO !!
WHERE'S SHIRON !?
HURRY UP AND GIVE HIM BACK!
I CAN'T BATTLE WITH-OUT HIM!
HE'S NOT HERE !!
STAY BACK !!
YOU'RE IN THE WAY !!
WHAT ...
...DID YOU SAY !?
HEY, HEY... A MOMENT'S DISTRAC-TION...

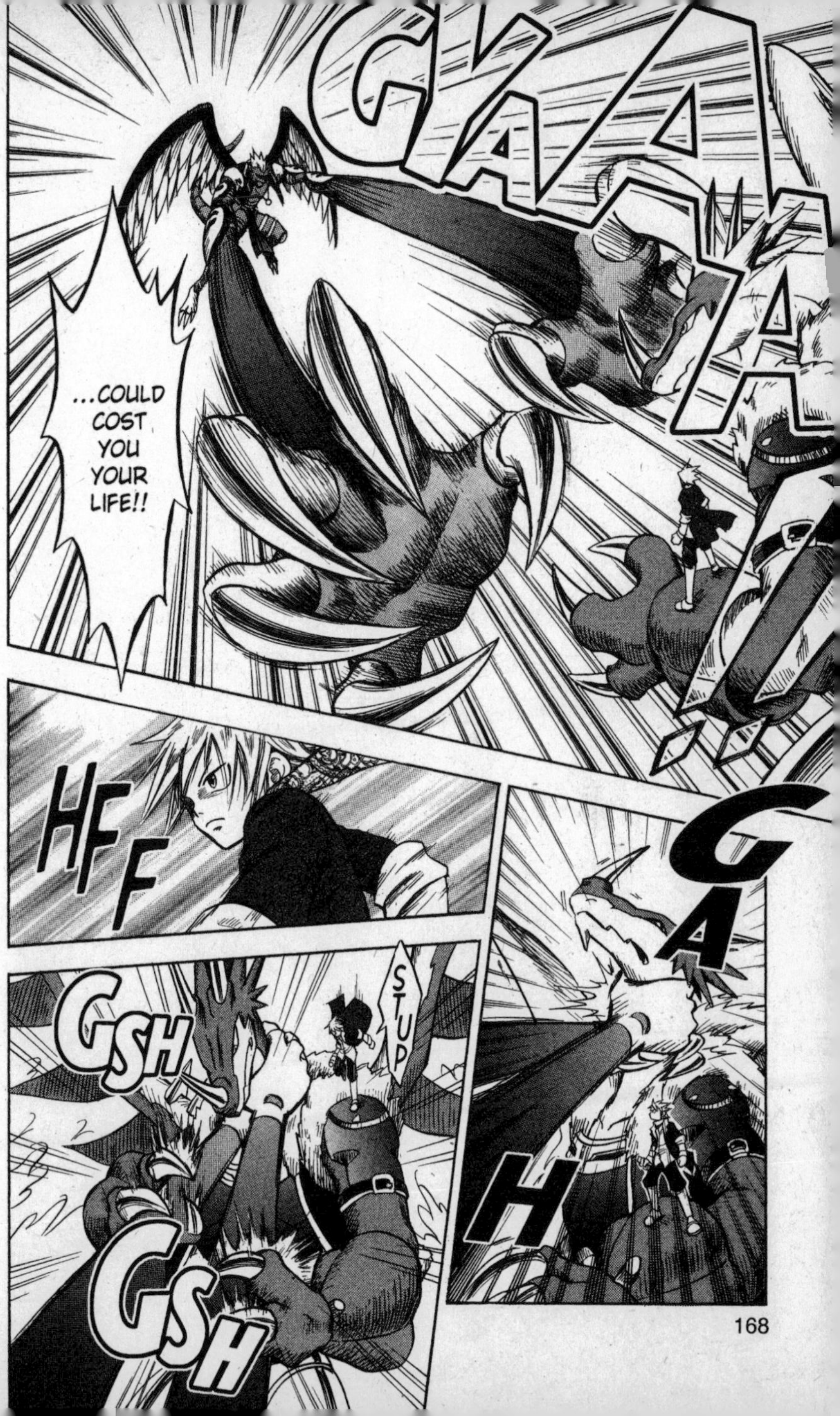
GAAAAAH
...COULD COST YOU YOUR LIFE!!
GAH
HFF
GSH
STUP
GSH

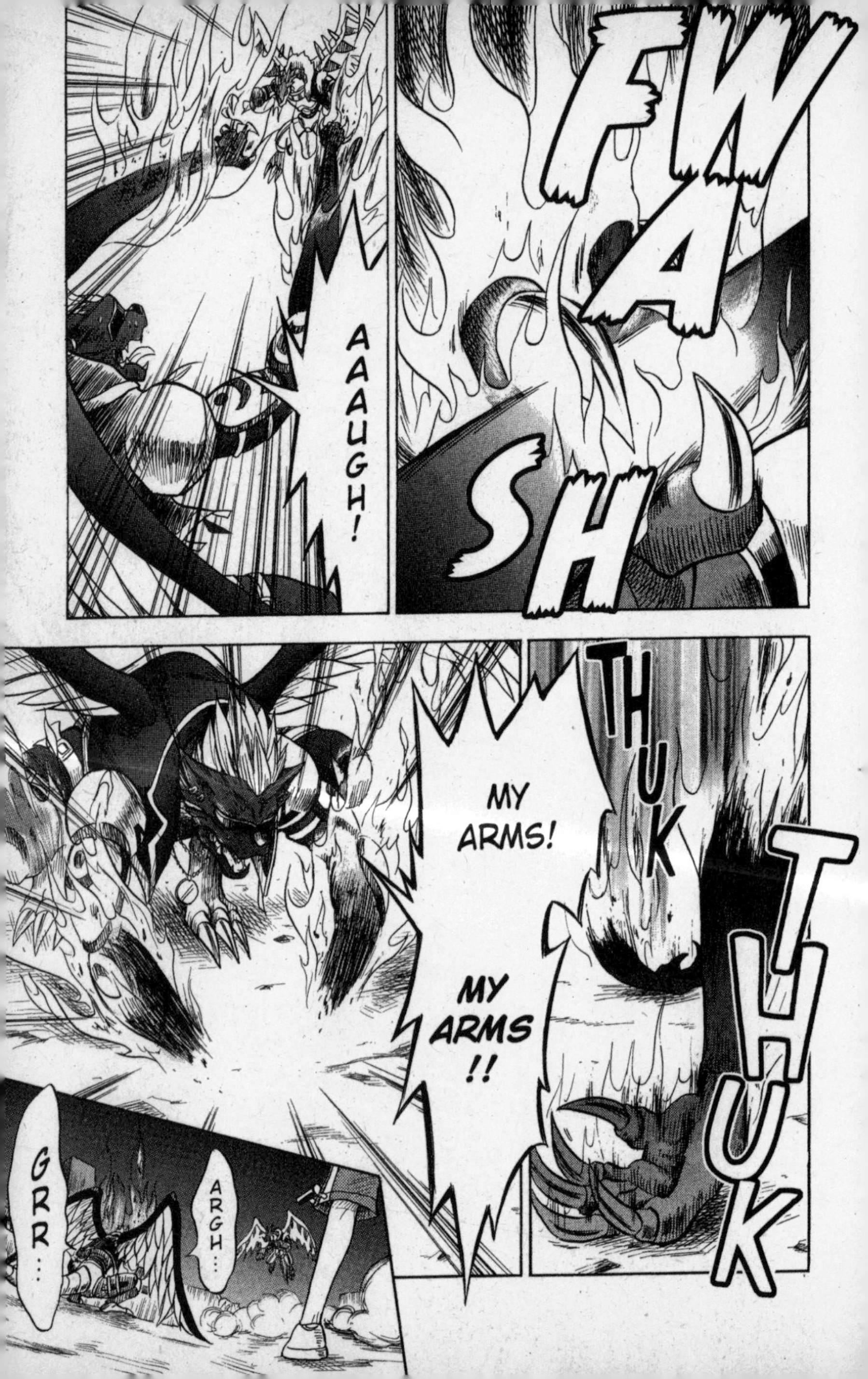
FWASH
AAAUGH!
THUK
THUK
MY ARMS!
MY ARMS!!
ARGH...
GRR...

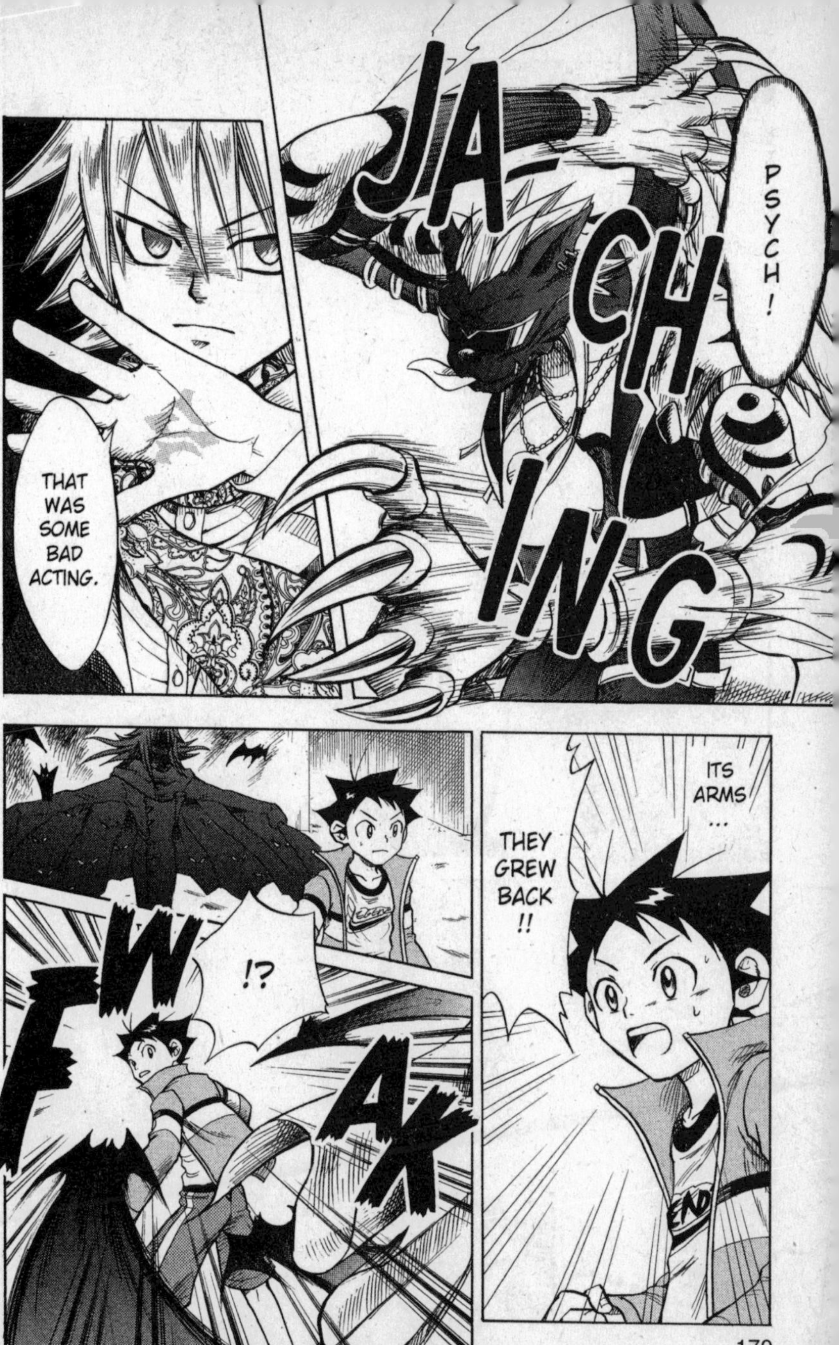
PSYCH!
JA-CH-ING
THAT WAS SOME BAD ACTING.
ITS ARMS...
THEY GREW BACK!!
!?
FWAK

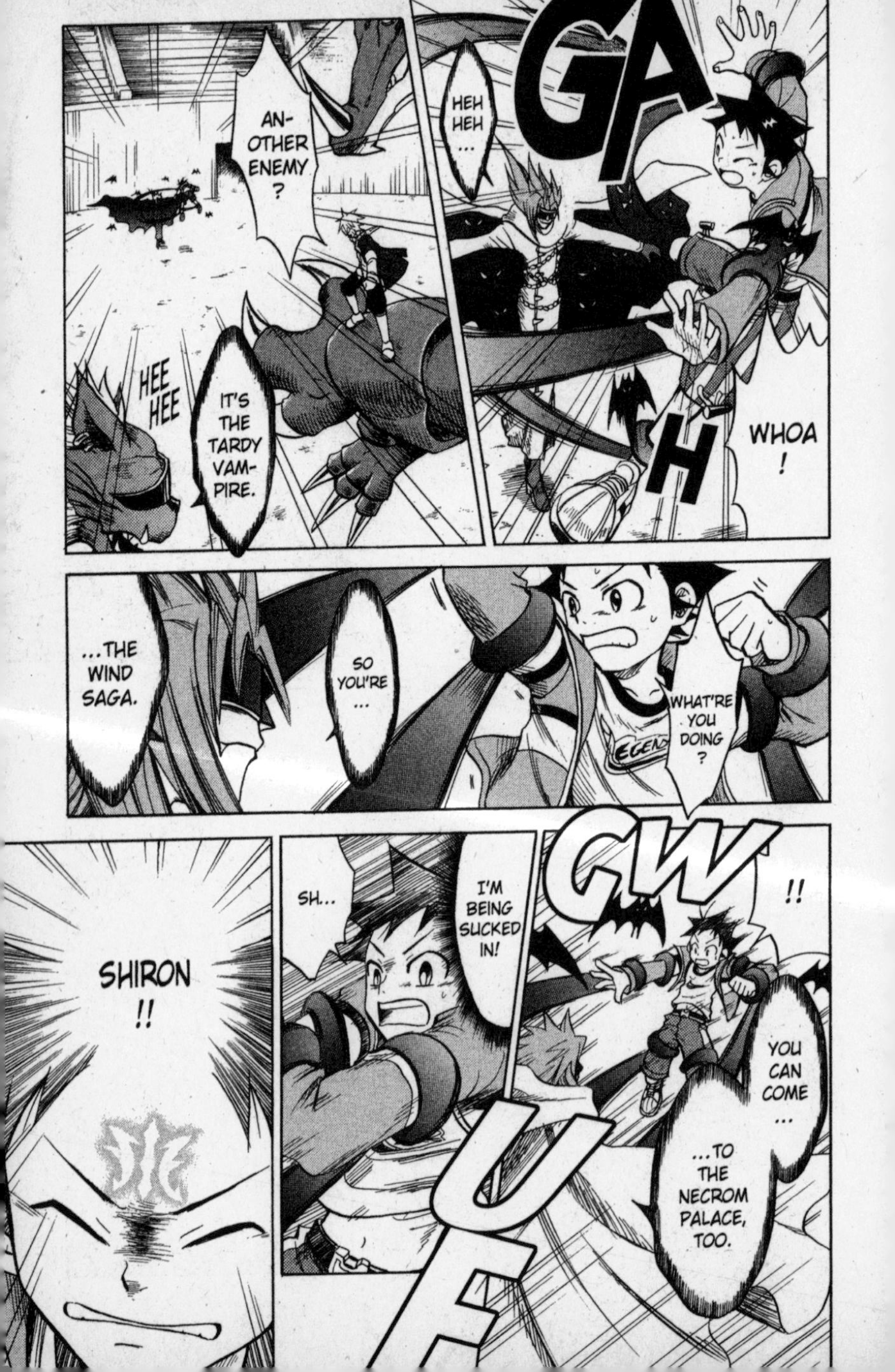
GA
HEH HEH ...
WHOA !
H
AN-OTHER ENEMY ?
IT'S THE TARDY VAM-PIRE.
HEE HEE
WHAT'RE YOU DOING ?
SO YOU'RE ...
...THE WIND SAGA.
GW
!!
I'M BEING SUCKED IN!
SH...
YOU CAN COME ...
...TO THE NECROM PALACE, TOO.
U
F
SHIRON !!

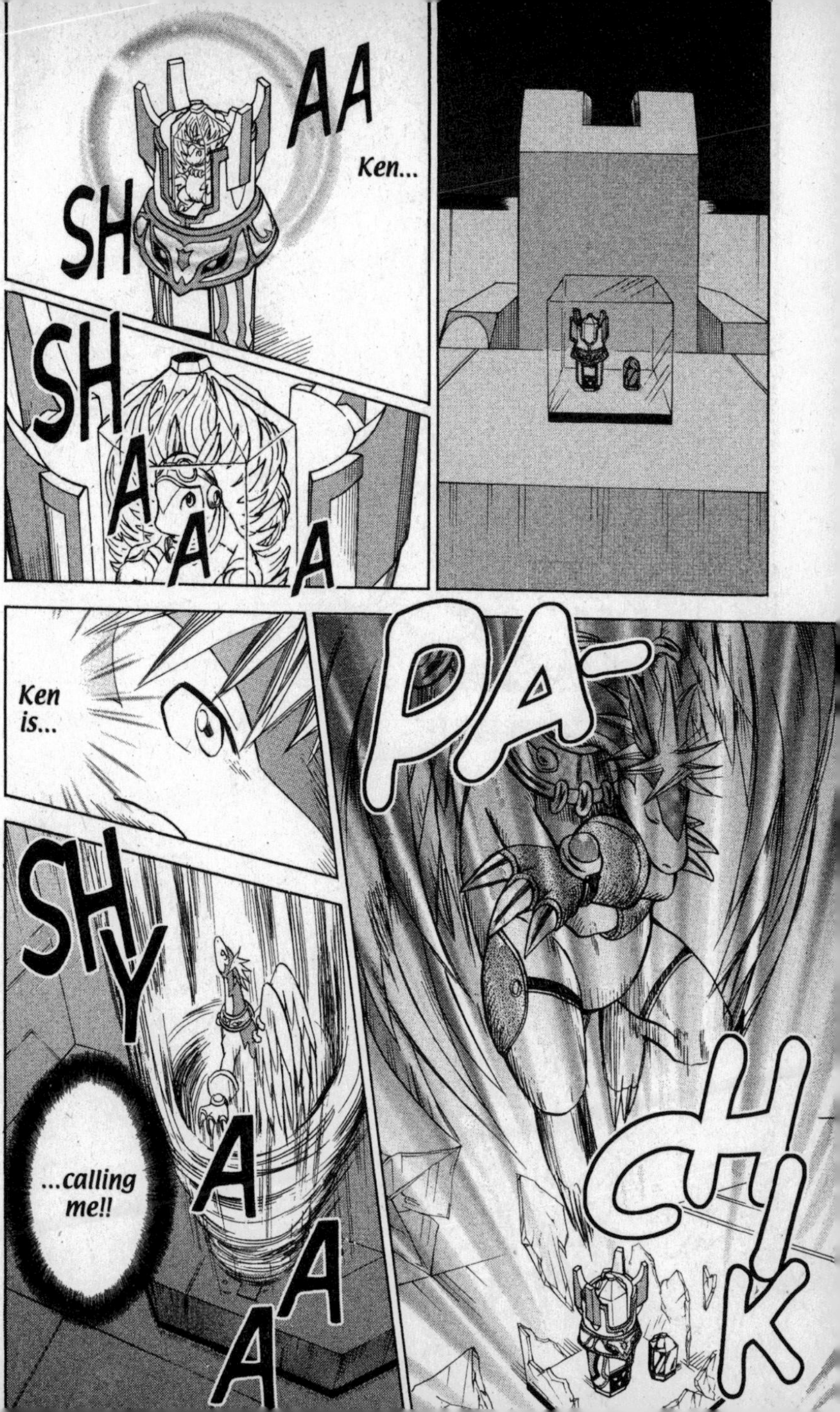
SHAA
Ken...
SHAAAA
PA-CHIK
Ken is...
SHYAAAA
...calling me!!

READ THIS WAY

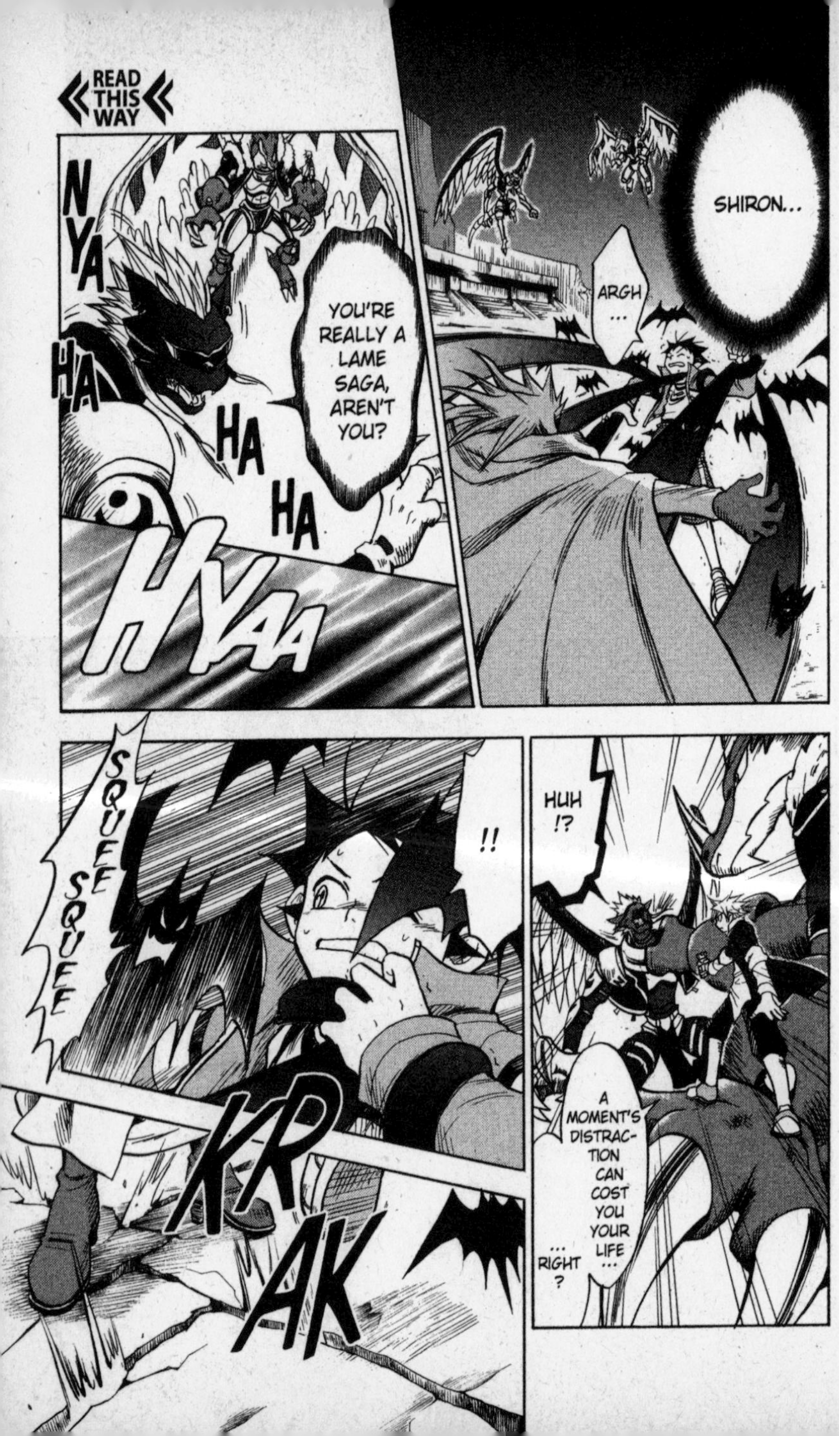
SHIRON...
ARGH ...
NYAHA
HA
HA
YOU'RE REALLY A LAME SAGA, AREN'T YOU?
HYAA
HUH !?
A MOMENT'S DISTRACTION CAN COST YOU YOUR LIFE ...
... RIGHT ?
!!
SQUEE SQUEE
KRAK

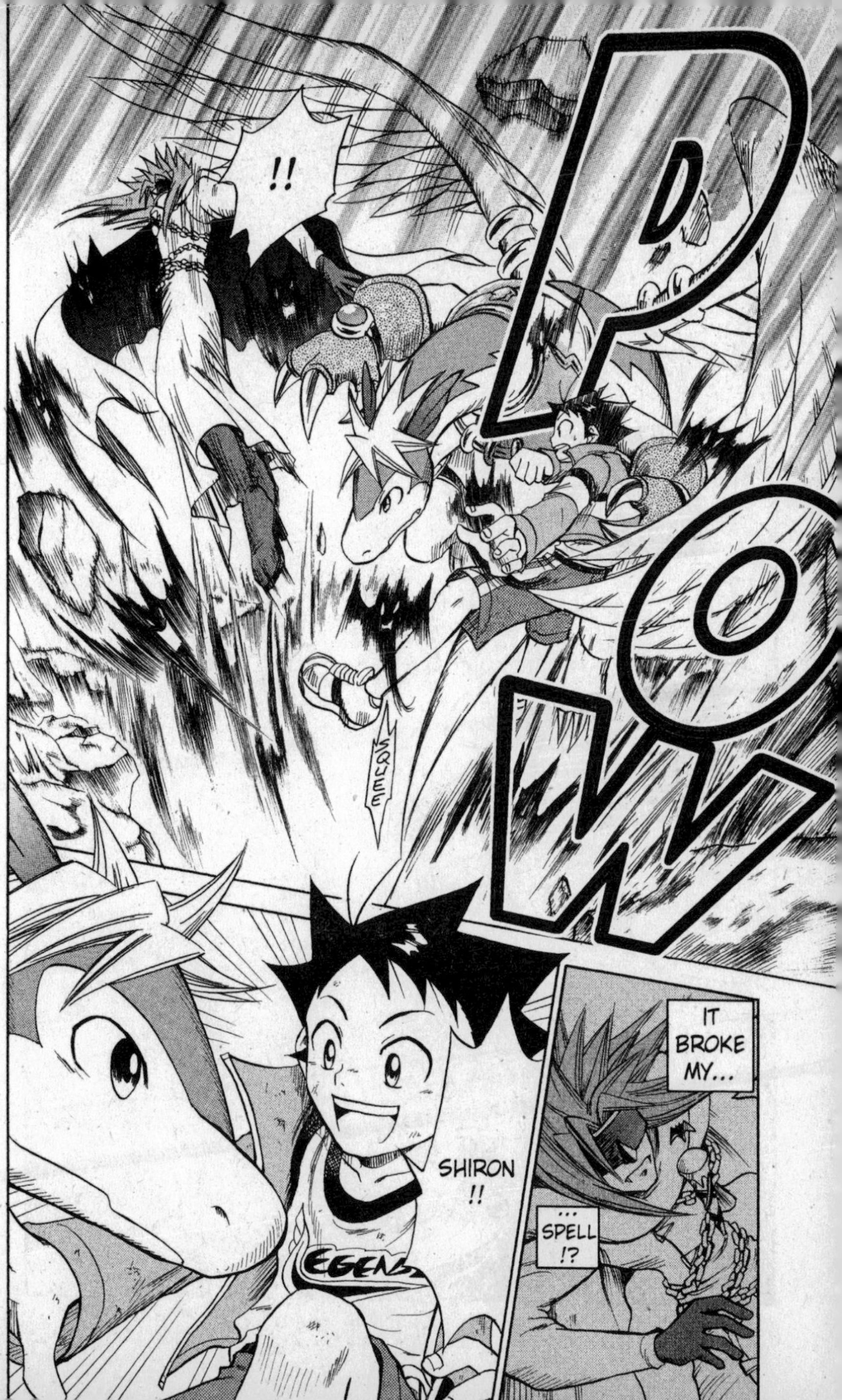
!!
POW
SQUEE
IT BROKE MY...
...SPELL!?
SHIRON!!

READ THIS WAY

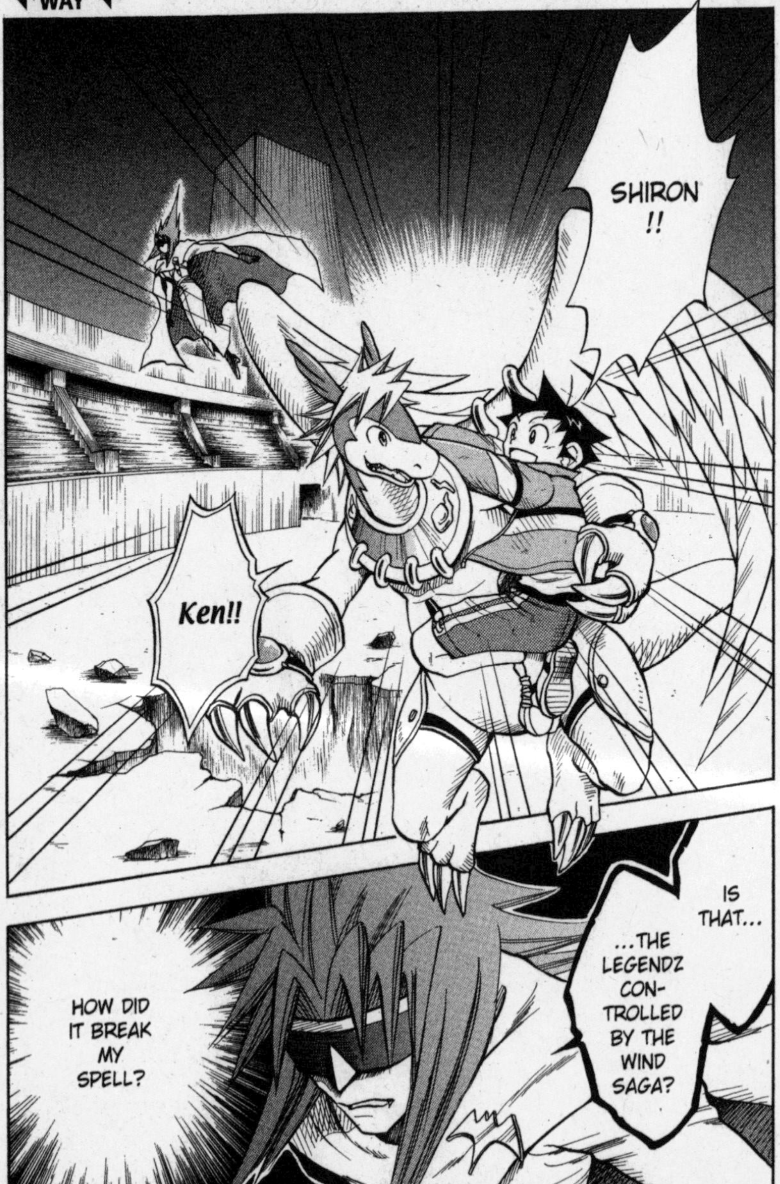
SHIRON !!
Ken!!
IS THAT...
...THE LEGENDZ CON-TROLLED BY THE WIND SAGA?
HOW DID IT BREAK MY SPELL?

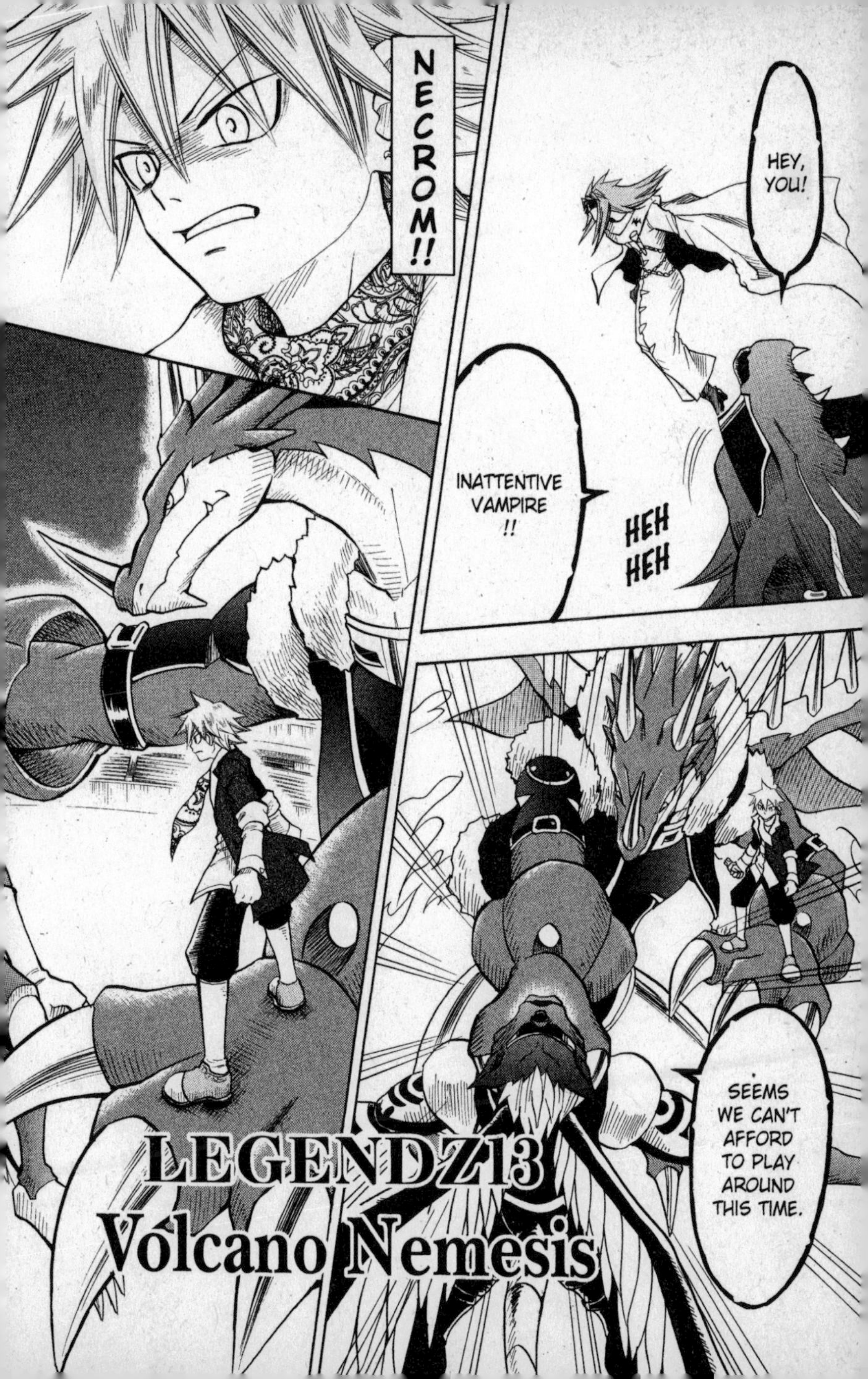
HEY, YOU!
INATTENTIVE VAMPIRE !!
HEH HEH
NECROM!!
SEEMS WE CAN'T AFFORD TO PLAY AROUND THIS TIME.
LEGENDZ 13
Volcano Nemesis

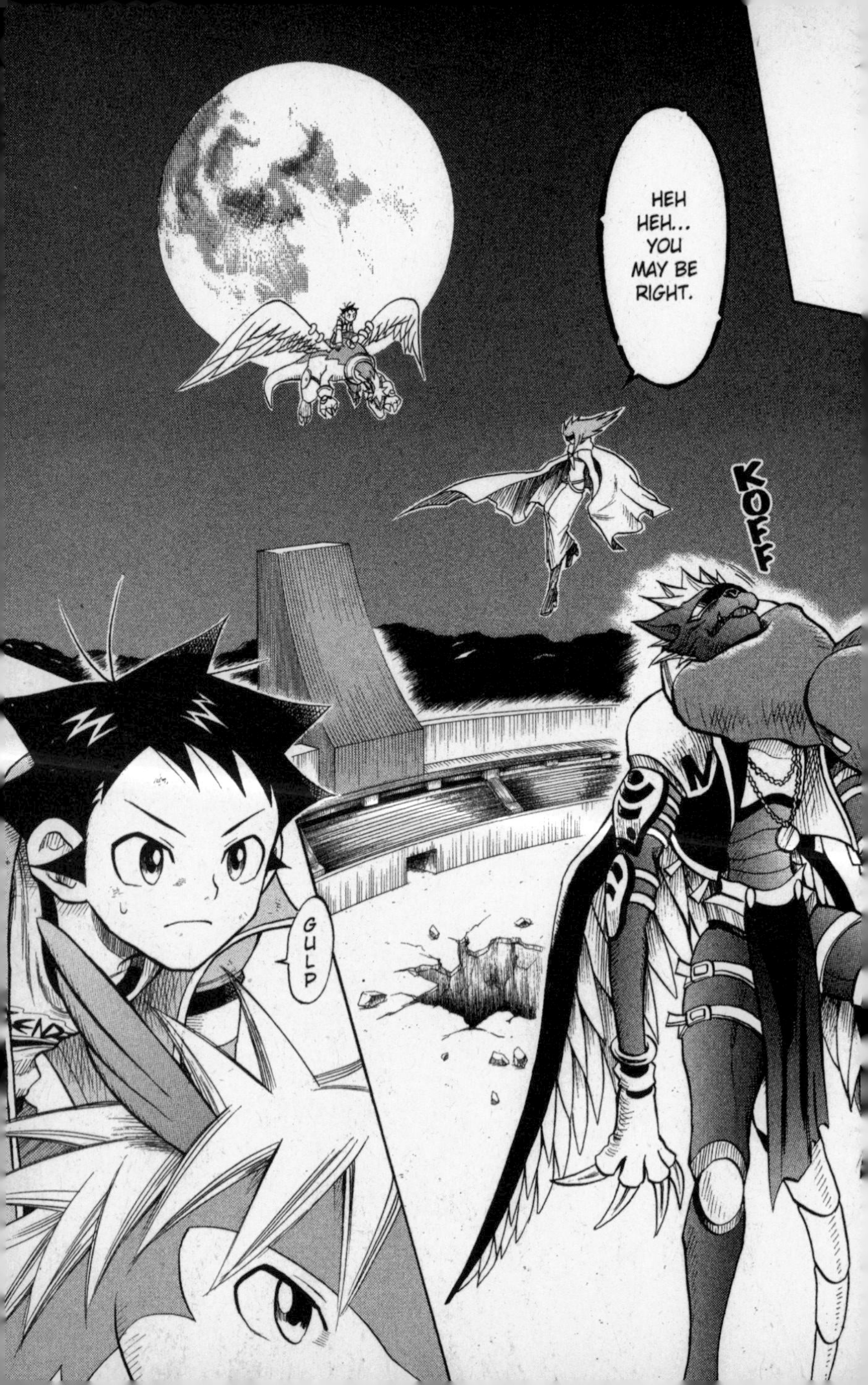
HEH HEH... YOU MAY BE RIGHT.
KOFF
GULP

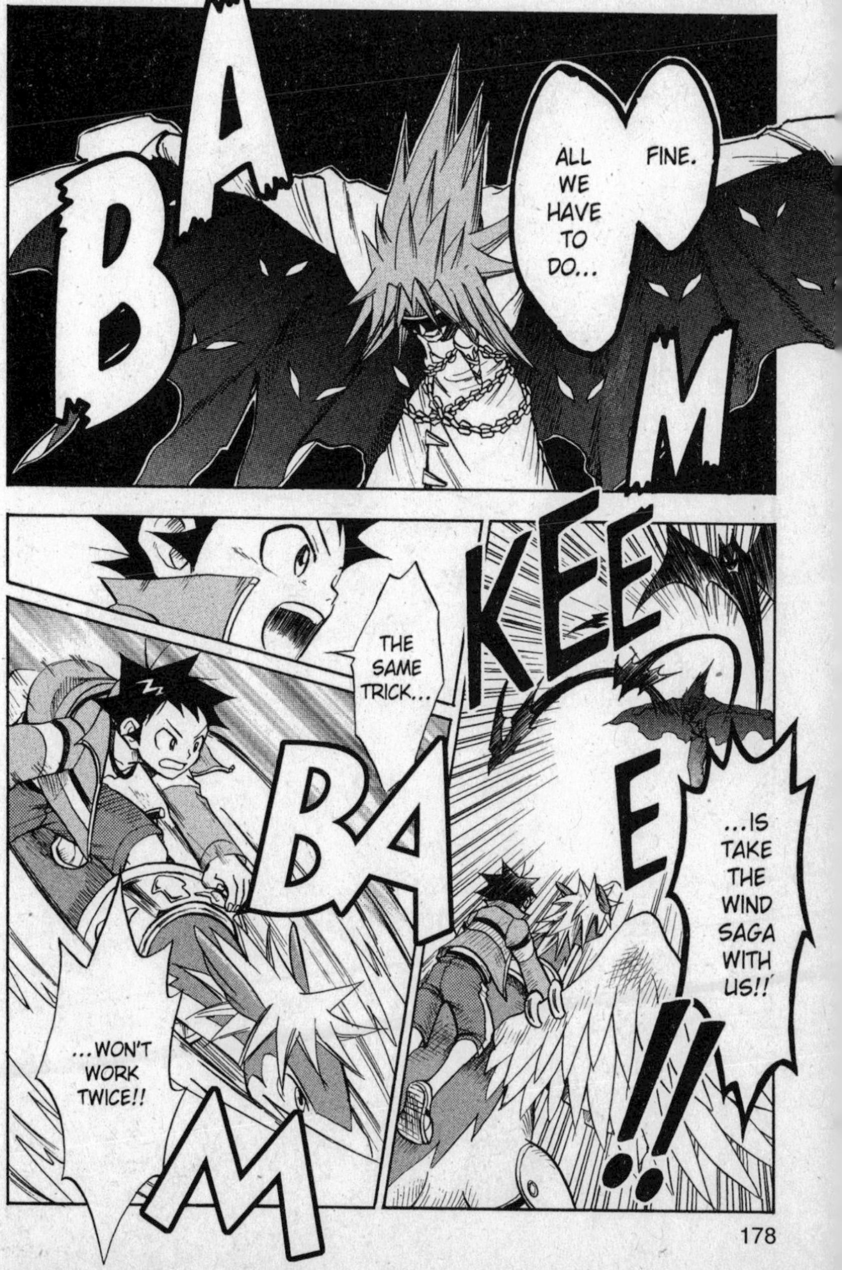

FINE.
ALL WE HAVE TO DO...
BAAM
KEEE!!
THE SAME TRICK...
...IS TAKE THE WIND SAGA WITH US!!
BAM
...WON'T WORK TWICE!!

READ THIS WAY

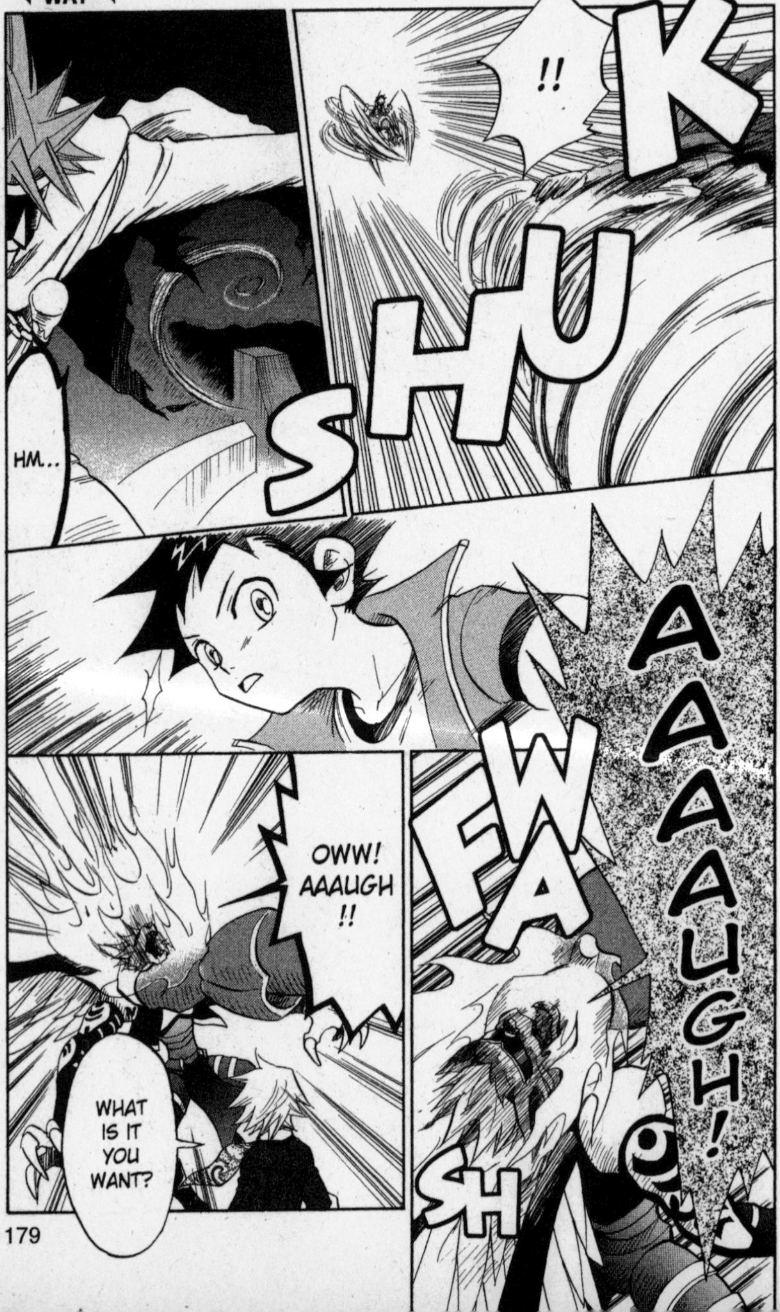
!!
SHUK
HM...
AAAAUGH!
FWA
SH
OWW! AAAUGH !!
WHAT IS IT YOU WANT?

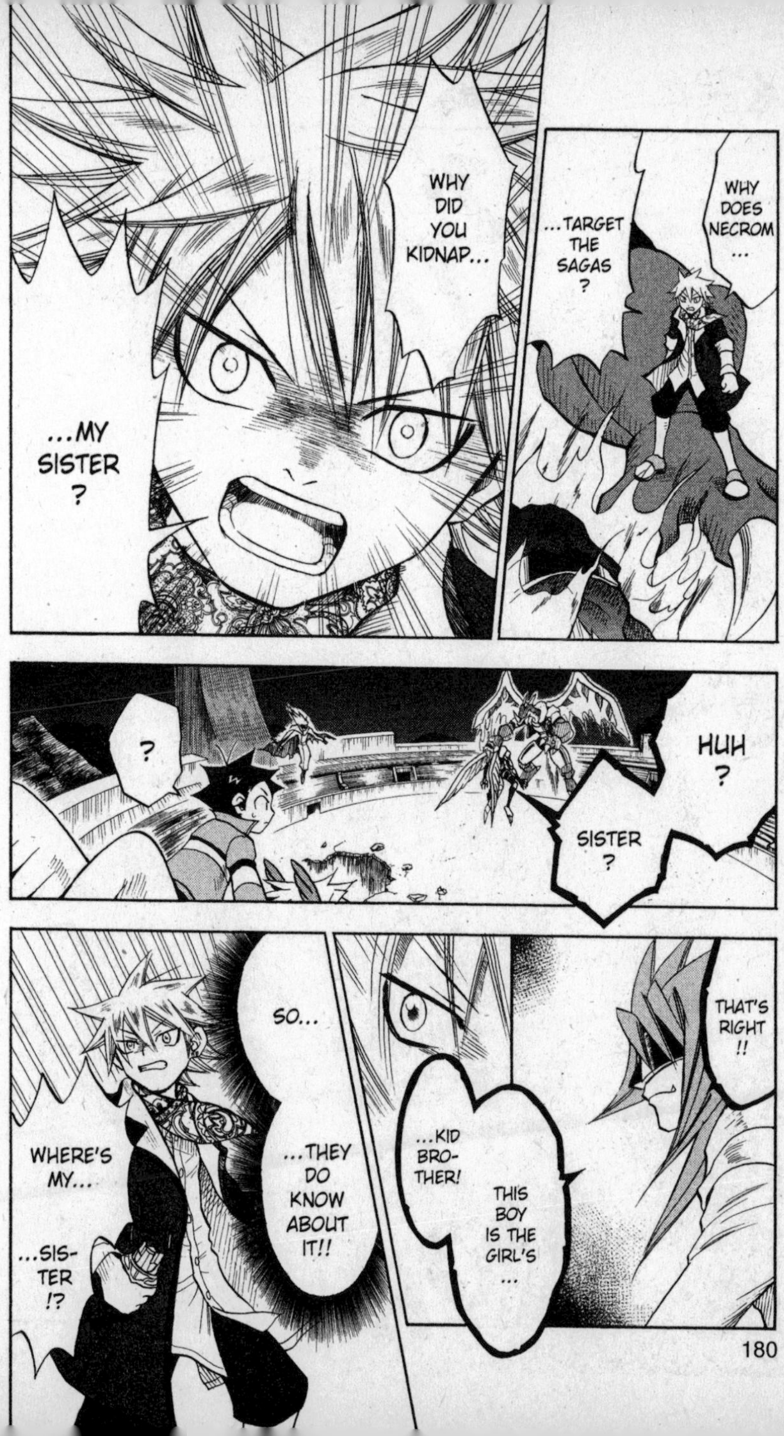
WHY DOES NECROM ...
...TARGET THE SAGAS ?
WHY DID YOU KIDNAP...
...MY SISTER ?
HUH ?
SISTER ?
?
THAT'S RIGHT !!
THIS BOY IS THE GIRL'S ...
...KID BRO- THER!
SO...
...THEY DO KNOW ABOUT IT!!
WHERE'S MY...
...SIS- TER !?

READ THIS WAY

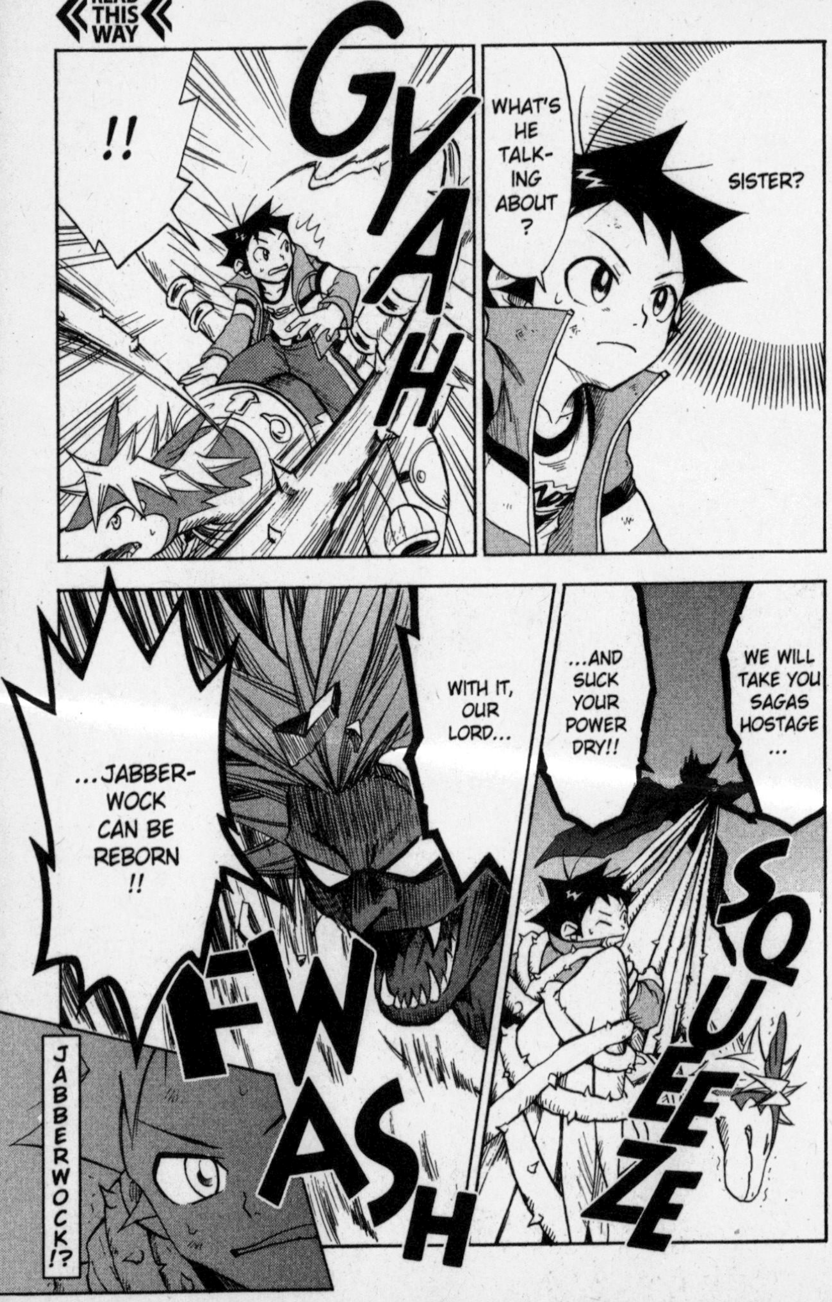

SISTER?
WHAT'S HE TALKING ABOUT?
GYAH
!!
WE WILL TAKE YOU SAGAS HOSTAGE...
...AND SUCK YOUR POWER DRY!!
SQUEEZE
WITH IT, OUR LORD...
...JABBERWOCK CAN BE REBORN!!
FWASH
JABBERWOCK!?

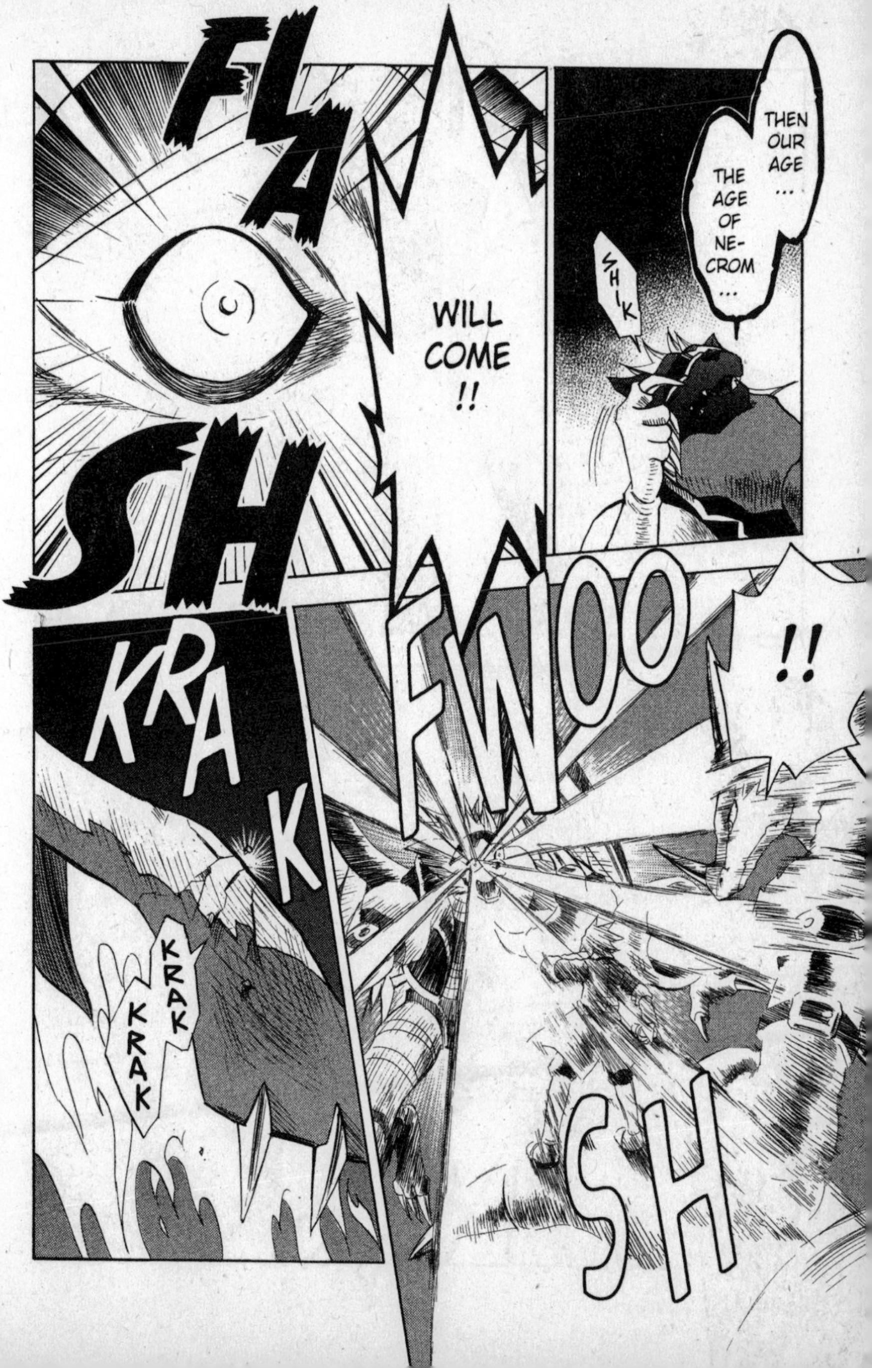
THEN OUR AGE ...
THE AGE OF NE-CROM ...
SHIK
FLASH
WILL COME !!
FWOOSH
!!
KRAK
KRAK
KRAK

READ THIS WAY

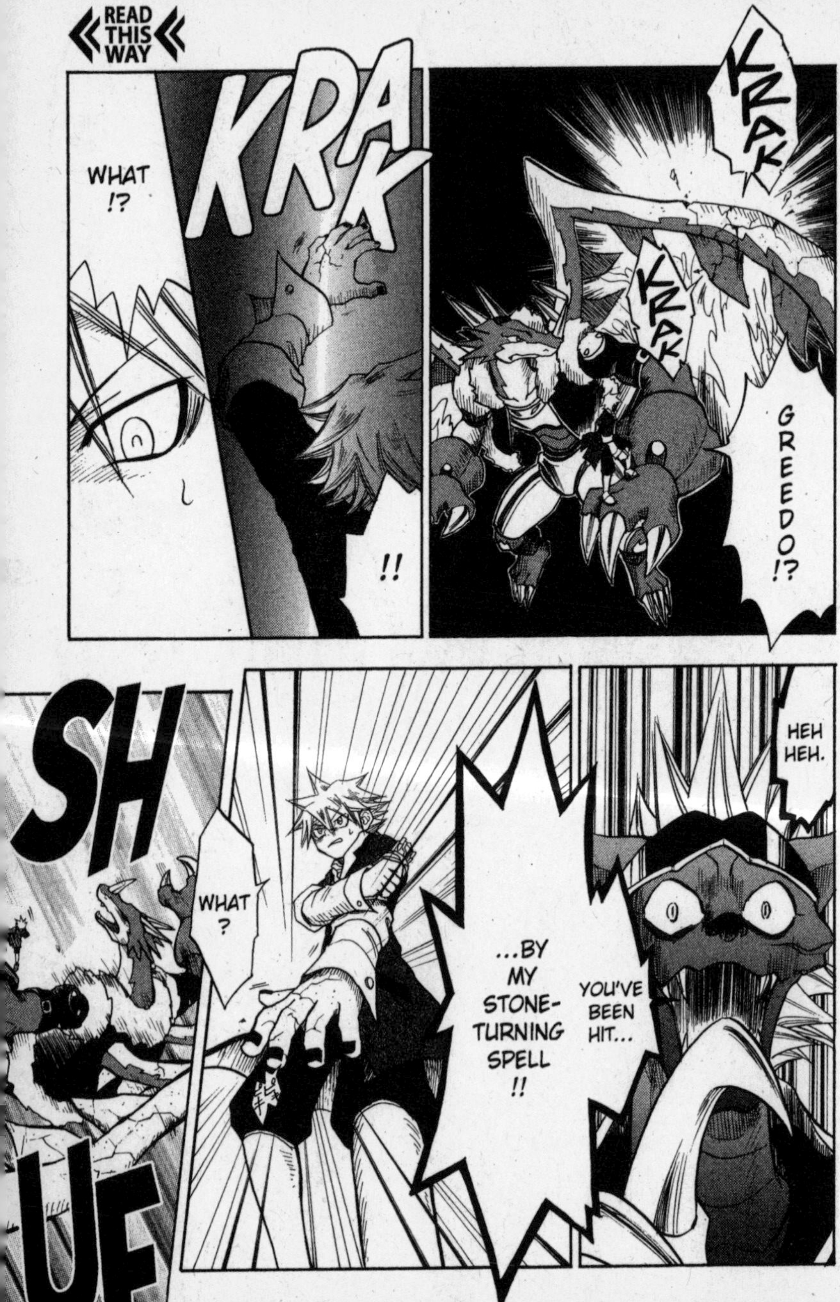
KRAK
KRAK
GREEDO!?
KRAK
WHAT !?
!!
HEH HEH.
YOU'VE BEEN HIT...
...BY MY STONE-TURNING SPELL !!
WHAT ?
SHUF

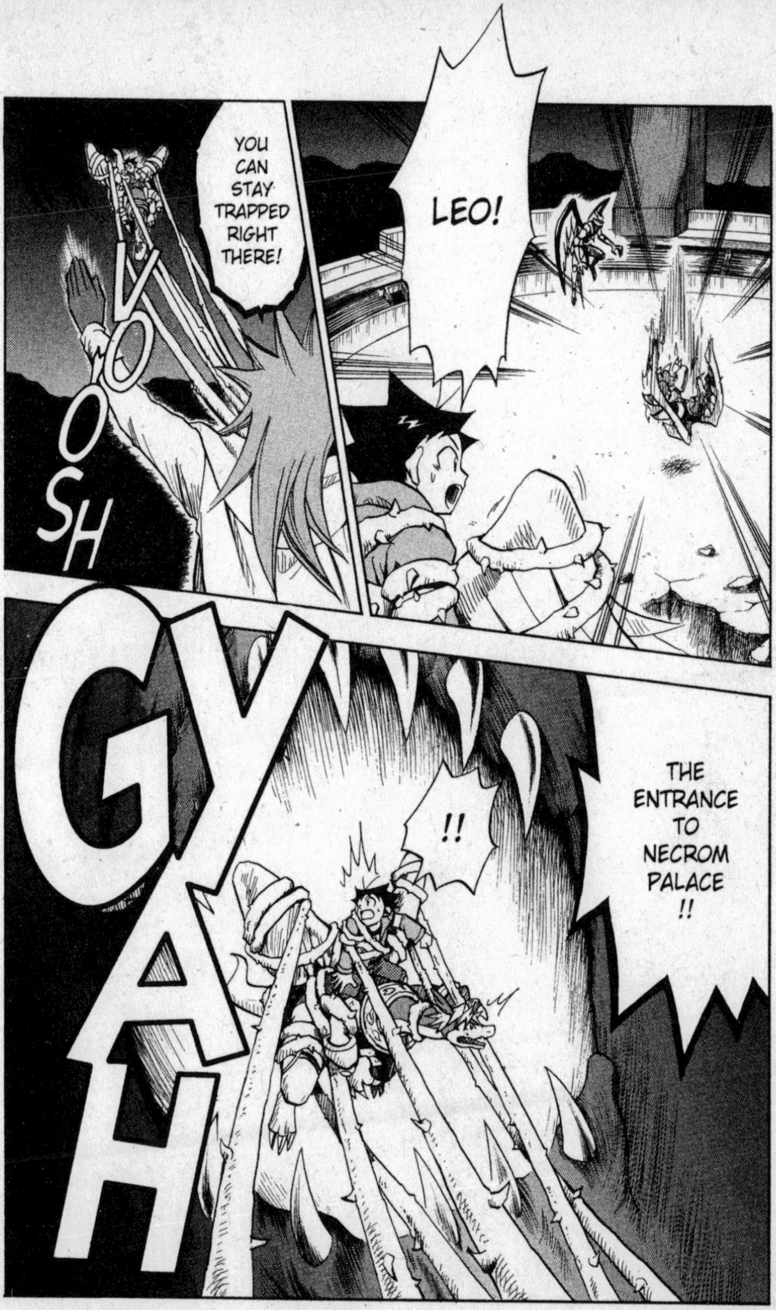
LEO!
YOU CAN STAY TRAPPED RIGHT THERE!
VOOOSH
THE ENTRANCE TO NECROM PALACE !!
!!
GYAH

READ THIS WAY

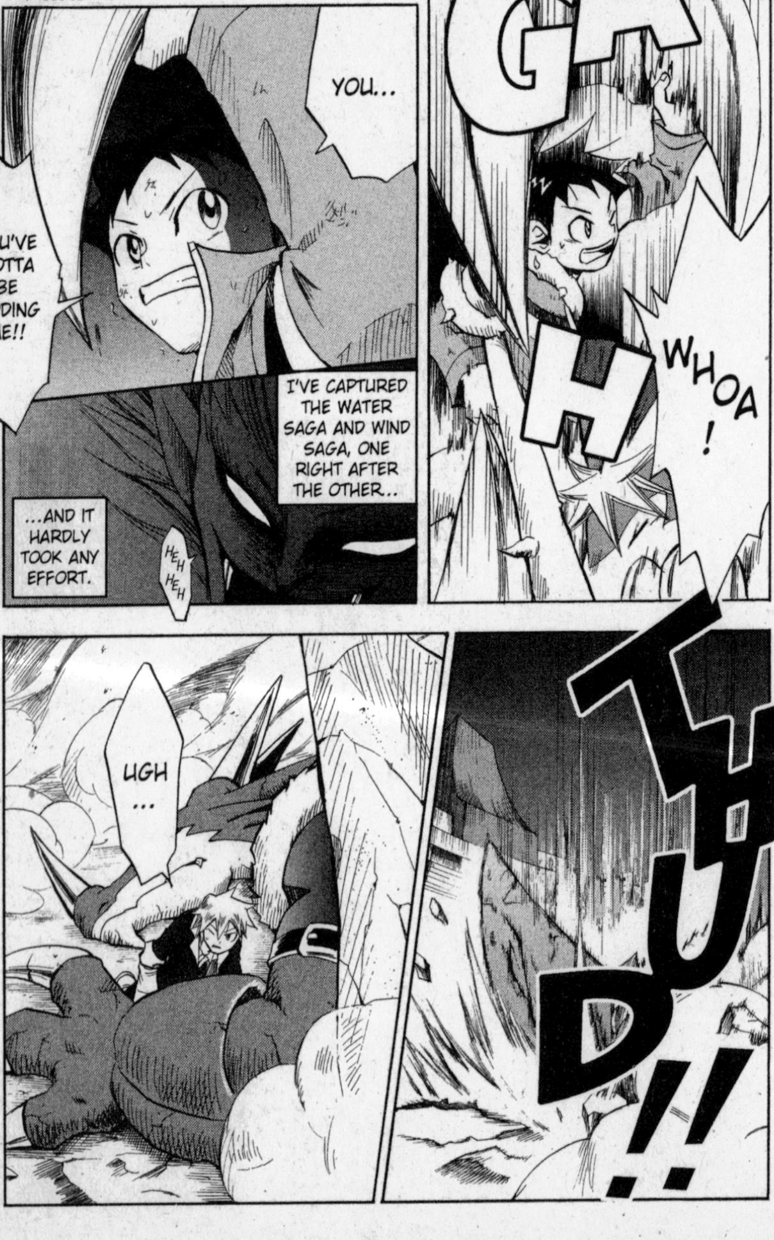
GA
H
WHOA!
YOU...
YOU'VE GOTTA BE KIDDING ME!!
I'VE CAPTURED THE WATER SAGA AND WIND SAGA, ONE RIGHT AFTER THE OTHER...
...AND IT HARDLY TOOK ANY EFFORT.
HEH HEH
THUD!!
UGH...

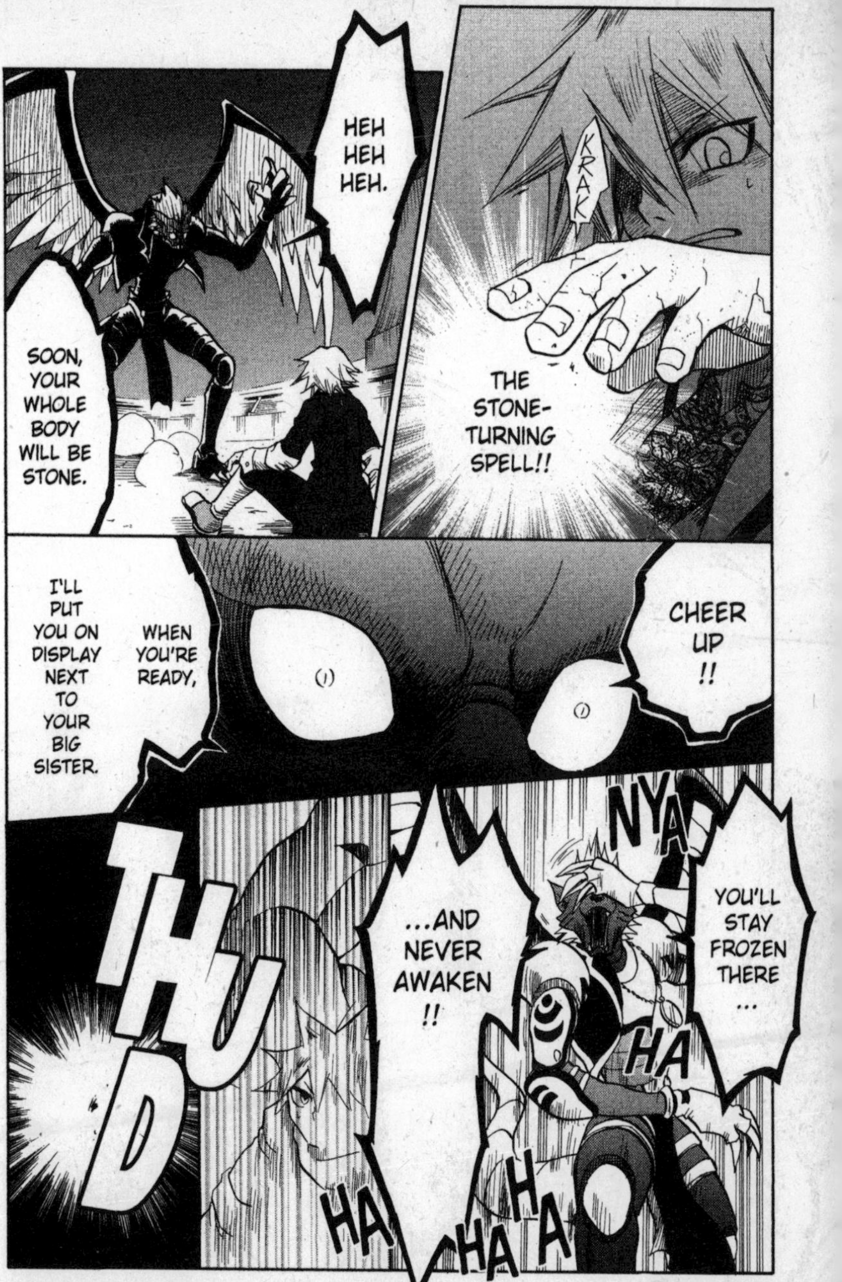
KRAK
THE STONE-TURNING SPELL!!
HEH HEH HEH.
SOON, YOUR WHOLE BODY WILL BE STONE.
CHEER UP!!
WHEN YOU'RE READY,
I'LL PUT YOU ON DISPLAY NEXT TO YOUR BIG SISTER.
NYA
YOU'LL STAY FROZEN THERE...
...AND NEVER AWAKEN!!
HA
THUD
HA
HA
HA
HA

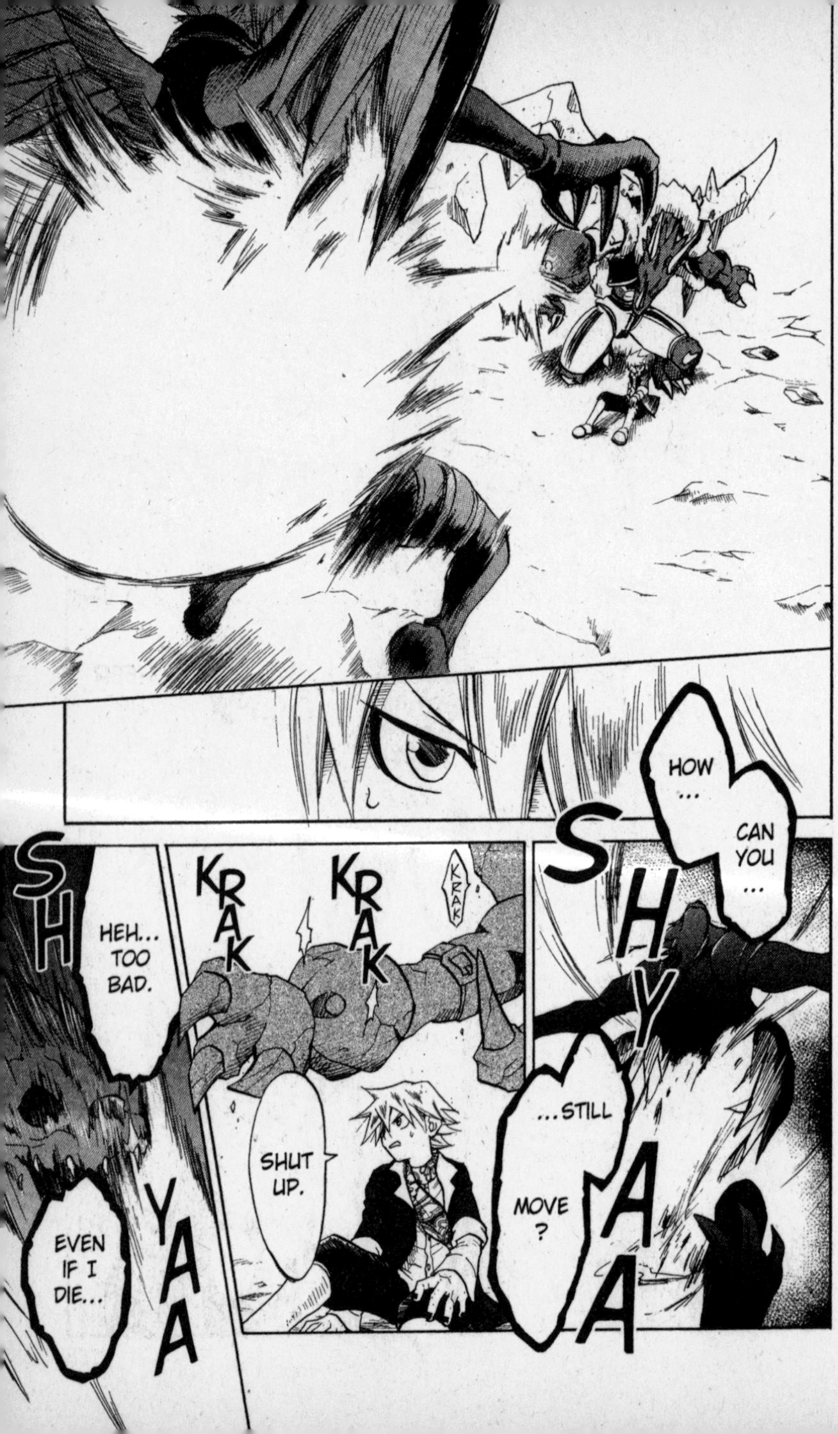
HOW... CAN YOU...
SHYAAA
...STILL MOVE?
KRAK
KRAK
KRAK
SHUT UP.
SHYAA
HEH... TOO BAD.
EVEN IF I DIE...

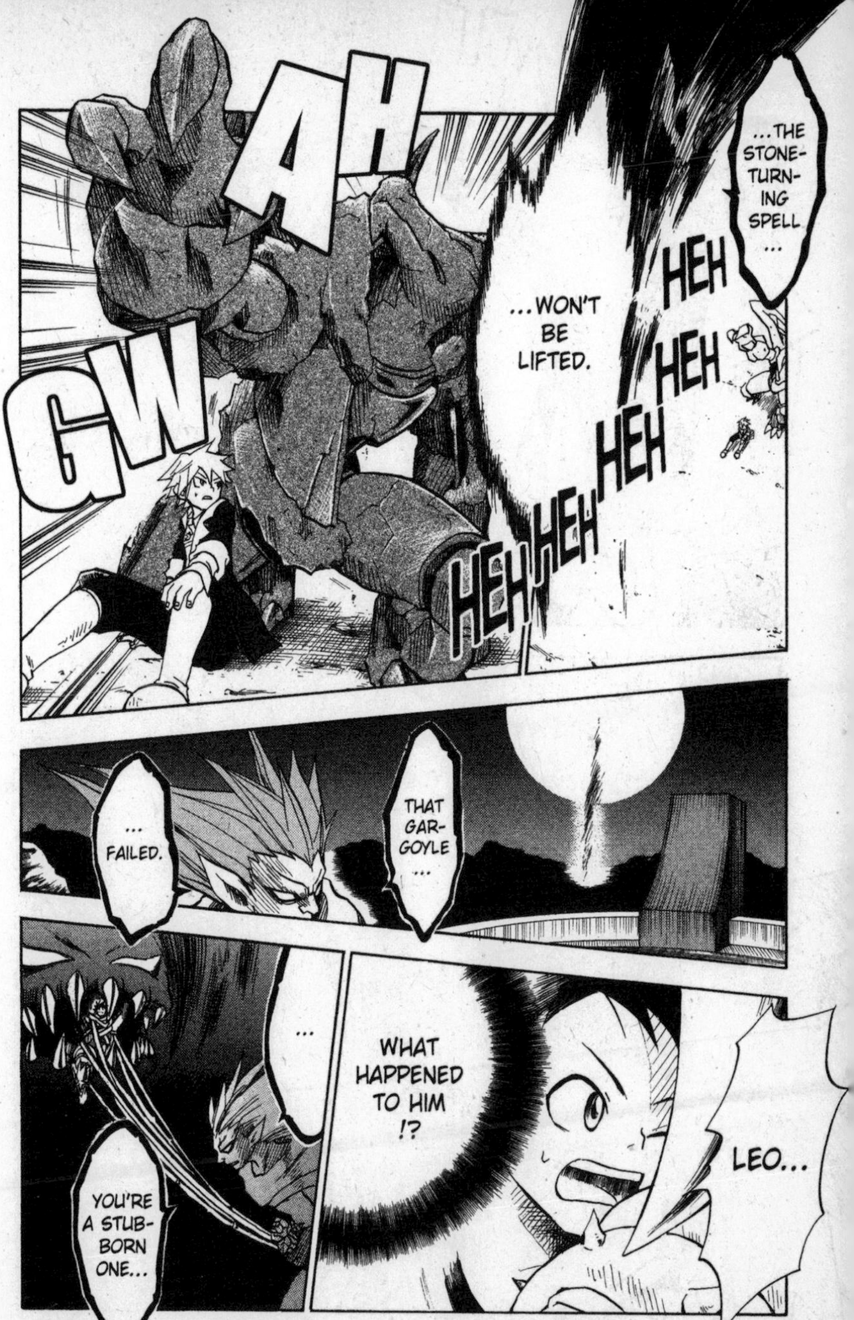

...THE STONE-TURNING SPELL...
HEH HEH HEH HEH HEH HEH
...WON'T BE LIFTED.
GWAH
THAT GARGOYLE...
...FAILED.
LEO...
WHAT HAPPENED TO HIM!?
...
YOU'RE A STUBBORN ONE...

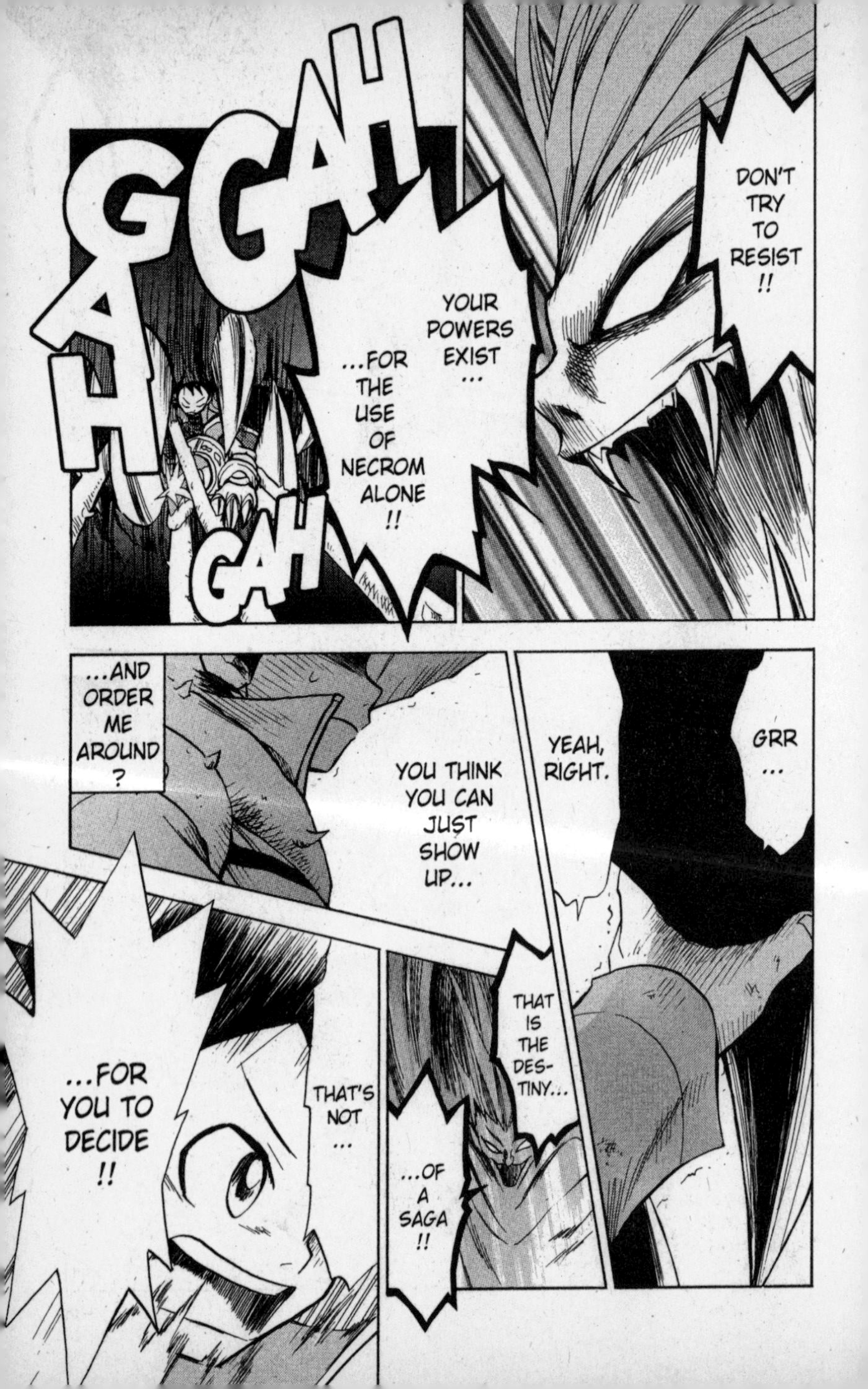
DON'T TRY TO RESIST!!
YOUR POWERS EXIST...
...FOR THE USE OF NECROM ALONE!!
GGAH
AH
GAH
GRR...
YEAH, RIGHT.
YOU THINK YOU CAN JUST SHOW UP...
...AND ORDER ME AROUND?
THAT IS THE DES-TINY...
...OF A SAGA!!
THAT'S NOT...
...FOR YOU TO DECIDE!!

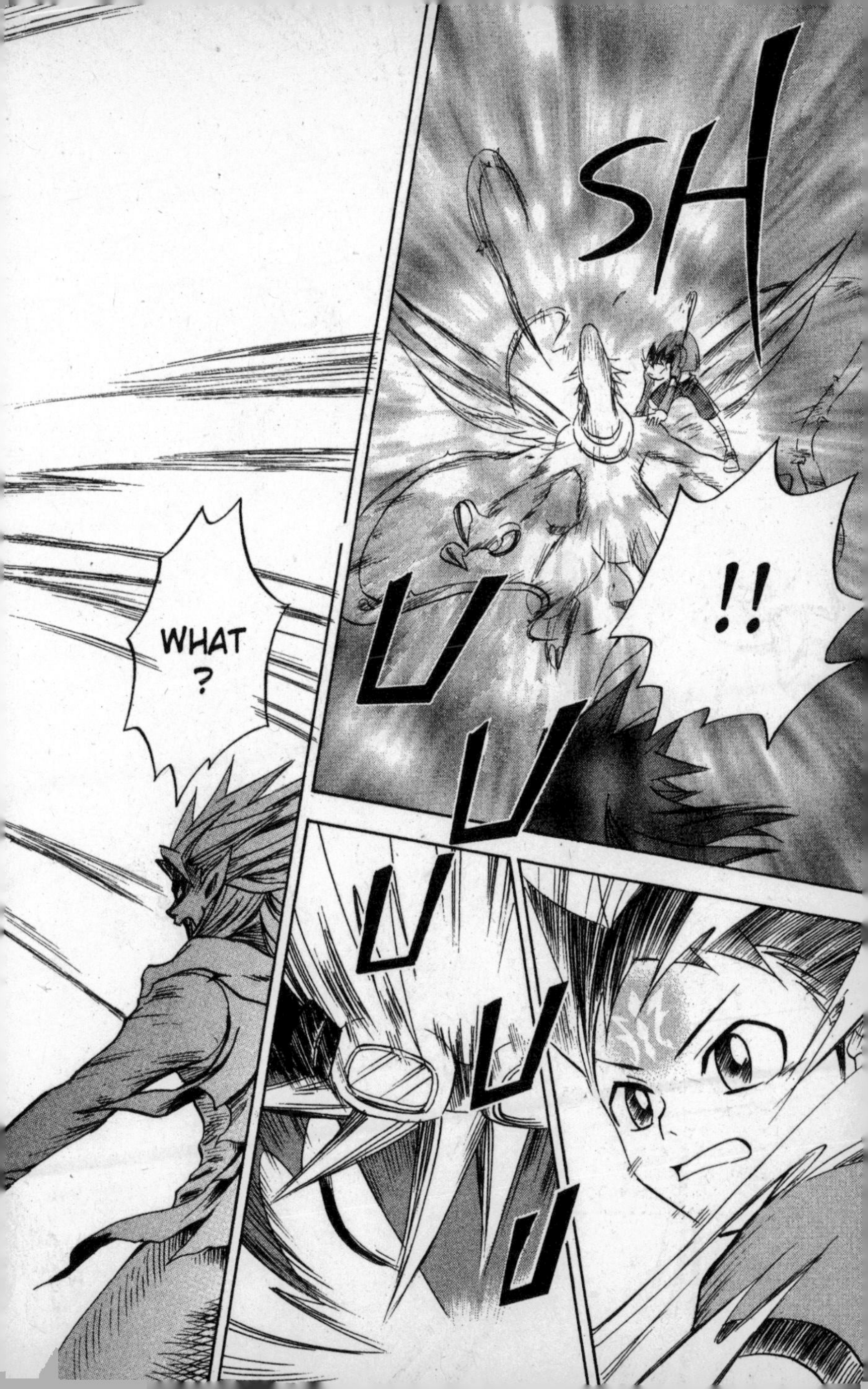
SHUUUUU
!!
WHAT ?

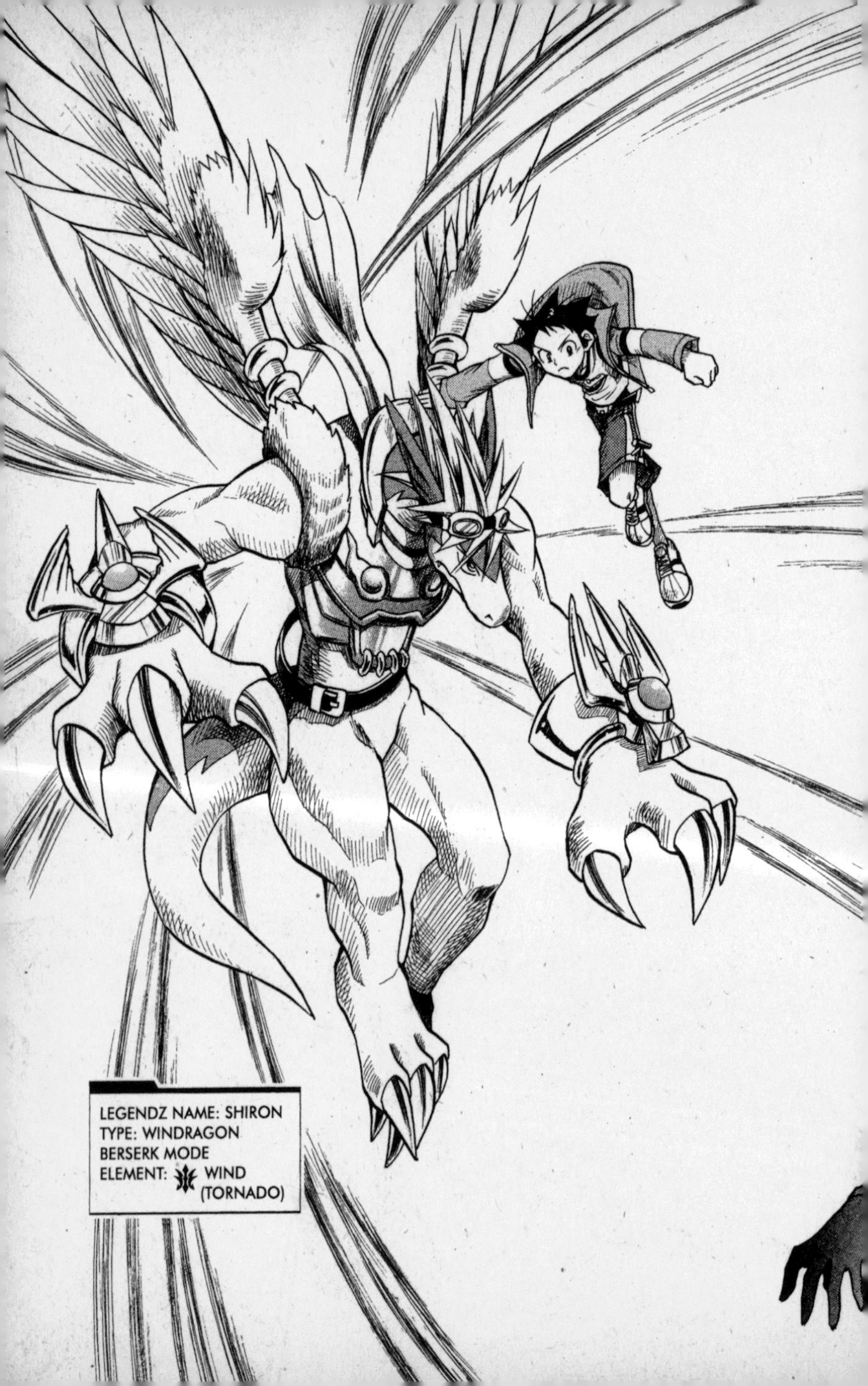
LEGENDZ NAME: SHIRON
TYPE: WINDRAGON
BERSERK MODE
ELEMENT: WIND (TORNADO)

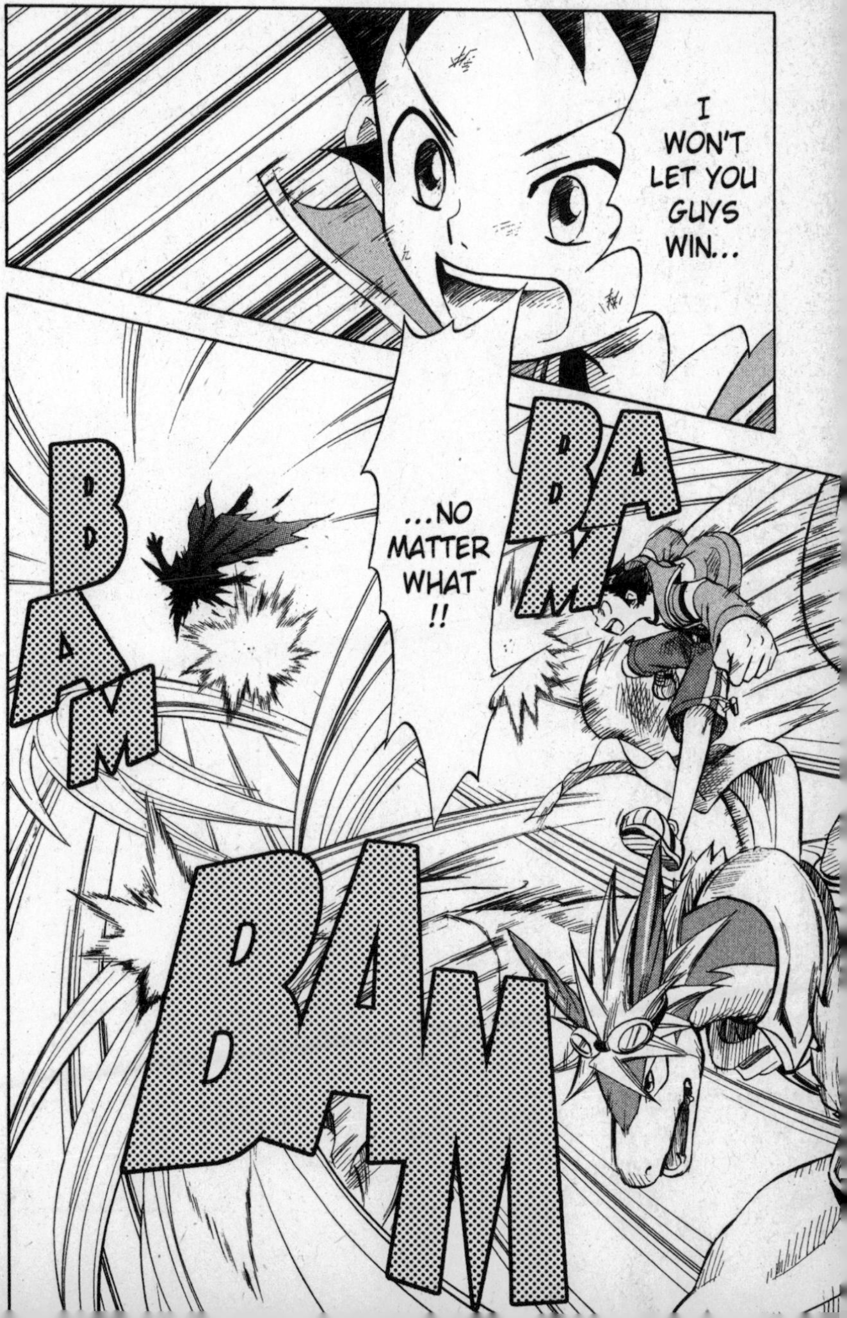
I WON'T LET YOU GUYS WIN...
...NO MATTER WHAT!!
BAM
BAM
BAM

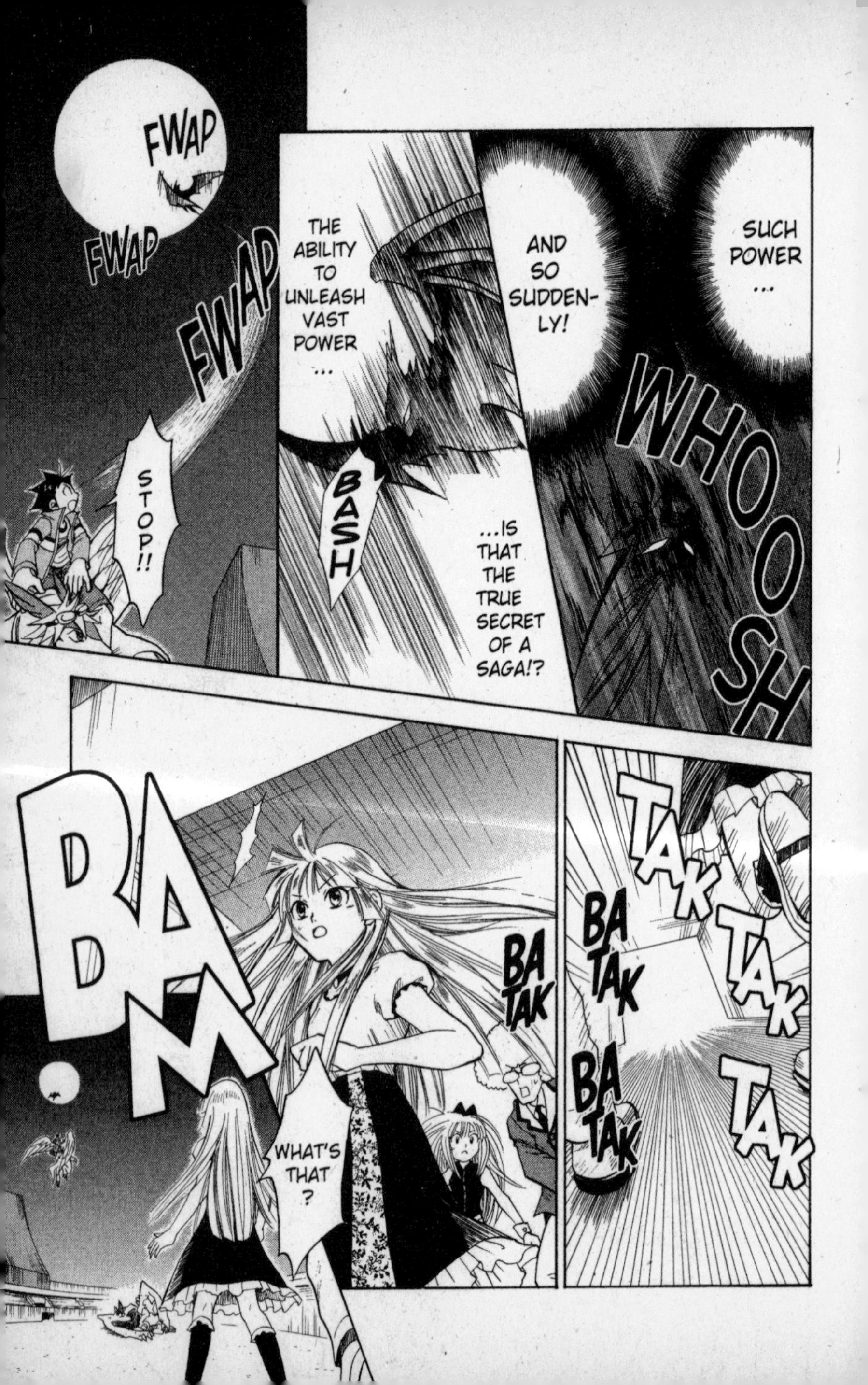
SUCH POWER ...
WHOOSH
AND SO SUDDEN-LY!
THE ABILITY TO UNLEASH VAST POWER ...
BASH
...IS THAT THE TRUE SECRET OF A SAGA!?
FWAP
FWAP
FWAP
STOP!!
TAK
TAK
TAK
BA TAK
BA TAK
BA TAK
BAM
WHAT'S THAT ?

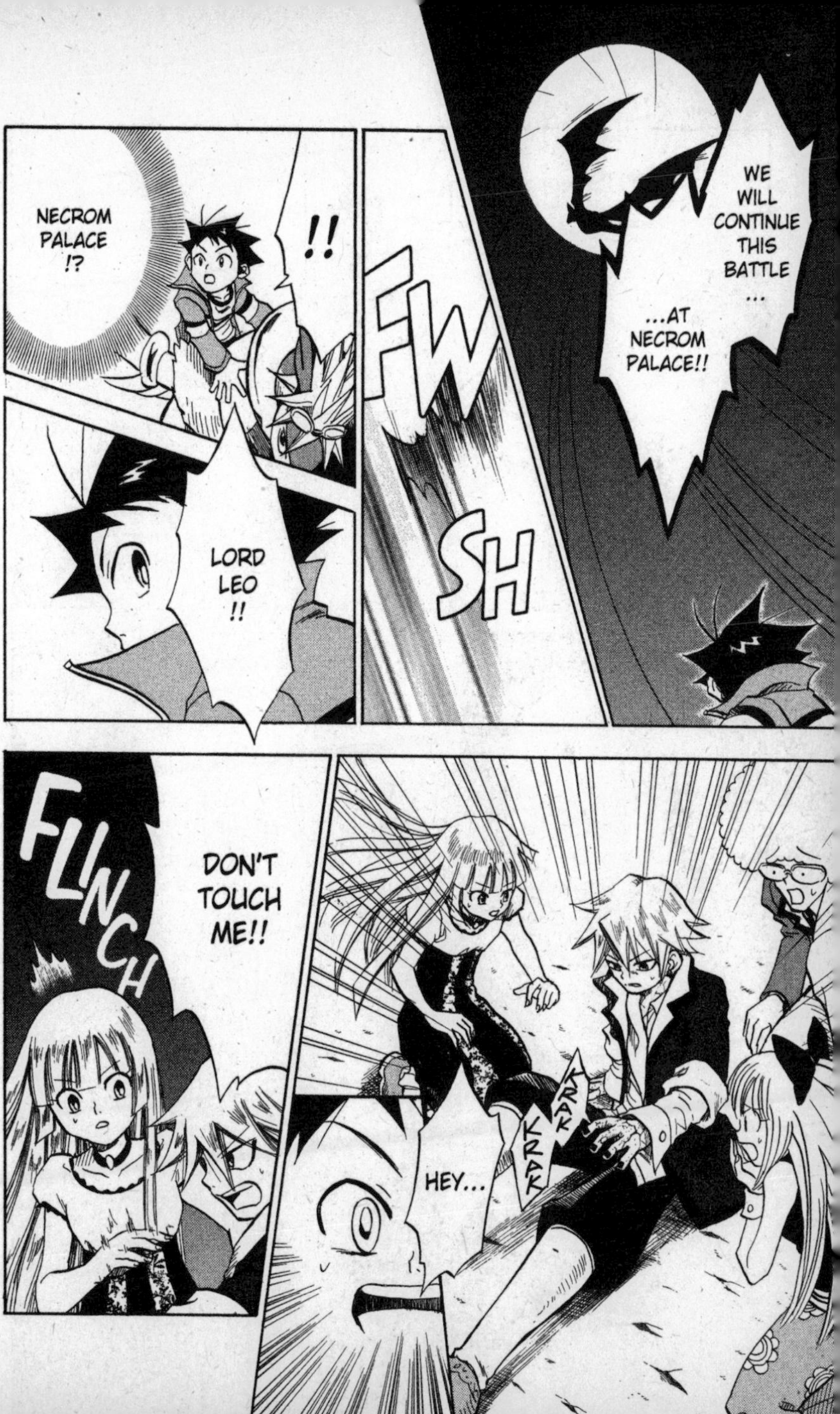
WE WILL CONTINUE THIS BATTLE ...
...AT NECROM PALACE!!
FWSH
!!
NECROM PALACE !?
LORD LEO !!
KRAK KRAK
HEY...
FLINCH
DON'T TOUCH ME!!

READ THIS WAY

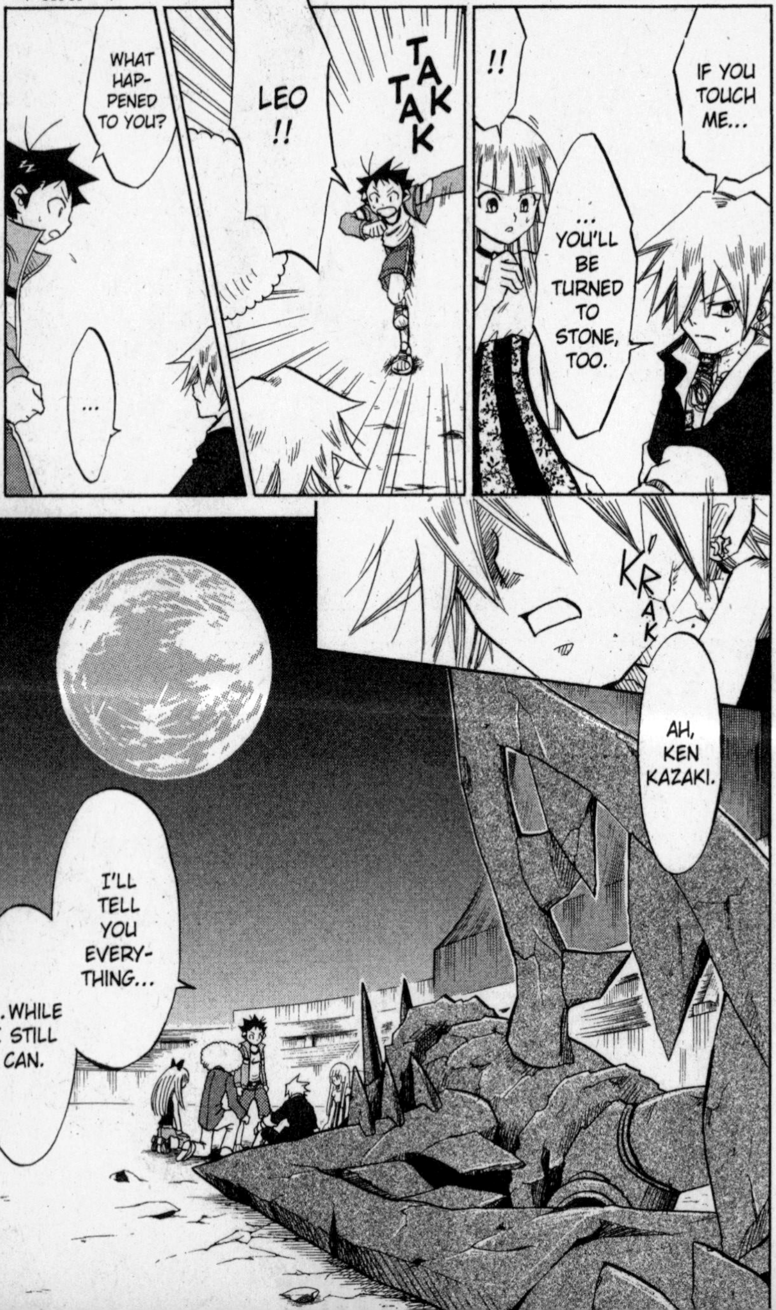
IF YOU TOUCH ME...
...YOU'LL BE TURNED TO STONE, TOO.
!!
TAK TAK
LEO !!
WHAT HAP-PENED TO YOU?
...
KRAK
AH, KEN KAZAKI.
I'LL TELL YOU EVERY-THING...
...WHILE I STILL CAN.

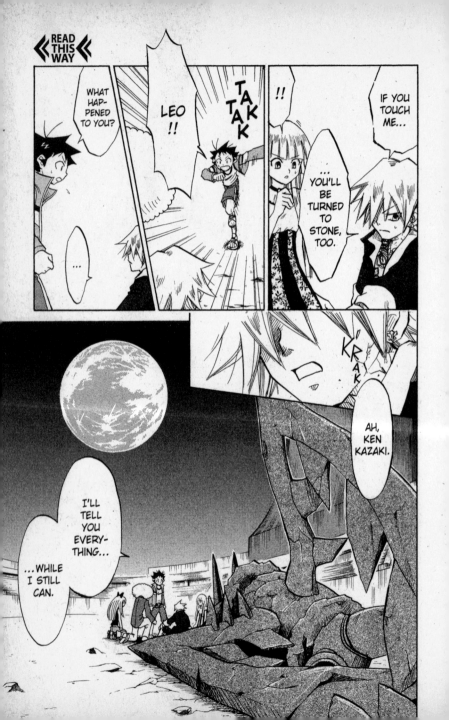

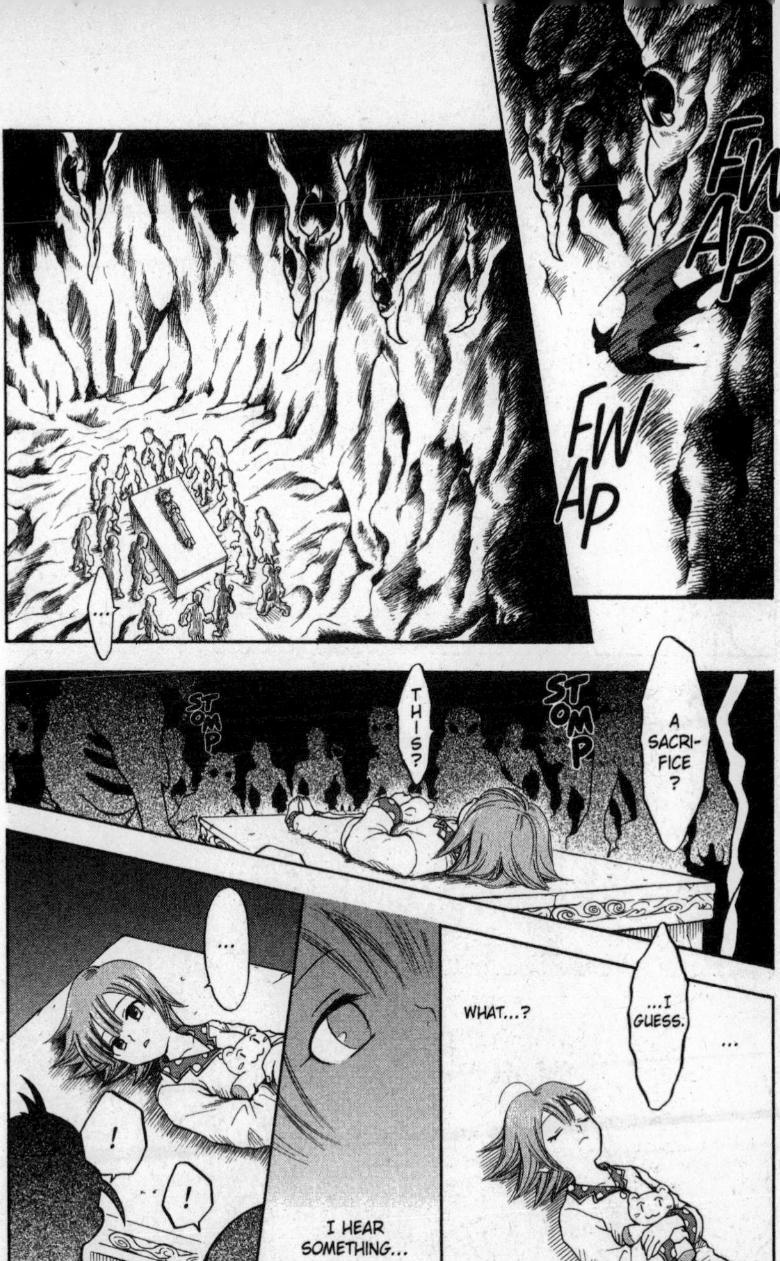
FWAP
FWAP
...
A SACRIFICE?
STOMP
THIS?
STOMP
...I GUESS.
...
WHAT...?
I HEAR SOMETHING...
...
!
!

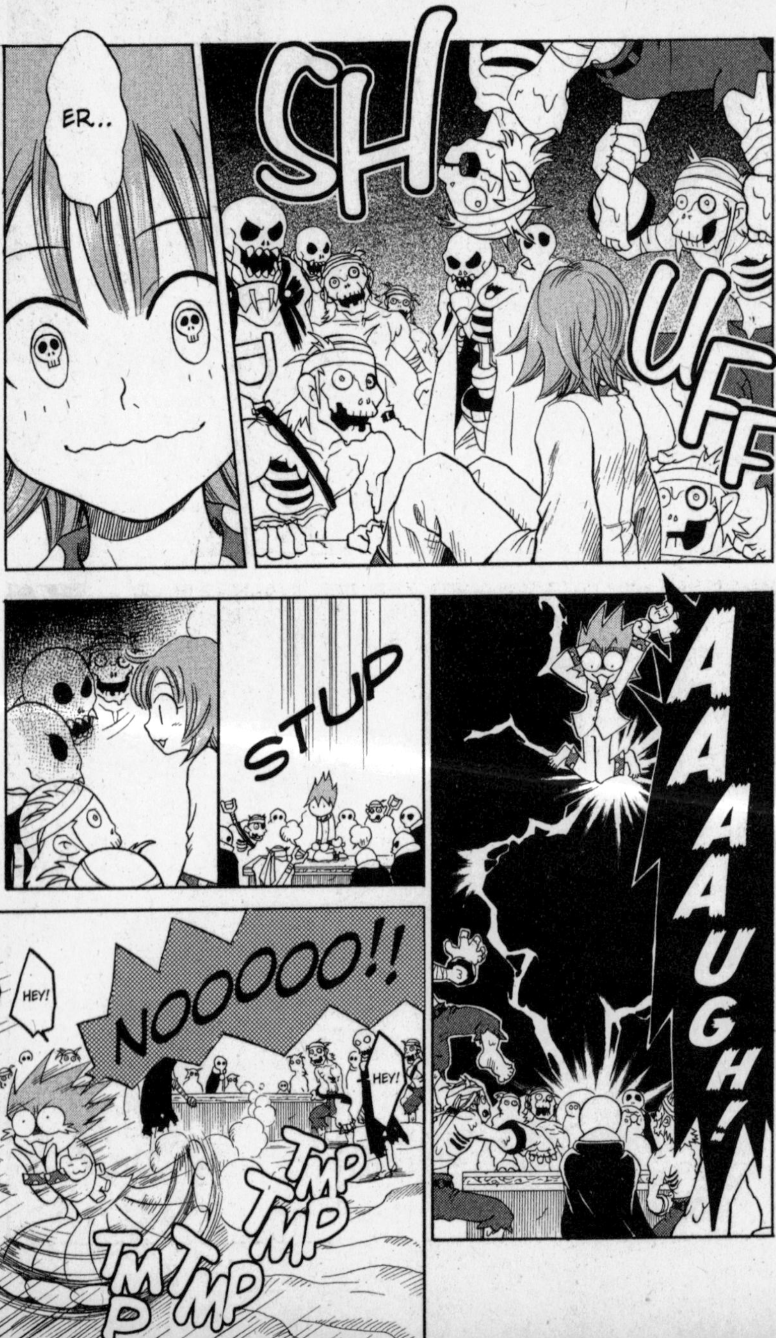
SHUFF
ER...
AAAAUGH!
STUP
NOOOOOO!!
HEY!
TMP TMP
HEY!
IT RAN AWAY.
TMP TMP

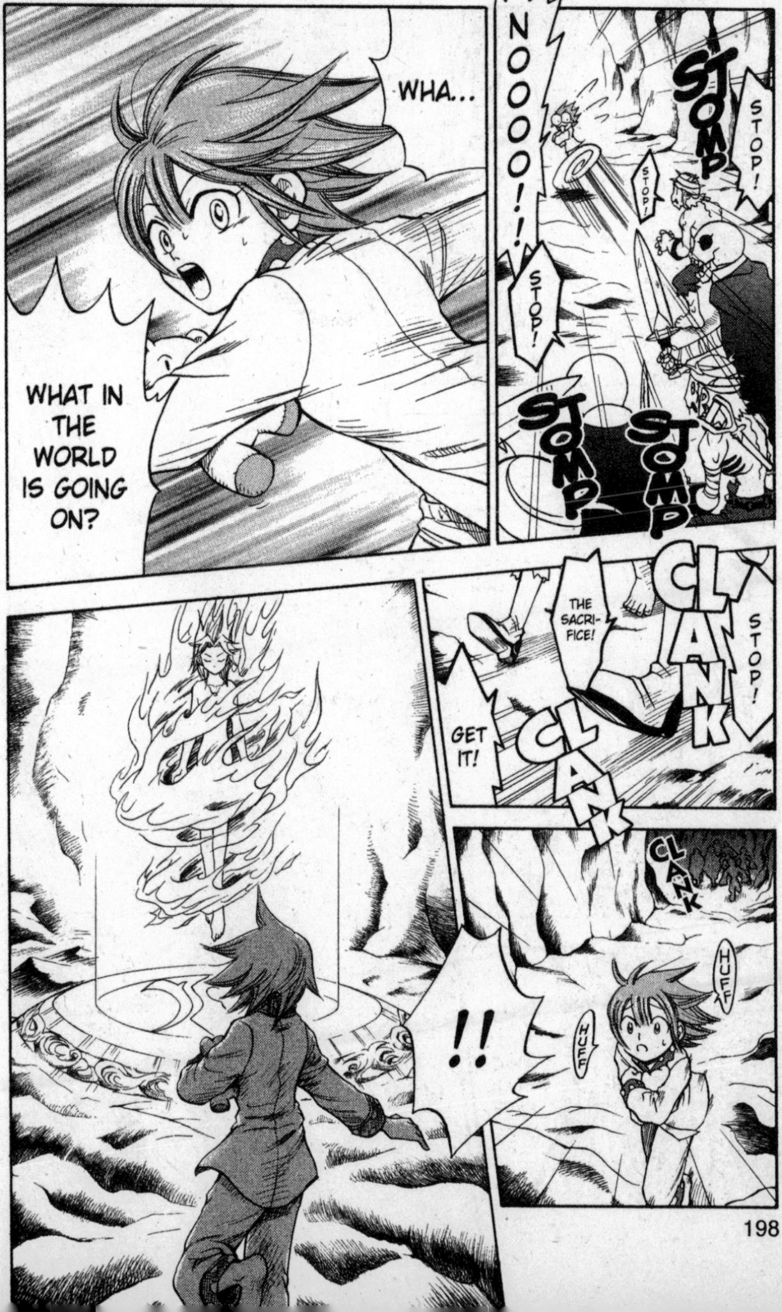
NOOOOO!!
STOMP
STOP!
STOP!
STOP!
STOMP
STOMP
WHA...
WHAT IN THE WORLD IS GOING ON?
CLANK
STOP!
THE SACRIFICE!
GET IT!
CLANK
CLANK
HUFF
HUFF
!!

READ THIS WAY

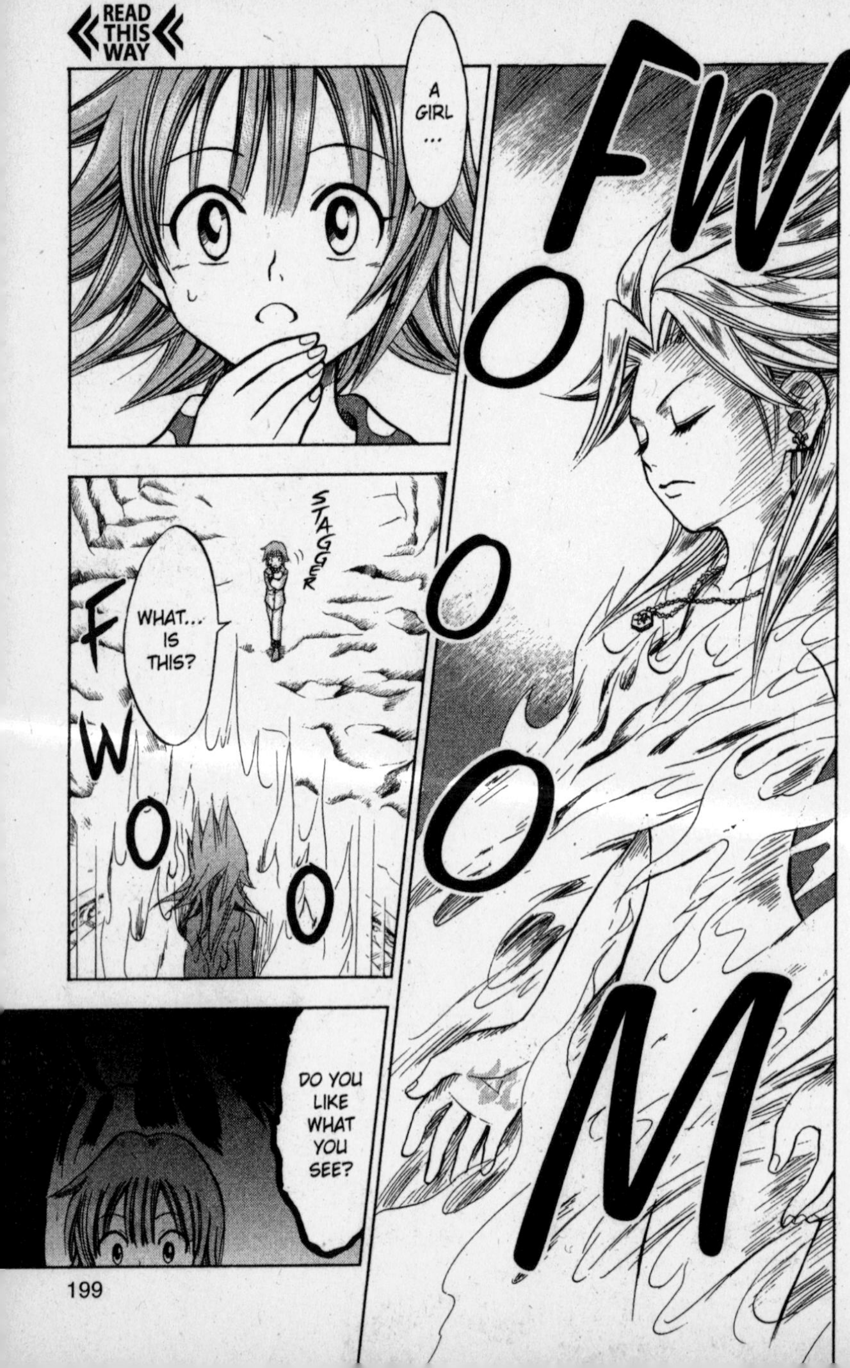

FWOOOM
A GIRL ...
STAGGER
WHAT... IS THIS?
FWOO
DO YOU LIKE WHAT YOU SEE?

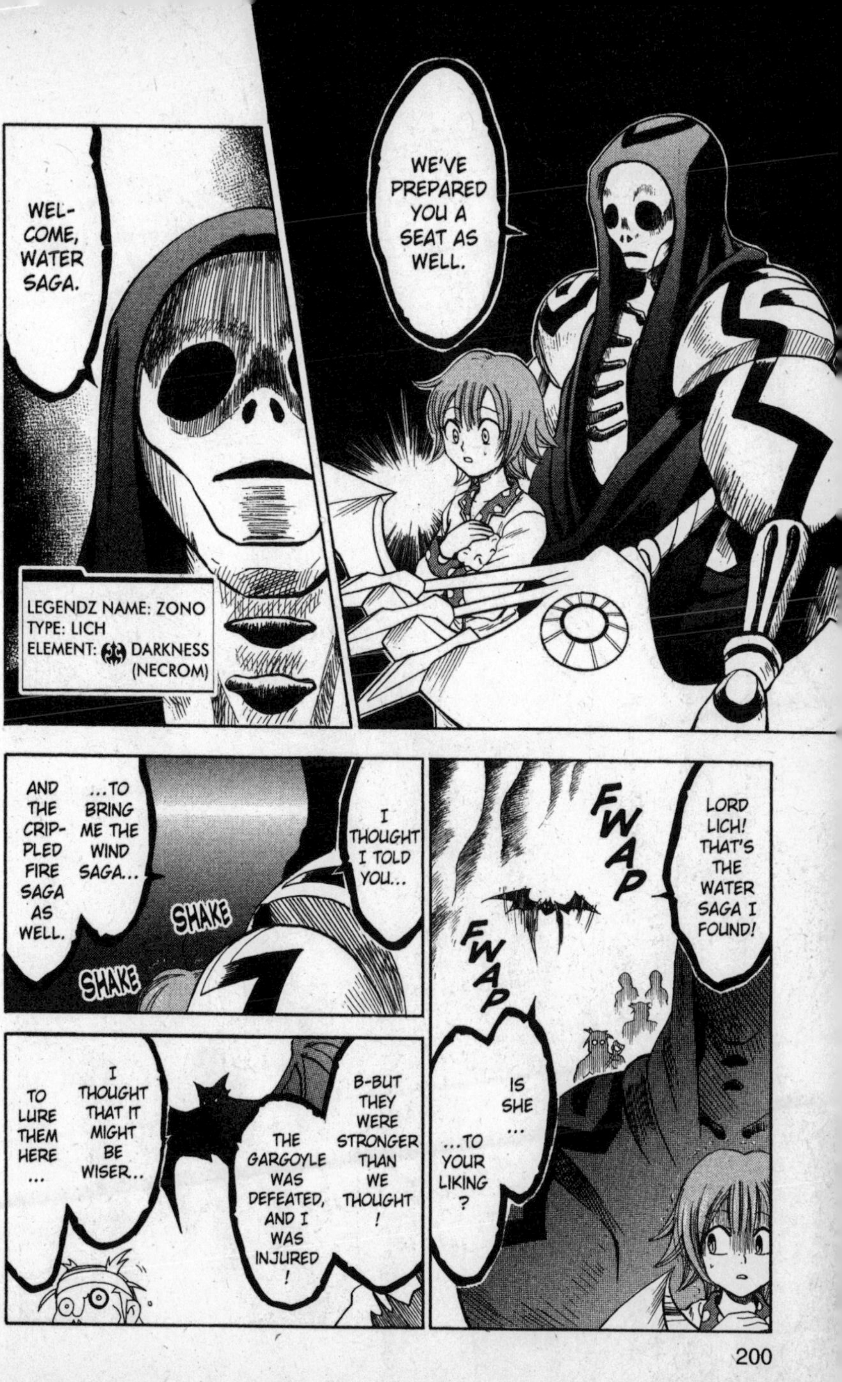
WE'VE PREPARED YOU A SEAT AS WELL.
WEL-COME, WATER SAGA.
LEGENDZ NAME: ZONO
TYPE: LICH
ELEMENT: DARKNESS (NECROM)
FWAP
FWAP
LORD LICH! THAT'S THE WATER SAGA I FOUND!
IS SHE ...
...TO YOUR LIKING?
I THOUGHT I TOLD YOU...
...TO BRING ME THE WIND SAGA...
AND THE CRIP-PLED FIRE SAGA AS WELL.
SHAKE
SHAKE
B-BUT THEY WERE STRONGER THAN WE THOUGHT!
THE GARGOYLE WAS DEFEATED, AND I WAS INJURED!
I THOUGHT THAT IT MIGHT BE WISER...
TO LURE THEM HERE...

READ THIS WAY

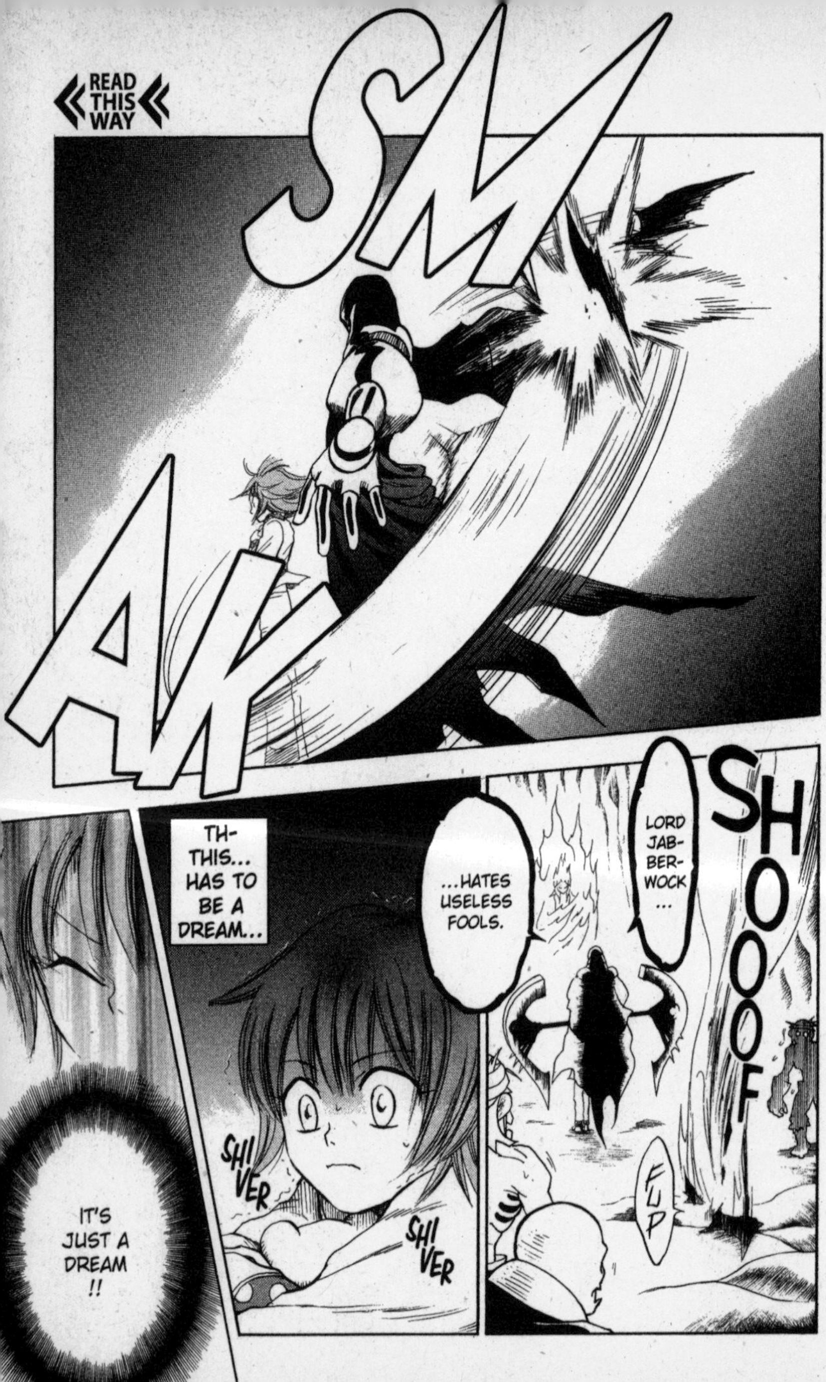
SMAK
SHOOOOF
LORD JABBERWOCK...
...HATES USELESS FOOLS.
FLIP
TH-THIS... HAS TO BE A DREAM...
SHIVER
SHIVER
IT'S JUST A DREAM!!

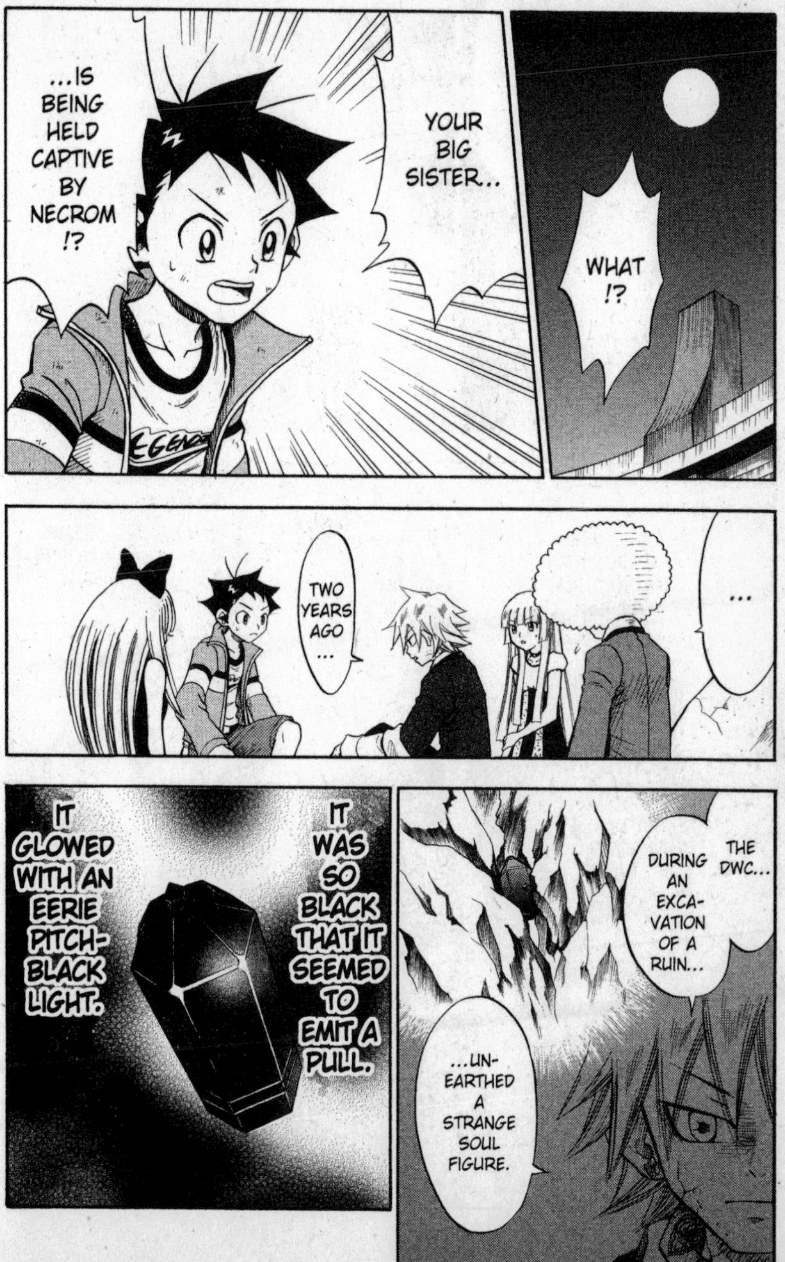
WHAT !?
YOUR BIG SISTER...
...IS BEING HELD CAPTIVE BY NECROM !?
...
TWO YEARS AGO ...
THE DWC...
DURING AN EXCA-VATION OF A RUIN...
...UN-EARTHED A STRANGE SOUL FIGURE.
IT WAS SO BLACK THAT IT SEEMED TO EMIT A PULL.
IT GLOWED WITH AN EERIE PITCH-BLACK LIGHT.

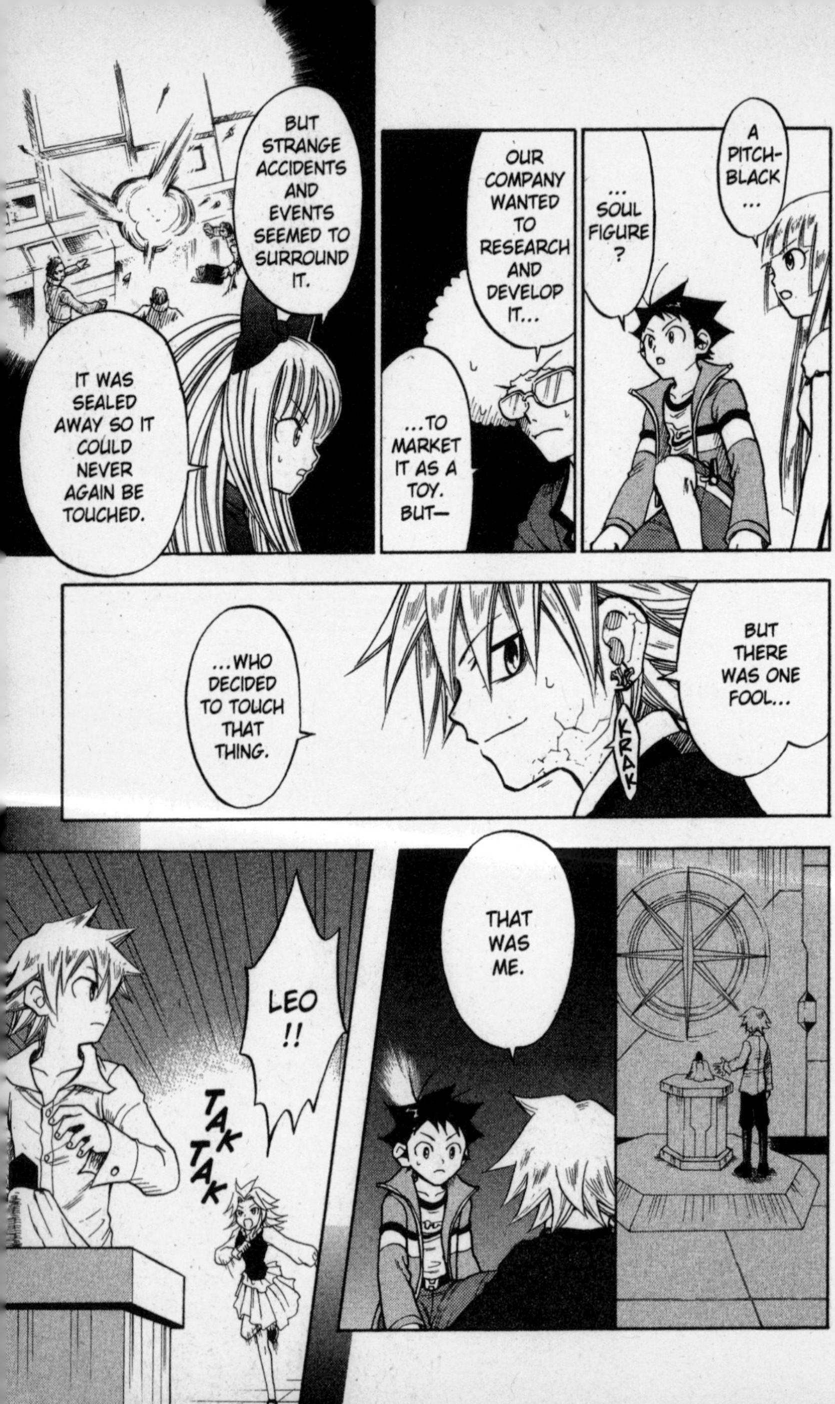

A PITCH-BLACK...
...SOUL FIGURE?
OUR COMPANY WANTED TO RESEARCH AND DEVELOP IT...
...TO MARKET IT AS A TOY. BUT—
BUT STRANGE ACCIDENTS AND EVENTS SEEMED TO SURROUND IT.
IT WAS SEALED AWAY SO IT COULD NEVER AGAIN BE TOUCHED.
BUT THERE WAS ONE FOOL...
KRAK
...WHO DECIDED TO TOUCH THAT THING.
THAT WAS ME.
LEO!!
TAK TAK

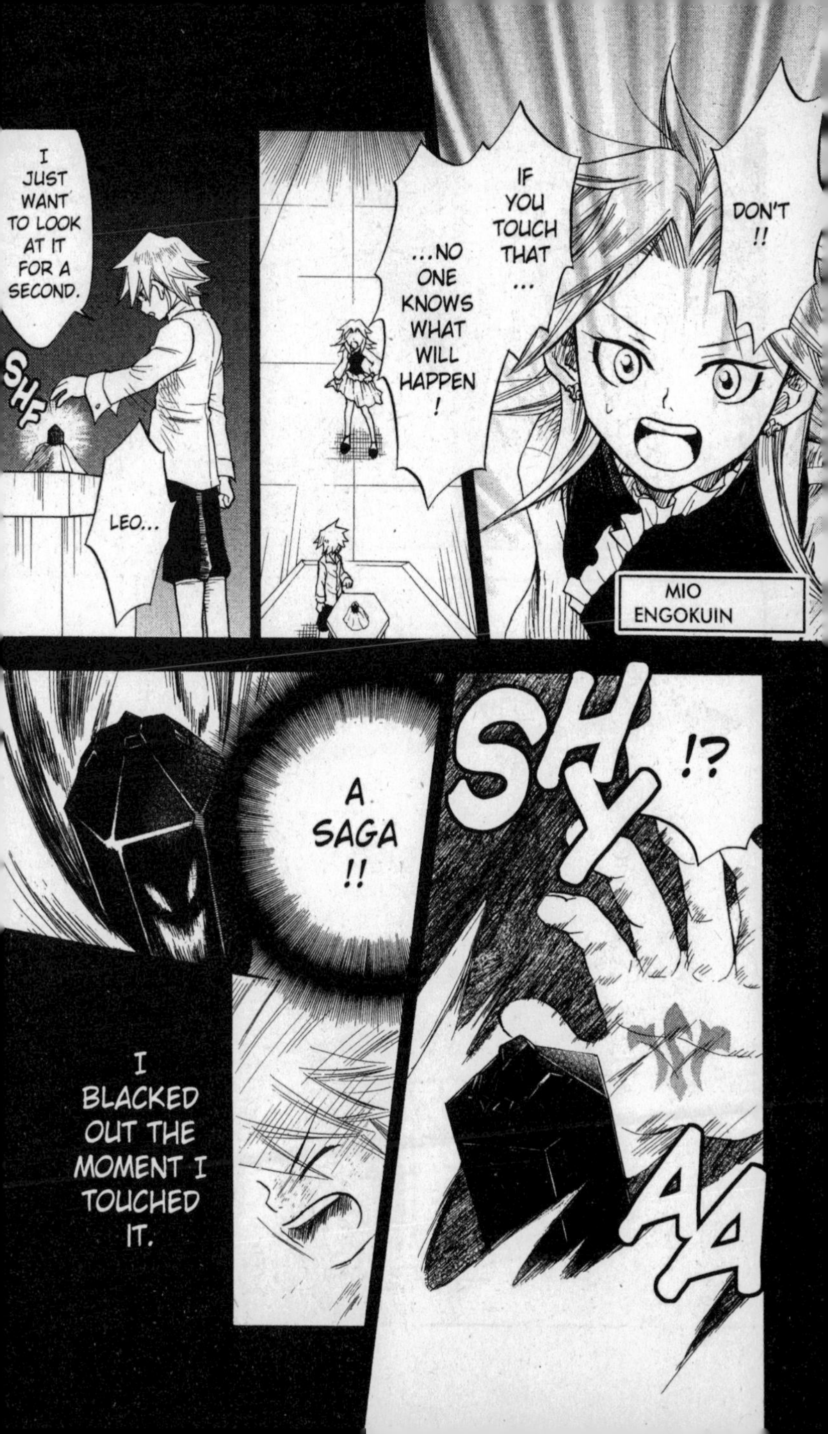
DON'T !!
IF YOU TOUCH THAT ...
...NO ONE KNOWS WHAT WILL HAPPEN !
MIO ENGOKUIN
I JUST WANT TO LOOK AT IT FOR A SECOND.
SHF
LEO...
SHY
!?
AA
A SAGA !!
I BLACKED OUT THE MOMENT I TOUCHED IT.

READ THIS WAY

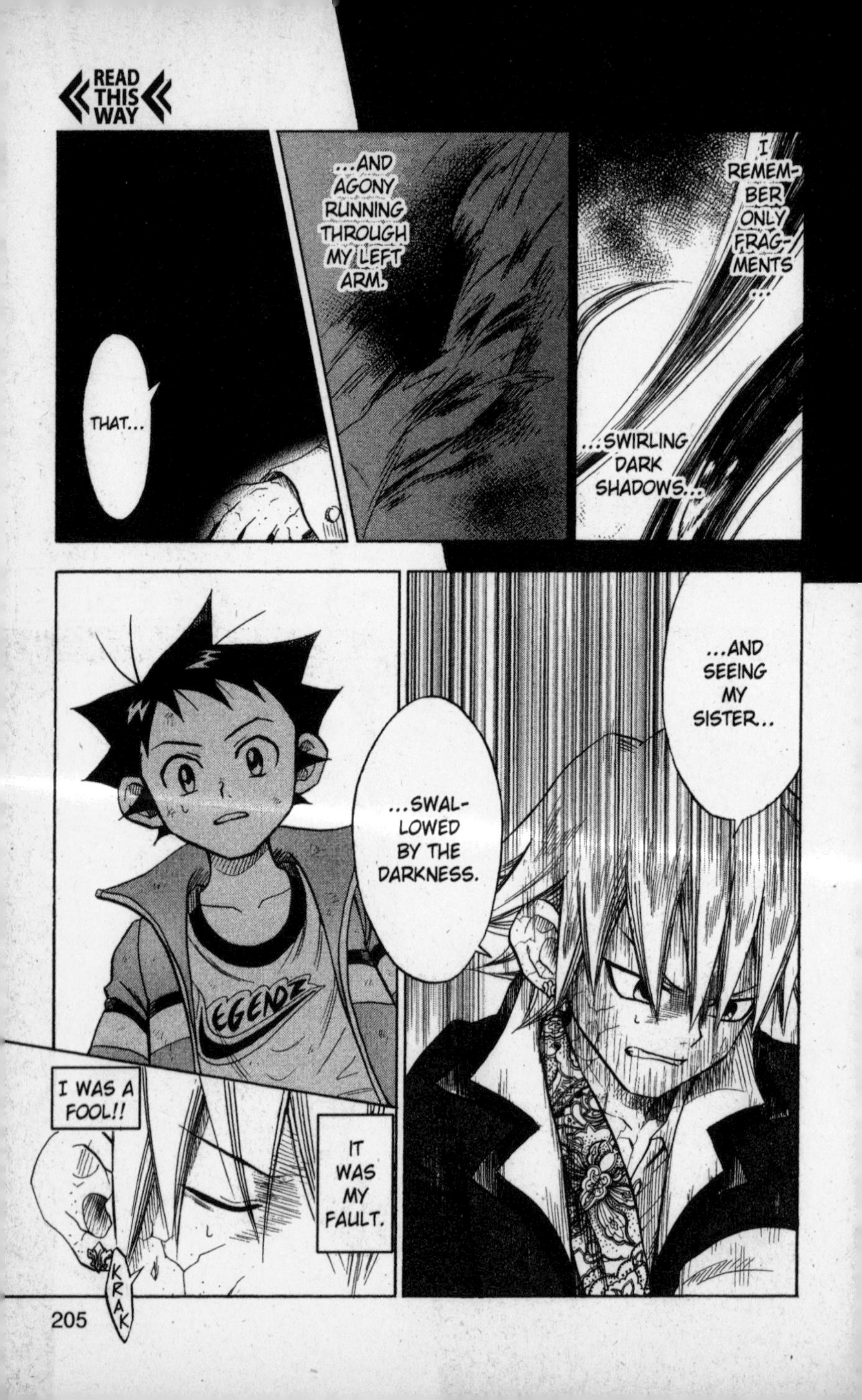
I REMEMBER ONLY FRAGMENTS...
...SWIRLING DARK SHADOWS...
...AND AGONY RUNNING THROUGH MY LEFT ARM.
THAT...
...AND SEEING MY SISTER...
...SWALLOWED BY THE DARKNESS.
IT WAS MY FAULT.
I WAS A FOOL!!
KRAK

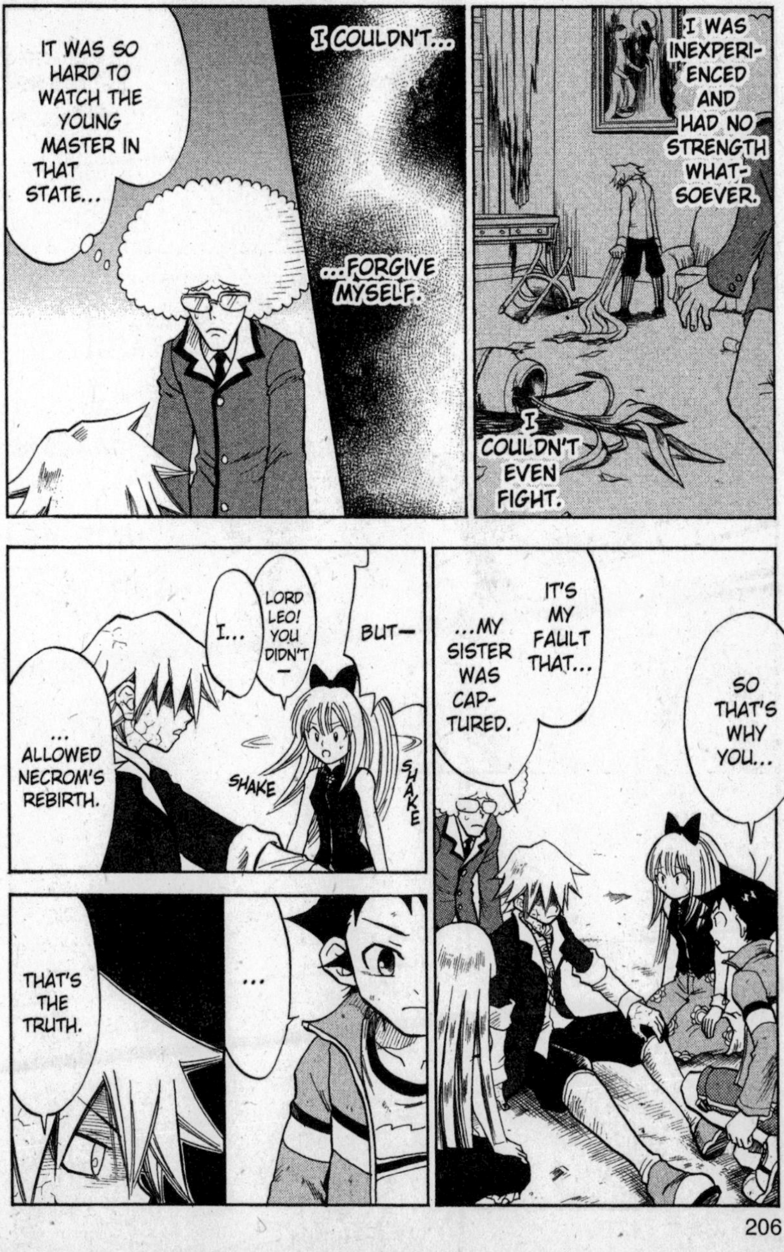
I WAS INEXPERIENCED AND HAD NO STRENGTH WHATSOEVER.
I COULDN'T EVEN FIGHT.
I COULDN'T...
...FORGIVE MYSELF.
IT WAS SO HARD TO WATCH THE YOUNG MASTER IN THAT STATE...
SO THAT'S WHY YOU...
IT'S MY FAULT THAT...
...MY SISTER WAS CAPTURED.
BUT—
LORD LEO! YOU DIDN'T—
I...
...ALLOWED NECROM'S REBIRTH.
SHAKE
SHAKE
...
THAT'S THE TRUTH.

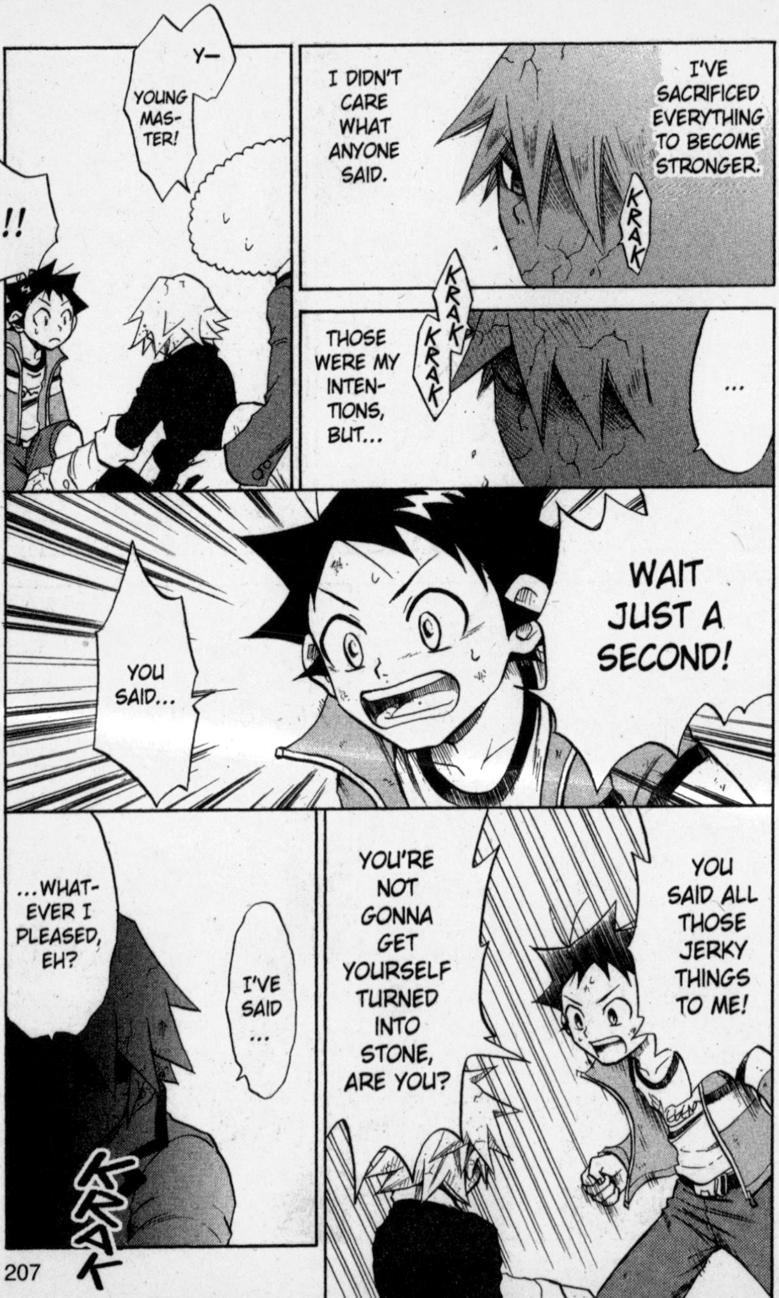
I'VE SACRIFICED EVERYTHING TO BECOME STRONGER.
KRAK
I DIDN'T CARE WHAT ANYONE SAID.
...
KRAK
KRAK
THOSE WERE MY INTENTIONS, BUT...
Y—
YOUNG MASTER!
!!
WAIT JUST A SECOND!
YOU SAID...
YOU SAID ALL THOSE JERKY THINGS TO ME!
YOU'RE NOT GONNA GET YOURSELF TURNED INTO STONE, ARE YOU?
I'VE SAID...
...WHATEVER I PLEASED, EH?
KRAK

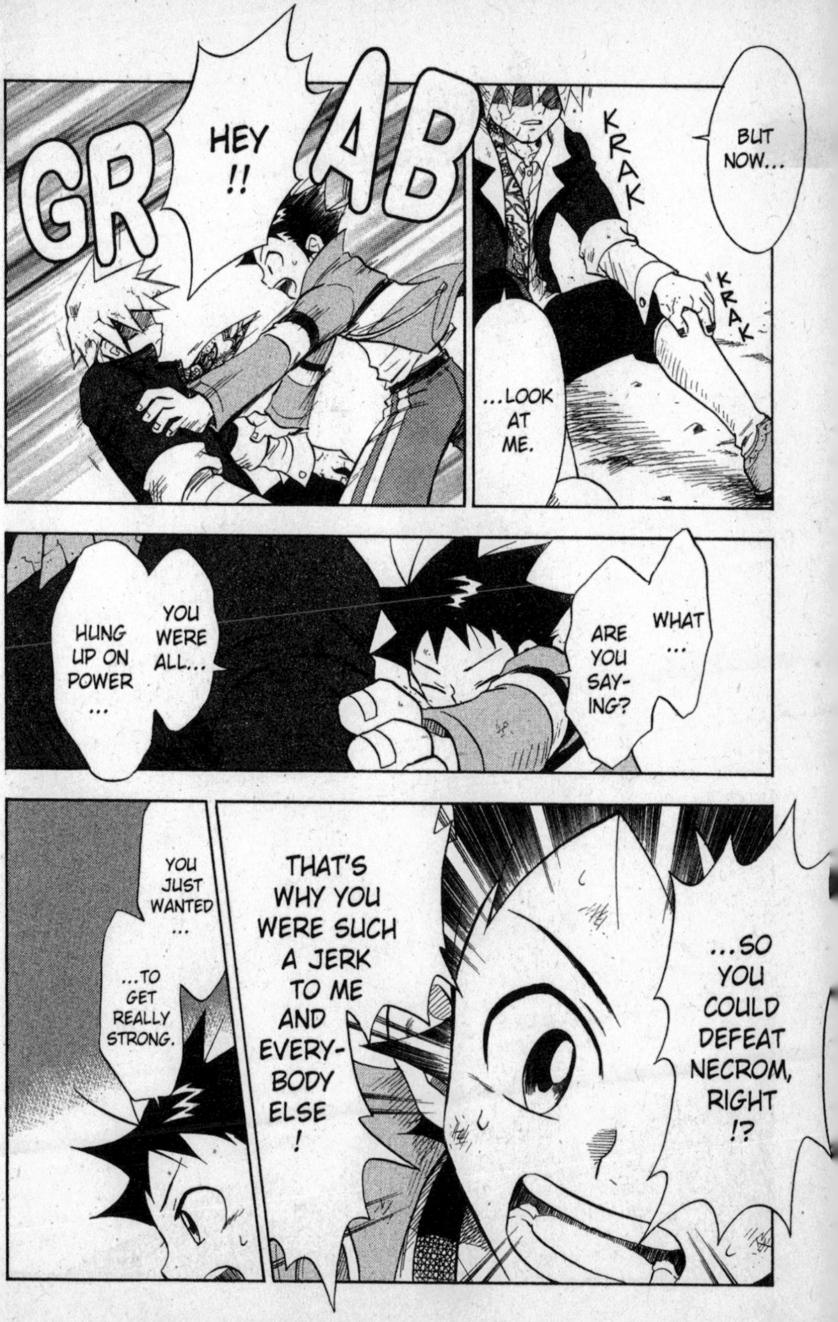
BUT NOW...
KRAK
KRAK
...LOOK AT ME.
GRAB
HEY !!
WHAT ... ARE YOU SAYING?
YOU WERE ALL... HUNG UP ON POWER ...
THAT'S WHY YOU WERE SUCH A JERK TO ME AND EVERYBODY ELSE !
...SO YOU COULD DEFEAT NECROM, RIGHT !?
YOU JUST WANTED ...
...TO GET REALLY STRONG.

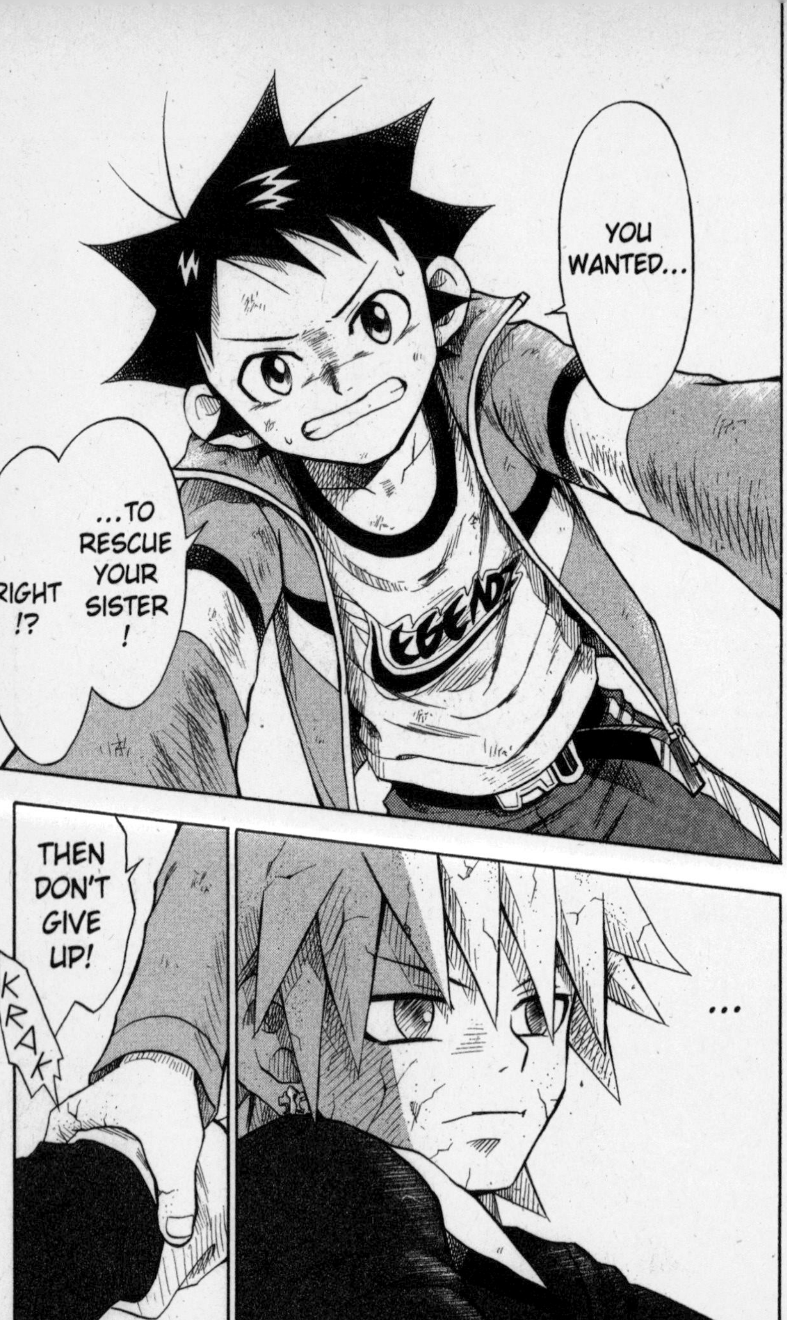
YOU WANTED...
...TO RESCUE YOUR SISTER!
RIGHT!?
...
THEN DON'T GIVE UP!
KRAK

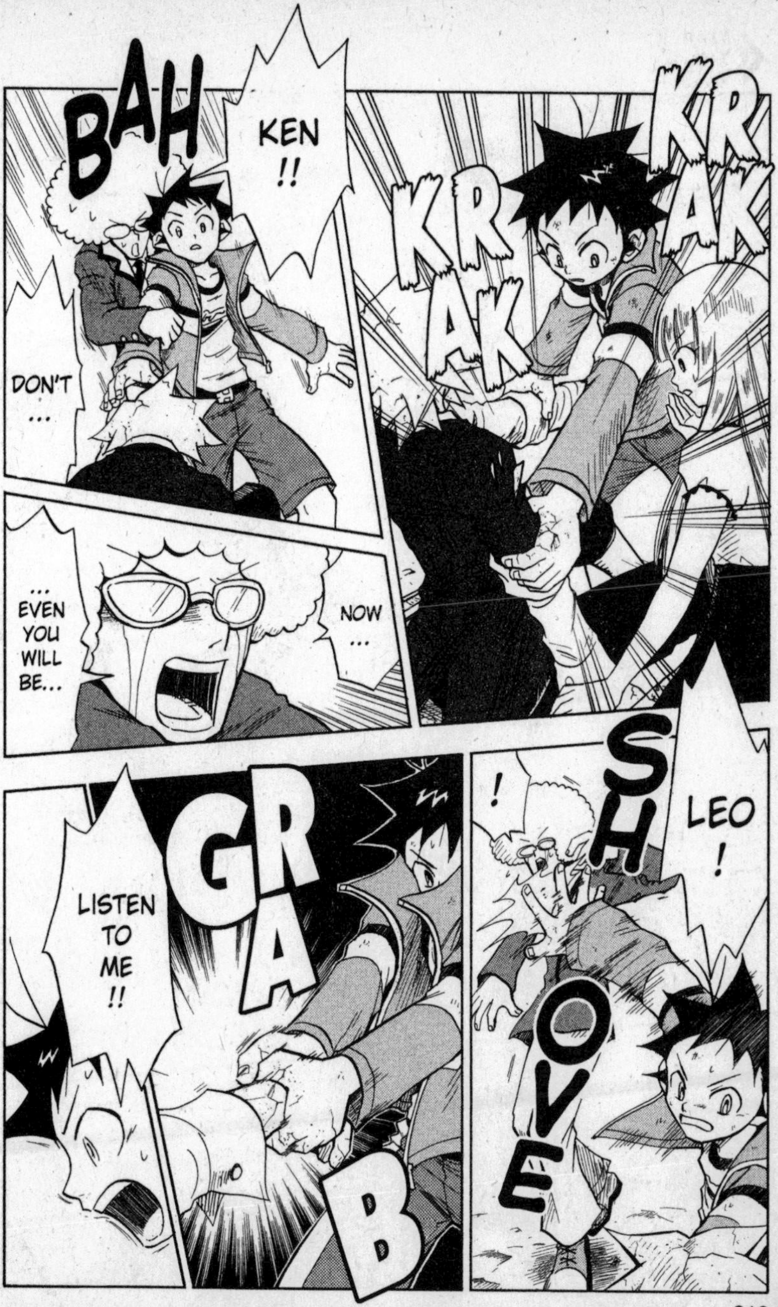
KRAK
KRAK
KEN !!
BAH
DON'T ...
NOW ...
... EVEN YOU WILL BE...
SHOVE
LEO !
!
GRAB
LISTEN TO ME !!

READ THIS WAY

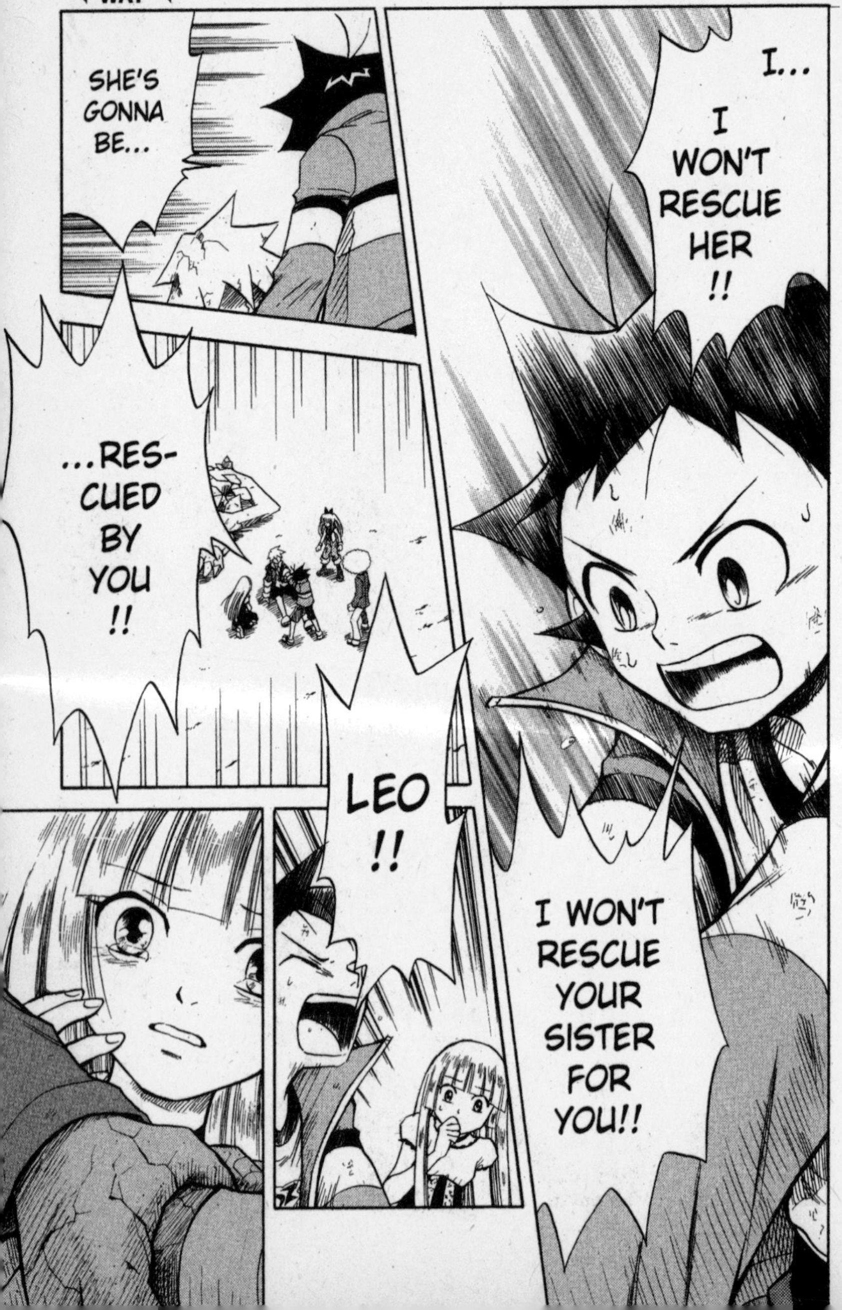

I...
I WON'T RESCUE HER !!
I WON'T RESCUE YOUR SISTER FOR YOU!!
SHE'S GONNA BE...
...RES-CUED BY YOU !!
LEO !!

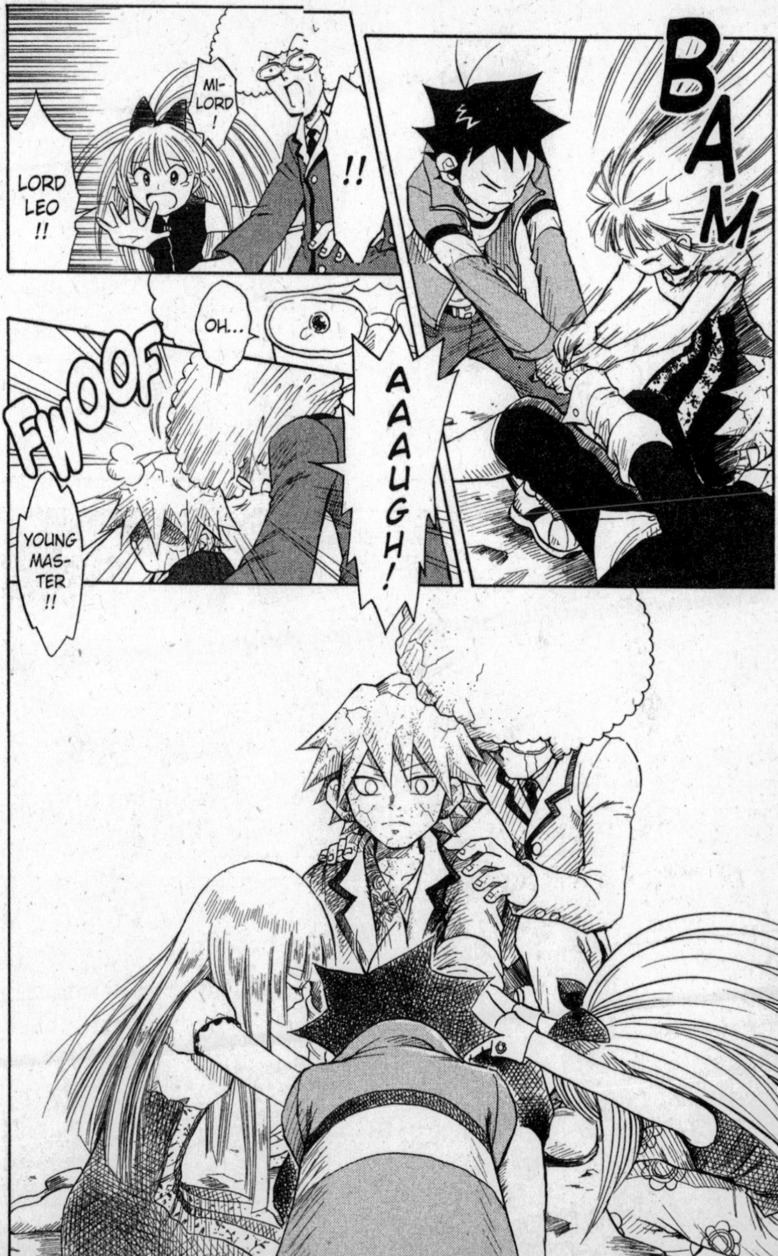
BAM
MI-LORD!
!!
LORD LEO!!
OH...
AAAUGH!
FWOOF
YOUNG MASTER!!

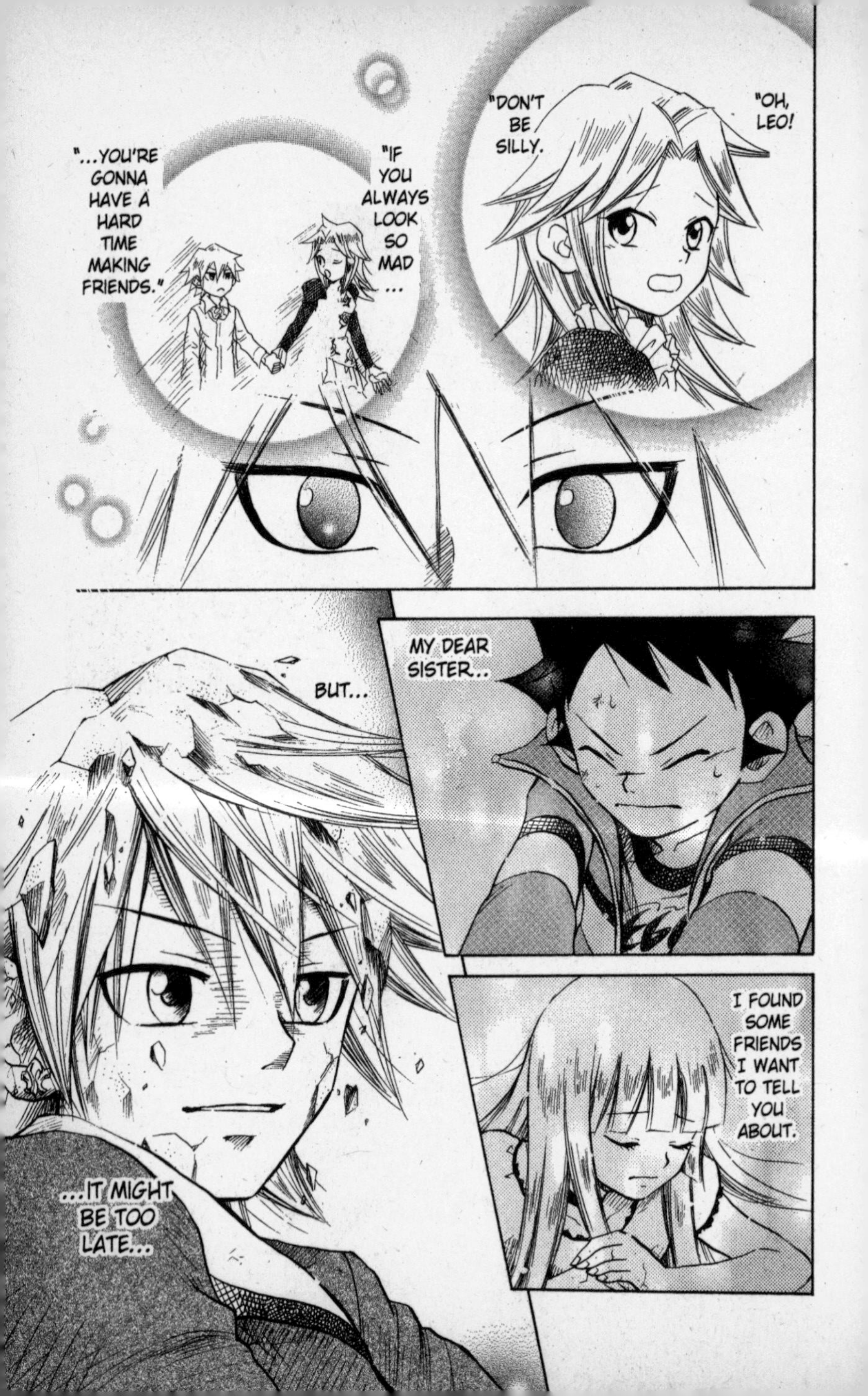
"OH, LEO!
"DON'T BE SILLY.
"IF YOU ALWAYS LOOK SO MAD...
"...YOU'RE GONNA HAVE A HARD TIME MAKING FRIENDS."
MY DEAR SISTER...
I FOUND SOME FRIENDS I WANT TO TELL YOU ABOUT.
BUT...
...IT MIGHT BE TOO LATE...

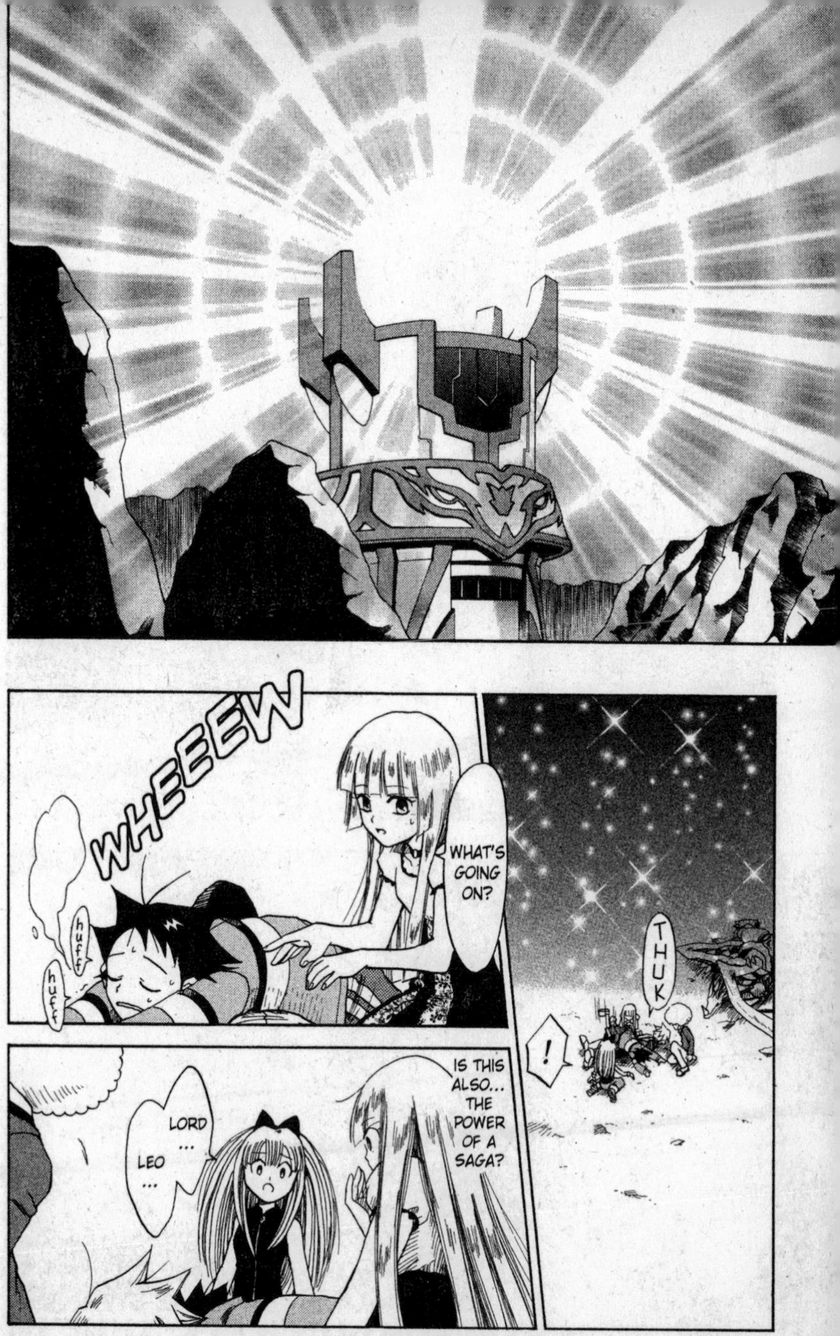
THUK
!
WHAT'S GOING ON?
WHEEEW
huff
huff
IS THIS ALSO... THE POWER OF A SAGA?
LORD ...
LEO ...

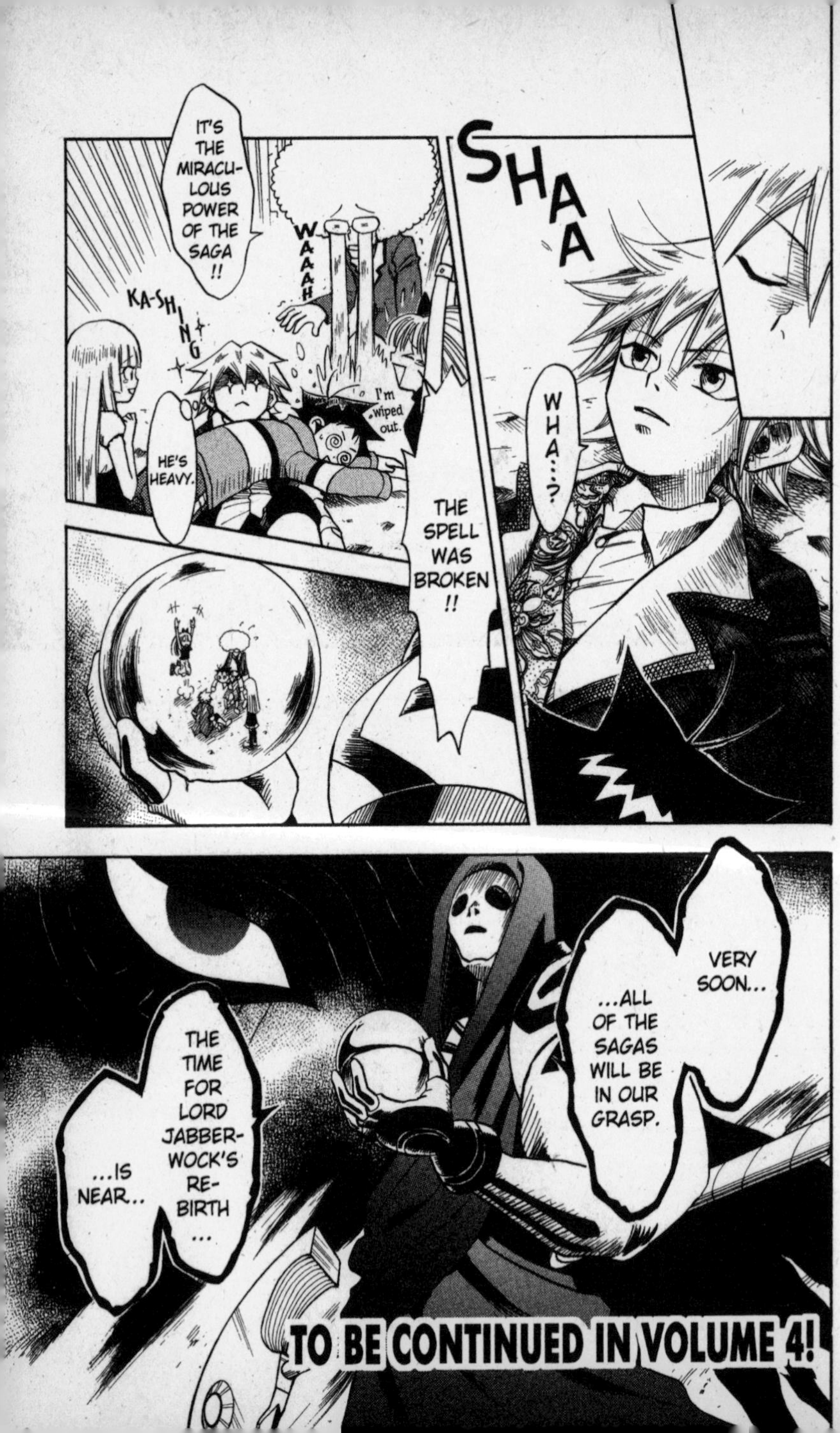
SHAA
WHA...?
WAAAAH
IT'S THE MIRACULOUS POWER OF THE SAGA!!
KA-SHING
I'm wiped out.
HE'S HEAVY.
THE SPELL WAS BROKEN!!
VERY SOON...
...ALL OF THE SAGAS WILL BE IN OUR GRASP.
THE TIME FOR LORD JABBERWOCK'S REBIRTH...
...IS NEAR...
TO BE CONTINUED IN VOLUME 4!

In the Next Volume...

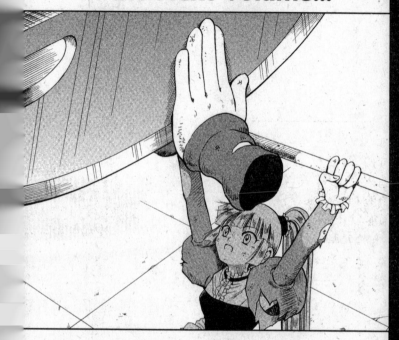

Ken, Kaoruko and Leo head to South America in search of Necrom Palace, where the forces of Darkness are holding Leo's sister and Ririko prisoner. They find the entrance high up in the mountains, but they trigger a trap and the entrance starts to disappear. Ken and Kaoruko make it inside just in time, but Necrom is lying in wait for them!

Coming in February 2006!

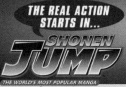
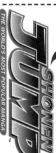
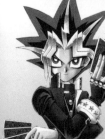

Check us out
on the web!

www.shonenjump.com

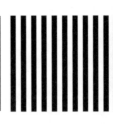
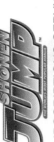

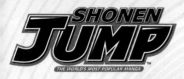

COMPLETE OUR SURVEY AND LET US KNOW WHAT YOU THINK!

☐ Please do NOT send me information about VIZ Media and SHONEN JUMP products, news and events, special offers, or other information.

☐ Please do NOT send me information from VIZ Media's trusted business partners.

Name: _____

Address: _____

City:_____ State:_____ Zip:_____

E-mail: _____

☐ Male ☐ Female Date of Birth (mm/dd/yyyy): ___ / ___ / ___ (Under 13? Parental consent required.)

① Do you purchase SHONEN JUMP Magazine?

☐ Yes   ☐ No

If **YES**, do you subscribe?
☐ Yes   ☐ No

If **NO**, how often do you purchase SHONEN JUMP Magazine?
☐ 1-3 issues a year   ☐ 4-6 issues a year   ☐ more than 7 issues a year

② Which SHONEN JUMP Manga did you purchase this time? (please check only one)

☐ Beet the Vandel Buster   ☐ Bleach   ☐ Bobobo-bo Bo-bobo
☐ Death Note   ☐ Dragon Ball   ☐ Dragon Ball Z
☐ Dr. Slump   ☐ Eyeshield 21   ☐ Hikaru no Go
☐ Hunter x Hunter   ☐ I"s   ☐ JoJo's Bizarre Adventure
☐ Knights of the Zodiac   ☐ Legendz   ☐ Naruto
☐ One Piece   ☐ Rurouni Kenshin   ☐ Shaman King
☐ The Prince of Tennis   ☐ Ultimate Muscle   ☐ Whistle!
☐ Yu-Gi-Oh!   ☐ Yu-Gi-Oh!: Duelist   ☐ Yu-Gi-Oh!: Millennium World
☐ YuYu Hakusho   ☐ Other _____

Will you purchase subsequent volumes?
☐ Yes   ☐ No

③ How did you learn about this title? (check all that apply)

☐ Favorite title   ☐ Advertisement   ☐ Article
☐ Gift   ☐ Read excerpt in SHONEN JUMP Magazine
☐ Recommendation   ☐ Special offer   ☐ Through TV animation
☐ Website   ☐ Other _____

4 Of the titles that are serialized in SHONEN JUMP Magazine, have you purchased the paperback manga volumes?

☐ Yes ☐ No

If **YES**, which ones have you purchased? (che

☐ Hikaru no Go ☐ Naruto g

☐ Yu-Gi-Oh!: Millennium World

If **YES**, what were your reasons for purchasing? (please pick up to 3)

☐ A favorite title ☐ A favorite creator/artist ☐ I want to read it in one go

☐ I want to read it over and over again ☐ There are extras that aren't in the magazine

☐ The quality of printing is better than the magazine ☐ Recommendation

☐ Special offer ☐ Other

If **NO**, why did/would you not purchase it?

☐ I'm happy just reading it in the magazine ☐ It's not worth buying the manga volume

☐ All the manga pages are in black and white, unlike the magazine

☐ There are other manga volumes that I prefer ☐ There are too many to collect for each title

☐ It's too small ☐ Other ______________________

5 Of the titles NOT serialized in the magazine, which ones have you purchased?
(check all that apply)

☐ Beet the Vandel Buster ☐ Bleach ☐ Bobobo-bo Bo-bobo ☐ Death Note

☐ Dragon Ball ☐ Dragon Ball Z ☐ Dr. Slump ☐ Eyeshield 21

☐ Hunter x Hunter ☐ I"s ☐ JoJo's Bizarre Adventure ☐ Knights of the Zodiac

☐ Legendz ☐ The Prince of Tennis ☐ Rurouni Kenshin ☐ Ultimate Muscle

☐ Whistle! ☐ Yu-Gi-Oh! ☐ Yu-Gi-Oh!: Duelist ☐ None

☐ Other ______________________

If you did purchase any of the above, what were your reasons for purchasing?

☐ A favorite title ☐ A favorite creator/artist

☐ Read a preview in SHONEN JUMP Magazine and wanted to read the rest of the story

☐ Recommendation ☐ Other

Will you purchase subsequent volumes?

☐ Yes ☐ No

6 What race/ethnicity do you consider yourself? (please check one)

☐ Asian/Pacific Islander ☐ Black/African American ☐ Hispanic/Latino

☐ Native American/Alaskan Native ☐ White/Caucasian ☐ Other

THANK YOU! Please send the completed form to:

VIZ Media Survey
42 Catharine St.
Poughkeepsie, NY 12601

VIZ MEDIA

All information provided will be used for internal purposes only. We promise not to sell or otherwise divulge your information.